ECONOMICS OF EMERGING MARKETS

ECONOMICS OF EMERGING MARKETS

LADO BERIDZE
EDITOR

Nova Science Publishers, Inc.
New York

LIBRARY OF CONGRESS CATALOGING-IN-PUBLICATION DATA
Economics of emerging markets / Lado Beridze (editor).
      p. cm.
ISBN-13: 978-1-60021-850-7 (hardcover)
ISBN-10: 1-60021-850-4 (hardcover)
1. Mixed economy--Developing countries--Case studies. 2. Developing countries--Economic conditions--Case studies. I. Beridze, Lado.
HC59.7.E3142   2007
330.9172'4--dc22   2007037196

Published by Nova Science Publishers, Inc. ✢ New York

CONTENTS

PREFACE

This new book presents recent significant research dealing the economics of emergin markets. The term emerging markets is commonly used to describe business and market activity in industrializing or emerging regions of the world. The term is sometimes loosely used as a replacement for emerging economies, but really signifies a business phenomenon that is not fully described by or constrained to geography or economic strength; such countries are considered to be in a transitional phase between developing and developed status. Examples of emerging markets include China, India, Mexico, Brazil, much of Southeast Asia, countries in Eastern Europe, parts of Africa and Latin America. An emerging market is sometimes defined as "a country where politics matters at least as much as economics to the markets." It appears that emerging markets lie at the intersection of non-traditional user behavior, the rise of new user groups and community adoption of products and services, and innovations in product technologies and platforms. The term "rapidly developing economies" is now being used to denote emerging markets such as The United Arab Emirates, Chile and Malaysia that are undergoing rapid growth.

Chapter 1 - This paper extends previous work by Ijiri (1995) by proposing the use of a stable composite currency in global financial reporting. Ijiri argues that transnational corporations should report financial statements using a composite currency rather than individual home currencies to avoid currency-dependent results. The authors propose a composite currency comprised of national currencies of different countries that is stable in value over time. Consistent with Ijiri, transnational corporations would benefit from a stable benchmark for measuring accounting values.

Chapter 2 - The objective of this chapter is to review the transmission mechanisms uniting equity market development and economic growth in developing countries. Overall, conclusions suggest that domestic development and international integration of equity markets have dissociated effects on economic welfare. At the domestic level, equity markets foster the mobilization and allocation of financial resources, and improve corporate governance subject to a satisfactory level of informational efficiency. However, equity market integration lowers the cost of capital, but increases financial vulnerability and exerts a non linear impact on capital flows. The authors summarize these ambiguous mechanisms in an 'equity market development triangle' and suggest a few directions for future research.

Chapter 3 - Asia presents one of the most vibrant economic environments in the world. China and India have emerged as the leaders in the Asian region due to their rapid growth and market size. Consequently, equity markets in both China and India have significantly developed following liberalization in the early 1990s. The rapid growth of these economies coupled with the development of their financial markets has attracted significant portfolio investment from U.S. investors. For example, U.S. equity portfolio flows have increased from 0.63 billion to 7.14 billion in China and from 0.5 to 11 billion in India between 1994 and 2005.

This research examines the dynamic nature of the relationship between U.S. portfolio equity flows and equity returns in China and India. To understand the linkages between equity flows, market returns, and other variables the authors dissect our empirical findings as follows: first, they examine the correlations between stock market returns and portfolio flows; second, they decompose flows into expected and unexpected components to analyze how returns are influenced by different flow components; and third, they explore the dynamic relationships among flows, returns, and related variables. Our findings show that flows are 'pulled' into China and India by returns greater than U.S. market returns. Additionally, the authors find that the Indian equity index is influenced by U.S. investment activity and dividend yields, whereas the Chinese equity index is statistically unaffected by foreign investor behavior and fundamental determinates of value. This supports the ideas espoused in the popular press that the Chinese government still plays a major role in determining equity prices. A unique finding of this research is that the variance of the flow sequence in both China and India is better explained by shock to fundamentals vs. shocks to returns. This indicates that large American investors are making portfolio allocation decisions not simply on the basis of simple 'return chasing', but are at least partially informed about the markets of China and India. The authors anticipate that the strong relationship between equity flows and fundamentals should strengthen in the future as information asymmetries decline and U.S. investors continue to develop more sophisticated methods of assessing underlying value in these markets.

Chapter 4 - This paper examines whether monetary policy shocks have any varying degrees of effect on the inflation, output and unemployment indicators of the European Union member countries. The authors hypothesize that a positive monetary policy shock increases the output and the price levels causing a decrease in unemployment. The results show that a one standard deviation positive shock in monetary policy positively affects inflation in France and Italy. Also there is negative response of unemployment to the monetary base in the case of Germany, France and Italy. They do not find any such significant relationship between output and monetary policy. Overall, monetary policy shocks have asymmetric effect on inflation and unemployment.

Chapter 5 - The authors examine how the precision of asset allocation increases when considering the higher order moments such as skewness and kurtosis. This is because the normality of equity returns are dubious as documented in the finance literature. Thus, they execute an empirical analysis of emerging equity markets by considering skewness and kurtosis. The authors believe that this is the first paper which considers until kurtosis in the empirical analysis of asset allocation. In the analysis, it is subject to the sequential quadratic programming based on a quasi-Newton updating method. As the covariance affects the asset allocation in the mean-variance model, it seems that the coskewness and cokurtosis affect the asset allocation in the mean-variance-skewness-kurtosis model. The authors find that if the investors' amounts are relatively small, the traditional mean-variance approach of asset allocation is acceptable. However, when considering large investments, they note a small but significant percentage change in investor satisfaction when using skewness and kurtosis.

Chapter 6 - This study investigates whether the Consumption-based Capital Asset Pricing Model (CCAPM) is consistent with the data from four Latin-American countries: Brazil, Chile, Colombia, and Mexico. Empirical results showed that there is a statistically significant relationship between mean excess returns and consumption betas in the countries cited above, with the exception of Mexico. Such results are, in part, similar to the results reported in previous studies for the United States of America.

Chapter 7 - The authors analyzed the presence of rational bubbles in Istanbul Stock Exchange (ISE) between 1998-2006 period by implementing linear and nonlinear unit root tests to 7 different indices. The first analysis is based on implementing augmented Dickey-Fuller unit root and KPSS stationary tests to the price-dividend ratios of the indices. The results are in favor of the presence of rational bubbles in the indices. The authors implemented a further test which enables time-varying discount rates. Generally the results of the loglinear model also support the previous results. The potential weaknesses of linear test methods as well as the advantages of nonlinear models motivated to use the bilinear test method. The evidence from the nonlinear test is in favor of the existence of rational bubbles in all indices in the sample period of 2nd March 1998–29th December 2006. But the results of the subperiods are contradictory for some indices. In the first and second subperiods the authors cannot accept unit root bilinearity for ISE National-Services index. The results also reject the significance of the bilinear term for ISE National-Industrials and ISE Investment Trusts indices in the second subperiod. As a result, they can conclude that as a general structure, the rational bubbles present in ISE.

Chapter 8 - This paper investigates the relative performance of local, foreign, and expatriate financial analysts on Latin American emerging markets. The authors measure analysts' relative performance with three dimensions: (1) forecast timeliness, (2) forecast accuracy and (3) impact of forecast revisions on security prices. The main findings can be summarized as follows. Firstly, there is a strong evidence that foreign analysts supply timelier forecasts than their peers. Secondly, analyst working for foreign brokerage houses (i.e. expatriate and foreign ones) produce less biased forecasts than local analysts. Finally, after controlling for analysts' timeliness, the authors find that foreign financial analysts' upward revisions have a greater impact on stock returns than both followers and local lead analysts forecast revisions. Overall, the results suggest that investors should better rely on the research produced by analysts working for foreign brokerage houses when they invest in Latin American emerging markets.

Chapter 9 - This chapter surveys the salient concepts relating to the role and development of emerging securities markets. It considers both general securities markets activity as well as the operations of exchanges which facilitate securities trading. The section relating to general securities activity discusses the liberalisation of securities markets in recent years, the risks related to portfolio investment in emerging markets and the impacts of the gradual integration of these markets with global ones.

Part of the business activity of securities exchanges is migrating overseas through the tendency for larger companies to cross-list on major exchanges. This chapter thus explores how emerging economy exchanges may assert their role in international financial markets through supplementing traditional business streams with new ones, enhancing liquidity and using appropriate technology. Finally, the chapter illustrates how securities activity in emerging economies should be supplemented by the appropriate legal and regulatory framework.

Chapter 10 - Campbell (2003) confirms the equity premium puzzle in an international context based on the Consumption-CAPM and cross-country evidence on implausibly large coefficients of relative risk aversion. In this paper the authors adopt a spectral approach to re-estimate the values of risk aversion over the frequency domain for six Latin American emerging markets. The authors complement our analysis with the traditional time series approach and confirm the results of existing literature of large coefficients of relative risk aversion. The frequency domain findings, however, indicate that at lower frequencies risk aversion falls substantially across countries, thus yielding in many cases reasonable values of the implied coefficient of risk aversion.

Chapter 11- In this chapter the authors examine how investor overconfidence and self-attribution bias affects the profitability of momentum strategies in emerging markets, in light of the assumptions made by Cooper et al. [2004] for the US stock market and later applied to the Spanish stock market by Muga and Santamaría [2006]. Consistent with the author's initial hypotheses, behavioural biases of this kind are found to have little influence in the emerging markets considered, (Argentina, Brazil, Mexico, and Chile) due to the impact of the periodical economic crises experienced by these countries during the study period (1994-2004). Nevertheless, a more detailed analysis of the winner and loser portfolios for the different strategies revealed some evidence of momentum consistent with the presence of disposition investors in these markets.

Chapter 12 - Recent financial crises suggest the importance of the diffusion mechanism, at an international level, of emerging bonds markets shocks. Using extreme value analysis for the sovereign debt spreads of emerging markets, the present paper explores the extreme dependence of the Colombian risk premium to international financial markets. The architecture of capital markets can lead a collapse of emerging markets, where fundamentals do not determine the position liquidation totally. The relation between the Colombian country risk and the United States asset markets shows that an increase in global uncertainty defines a *"Flight to quality"* and therefore an additional increase in the contagion probability for the emerging markets bonds.

Chapter 13 - There is evidence that value stocks have higher returns than growth stocks in markets around the world. Not much is known, however, about the performance of value strategies in the Brazilian market. The purpose of this paper is to analyze the performance of a very simple investment strategy based on the dividend yield. Using data from a 10-year period from 1995 to 2004, we provide evidence that the dividend yield has a moderate power to explain stock returns. The results using the Jensen alpha, and the Treynor and Sharpe ratios indicate that the most diversified portfolios do achieve risk-adjusted excess returns. All betas are significant and below unity suggesting that the dividend strategy has a lower risk than investing in the market. Building portfolios with the highest yielding stocks present more bull months (positive returns) than bear months (negative returns). Further, the magnitude of the returns in bull months is higher than in bear months.

Chapter 14 - This study examines whether the financial performances of companies in Taiwan differ when the firms adopt employee stock ownership plans (ESOPs). The results of analyzing the market reactions, as reflected in the stock returns when an announcement is made in a board meeting regarding the adoption of an ESOP, indicate that the electronics and non-electronics industries differ significantly on terms of the ROE, profit margin and equity multiplier during the pre- and post-event periods. The total asset turnover rate in the non-electronics industry, however, does not differ significantly during the pre- and post-event periods. Reactions toward the adoption of an ESOP are observed in the market before the event occurs, and the electronics industry accounts for the most significant reaction. Moreover, the authors find that a negative relationship exists between the CAAR and firm size, and that there is a positive relationship between the CAAR and the market-to-book ratio and the debt ratio.

In: Economics of Emerging Markets
Editor: Lado Beridze, pp. 1-4

ISBN: 978-1-60021-850-7
© 2008 Nova Science Publishers, Inc.

Expert Commentary A

MONETARY POLICY AND DIVERSIFICATION BENEFITS OF INVESTING IN EMERGING MARKETS

Partha Gangopadhyay
St. Cloud State University, Minnesota, USA

There is extensive evidence in the academic literature that monetary policy in the U.S. influences contemporaneous and expected stock returns [for a partial list of studies see Rozeff (1974 and 1975), Geske and Roll (1983), James, Koreisha, and Partch (1985), Smirlock and Yawitz (1985), Kaul (1987), Zweig (1986), Thorbecke and Alami (1992), Jensen and Johnson (1995), Jensen, Mercer, and Johnson (1996), Patelis (1997), Thorbecke (1997), Jensen, Johnson, and Mercer (1998), Park and Ratti (2000), Jensen and Mercer (2002), and Gangopadhyay (2007)]. The evidence presented in these papers suggests that U.S. stock and bond returns are significantly higher during time periods when the Federal Reserve pursues expansive monetary policy, compared to periods of restrictive monetary policy. Several authors report that stock returns are in fact negative during restrictive monetary policy. Gangopadhyay (2007) reports that the average annual monetary policy premium in U.S. stock returns (market return during expansive monetary policy minus return during restrictive monetary policy) was 14.98% between 1929 and 2001. The size of the monetary policy premium seems to have increased over time (18.32% average premium between 1963 and 2001). From an asset pricing angle the general conclusion is that monetary stringency significantly impacts equity risk premiums (Thorbecke, 1997, Jensen and Mercer, 2002, Gangopadhyay, 2007). Jensen, Johnson, and Mercer (1998) also provide compelling evidence that size and value premiums in stock returns exist only in time periods when the Federal Reserve pursues expansive monetary policy.

How are Federal Reserve monetary policy shocks channeled to the equity markets? In an early study, Smirlock and Yawitz (1985) argue that changes in monetary policy affect stock returns by influencing interest rate forecasts, the cost of capital, and investors' expectations of corporate profitability. In two widely cited more recent papers, Bernanke and Gertler (1989 and 1995) argue that monetary policy affects corporate profitability through two different channels: a balance sheet channel (or net worth channel), and a bank lending channel. Interest rate hikes by the Federal Reserve worsen firms' balance sheets by increasing interest expenses, reducing net cash flows and profits, and reducing value of assets that the firm may have used as collateral for external financing. Short-term borrowing (working capital financing) also rises following monetary tightening (Friedman and Kuttner, 1993, Gertler and Gilchrist, 1994, and Bernanke and Gertler, 1995). This additional need for external financing arises (internal financing may be inadequate due to low corporate profits) precisely at times when such financing is more expensive. Monetary tightening also works through the bank lending channel - by draining reserves and deposits from the banking system, the supply of bank loans is reduced and agency costs of lending are magnified. The effect of corporate cash flow squeeze and reduced supply of (costlier) bank loans places more financial burden on small firms than on large firms. Large firms may be better collateralized (and in better overall financial condition) and have recourse to commercial paper and other sources of short-term credit. Since stock prices are weighted average of expected future cash flows, in an efficient market, stock prices should quickly incorporate the real effects of monetary policy. Monetary tightening by the Federal Reserve, therefore, predicts lower expected stock returns in the short run, especially for small firms. Thorbecke (1997) finds empirical support for Bernanke and Gertler's (1989 and 1995) hypotheses. Thorbecke (1997) concludes that " .. expansionary monetary policy exerts real effects by increasing future cash flows or by decreasing the discount factors at which those cash flows are capitalized". Gangopadhyay (2007) examines the impact of monetary policy shocks on market-wide cash flows and discount rates. He reports that monetary policy shocks are primarily transmitted to the stock market through their impact on market cash flows. Market discount rates are also impacted, but for 1929-2001, the primary channel of monetary policy transmission has been the impact of policy shocks on market cash flows. Park and Ratti (2000) present empirical evidence that positive output shocks (growth in industrial production) lead to higher inflation and to monetary tightening. Monetary tightening, in turn, causes an immediate decline in expected real stock return. Thus Park and Ratti (2000) establish empirical cause and effect relationships among real economic activity, inflation, monetary policy, and expected stock return.

The papers cited above provide evidence that expansive (restrictive) Federal Reserve monetary policy increases (decreases) U.S. stock and bond returns. Ahmed, Gangopadhyay and Nanda (2003) examine the impact of Federal Reserve monetary policy on U.S. based emerging market stock and bond mutual funds. They provide compelling evidence that emerging market funds perform significantly better in restrictive Federal Reserve monetary policy environments than in expansive environments. This pattern of reaction is the exact opposite of what has been generally observed in U.S. financial markets. Ahmed et al (2003) report that the average annual premium (restrictive policy-period return minus expansive policy-period return) during 1980-2000 ranges from a low of 19% for Pacific (excluding Japan) funds to a high of 31% for Diversified Emerging Market Funds. Average annual emerging market bond fund returns are 5% during expansive U.S. monetary policy and 30% during restrictive monetary policy. Since these reaction patterns are exact opposite of what have been observed in U.S. financial markets, Ahmed et al (2003) conclude that U.S. investors can reap sizable diversification benefits from investing in emerging market stock and bond funds. These funds provide handsome returns at time periods when the Federal Reserve hikes interest rates in the U.S., which overlaps with a period of negative returns in U.S. equity markets.

Ahmed at al (2003) examine U.S. based emerging market funds that are accessible to U.S. investors. Their results are consistent with the notion that American investors understand these diversification benefits and channel funds to emerging markets when the outlook for U.S. equity markets looks bleak, because of interest rate hikes by the Federal Reserve. Much of the money that is invested in emerging markets probably returns to the U.S. when the Federal Reserve begins lowering interest rates in the U.S. The evidence in Ahmed et al (2003) is consistent with the idea that emerging financial markets experience significant flow of funds from the U.S. when the Federal Reserve pursues anti-inflationary monetary policy. Much of these funds probably leave emerging markets when the Federal Reserve switches to expansive monetary policy.

To properly ascertain diversification benefits of investing in emerging markets, one needs to jointly examine the impact of monetary policy of the Federal Reserve and of central banks of emerging countries. To the best of my knowledge, this has not been examined yet. Emerging countries do not necessarily coordinate their monetary policies with the U.S. Federal Reserve. Ahmed et al (2003) argue that Federal Reserve monetary policy influences flow of U.S. funds to emerging countries. However, as in the U.S., domestic monetary policy in emerging countries probably has significant impact on expected firm cash flows, and on discount rates at which expected cash flows are capitalized. If one can generalize Bernanke and Gertler's (1989 and 1995) hypotheses about channels of monetary policy transmission (in the U.S.) to emerging markets, then domestic monetary policy shocks could have sizable impact on emerging equity market returns. Suppose that the central bank of emerging country X and the U.S. Federal Reserve simultaneously pursue restrictive monetary policy. Restrictive domestic monetary policy will probably depress stock prices in country X through the policy's impact on firms' balance sheets and supply of bank loans. To understand this, one needs to study the impact of domestic monetary policy on firm cash flows and discount rates in emerging countries. A few studies have examined this in the U.S., but this has not been investigated for emerging markets (to the best of my knowledge). Restrictive U.S. monetary policy will simultaneously increase the flow of funds to country X, boosting their financial markets. If both central banks pursue restrictive policy simultaneously, then what is the net impact on country X's markets? What is the net impact if the two central banks simultaneously pursue expansive policy (or if they pursue divergent policies)? To properly ascertain diversification benefits of investing in emerging markets, a country-by-country analysis of the combined effect of Federal Reserve and country X's monetary policies on different types of firms in country X (small vs. big, value vs. glamour) needs to be undertaken. This appears to be a promising avenue of future research.

REFERENCES

Ahmed, P., P. Gangopadhyay, and S. Nanda, 2003, Investing in emerging market mutual funds, *Journal of Business and Economic Perspectives*, 29, 5-15.

Bernanke, B. S. and M. Gertler, 1989, Agency costs, net worth, and business fluctuations, *American Economic Review*, 79, 14-31.

Bernanke, B. S. and M. Gertler, 1995, Inside the black box: The credit channel of monetary policy transmission, *Journal of Economic Perspectives*, 9, 27-48.

Friedman, B. M. and K. N. Kuttner, 1993, Economic activity and the short-term credit market: An analysis of prices and quantities, *Brookings Papers on Economic Activity*, 2, 193-266.

Gangopadhyay, P., 2007, Monetary policy and pricing of cash-flow and discount- rate risk, Working Paper, St. Cloud State University.

Gertler, M. and S. Gilchrist, 1994, Monetary policy, business cycles, and the behavior of small manufacturing firms, *Quarterly Journal of Economics*, 109, 310-338.

Geske, R. and R. Roll, 1983, The fiscal and monetary linkage between stock returns and inflation, *Journal of Finance*, 38, 1-33.

James, C., S. Koreisha, and M. Partch, 1985, A VARMA analysis of the causal relations among stock returns, real output, and real interest rates, *Journal of Finance*, 40, 1375-1384.

Jensen, G. R. and R. R. Johnson, 1995, Discount rate changes and security returns in the U.S., 1962-1991, *Journal of Banking and Finance*, 19, 79-95.

Jensen, G.R., J.M. Mercer, and R.R. Johnson, 1996, Business conditions, monetary policy, and expected security returns, *Journal of Financial Economics*, 40, 213-237.

Jensen, G.R., R.R. Johnson, and J.M. Mercer, Winter 1998, The inconsistency of small-firm and value stock premiums, *Journal of Portfolio Management*, 24, 27-36.

Jensen, G.R. and J.M. Mercer, 2002, Monetary policy and the cross-section of expected stock returns, *The Journal of Financial Research*, 25, 125-139.

Kaul, G., 1987, Stock returns and inflation: The role of the monetary sector, *Journal of Financial Economics*, 18, 253-276.

Patelis, A.D., 1997, Stock return predictability and the role of monetary policy, *Journal of Finance*, 52, 1951-1972.

Park, K. and R. A. Ratti, 2000, Real activity, inflation, stock returns, and monetary policy, *The Financial Review*, 35, 59-78.

Rozeff, M., 1974, Money and stock prices: Market efficiency and the lag in effect of monetary policy, *Journal of Financial Economics*, 1, 245-302.

Rozeff, M., 1975, The money supply and the stock market: The demise of a leading indicator, *Financial Analysts Journal*, 31, 18-20, 22-24, 26, 76.

Smirlock, M. and J. Yawitz, 1985, Asset returns, discount rate changes, and market efficiency, *Journal of Finance*, 40, 1141-1158.

Thorbecke, W. and T. Alami, 1992, The federal funds rate and the arbitrage pricing theory: Evidence that monetary policy matters, *Journal of Macroeconomics*, 14, 731-744.

Thorbecke, W., 1997, On stock market returns and monetary policy, *Journal of Finance*, 52, 635-654.

Zweig,M., 1986, *Martin Zweig's Winning on Wall Street* (Warner Books: New York).

In: Economics of Emerging Markets
Editor: Lado Beridze, pp. 5-7
ISBN: 978-1-60021-850-7
© 2008 Nova Science Publishers, Inc.

Expert Commentary B

IMPACT OF GLOBALIZATION ON THE INTEGRATION OF ARAB STOCK EXCHANGES

Shahira Abdel Shahid

Cairo and Alexandria Stock Exchanges, Cairo, Egypt

Globalization is a fact that cannot be ignored and its impact on countries, economies, markets, governments etc. is quite notable, particularly in the last decade. Globalization refers to the increasing integration of economies around the world, particularly through trade and financial flows. In specific, it refers to the movement of people (labor) and knowledge (technology) across international borders. The most striking aspect of globalization has been the integration of financial markets made possible by modern electronic communication.

The impact of globalization on financial markets was remarkable and is reflected in various aspects. First, technology advancements, whereby information has become readily available due to the Internet and computer based trading, which have revolutionized investment and chattered geographical boundaries and thus investors can now via a click of a mouse conduct trades in several markets instantaneously. Furthermore, deregulation of markets, as reflected in reducing foreign exchange controls, relaxing restrictions on the purchase of domestic securities by foreign investors and reducing taxes imposed on foreign investors, all have led to the liberalization of capital flows across the globe. This was however accompanied by increased volatility of markets, bubbles, crashes as witnessed in South East Asia crisis in 1997, Russia crisis 1998, Brazil crisis 1999 and most recently Emerging Gulf Markets in March 2006. Another important feature of globalization was the mergers and acquisitions in the financial services industry that led to the emergence of few financial global conglomerates that provide a multitude of services e.g. commercial banking, investment banking, insurance, real estate, property services etc. such as Morgan Stanley, Merrill Lynch, UBS, Citigroup etc. Moreover, in the early 1990's, stock exchanges started changing their governance structure and have become demutualized i.e. changed from mutual, non-profit organizations that are run by their members into for-profit companies that are owned by member firms, investors, issuers and the public at large and are held accountable to shareholders. This has intensified competition among stock exchanges and as a result, it is expected that the number of stock exchanges will be reduced and we will end up in the next decade having few mega exchanges and the remaining smaller exchanges will focus on specific or niche markets.

Furthermore, a wave of mergers, acquisitions and takeovers among world exchanges that started in the late 1990's witnessed a surge in 2006 with multi-billion dollar deals, the most eminent of which, was the friendly takeover of New York Stock Exchange of Euronext ($20 billion deal). This wave of mergers and alliances among exchanges will continue if those exchanges wanted to maintain their growth potentials and remain competitive. Nevertheless, the same period witnessed several failures in merging stock exchanges, the most well-known of which was the several failed merger attempts between London Stock Exchange and Deutsche Borse, due to lack of commitment of management, resistance from shareholders, differences in cultures and differences in the implemented rules and regulations etc.

Globalization was also accompanied by the rise of importance of corporate governance. Corporate governance is a broad term that encompasses rules and market practices, which determine how widely held companies, make decisions, the transparency of their decision-making processes, the accountability of their directors, managers and employees, the information they disclose to investors and the protection of minority shareholders.

Globalization is forcing many companies to tap international financial markets and thus face greater competition. In an increasingly globalized economy, firms need to tap domestic and international capital markets for capital and investment and the quality of corporate governance is increasingly becoming the criterion for investment and lending. Many shareholders now compare ownership rights and governance as part of their due diligence reviews of companies. International investors are also convinced that the appropriate governance structure reduces risk and promote performance and that shareholder participation can motivate boards to produce higher long-term returns. Companies that enjoy good corporate governance have a competitive advantage in attracting capital over those whose practices discourage shareholder participation. Corporate governance is a significant factor considered by institutional investors when making investment decisions and ownership stakes.

In summary, globalization resulted in investors investing globally in any market, member firms (broker-dealers) trading across various exchanges and issuers (listed companies) having multiple listings on several exchanges at the same time.

Referring to the integration among Arab stock exchanges, it could be a viable but is a long-term process that requires vision, determination, commitment and strategic planning. It should be pointed out that that Arab economic integration was not that successful although it started, during the same period early 1950's, when European Union began, but the later was very successful, whereas Arab countries intra-regional trade amounted to a mere 8% compared to NAFTA 48%, EU 67% and ASEAN countries 55% in 2004.

The reasons for achieving minimal Arab economic integration were mainly due to: greater emphasis was placed upon the notion of integration by the political leaders without considering the economic rationale, lack of political determination of the parties that wanted to integrate, the small size of Arab trade compared to world trade, for example the size of Arab countries' collective GDP amounts to less than the GDP of Spain, similarity of products in the Arab region resulted in having limited mutual trade benefits among Arab countries, weak infrastructure links, the lack of executive institutions that could help in enforcing the integration agreements etc. Learning from the above, prior to Arab stock exchanges integration, there should be first harmonization in the trading, listing and membership rules as well as tackling of the differences in capital controls, openness of markets, exchange rates etc. Furthermore, Arab Exchanges must change their structure and governance from mutual or government owned entities to become private companies as happening all over the world. The only stock exchange that privatized was Dubai Financial Market, which had a very successful Initial Public Offering (IPO) in December 2006 that was oversubscribed 300 times.

Private exchanges that have private boards and are run by private management are much better in deciding on which exchanges to merge or integrate with or remain on a stand-alone basis, given their own strategic and economic objectives, as shown in the successful international examples of world exchanges. The exchanges in a merger talk need first resolve several issues such as agreeing on the trading platform that will be used which is a major decision, obtaining approval of the shareholders of both entities is crucial to its success, reconciling different cultures and styles are just some of the subject matters that need to be tackled.

Exchanges will choose to integrate only if the integration or merger is expected to provide value, synergies and growth to the merged entities, otherwise it will be a futile exercise. Regrettably, great emphasis is now placed upon the notion of Arab stock exchanges integration by politicians without considering the process, economics and practicalities involved in achieving integration.

A final point to conclude with is that experience showed that gradual integration is advisable and more effective. Thus, two or three exchanges integrate first and later other exchanges may join them as was the case in Euronext (it originally started with the merger between Paris, Brussels and Amsterdam Exchanges and then later added Lisbon and Liffe Exchanges). In other words, proposing the integration of ten or more Arab exchanges is simply impossible, which also failed when the European Commission tried in the early 1990's to have a Pan European Exchange, instead of the existing thirty European exchanges at that time.

In: Economics of Emerging Markets
Editor: Lado Beridze, pp. 9-24

ISBN: 978-1-60021-850-7

Chapter 1

MEASUREMENT PROBLEMS IN GLOBAL FINANCIAL REPORTING: THE NEED FOR A STABLE COMPOSITE CURRENCY

Nikolai V. Hovanov, James W. Kolari[*],
and Mikhail V. Sokolov
St. Petersburg State University, Texas A&M University,
AVK Securities and Finance Limited, USA

ABSTRACT

This paper extends previous work by Ijiri (1995) by proposing the use of a stable composite currency in global financial reporting. Ijiri argues that transnational corporations should report financial statements using a composite currency rather than individual home currencies to avoid currency-dependent results. We propose a composite currency comprised of national currencies of different countries that is stable in value over time. Consistent with Ijiri, transnational corporations would benefit from a stable benchmark for measuring accounting values.

Keywords: Composite currency; Stable aggregate currency; Global financial reporting; Foreign currency translation; Reporting currency; Exchange rates; Currency invariance

Work by Ijiri (1995) proposes the use of a composite currency in global financial reporting to resolve measurement problems inherent in local currencies. Ijiri demonstrates that for a transnational corporation (TNC), which typically invests in different countries, the currency of account should not be the national currency of a single country. In this regard, accounting information can vary considerably for different local currencies (e.g., U.S. dollars versus European euros) used to denominate prices, such that financial reports are currency dependent. Instead of using local currencies, he recommends denomination of prices in a composite currency comprised of a basket of national currencies to measure accounting information over time. More specifically, he proposes that currencies' amounts in the multiple-currency basket should be proportional to corresponding volumes of assets of a TNC in different countries. We will refer to this proportional currency-basket by using the abbreviation PIM (Proportional Ijiri Money). He further recommends that each TNC should develop its own specific PIM. As such, accountants would measure the values of goods and services using noncomparable units of account for different TNCs – for example, IBM-PIM, Toshiba-PIM, Siemens-PIM, etc.

In this paper we propose a simplified approach based on a basket of currencies that is relatively stable in value over time. We follow Hovanov, Kolari, and Sokolov (2004), who derive an optimal minimum-variance currency basket that can be considered a stable aggregate currency (hereafter *SAC*). In this regard, Hovanov et al. show that *SAC* is almost 40 times more stable in value that the U.S. dollar in the period 1981-1998.

Relevant to *SAC* as a unit of account, international accounting standards employ constant currency accounting to adjust income statement and balance sheet figures for changing currency values over time. Constant currency accounting assumes that the exchange rate at the end of an accounting period is the same as at the beginning of the period. Of course, comparing accounting data over time would be facilitated by denominating figures in a relatively constant money such as *SAC*. This *global approach* to constant currency accounting adjusts income statement and balance sheet data using *world money units* comprised of an optimal minimum-variance basket of international currencies. By contrast, current constant currency methods utilize a *local approach* that adjust data using *national currency units*. *SAC* solves the problem of choosing a local currency to denominate accounting data. As Ijiri points out, the application of different alternative base currencies creates ambiguity in time series observations of goods' and services' values. Transnational corporations with revenues and costs in multiple currencies need a composite currency that is global in nature. We believe that *SAC* can serve the role of common *numeraire* currency due to its extremely low volatility and construction from world currencies. Rather than a single world currency, we propose a numeraire currency comprised of national currencies of different countries. This proposal is consistent with work by Nobel Laureate Robert Mundell (2000a, 2000b, 2000c, 20001), who argues for the development of a common numeraire based on a currency basket containing the U.S. dollar, European euro, and Japanese yen. According to Mundell, denominating the values of goods and services in currency basket terms would increase the transparency and comparability of prices in international transactions.

In the next section we provide a simple accounting model of goods exchange. This model serves as a foundation for developing *SAC*. Subsequently, we compare the volatility of *PIM* versus *SAC* using historical exchange rates for the U.S. dollar (*USD*) and European euro (*EUR*).

* Corresponding author: Dr. James W. Kolari, JP Morgan Chase Professor of Finance, Texas A&M University, Finance Department, College Station, TX 88843-4218; Office phone: 979-845-4803; Fax: 979-845-3884; Email address: j-kolari@tamu.edu

A SIMPLE ACCOUNTING MODEL OF GOODS AND SERVICES

Here we review work by Kolari, Sokolov, Fedotov, and Hovanov (2001) concerning a simple accounting model of the real economy. A basic concept in our model is that all goods' values are in reality exchange rates. For example, when you purchase any good or service, the price indicates how much one unit costs per unit of a particular currency. Of course, goods can be traded for other goods, and currencies exchanged for other currencies. However, a basic problem in all of these exchange rates is that there is no stable benchmark to use as a starting point in setting all of their values. With no stable benchmark, we argue that accounting for goods and services values has measurement problems. In this section we provide a basic framework for accounting measurement.

Suppose that there is a fixed finite set of infinitely divisible goods (commodities, services, currencies, etc.) $G = \{g_1, ..., g_n\}$, with amount (quantity, volume) of ith good being determined by a real number $q_i \geq 0$. In other words, any amount of ith good may be represented in the form $q_i u_i$, where the positive real number q_i is the good's quantity, and the measurement unit u_i describes the quality of the good (Bridgman, 1931).

The amount q_i of any simple good g_i from the set G can be measured by a *scale of ratios* with a precision of a measurement unit $u_i = a_i u_i'$, which is an increasing linear homogeneous transformation $q_i' = a_i \cdot q_i$ (Abdel-Magid et al., 1986). It is important to keep in mind that these two real numbers q_i, and q_i' representing a fixed amount of simple good g_i on two corresponding numerical scales (e.g., U.S. dollars and European euros) are simple transformations of one another. Therefore, a researcher can manipulate their numerical data by choosing the most convenient measurement scale or measurement unit.

Any pair of goods g_i, g_j from the set $G = \{g_1, ..., g_n\}$ may be exchanged *directly* without the necessity of any medium of exchange in the form of another good or use of money. Moreover, this direct barter exchange of goods g_i, g_j, which are taken in any finite amounts $q_i > 0$, $q_j > 0$, is quantitatively defined by a positive *exchange coefficient* c_{ij}. The exchange coefficient gives the amount c_{ij} of good g_j that one can exchange for one unit u_i of good g_i, which can be written as the ratio $c_{ij} = q_j / q_i$ of exchangeable quantities q_i, q_j of corresponding goods g_i, g_j.

In the case when goods under exchange are currencies, the coefficient c_{ij} is the exchange rate between the ith currency and the jth currency. In other words, dimensional coefficient $c_{ij} \cdot u_j / u_i$ shows the price of one unit u_i of currency g_i represented in units u_j of currency g_j. The totality of all exchange coefficients c_{ij}, $i, j = 1, ..., n$ may be represented in the form of an exchange rate matrix $C = (c_{ij})$ with positive elements. The matrix $C = (c_{ij})$ is *transitive*, i.e., the relation $c_{ij} \cdot c_{jk} = c_{ik}$ takes place among every three elements c_{ij}, c_{jk}, c_{ik}, $i, j, k = 1,..., n$ of the matrix (e.g., yen/dollar x dollar/euro = yen/euro). Trivial implications from transitivity of exchange matrix $C = (c_{ij})$ are *reflexivity* ($c_{ii} = 1$, $i = 1,..., n$), and *reciprocal symmetry* ($c_{ji} = 1/c_{ij}$, or $c_{ij} \cdot c_{ji} = 1$).

So far, our simple accounting model of goods and services can be summarized by the ordered set (G, U, C), where $G = \{g_1,..., g_n\}$ is a fixed finite set of all simple goods under investigation, $U = \{u_1,..., u_n\}$ is a fixed set of measurement units for amounts of the corresponding goods, and $C = (c_{ij})$ is a fixed positive transitive matrix of exchange coefficients. Now consider the situation when an amount q_i of units u_i of ith good is exchanged for an amount q_j of units u_j of jth good. These goods can be set equal to one another by means of a fixed quantity of money, which Adam Smith (1976) referred to as the "value in exchange." This exchange of goods is an equivalence relation with reflexive, symmetric, and transitive binary properties (Kuratowski and Mostowski, 1967). We will write this relation for the pair of goods' amounts $q_i u_i$, $q_j u_j$ as $q_i[u_i] \equiv q_j[u_j]$. Next, assume that this value in exchange can be measured by a numerical scale represented by a fixed money denoted by the numerical function $Val(q; u)$ of a good's amount q (measured by the unit u). Thus, we have the *condition of exchangeability* defined as $q_i[u_i] \equiv q_j[u_j]$ if and only if $Val(q_i; u_i) = Val(q_j; u_j)$.

It is reasonable to suppose that $Val(q; u)$ is an additive and increasing function of q. From these conditions the explicit formula $Val(q; u) = q \cdot Val(1; u)$ for the value function may be derived (see Aczél, J. and J. Dhombres, 1989, chapter 2.1). One can treat the function $Val(q; u)$ as an indicator (index) of value in exchange of an amount qu of a good from the set $G = \{g_1,..., g_n\}$. When all goods under investigation are currencies, the function $Val(q; u)$ may be interpreted as an indicator (index) of exchange rate of a corresponding currency. Consequently, we can write:

$$\frac{Val(1; u_i)}{Val(1; u_j)} = \frac{q_j}{q_i} = c_{ij}, \tag{1}$$

which determines element c_{ij} of the exchange-matrix $C = (c_{ij})$, $i, j = 1,..., n$. So, an observable proportion c_{ij} of two goods exchange may be treated as a ratio of two corresponding non-observable values in exchange $Val(1; u_i)$, $Val(1; u_j)$ of the goods' units. Such a theoretical interpretation of the empirical data c_{ij}, $i, j = 1,..., n$ in terms of values of the function $Val(q; u)$ raises the question as to whether there exists a *one-argument* function

$Val(q;u)$, such that equation (1) holds for all exchange-coefficients treated as values of a *two-argument* function $c(i,j) = c_{ij}$, $i,j = 1,...,n$? In this regard, all elements of an exchange-matrix $C = (c_{ij})$ may be represented as corresponding ratios of values of a one-argument value-function $Val(q;u)$ if and only if the matrix is *transitive* (e.g., see Kolari et al., 2001), i.e., the relation $c_{ij} c_{jk} = c_{ik}$, $i,j,k = 1,...,n$ holds for every three elements c_{ij}, c_{jk}, c_{ik} of the matrix.

Now we can introduce estimations of value in exchange for units $u_1,...,u_n$ of goods under exchange. For example, elements of jth column of the exchange matrix may be taken as the required estimations $Val_{ij} = c_{ij}$, $i = 1,...,n$. Setting $Val_{jj} = c_{jj} = 1$, the jth good's unit u_j becomes a *unit of account* (i.e., numeraire, standard good, standard of value, etc.) in relation to which accounting values of all other goods and services are measured.

CONSTRUCTING STABLE INDICES OF VALUE

The fact that values in exchange Val_{ij}, $i = 1,...,n$ are dependent on the choice of a standard good g_j creates problems for comparing values when measured at different moments of time. For example, the value of any particular good in U.S. dollars differs over time from its value denominated in European euros or Japanese yen. The chosen base currency substantially changes the value of any good over time. To overcome this problem inherent in index Val_{ij}, Hovanov et al. (2004) provide a modified indicator of value in exchange, or *normalized value in exchange*

$$NVal_{ij} = \frac{Val_{ij}}{\sqrt[n]{\prod_{r=1}^{n} Val_{rj}}} = \frac{c_{ij}}{\sqrt[n]{\prod_{r=1}^{n} c_{rj}}} = \sqrt[n]{\prod_{s=1}^{n} c_{is}} \qquad (2)$$

The normalized index $NVal_{ij}$ of value in exchange of ith good's unit u_i is represented in the form of a simple fraction, where numerator is equal to exchange coefficient c_{ij}, and the denominator equals the geometric mean of exchange coefficients $c_{1j},...,c_{nj}$ (i.e., elements of the jth column of exchange-matrix $C = (c_{ij})$). This index may be represented in the form of geometric mean of exchange coefficients $c_{i1},...,c_{in}$ (i.e., elements of the ith row of exchange-matrix $C = (c_{ij})$).

The most important property of $NVal_{ij}$ is its independence from the choice of a standard currency g_j: $NVal_{ij} = NVal_{ik}$ for all $j,k = 1,...,n$. Thus, it is invariant in relation to alternative choices of standard currencies. As an example, given the dollar value of a good, if we convert its value to euros or yen as the base currency, its value would be the same. In effect, we have converted dollars scaled in euros or scaled in yen to a single dollar scale. An analogy would be to create a formula that could convert temperature in Fahrenheit or centigrade to the some alternative temperature scale. Since normalized value in exchange $NVal_{ij}$ is independent of a standard currency g_j, we will use the notation $NVal_i = NVal_{ij}$.

$NVal_i$ can be used in empirical investigations of $c_{ij}(t)$, $i,j = 1,...,n$, $t = 1,...,T$, or currencies' rates of exchange. It is convenient to set this index equal to 1 at some initial point in time. In this regard, the normalized value in exchange of ith currency at the moment t can be written as

$$NVal_i(t) = \frac{c_{ij}(t)}{\sqrt[n]{\prod_{r=1}^{n} c_{rj}(t)}} = \sqrt[n]{\prod_{s=1}^{n} c_{is}(t)} \ , \tag{3}$$

and the *reduced* (to the time t_0) normalized value in exchange is

$$RNVal_i(t/t_0) = \frac{NVal_i(t)}{NVal_i(t_0)} = \sqrt[n]{\prod_{s=1}^{n} \frac{c_{is}(t)}{c_{is}(t_0)}} \ , \tag{4}$$

where the time t_0 is set as the starting point by the researcher, i.e., $RNVal_i(t_0/t_0) = 1$ for all $i = 1,...,n$.

While $RNVal_i(t/t_0)$ provides a single value (for example) of a dollar-denominated good no matter what base currency is used (e.g., euros or yen), it will tend to have fairly large fluctuations over time due to changes in the dollar's value in world currency markets. As Adam Smith (1976, p. 48) observed, a commodity that substantially changes value over time should not be used to measure the value of other commodities. According to Davies (1996), many authors have sought a stable unit of account, including gold and silver money of mercantilists, labor of Smith and Ricardo, abstract labor of Marx, wage unit of Keynes, standard commodity and common labor of Sraffa, unit of consumption as well as ideal price in equilibrium between demand and supply of neo-classical economics, energy unit, etc. (e.g., see Bonar, 1909; Debreu, 1959; Sraffa, 1960; Georgescu-Roegen, 1976; and Passinetti, 1981). The basic problem is that we need a *measuring stick* (or unit of account) that does not change length (or dimension) over time. When measuring height, weight, speed, etc., we always assume that our measuring stick is constant over time. Unfortunately, even hard currencies of major industrial countries experience large swings in their currencies' values over time. For example, in the last eight years the European euro's value has fluctuated from about 0.80 dollars to over 1.40 dollars, which implies that it rose about 75 percent in this short period of time. If business, government, and nonprofit entities' activities were measured in euros or dollars, it is immediately obvious that it is unreasonable to suppose that their relative accounting valuations could change by one-half in just a few years![1]

In an effort to develop a stable money for measurement purposes, Hovanov et al. (2004) construct a minimum variance composite (basket) currency for a fixed market of goods and for a fixed period of time. This stable aggregate currency (*SAC*) is constructed from the national currencies of countries taken from a fixed set $G = \{g_1,...,g_n\}$ in fixed amounts $q_i > 0$, $i = 1,...,n$. An aggregate currency is determined by a vector $\overline{q} = (q_1,...,q_n)$ of the currencies' amounts (e.g., 1.00 dollar, 1.20 euros, and 100 yen with these amounts fixed over time). There are a number of well-known composite currencies which have been in practical use in the second part of the 20th century as numeraire – namely, the EUA (European Unit of Account) until 1979, ECU (European Currency Unit) from 1979 to 1999, SDR (Special Drawing Rights) of the International Monetary Fund since 1970, etc. (see Mussa et al., 1996).

We next turn to a mathematical solution that seeks an optimal, stable currency basket based on well-known diversification principles developed by Nobel Laureate Harry Markowitz (1952). For a fixed time t value in exchange $Val_j(\overline{q};t)$ of an aggregate currency $\overline{q} = (q_1,...,q_n)$ is defined by the formula

$$Val_j(\overline{q};t) = \sum_{i=1}^{n} q_i\, Val_{ij}(t) = \sum_{i=1}^{n} q_i c_{ij}(t), \tag{5}$$

with value in exchange being measured in units u_j of currency g_j.[2] [2]Normalized index $NVal_j(\overline{q};t)$ of value in exchange of the aggregated currency is

$$NVal_j(\overline{q};t) = \frac{Val_j(\overline{q};t)}{\sqrt[n]{\prod_{r=1}^{n} c_{rj}(t)}} = \sum_{i=1}^{n} q_i \frac{Val_{ij}(t)}{\sqrt[n]{\prod_{r=1}^{n} c_{rj}(t)}} = \sum_{i=1}^{n} q_i \sqrt[n]{\prod_{r=1}^{n} c_{ir}(t)} = \sum_{i=1}^{n} q_i\, NVal_i(t)$$

$$\tag{6}$$

---

[1] Ijiri (1995) cites work by Abdel-Magid and Cheung (1986), Mehta and Thapa (1991), and Kirsch and Johnson (1991) to support the argument that comparing multinationals is difficult due to the use of different national or local currencies and frequent changes in functional currencies.

[2] Here we use only the simplest additive form of a composite good's (aggregated currency's) index of value. Interesting approaches to this fundamental problem of a composite good's (i.e., a set of commodities and services, a collection of currencies, a portfolio of securities, etc.) value estimation are available, for example, in works by Leontief (1936), Hicks (1939, Chapter II), Markowitz (1952), Sraffa (1960), Samuelson and Swamy (1974), and Sharpe (1995).

It is evident that normalized index $NVal_j(\overline{q};t)$ has the advantage that it does not depend on unit u_j of standard currency g_j, i.e., for all $j,k=1,...,n$ the equality $NVal_j(\overline{q};t) = NVal_k(\overline{q};t) = NVal(\overline{q};t)$ holds.

Similar to equation (4) above, it is convenient to reduce the value of the composite currency to the value 1.0 at the time t_0, or

$$RNVal(\overline{q};t/t_0) = \frac{NVal(\overline{q};t)}{NVal(\overline{q};t_0)} = \sum_{i=1}^{n} w_i RNVal_i(t) = RNVal(\overline{w};t/t_0), \qquad (7)$$

where weight-coefficient ("weight") w_i ($w_i \geq 0$, $w_1 + ... + w_n = 1$) is determined by formula

$$w_i = \frac{q_i NVal_i(t_0)}{\sum_{r=1}^{n} q_r NVal_r(t_0)} = \frac{q_i Val_i(t_0)}{\sum_{r=1}^{n} q_r Val_r(t_0)} = \frac{q_i c_{ij}(t_0)}{\sum_{r=1}^{n} q_r c_{rj}(t_0)}. \qquad (8)$$

Definition (7) implies that $RNVal(\overline{q};t_0/t_0)=1$ for any aggregated currency $\overline{q} = (q_1,...,q_n)$.

We are now in a position to solve for an aggregated currency $\overline{q} = (q_1,...,q_n)$ with minimal volatility of the corresponding time series $RNVal(\overline{q};t) = RNVal(\overline{w};t)$, $\overline{w} = (w_1,...,w_n)$ for a fixed set of goods $G = \{g_1,...,g_n\}$, a fixed period of time $[1,T] = \{1,2,...,T\}$, and given time series $c_{ij}(t)$, $i,j = 1,...,n$, $t = 1,...,T$). Volatility of the time series can be measured by the sample variance

$$S^2(\overline{w}) = Var(RNVal(\overline{w};t)) = \frac{1}{T}\sum_{t=1}^{T}[RNVal(\overline{w};t) - ERNVal(\overline{w})]^2, \qquad (9)$$

where

$$E[RNVal(\overline{w})] = \frac{1}{T}\sum_{t=1}^{T} RNVal(\overline{w};t) \qquad (10)$$

,

is the mathematical expectation of time series $RNVal(\overline{w};t)$, $t = 1,...,T$.[2]

Following Markowitz's diversification principles, the optimal weight-vector $\overline{w}^* = (w_1^*,...,w_n^*)$ minimizes variance $S^2(\overline{w}) = Var(RNVal(\overline{w};t))$ under the constraints $w_i \geq 0$, $i=1,...,n$, $w_1 + ... + w_n = 1$. Here the optimization problem involves minimizing quadratic form $S^2(\overline{w})$ given linear constraints, rather than the usual portfolio problem of minimizing variance conditional on the mean level. That is, we seek to solve for the global minimum point on Markowitz's efficient frontier. There exist many alternative numerical methods to solve this optimization problem. We use Solver.xla in MS Excel 7.0.

The aggregate stable currency with minimal variance $S^2(\overline{w}*)$ is determined by the optimal weights $w_1*,...,w_n*$. The optimal amounts $q_1*,...,q_n*$ of the currencies, which are contained in the optimal currency basket, are proportional to corresponding optimal weight-coefficients $w_1*,...,w_n*$ and may be represented in the form $q_i* = \mu \cdot w_i* / c_{ij}(t_0)$, $i = 1,...,n$, where μ is an arbitrary positive constant (hereafter we utilize $\mu = 1$ as it provides the equality $Val(1\,\text{unit of }SAC; t_0) = Val(1\,\text{unit of currency } g_j; t_0))$ (Hovanov et al., 2004).

Thus, any vector $\overline{q} = (q_1,...,q_n)$ of the currencies' amounts, which are proportional to the components of optimal weight-vector $\overline{w}* = (w_1*,...,w_n*)$, determines a required stable aggregate currency (SAC) with minimal variance $S^2(\overline{w}*)$, which is associated with time series $RNVal(\overline{w}*;t)$, $t = 1,...,T$. SAC provides a relatively constant *measuring stick* that we can use to reliably measure the values of goods and services without the problem of changing dimension as reflected by changes in national currency values over time.

A COMPARISON OF *PIM* AND *SAC* VOLATILITY

In this section we compare the volatility of SAC and PIM (Proportional Ijiri Money). Similar to Ijiri's example, consider two transnational corporations X and Y in 2003 holding assets in Euro-zone countries and the U.S. More specifically, firm X has 160 million euros and 40 million dollars, and firm Y has 40 million euros and 160 million dollars. Using previous notation and expressing units in millions, this means that X-PIM should be determined by $\overline{q}_X = (160\,EUR, 40\,USD)$ with corresponding weight vector $\overline{w}_X = (80.56\%, 19.44\%)$, while Y-PIM is determined by $\overline{q}_Y = (40\,EUR, 160\,USD)$ with corresponding weight vector $\overline{w}_Y = (20.58\%, 79.42\%)$ (i.e., we have used equation (8) with $c_{12}(t_0) = 1.036\,USD/EUR$, $t_0 = 1$: January 1, 2003).

Comparative analyses of volatility are based on day-to-day exchange rates of currencies (EUR, USD) from January 1, 2003 to December 31, 2003. Data are gathered from the Pacific Exchange Rate Service (http://fx.sauder.ubc.ca/data.html). Two time series of reduced (to the time $t_0 = 1$: January 1, 2003) normalized indices of value in exchange were calculated, or $RNVal_i(t/1)$, $i = 1(EUR), 2(USD)$, $t = 1,...,250$. Solving for the minimum variance basket of euros and dollars, the optimal currency weights are $w* = \{52.79\%\ EUR,\ 47.21\%\ USD\}$. Any basket containing euros and dollars in these proportions would be relatively stable over time (e.g., a basket containing 52.79 euros and

47.21 dollars). To compare the stability over time of this minimum variance basket to *PIM* currency baskets for firms X and Y, three time series of reduced normalized indices of value in exchange were calculated: $RNVal(SAC; t/1)$, $RNVal(X-PIM; t/1)$, $RNVal(Y-PIM; t/1)$, $t = 1,...,T = 1,...,251$, for *SAC*, *X-PIM*, and *Y-PIM*, respectively. Figure 1 illustrates these basket currencies' time series, in addition to the normalized values of the dollar and euro over time. It is obvious that *SAC* is much more stable over time than *X-PIM*, *Y-PIM*, *EUR*, and *USD*.

Next, sample standard deviations and sample coefficients of correlation for simple (*EUR*, *USD*) and aggregated (*SAC, X-PIM, Y-PIM*) currencies are calculated. Table 1 reports these results for the following five time series: $RNVal(SAC; t/1)$, $RNVal(X-PIM; t/1)$, $RNVal(Y-PIM; t/1)$, and $RNVal_i(t/1)$, $i = 1,2$ for the dollar (*USD*) and euro (*EUR*). Here we see that *SAC* is more than 40 times more stable than *X-PIM,* and *Y-PIM* and more than 70 times more stable than *EUR*, and *USD* in our sample period. It is clear that *SAC* is far more stable in terms of smaller standard deviation than *X-PIM* and *Y-PIM*. Also, *SAC* is virtually uncorrelated with the simple currencies *EUR* and *USD*, which are contained in the *SAC* basket. We infer that composite currency *SAC* with demonstrated low volatility can be considered a *stable unit of account* not only for both X and Y transnational corporations but for any other *TNC*s holding assets in euros and dollars in 2003.

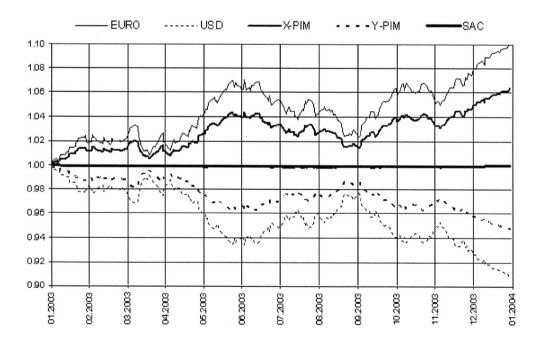

Figure 1. Values of reduced normalized indices of value in exchange of simple $RNVal_i(t/1)$, $i = 1$ (*EUR*), 2 (*USD*) and aggregated $RNVal(X-PIM; t/1)$, $RNVal(Y-PIM; t/1)$, $RNVal(SAC; t/1)$ currencies in the sample period January 1, 2003 – December 31, 2003.

Table 1. Correlation coefficients and standard deviations of simple (*EUR*, *USD*) and aggregated (*X-PIM, Y-PIM, SAC*) currencies in the sample period January 1, 2003 – December 31, 2003

	EUR	*USD*	*X-PIM*	*Y-PIM*	*SAC*	*St. Dev.*
EUR	+1.00	-1.00	+1.00	-1.00	+0.01	0.0232
USD	-1.00	+1.00	-1.00	+1.00	+0.01	0.0212
X-PIM	+1.00	-1.00	+1.00	-1.00	+0.02	0.0146
Y-PIM	-1.00	+1.00	-1.00	+1.00	+0.02	0.0121
SAC	+0.01	+0.01	+0.02	+0.02	+1.00	0.0003

To check the stability of *SAC* outside the 2003 sample year, consider the asset structure of transnational corporation IBM in 2000 and 2001. Suppose that IBM holds its assets mainly in euros and dollars ($g_1 - EUR$, $g_2 - USD$). Let's assume that in 2000 IBM holds 43.139 billion euros and 45.21 billion dollars (see World Investment Report, 2002). In this case IBM-*PIM* should be determined by weight-vector $\overline{w} = (w_1, w_2)$ with almost equal components: $w_1 = 48.83\%$, $w_2 = 51.17\%$.

For the optimal basket *SAC* in the period January 1, 2000 to December 31, 2000, we use the optimal 2002 weights above, or $w^* = \{52.79\%\ EUR, 47.21\%\ USD\}$. Table 2 and Figure 2 show the results of the comparative analysis of simple (EUR, USD) and aggregated (SAC, $IBM - PIM$) currencies. As in the previous example, it is obvious that *SAC* is far more stable than IBM-*PIM* and is almost practically uncorrelated with the simple currencies (EUR, USD). Hence, *SAC* preserves its stability property in out-of-sample periods, which means that it is an appropriate metric for accounting values from year-to-year.

Finally, let's consider IBM's asset structure at 2001. Suppose it has changed to 32.8 billion euros and 55.513 billion dollars, which corresponds to IBM-*PIM* with weight-vector $w_1 = 37.14\%$, $w_2 = 62.86\%$. Again, two time series of reduced (to the moment $t_0 = 1$: January 1, 2001) normalized indices of value in exchange $RNVal_i(t/1)$, $i = 1, 2$, $t = 1,...,T = 1,...,251$, are calculated, and the optimal SAC basket $w^* = \{51.45\%\ EUR, 48.55\%\ USD\}$ is obtained.

Table 2. Correlation coefficients during the in-sample period January 1, 2000 – December 31, 2000 and standard deviations during the in-sample period January 1, 2000 – December 31, 2000 and out-of-sample period January 1, 2001 – December 31, 2001 of simple (*EUR*, *USD*) and aggregated (*IBM-PIM, SAC*) currencies

	EUR	*USD*	*IBM-PIM*	*SAC*	*St. Dev. (2000)*	*St. Dev. (2001)*
EUR	+1.00	-1.00	-0.98	+0.02	0.0259	0.0136
USD	-1.00	+1.00	+0.99	+0.01	0.0290	0.0157
IBM-PIM	-0.98	+0.99	+1.00	+0.18	0.0022	0.0011
SAC	+0.02	+0.01	+0.18	+1.00	0.0004	0.0002

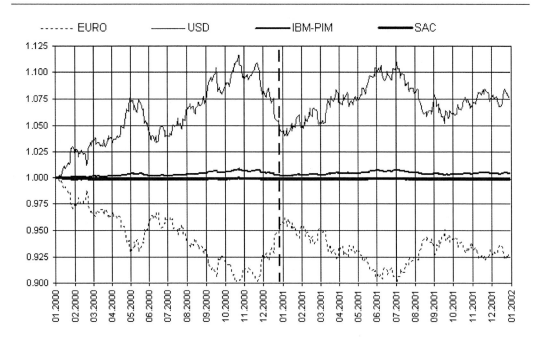

Figure 2. Values of reduced normalized indices of value in exchange of simple $RNVal_i(t/1)$,

$i = 1$ (*EUR*), 2 (*USD*) and aggregated $RNVal(IBM-PIM; t/1)$, $RNVal(SAC; t/1)$ currencies in the in-sample period January 1, 2000 – December 31, 2000 and out-of-sample period January 1, 2001 – December 31, 2001.

As shown in Table 3 and Figure 3, *SAC* is much less volatile than the euro and dollar as well as the aggregated currency IBM-*PIM* for in-sample and out-of-sample periods. Indeed, it changes little in value over time, which is not true for the proportional IBM multi-currency unit.

Table 3. Correlation coefficients during the in-sample period January 1, 2001 – December 31, 2001 and standard deviations during the in-sample period January 1, 2001 – December 31, 2001 and out-of-sample period January 1, 2002 – December 31, 2002 of simple (*EUR, USD*) and aggregated (*IBM-PIM, SAC*) currencies

	EUR	*USD*	*IBM-PIM*	*SAC*	*St. Dev.* (2001)	*St. Dev.* (2002)
EUR	+1.00	-1.00	-1.00	+0.01	0.0142	0.0280
USD	-1.00	+1.00	+1.00	+0.01	0.0150	0.0280
IBM-PIM	-1.00	+1.00	+1.00	+0.03	0.0042	0.0074
SAC	+0.01	+0.01	+0.03	+1.00	0.0001	0.0007

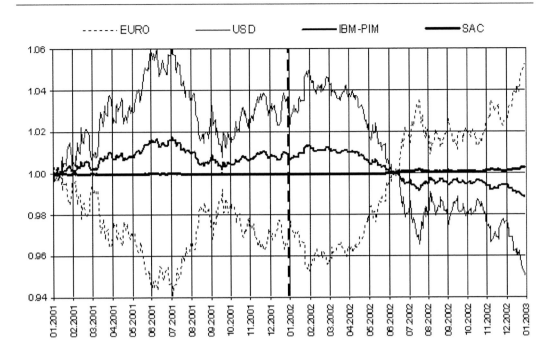

Figure 3. Values of reduced normalized indices of value in exchange of simple $RNVal_i(t/1)$, $i = 1$ (*EUR*), 2 (*USD*) and aggregated $RNVal(IBM-PIM;t/1)$, $RNVal(SAC;t/1)$ currencies in the in-sample period January 1, 2001 – December 31, 2001 and out-of-sample period January 1, 2002 – December 31, 2002.

PRACTICAL AND RESEARCH IMPLICATIONS
OF STABLE COMPOSITE CURRENCIES

SAC's relative stability for in-sample and out-of-sample periods suggests that it is more stable unit of account than national or local currencies. Like any money, *SAC* could be used as a medium of exchange in actual transactions in that international businesses could arrange payments in this optimal currency basket. Also, *SAC* could be employed to denominate debt contracts and substantially reduce exchange rate risks associated with interest and principle payments that fluctuate with currency movements. While these potential applications of *SAC* are possible in the future, we believe that *SAC* has immediate relevance to accounting as a stable unit of account. How is it possible to know if a firm grew in size or profits from one period to the next if the measuring stick (e.g., the dollar or another national currency) is changing over time. Imagine measuring the growth of a person with a ruler that randomly changes in length over time. While this practice sounds absurd, we measure the value of assets, liabilities, revenues, costs, etc. with a measuring stick (e.g., the dollar and euro) that changes randomly in value over time. *SAC* mitigates this age-old problem of a stable numeraire by remaining relatively constant in value over time.

It is a simple process to convert accounting values denominated in national currencies to the optimal basket currency *SAC*. For example, using the optimal weights

$w^* = \{52.79\%\ EUR,\ 47.21\%\ USD\}$, we can compute on any day t the dollar/optimal currency basket exchange rate as $USD/SAC_t = 0.5279\ (USD/EUR_t) + 0.4721\ (USD/USD = 1)$, where USD/EUR_t is the dollar/euro exchange rate on day t. By inverting this exchange rate to get SAC/USD_t, we can now easily convert values in USD to values denominated in SAC. Since SAC is a world money unit based on multiple national currencies, it provides a global, as opposed to local, approach to measuring the accounting values of goods and services. In the present paper we used the dollar and euro to construct SAC, but other major currencies (e.g., the British pound, Japanese yen, etc.) could readily be included in this optimal currency basket. In this regard, an empirical issue for future study is to explore different potential combinations of local currencies to find the most stable (minimum variance) composite currency.

Shiller (1993, 1998) argues that many common indices, such as consumer price indices, stock price indices, money stock measures, national income indices, etc., were initially theoretical concepts of interest to only a small group of researchers and specialists. However, over time they became accepted into everyday practice due to repeated usage and familiarity. According to Shiller, these indices are important because they have led to the development of new financial/economic information that is used by decision makers, government, and others. Analogously, the notion of denominating accounting values in composite currencies is a valuable indexation of financial data. Did a firm's assets and profits grow because it increased its size or earnings or was it simply due to a change in the value of the currency used to denominate these accounting items? To abstract from movements in currency values and avoid currency-dependent financial reporting, not only transnational but all firms would benefit from using a stable composite currency to denominate accounting information. Consistent with Ijiri's recommendation, in this way financial reporting could be harmonized across countries not only in terms of language and accounting standards but currency also.

REFERENCES

Abdel-Magid, M. and J. Cheung. "Ratio Scales, Foreign Exchange Rates, and the Problem of Foreign Currency Translation: An Analytical-Empirical Perspective." *International Journal of Accounting*, 22 (1), 1986, 33-49.

Aczél, J. and J. Dhombres. *Functional Equations in Several Variables with Applications to Mathematics, Information Theory and to the Natural and Social Sciences*. Cambridge: Cambridge University Press. 1989.

Bonar, J. *Philosophy and Political Economy*. New York: Macmillan, 1909.

Bridgman, P. *Dimensional Analysis*. New Haven: Yale University Press, 1931.

Davies, G. *A History of Money from Ancient Times to the Present Day*. Cardeff: University of Wales Press, 1996.

Debreu, G. *Theory of Value: An Axiomatic Analysis of Economic Equilibrium*. London: Wiley and Sons, Inc., 1959.

Georgescu-Roegen, N. *Energy and Economic Myths*. Oxford: Pergamon Press, 1976.

Hicks, J. *Value and Capital*. Oxford, Oxford University Press, 1939.

Hovanov, N. "Stable Units of Account – A Base of Informational Support for Financial Economics." *Abstracts of the 7-th International Conference on Regional Informatics*. St. Petersburg, Russia, 2000, 95. (In Russian)

Hovanov, N. "Models of Composite Goods Value Indices Construction: A Short Survey of Nobel Prize Laureates' Works." *Proceedings of the International Symposium on the Nobel Prize Laureates and Russian Scientific Schools in Economics*. St. Petersburg, Russia, 2003, 189-191. (In Russian)

Hovanov, N., J. Kolari, and M. Sokolov. "Aggregated World Currency of Minimal Risk." *Proceedings of the International Scientific School on Modeling and Analysis of Safety and Risk in Complex Systems*. St. Petersburg, Russia, 2002, 200-203.

Hovanov, N. V., J. W. Kolari, and M. V. Sokolov. "Computing Currency Invariant Indices with an Application to Minimum Variance Currency." *Journal of Economic Dynamics and Control*, 28 (8), 2004, 1481-1504.

Ijiri, Y. "Global Financial Reporting Using a Composite Currency: An Aggregation Theory Perspective." *The International Journal of Accounting*, 30 (2), 1995, 95-106.

Kirsch, R. J. and W. Johnson. "The Impact of Fluctuating Exchange Rates on U.S. Multinational Corporate Budgeting for, Performance Evaluation of, Foreign Subsidiaries. *International Journal of Accounting*, 26 (3), 1991, 149-173.

Kolari, J., M. Sokolov, Y. Fedotov, and N. Hovanov. "A Simple Model of Exchange: Indices of Value in Exchange. *Proceedings of St. Petersburg State University*, 13, 2001. 141-147. (In Russian).

Krause, U. *Money and Abstract Labour*. London: Verso, 1982.

Kuratowski, K. and A. Mostowski. *Set Theory*. Amsterdam: North-Holland Publishing Co., 1967.

Leontief, W. "Composite Commodities and the Problem of Index Numbers." *Econometrica*, 4 (1), 1936, 39-59.

Markowitz, H. "Portfolio Selection." *The Journal of Finance*, 7 (1), 1952, 77-91.

Mehta, D. R. and S. B. Thapa. "FAS-52, Functional Currency, and the Non-Comparability of Financial Reports." *International Journal of Accounting*, 26 (2), 1991, 71-84.

Mundell, R.. "Currency Areas, Exchange Rate Systems, and International Monetary Reform." Speech delivered at Universidad del CEMA, Buenos Aires, Argentina (April) (*www.columbia.edu/~ram15/cema2000.html*), 2000a, 1-23.

Mundell, R.. "A Reconsideration of the Twentieth Century." *American Economic Review*, 90, 2000b, 327-340.

Mundell, R. "Exchange Rates, Currency Areas and the International Financial Architecture." Speech delivered at an IMF panel, Prague, Czech Republic (September 22) (*www.usagold.com/gildedopinion/mundellprague.html*), 2000c, 1-7.

Mundell, R. and M. Friedman. "One World, One Currency?" *Options Politiques*, May 2001, 10-30.

Mussa, M., J. M. Boughton, and P. Isard. *"The Future of the SDR in the Light of Changes in the International Monetary System."* Washington, DC: International Monetary Fund, 1996.

Passinetti, L. Structural Change and Economic Growth: A Theoretical Essay on the Dynamics of the Wealth of Nations. Cambridge: Cambridge University Press, 1981.

Samuelson, P. and S. Swamy. "Invariant Economic Index Numbers and Canonical Duality." *American Economic Review*, 64 (4), 1974, 566-593.

Seton, F. *The Economics of Cost, Use and Value: The Evaluation of Performance, Structure, and Prices across Time, Space, and Economic Systems*. Oxford: Claredon Press, 1992.

Sharpe, W. *Investments*, 5th edition. Englewood Cliffs, NJ: Prentice Hall, 1995.

Smith, A. *An Inquiry into the Nature and Causes of the Wealth of Nations*. Oxford: Oxford University Press, 1976.

Shiller, R. J. *Macro markets*. Oxford, Oxford University Press, 1993.

Shiller, R. J. "Indexed Units of Account: Theory and Assessment of Historical Experience." *NBER working paper 6356* (January), 1998.

Sraffa, P. *Production of Commodities by Means of Commodities: Prelude to a Critique of Economic Theory*. Cambridge: Cambridge University Press, 1960.

World Investment Report 2002: Transnational Corporations and Export Competitiveness, *United Nations Conference on Trade and Development*, United Nations, Geneve and New York (*http://www.unctad.org/en/docs/wir2002_en.pdf*).

In: Economics of Emerging Markets
Editor: Lado Beridze, pp. 25-66

ISBN: 978-1-60021-850-7
© 2008 Nova Science Publishers, Inc.

Chapter 2

EQUITY MARKETS AND ECONOMIC DEVELOPMENT: WHAT DO WE KNOW?

Thomas Lagoarde-Segot[*,1] *and Brian M. Lucey* [2]

[1]Euromed Marseille Ecole de Management and DEFI, Université de la Méditerranée
[2]School of Business Studies and Institute for International Integration Studies, Trinity College Dublin.

ABSTRACT

The objective of this chapter is to review the transmission mechanisms uniting equity market development and economic growth in developing countries. Overall, conclusions suggest that domestic development and international integration of equity markets have dissociated effects on economic welfare. At the domestic level, equity markets foster the mobilization and allocation of financial resources, and improve corporate governance subject to a satisfactory level of informational efficiency. However, equity market integration lowers the cost of capital, but increases financial vulnerability and exerts a non linear impact on capital flows. We summarize these ambiguous mechanisms in an '*equity market development triangle*' and suggest a few directions for future research.

JEL classification: G11;G12;G15
Keywords: Equity Markets, Economic Development.

1. INTRODUCTION

Sixty years after Keynes' demise, the relationship uniting equity markets and economic development is still highly controversial. Countries embarking on financial reforms usually bear two objectives in mind: (a) to raise the level of saving and investment; and (b) to improve the allocation of investment resources in consistency with certain economic and

---

[*] Corresponding Author: thomas.lagoarde-segot@euromed-marseille.com. Telephone: +33 (0) 491 827 390.

social objectives. Nevertheless, equity market development constitutes a separate component of financial liberalization policies, and its economic impact remains ambiguous.

On the one hand, standard transmission mechanisms include increased resource mobilization, better allocation of capital, and improved corporate governance (Cho, 1986; Stulz, 1999). However, not only are these theoretical arguments under-investigated at the empirical level, but a number of arguments also suggest that policy makers should remain cautious with equity market development. First, equity markets fail to allocate resources to the most desirable uses in the presence of information asymmetries (Stiglitz, 1989; Mayer, 1990). Second, shareholder dominance may disturb the implementation of long-run objectives and the necessary balance between stakeholders, both within the firm and the economy (Jeffers, 2005). Third, capital flow volatility and international financial contagion to emerging markets have underlined the risks associated to equity market integration (Calvo and Mendoza, 2000). These observations have led some economists to argue that equity markets constitute *"costly irrelevances which (developing countries) can ill afford"* (Singh, 1999; Singh & Weiss, 1998). Taken together with certain dissatisfaction with the Washington Consensus policies, this lack of empirical evidence has made criticism of equity markets a cornerstone of the *alter-globalisation* movement[1].

This chapter thus aims to survey a large body of theoretical and empirical literature on equity markets and development in an effort to identify potential lessons for policy making, and to suggest areas for future research. It is structured as follows. The first section reviews the internal effects of capital market reforms in emerging countries. The second section focuses on equity market integration and its associated effects. The third section summarizes our findings by considering the intersection of these analyzes, and the fourth section identifies promising research ideas.

2. REVIEW OF INTERNAL IMPLICATIONS

2.1. Mobilization and Allocation of Financial Resources

The pioneering work of Goldsmith (1969), Shaw (1973) and McKinnon (1973) underlined the role of finance in economic development. These authors argued that domestic financial liberalization would lead to higher savings, improved resource allocation and economic growth. However, in their work the emphasis was on the liberalization of the commercial banking system, as opposed to equity markets. Their reasoning was based on the neoclassical assumption of an identity relationship between aggregate investment and aggregate savings, which in turn are positively correlated to interest rates.

To illustrate this point one can suppose a 'financial repression' situation in which interest rates ceilings prevail, so that the interest rate is $r1$ such as $r1 < r^*$, where r* is the natural equilibrium rate. This interest rate corresponds to a savings rate $S1 < S^*$, which ultimately leads to an investment rate $I1 < I^*$; where I^* and S^* are the equilibrium investment and savings rate, respectively. The direct consequence is that a fraction (I^*-I1) of investment projects

---

[1] Over the past ten years, many non-governmental organizations have attempted to provide a 'citizen expertise' on the social and economic consequences financial globalisation. See, for instance, www.attac.org or www.macroscan.com.

cannot be financed. Moreover, credit rationing may also lead banks to minimize risk and allocate savings to projects carrying a lower level of risk. As a consequence, the unsatisfied investment demand segment (I^*-$I1$) tends to gather projects with the highest potential returns, i.e. the most socially useful projects. This magnifies the aggregate welfare loss for the economy. By contrast, the increase in interest rates that result from financial liberalization may lead to an improved mobilization and allocation of domestic resources.

However, these initial models of 'financial repression' have been criticized for overlooking the possibility that endogenous constraints in the credit market may constitute obstacles to the allocative efficiency of investment (Stiglitz and Weiss, 1981). In a seminal model, Cho (1986) assumed that banks and equity investors have the same level of information about firms. In addition, information asymmetries in the credit market imply that although individual borrowers can be sorted according to their expected productivities, their degrees of risk are unknown, so that banks cannot identify the individual risk characteristics of firms. As a consequence, lenders aggregate borrowers into groups, and base their decisions on the expected variance in the distribution of risk for each group of borrowers.

In this context, the banking sector's expected return is a function of a fixed interest rate r^* and of the default risk. The model further supposes that a group of firms j are innovative and highly productive while a group of firms i are less productive, but have established customer relations with banks. Other things equal, the bank's subjective expected variance in the distribution of the risk of group j should be larger than the other group i. As a consequence, the banks' expected return from lending to group i may be higher than that of lending to group j (i.e., $E\Pi i^* \rangle E\Pi j^*$), although the expected productivity of the latter is higher than that of the former (i.e., $Ri \langle Rj$). This results in a suboptimal allocation of savings.

However, equity market investors do not take default risk into account, as their expected returns $E\Pi j^*$ are equivalent to the project's expected return, i.e. $E\Pi j^* = Rj$. In other words, shareholders make their investment decisions based on the comparison of expected productivities, which are known. This allows groups with more risk (such as group j) to obtain financing. Overall, the model suggests that equity market development is a necessary complement to reforms in the banking sector, as it contributes to better resource mobilization in the presence of information assymetries in the credit market (Cho, 1986).

Recent contributions in institutional economics have also highlighted a number of intuitive mechanisms through which market development may positively impact on the allocation of mobilized resources in developing countries. One argument is that banking systems in such countries are often characterized by a high ownership structure resulting in oligopolistic practices. As a consequence, the selection of investment projects based on expected operating results can be disturbed by strategic political interactions between agents, which ultimately results in suboptimal investment decisions and in a weak corporate sector. The poor allocative performance of the bank-based financial structure magnifies the relative advantages of equity markets (Henry and Springborg, 2004).

Other studies have underlined the liquidity–enhancing function of equity markets. For instance, the creation of a domestic stock market in developing countries may provide households with an additional instrument which may better meet their risk preferences and liquidity needs (Dailami and Atkin, 1990). Domestic stock investment may thus constitute an alternative to consumption, the purchase of land and real estate, or the seeking of more profitable investment abroad, and ultimately results in a better mobilization and allocation of savings (Oshikoya and Ogbu, 2003). Similarly, other authors have underlined the role of a large and active secondary market in mitigating the problem of the availability of long-term funds: investors and corporations tend to have conflicting concerns over the optimal degree of liquidity of financial transactions. Investors may indeed prefer high liquidity, whereas corporations need to be assured of long-term credits to match their long term assets. Transactions in the secondary markets may permit the reconciliation of these conflicting concerns and allow new equity issues in the primary markets to be successful. In other words, equity market development may ease the tension between savers' preference for liquidity and entrepreneurs' need for long-term finance (Ndikumana, 2001).

2.2. Corporate Governance

It should also be noted that foreign equity participation may promote further development of the domestic securities market. For instance, Errunza (1999) argued that foreign portfolio investment fosters managerial efficiency. There are five main mechanisms through which stricter governance rules are implemented following foreign equity investment (Stulz, 1999). *First*, firms tapping into foreign capital markets need to minimize agency problems and therefore tend to have an active board of directors that are independent of management. *Second*, international stock issuance requires managers to hire investment bankers. Such bankers have certain responsibilities within global capital markets, and thus play a key certification role in monitoring management. *Third*, globalization allows foreign shareholders to participate significantly in local firms. The introduction of foreign standards may be assimilated to a knowledge transfer from the foreign shareholder to the developing country corporation, which may then spill over to the rest of the economy through job turnover. *Fourth*, opening up to foreign capital creates a market for corporate control, in which fear of takeover or effective takeover fosters managerial discipline and increases efficiency. *Fifth*, local firms cross-listed in countries that better protect minority shareholders may face legal action from foreign shareholders. This constitutes an incentive for the convergence of domestic legal systems towards the highest international standards.

Overall, it is expected that improved institutions, shareholder protection, disclosure standards, along with the active participation of foreign investors,- i.e., the emergence of a local 'equity culture'- would instil confidence among local investors and contribute to further market development and greater managerial efficiency, ultimately resulting in higher economic growth.

2.3. Pervasive Effects

Nevertheless, there are also downsides to equity market development. More specifically, one problem with financial markets is that they tend to be biased towards the short run. This is magnified by the growing importance of institutional investors. Mutual funds managers who benchmark portfolio performance indeed tend to focus on market momentum rather than long-term prospects. In doing so, analysts prioritize quarterly as opposed to annual company reports (a situation described as a "*quarterly report dictatorship*" (Albert, 1995)). This short-term bias is magnified by portfolio diversification: managers can easily cancel some of their positions when their other holdings are well balanced.

By contrast, the identification of sound investment opportunities by a company's management requires a longer time horizon. The design and implementation of sound economic policy also requires a significantly slower pace. Overall, equity market development may favour shorter temporal horizons, in the economy, which may conflict with governmental and managerial timelines. Such a dynamic can be particularly harmful in developing countries, where economic challenges are extremely demanding.

Concurrently, while a lack of market liquidity is generally perceived as a fundamental cause of brutal variations in price, an informal view suggests that in some circumstances, too much liquidity can prove destabilizing. In the context of an underdeveloped financial market, additional liquidity may positively affect price variation by fostering market participants' ability to accommodate order flows. This positively impacts on the adjustment of prices to new information, and may generate a multiplier effect on volatility transmission in times of turmoil. Increased liquidity may induce a reciprocal loop between prices and orders, thereby amplifying market responses. This results in bubble-like booms in asset prices, and in magnified distress when the market plummets (Kenny and Moss, 1998). By contrast, the transmission of market effects is negligible where there are low levels of liquidity (Piesse and Hearn, 2001).

Besides, certain authors have questioned the impact of shareholder dominance on corporate governance. In a world of perfect capital mobility, the dominance of foreign shareholders may lead managers to focus on *one-dimensional* corporate performance measures (e.g. stock prices, return on equity). This tends to bias companies toward adaptive rather than innovative strategies. According to Lazonick and O'Sullivan (1996), shareholder dominance implies the pursuit of liquidity, which is incompatible with the financial commitment required by innovation. These authors do not recognize shareholders as 'principals' who benefit from residual revenue because '*given their quest for liquidity, of all the stakeholders in the modern industrial corporation, shareholders are the ones with the least stake in a particular company as an ongoing entity because, via the stock market, shareholders have the easiest conditions for exit of any stakeholders*' (p.58). Rejecting projects whose returns fail to satisfy investor demand for rapid payoffs may result in a shift of research away from projects with longer-term payoffs. This impacts on innovation and weakens technological development. For example, according to a survey of US companies, the average length of research projects decreased from 21.6 months in 1991 to 16.7 months in 1996 (OECD, 1999).

The pressure to generate returns for shareholders may also be detrimental to other stakeholders, and tends to reduce corporate governance to the sole relationship between shareholders and management (Jeffers, 2005). Other groups, such as employees, customers and suppliers, the state and society in general, are not properly taken into consideration. Environmental issues constitute a good example. Environmental economics theory states that social and environmental sustainability requires companies to internalize all types of costs into their decision function. However, lenders' portfolio decisions are solely based on the expected risk-return characteristics associated with borrowers' projects. Therefore, unless the existing regulatory regime causes product market capital-seekers to fully internalize all types of costs, the non-internalized costs and benefits of prospective investments will not figure into the capital suppliers' decision function. This may result in a sub-optimal resource allocation and in negative social and environmental externalities (Goldstein, 2001). Some authors have also suggested that this problem might be aggravated by the dynamic of financial globalization. For instance, Kim and Wilson (1997) developed a theoretical model in which independent welfare-maximizing governments may regulate pollution emissions from production activities, and tax residential labour and mobile capital in order to finance public good expenditures. Their results suggested that intergovernmental competition for mobile capital may lead to inefficiently lax environmental and social standards. They concluded that financial globalization may lead to a social and environmental 'race to the bottom'. Overall, these observations have led some economists to argue that equity markets constitute '*costly irrelevances which (developing countries) can ill afford*' (Singh, 1997).

2.4. Informationnal Efficiency

However, the mechanisms uniting equity market development and the allocation of investment appear more complex when one incorporates information costs and the informational requirements they impose on the individual equity investor. In line with the financial repression paradigm, proponents of *market efficiency* argue that financial markets collect and allocate savings to the most socially desirable economic projects. Nevertheless, the hypotheses underlying this reasoning are still the object of considerable debate.

2.4.1 Definition

In the broadest sense, market efficiency requires the simultaneous presence of three types of efficiency: *risk-diversification efficiency*, which states that markets fully diversify risks in line with the predictions of the Arrow-Debreu theorem; *valuation efficiency*, which refers to the market's capacity to reflect the fundamental value of financial assets; and *informational efficiency*, which states that active portfolio management strategies are ineffective. Within this framework, there is a direct causality link between informational efficiency, valuation efficiency and allocative efficiency (Aglietta, 2001). This has placed the notion of informational efficiency at the forefront of finance research over the last three decades. In a general sense, informational efficiency implies that the pricing of securities reflects all available information that is relevant to their valuation. However, Fama (1970) identified three types of market information and subsequently suggested three forms of market efficiency: strong, semi-strong, and weak.

'Strong form' efficiency states that all public and private historical information is entirely reflected in asset prices. This implies first, that private information (inside information) is difficult to obtain due to the competition among active investors in the market; and second, that even investors that manage to access private information are unable to achieve abnormal rates of returns. This, however, is unlikely to happen in reality, so that the strong form of efficiency is unlikely to hold.

The semi-strong form of efficiency states that current market prices reflect all publicly available information, including both macroeconomic information (money supply, exchange rate, interest rates...) and corporate information (announcement of dividends, annual earnings, stock splits). In this form of market efficiency, market prices instantaneously adjust to any good or bad news contained in such information as they are revealed. As a consequence, market participants cannot make consistently superior returns by analyzing publicly available information: only insiders may achieve abnormal profits.

Finally, the weak form of efficiency constitutes the most restrictive definition of the concept. It implies that asset prices reflect all past available information relevant to their valuation, so that the analysis of past prices cannot help predicting future patterns. Therefore, it is not possible for a trader to make abnormal returns based on technical analysis. Rejecting the weak-form of efficiency automatically implies rejecting the 'semi strong' and 'strong' forms. As a consequence, the weak-form definition of market efficiency constitutes the main operational definition for efficiency studies (Mobarek & Keasey, 2000). At the theoretical level, weak-form efficiency can be related to the 'random walk model' developed by Fama (1970).

2.4.2 Consequences of Informational Efficiency

The idea that a lack of informational efficiency may disturb the market-based system of incentives and affect the investment allocation process was originally popularized by J.M Keynes (1883-1946) in his description of the 'beauty contest'. Over the last decade however, a set of additional transmission mechanisms has been put forward to account for this phenomenon.

First, a firm may not be able to raise the outside funds necessary to undertake a worthy investment project if a manager cannot fully and credibly reveal information to outside investors and lenders (Myers and Majluf, 1984). *Second*, asymmetries of information between managers and outsiders may lead to diverging perceptions of asset pricing. For instance, given the alternative of financial leverage, managers may then issue new equity only if they assume that stock prices are overvalued. As a consequence, risk-averse investors may be reluctant to invest in new equity issues (Stiglitz, 1989; Franks and Mayer, 1990; Hubbard, 2000). Similarly, entrepreneurs may also hesitate to implement public offerings as a result of high transaction costs or the uncertainty of getting a fair price (Bekaert and Harvey, 1997). *Third*, inefficient markets are often characterized by the absence of reliable accounting standards and usually lack a regular, adequate and reliable disclosure of information. This magnifies the informational advantage of insiders, who are able to manipulate stock prices in order to make extra profits. For instance, better-informed investors may gain inside information about firm productivity. This advantage may be used to retain the high-productivity firms and to sell the low-productivity ones to partially informed savers, resulting in a misallocation of domestic savings (Razin, Sadka and Yuen, 1999). *Fourth*, market efficiency constrains the impact of stock market development on corporate governance. Tying the managers' income to biased market prices would result in a set of wrong managerial incentives, and would ultimately introduce disturbances in the corporate governance mechanism (Pollin, 2002). *Fifth*, market cycles tend to be particularly pronounced in inefficient markets. A lack of reliable information favours noise and herding behaviour among investors, increasing the probability of sudden opinion reversals (Singh, 1997). The negative consequences of market volatility are well known. The cost of capital for corporations may increase due to market fluctuations, which discourages risk-averse investors (Caporale, Howells and Soliman, 2004). Major booms and busts in the secondary market may also undermine the confidence of investors and affect the ability of companies to raise additional funds in the primary market. *Sixth*, speculative bubbles and crashes in the equity market may undermine the whole financial system and generate financial crises with very large economic and social costs (Agénor, 2003). It should also be noted that general equilibrium models have also underlined the positive relationship between informational efficiency and economic development (Capasso, 2004). Taken together, these intuitions constitute considerable backing for the idea that the market efficiency hypothesis largely conditions the economic impact of equity market liberalization policies.

2.4.3 Efficiency in Emerging Markets
In the context of developing markets, it should be noted that a number of specific factors may hinder the flow of information and imply departure from efficiency. Structural and institutional specificities, such as the fragmentation of capital markets, or the presence of political and economic uncertainties, may account for low efficiency (El-Erian and Kumar, 1995). Nonetheless, 'de jure' financial liberalization may not be a sufficient condition for informational efficiency. For instance, Kawakatsu and Morey (1999) investigated market efficiency before and after financial liberalization. They used two sets of dates and data from nine different countries, and found that market efficiency levels were unaffected by the selected events. However, 'de facto' levels of market development may exert a more significant impact on informational efficiency. The low degree of competition in thinly traded markets may indeed result in the presence of dominant players who can cause stock prices to deviate from their intrinsic value (Mobarek and Keasey, 2000). Such a phenomenon is likely to be accompanied by a lack of market transparency, as reflected by corporate information scarcity, low auditing experience, lax disclosure requirements, and overall weak regulations, which together result in truncated fundamental information and favour insider strategies (Blavy, 2002). By contrast, an increase in market capitalization and in the number of listed firms generally results in an enlarged investor base, whose informational needs may foster the development of an individual stock and market-wide research industry.

Insufficient liquidity levels may also affect the market's ability to accommodate orders, and hence weaken the link between prices and information. For instance, Brown and Zhang (1997) discussed the impact of liquidity on informational efficiency by comparing a dealer market and a limit-order book. In their theoretical model, dealers may be better informed than other traders, but the introduction of a limit-order book lowers the execution-price risk faced by speculators, and allows them to react more aggressively to information flows. The introduction of the limit order book thus simultaneously diminishes dealers' profits and increases informational efficiency. More generally, the development of an 'equity culture' in emerging countries societies appears to be an overarching requirement for establishing the conditions of market efficiency (Aloui, 2003).

2.5 Empirical Evidence

Empirical studies related to the theoretical processes discussed above can be divided into two main components: (i) financial development studies, and (ii) informational efficiency studies.

2.5.1 Financial Development Studies
As underlined in Demirgüc-Kunt and Levine (1996), the scarcity of data on stock markets in developing countries has led most research on the ties between financial development and

economic growth to focus on the impact of the banking sector. For instance, King and Levine (1993) examined the relationship between financial intermediation and long-run economic growth in eighty countries from 1960 to 1989. They found that the level of financial intermediary development was strongly linked to long-run growth, even after controlling for many other factors associated with long run growth.

Turning to capital market development, Haber (1991), using a historical analysis, documented the positive impact of capital market reforms on competition and industrialization using evidence from Brazil, Mexico, and the United States during the nineteenth and early twentieth centuries. Atje and Jovanovic (1993) were the first to formally investigate the impact of stock market development on economic growth. Using a sample of forty countries over the 1980-1988 period, they reported a strong relationship between a stock market development indicator (value traded as a percent of GDP) and economic growth. Levine and Zervos (1998) constructed aggregated indexes of overall stock market development and found that stock markets remained positively and significantly correlated to long-run growth over the 1976-1993 period for a wide number of developing countries, even after controlling for development level and economic policy variables. More recent empirical work has also suggested that equity market liberalization is associated with higher real growth, in the range of one percent per annum for the average emerging nation (Bekaert, Harvey and Lundblad, 2001).

Other studies have attempted to compare the respective impact of banks and equity markets. For instance, Demirgüc-Kunt (1992) highlighted a positive and significant relationship between firm leverage and stock market development, suggesting that equity finance may increase the borrowing capacity of firms through risk sharing and raise the quality and quantity of bank lending through timely and systematic information flows. Demirgüc-Kunt and Levine (1995) underlined that the level of stock market development is highly correlated to the development of banks, nonbanks, insurance companies and private pension funds. Their results indicated that, as an economy develops, its aggregate debt-to-equity ratio tends to diminish.

Along similar lines, Demirgüc-Kunt and Maksimovic (1998) explored the effect of stock market development on firms' financing choices. Looking at a sample of thirty industrial and developing economies, they observed that the effect of stock market development on firm debt-to-equity ratios depends on the initial level of stock market development. These empirical studies echo Boyd and Smith's (1996) theoretical model, which showed that the negative association between financial leverage and economic growth can be explained by rising aggregate investment monitoring costs. These are due to the adoption of more complex technology. In other words, the adoption of monitoring costs minimization strategies, as firms move up the value chain, may skew the economy's aggregate financial structure towards equity rather than debt. Recently, a few microeconomic investigations have also suggested that equity market liberalization leads to a modification of the pattern of corporate financing in emerging countries. For instance, Bekaert and Harvey (2000) investigated the impact of financial liberalization on asset pricing in a sample of 20 emerging countries and found that the cost of capital - as measured by dividend yields - always decreased after liberalization but that the effect was relatively weak (0.15%). Errunza and Miller (1998) used a sample of 126 firms from 32 countries and documented a reduction of 42.2 % in long run returns as well as significant positive returns around the announcement of ADR offerings. More recently, Patro and Wald (2005) investigated a panel of 18 emerging markets and found an average decrease in returns of 2.88% per month during the 36 month period starting three and a half year afters the liberalisation date, suggesting a significant decrease in the cost of capital. This result echoes that of Chari and Henry (2004), who used a similar dataset and an international asset pricing modelling framework to obtain similar results, while also underlining the role of firm-specific risk sharing characteristics in corporate valuation. This set of studies hence suggests that equity market development slackens the financial constraint in developing countries by inducing a significant decrease in the cost of capital[2].

Overall, financial development studies have underlined that equity markets have a role to play in financial liberalization policies, as a necessary complement to the banking sector.

2.5.2 Informational Efficiency

Informational efficiency studies have used various datasets and methodologies and can be divided into three main components. One first group of papers tested for the random walk hypothesis based on variance ratio and seasonality tests. A second group of papers directly examined the performance of technical trading rules in predicting price changes. Finally, a third group of papers investigated microstructures in emerging markets.

2.5.2.1 Variance Ratio and Seasonality Tests

Market efficiency tests through the random walk constitute a voluminous amount of literature, which can be chronologically described as follows. In a seminal paper, Urrutia (1995) implemented variance ratio and run tests using monthly data for market indexes in Argentina, Brazil, Chile and Mexico during the 1975-1991 period and yielded contrasting results. Fawson (1996) implemented a wide battery of tests including autocorrelation tests, run tests and unit root analysis to test for the random walk hypothesis in the Taiwan Stock Exchange using monthly stock market returns for the 1967-1993 periods. He was unable to reject the weak form efficiency hypothesis. Similarly, Dockery and Vergari (1997) were unable to reject the weak form efficiency hypothesis in the case of the Budapest Stock Exchange, using weekly stock market indexes covering the 1991-1995 period.

By contrast, Grieb and Reyes (1999) implemented variance ratio tests in the Brazilian and Mexican stock exchanges during the 1988-1995 periods, and significantly rejected the weak form efficiency hypothesis for all market indexes and most individual stocks. Mobarek and Keasey (2000) also attempted to assess the behaviour of stock price movement in the Dhaka Stock Exchange in Bangladesh for the 1988-1997 period and reported market inefficiency based on a runs test, an autocorrelation test, an auto-regression test and an auto-regressive integrated moving average model. However, Chang and Ting (2000) implemented a variance ratio analysis using weekly, monthly, quarterly and yearly returns for the Taiwanese market index for the period from 1971 to 1996. They were unable to reject the random walk hypothesis for all series, except weekly series. Cheung and Coutts (2001) also investigated weak form efficiency in the Hong Kong stock exchange based on variance ratio analysis, using daily data over the 1985-1997 period. They were unable to reject the random walk hypothesis. However, Groenewold et.al (2003) implemented autocorrelation and unit root tests using daily return series for seven indices of the Shangai and Shenzen Chinese stock exchanges and significantly rejected the random walk hypothesis. Lima and Tabak (2004) also applied a variance ratio analysis to daily stock price indexes for Shangai, Shenzen, Hong

---

[2] The underlying theoretical mechanisms have been described by Stulz (1999).

Kong, and Singapore stock exchanges from 1992 to 2000 and rejected the null hypothesis of efficiency in the case of Singapore. Finally, Seddighi and Nian (2004) used autocorrelation, unit root and auto regressive conditional heteroskedasticity models and were unable to reject the null of a random walk in the Shangai stock exchange using daily data from the market index and eight individual shares for the year 2000.

Concurrently, a few authors have tested for day-of-the-week effects in emerging markets. Aggarwal and Rivoli (1989) examined seasonal and daily patterns in equity returns in Hong Kong, Singapore, Malaysia and the Philippines using daily data for the 1976-1988 period. Their results suggested the presence of a robust January effect (higher returns) and Monday effects (lower returns) in all markets except the Philippines. Nath and Dalvi (2004) examined the anomaly in the Indian equity market for the period from 1999 to 2003 using high frequency and end of the day data, and found significant Monday and Friday effects. Finally, Basher and Sodorsky (2006) investigated the day-of-the-week effect in 21 emerging stock markets using daily data for the 1992-2003 period, and found significant support for such effects in the Philippines, Pakistan and Taiwan, Argentina, Malaysia, Thailand and Turkey. Overall, it appears that variance ratio and seasonality tests have raised very mixed results.

2.5.2.2 Technical Trading Rules

An alternative way to check for the random walk hypothesis is to examine the outcomes of technical analysis. The latter can be defined as the deliberate study of market price history, with a view to predicting price changes and enhancing trade profitability. In a seminal paper, Brock et al. (1992) demonstrated profitable moving average trading rules using the Dow Jones Industrials Average from 1897 to 1986. Bessembinder and Chan (1998) assessed whether technical analysis can predict stock price movement in Malaysia, Thailand, Taiwan, Hong Kong and Japan. They found that trading rules are successful in the least developed markets (Malaysia, Thailand and Taiwan), but have less explanatory power in the more developed markets (Hong Kong and Japan). Ratner and Leal (1999) applied technical trading rules to ten emerging equity markets in Latin America and Asia from January 1982 through April 1995. Their results suggested that trading strategies may be profitable in Taiwan, Thailand and Mexico, but not in other markets. Similarly, Parisi and Vasquez (2000) adopted a similar methodology using daily closing prices for the 1987–1998 periods in the Chilean stock market and provided strong support for the technical strategies. Finally, Chang et.al (2004) implemented a comprehensive technical trading analysis, testing for different sub-samples and analyzing returns in bear and bull markets in 11 emerging markets for the 1991-2004 periods. Their results suggested that emerging equity indices do not resemble a random walk, as opposed to more developed markets such as the USA and Japan.

2.5.2.3 Institutions and Efficiency

In light of current theory, authors have attempted to measure the impact of institutions on price patterns. For instance, one first group of studies documented a mutually reinforcing relationship between market efficiency and liquidity levels. Demirgüc-Kunt and Levine (1996) suggested a positive correlation between liquidity, institutional development and market efficiency using data for 41 emerging countries from 1986 to 1993. In developed markets, Jones (2001) assembled an annual time series of bid-ask spreads on Dow Jones stocks from 1900 to 2000, and showed that time varying spreads and turnovers are important determinants of conditional expected stock market returns.

It should also be noted that liquidity levels also have legal and political origins. Using a price-based measurement of liquidity, Lesmond (2005) underlined that countries with weak political and legal institutions have significantly higher liquidity costs than countries with strong political and legal systems: higher incremental political risk tends to be associated with a 10 basis point increase in transaction costs. In a similar vein, Khwaja and Mian (2005) investigated the relationship between poor regulatory environments and the presence of abnormal returns among brokers in Pakistan using trade level data. Their results highlighted a possible manipulation of stock prices by collusive brokers: when prices are low, brokers tend to trade amongst themselves in order to artificially raise prices and attract positive-feedback traders. Once prices have risen, the former exit and leave the latter to suffer the ensuing price fall. These authors underlined that brokers may earn annual rates of return that are 50-90 percentage points higher than those earned by outside investors. These large rents may explain why market reforms are hard to implement, and why emerging equity markets often remain marginal with few outsiders investing and little capital raised.

Another group of papers studied the bid-ask spread price patterns. Cajueiro and Tabak (2005) investigated the causes of long-range dependence in bid–ask prices for all stocks traded in the Brazilian financial market from January 1998 through November 2003. Their findings suggested that price patterns are not solely driven by fundamentals but also by other market characteristics such as capitalization measures (a proxy for liquidity), dividends payments, return on equity (ROE) and financial leverage. Speculative behavior (for example, technical analysis) and speculative bubbles in stock markets have important roles in the determination of prices. Finally, Gorkittisunthorn et.al (2006) examined 104 stock splits that occurred in the Stock Exchange of Thailand during the 2000–2004 period and documented a negative and statistically significant relationship between insider ownership level and change in the percentage bid–ask spread. This further highlights the link between corporate governance structure and equity market efficiency in emerging countries. Overall, empirical investigations of efficiency have yielded mixed results.

Taken together, theoretical and empirical studies suggest that the economic impact of internal equity market development is ambiguous. On the one hand, standard transmission mechanisms include better mobilization and allocation of domestic financial resources, as well as improved corporate governance. Recent empirical macroeconomic and microeconomic models seem to confirm these theoretical intuitions. On the other hand, informational efficiency should be considered as a *relative* rather than *absolute* phenomenon, and is linked to institutional developments.

Overall, the material reviewed in this section suggests that equity market development is an appropriate strategy to foster the mobilization and allocation of domestic financial resources in developing countries. However, such policies must simultaneously tackle insufficient levels of informational efficiency by setting up adequate institutions.

Nonetheless, the trend towards financial globalization generates a number of additional effects with powerful impact on domestic financial systems. These are discussed in the next section.

3. REVIEW OF EXTERNAL IMPLICATIONS

The globalization of financial services has, over the last decade, given rise to a voluminous amount of academic work analyzing both the extent and the consequences of international market integration for financial systems in developing countries. The objective of this section is to discuss the main conclusions from this literature. It is structured as follows. The first sub-section defines equity market integration. The second sub-section derives its main theoretical consequences. The third sub-section reviews the associated empirical literature.

3.1 Equity Market Integration: Definition

Although mostly used by empiricists, the concept of 'equity market integration' is embedded in asset pricing theory. Asset pricing models have highlighted three possible situations: full segmentation, mild segmentation and full integration of equity markets (Bekaert and Harvey, 1995).

3.1.1 Full market segmentation
Full equity market segmentation can be described based on the standard Capital Asset Pricing Model (CAPM), as developed by Sharpe (1964) and Lintner (1965). In this framework, the relevant risk faced by investors is the asset's contribution to the variance of a diversified portfolio within the domestic country. For any individual stock in the segmented stock market we have:

$$\begin{cases} E(R_i) = r_f + \beta_{im}\left[E(R_m) - r_f\right] \\ \left[E(R_m) - r_f\right] = \gamma(W)\sigma_m^{2} \\ E(R_i) = r_f + \gamma(W)COV(R_i, R_m) \end{cases} \qquad (1)$$

Where $E(R_i)$ is the required rate of return on firm i's stock, r_f is the risk-free rate in the domestic market, β_{im} is the beta coefficient of firm i with the domestic market portfolio, and $E(R_m)$ is the expected return on the domestic market. The aggregate risk premium can be established as the product of the coefficient of relative risk-aversion $\gamma(W)$ by the variance of the domestic market portfolio σ_m^{2}. $COV(R_i, R_m)$ is the covariance between the individual stock and the domestic portfolio.

3.1.2 Mild Segmentation
Mild segmentation constitutes an intermediary situation which was initially described by Errunza and Losq (1985). In their analysis, under mild segmentation governments maintain one restriction on financial liberalization: while domestic investors are allowed to invest in the world market portfolio, foreign investors can only hold a subset of domestic equities. This

corresponds to a hybrid CAPM in which assets are divided into freely tradable and restricted assets. Freely tradable assets are priced according to the world factor, which is the relevant source of systematic risk for foreign investors. The pricing of investible securities under mild segmentation is thus given by: $E(R_i) = r_f + \beta_{iw}[E(R_w) - r_f]$. However, the pricing of non-investible securities includes a 'super risk premium', which compensates domestic investors for bearing the risk associated with holding all of the non investible stocks. For any individual restricted stock, we have:

$$E(R_i) = r_f + \gamma_u(W)COV(R_i, R_w) + \gamma(W)COV(R_i, R_n | R_I) \qquad (2)$$

In equation (2), R_n and R_I are the returns on the portfolio non-investible and investible securities, respectively. The variable $COV(R_i, R_n | R_I)$ represents the covariance of firm i's return with the return on the portfolio of non-investible stocks, taking the return on the investible securities as given. γ and γ_u are risk aversion coefficients for restricted international investors and unrestricted domestic investors, respectively.

3.1.3 Market Integration

Finally, full integration means that the domestic equity market becomes a part of the global equity market. As a consequence, domestic assets are rewarded according to their covariance with the world portfolio, as the risk premium on any asset is proportional to its world beta. In other words, risk is measured through asset contribution to the world portfolio. The international version of the CAPM was proposed by Solnik (1974). For any local firm, we have:

$$\begin{cases} E(R_{i*}) = r_{f*} + \beta_{iw}[E(R_w) - r_{f*}] \\ [E(R_w) - r_{f*}] = \gamma(W)\sigma^2 w \\ E(R_{i*}) = r_{f*} + \gamma(W)COV(R_{i*}, R_w) \end{cases} \qquad (3)$$

Where β_{iw} denotes firm i's beta with the world market, $E(R_w)$ denotes the required rate of return on the world equity market portfolio, $\sigma^2 w$ denotes the variance of the return of the world portfolio and r_{f*} is the world risk-free rate. In other words, expected local returns $E(R_i)$ in a fully integrated market depend solely on non-diversifiable international factors.

3.2 Main Theoretical Implications

From a theoretical point of view, equity market integration affects (i) the dynamics of international diversification opportunities, and (ii) the domestic market's sensitivity to international shocks.

3.2.1 International Diversification Opportunities

Modern finance theory shows that including weakly correlated assets in a domestic portfolio reduces risk and maximizes long run yields (Markowitz, 1952, 1959). In this context, two main factors explain the attractiveness of international diversification for portfolio managers. First, the correlations between the returns of the securities that make up a portfolio are crucial in determining the associated level of risk. Generally, the lower the correlation between securities, the lower the portfolio risk, and risk-averse investors tend to select securities with low correlation (Markowitz, 1959). Second, the correlation between domestic and foreign returns is expected to be lower than that between purely domestic securities. This is due to the monetary, fiscal, and industrial policies varying from country to country, which add up to differing industrial compositions of stock market and countries and result in significant differentials in country returns dynamics. International diversification is thus beneficial to both value stability and long run yields because it facilitates the selection of foreign investment projects that exhibit very low correlation with the domestic portfolio.

The relationship uniting market integration, correlation and diversification has been recently formalized by Arouri (2003). The model proceeds from a dynamic representation of the International Asset Pricing Model risk premium (Solnik, 1974). and shows that the gains from international diversification are a negative function of the conditional correlation coefficient between the domestic portfolio and the global portfolio:

$$E\left(R_I - R_i \,/\, \Omega_{t-1}\right) = \delta_{t-1} * \left(1 - p_{i,w,t-1}\right) * VAR\left(R_{i,t} \Omega_{t-1}\right) \tag{1}$$

In (1), I represents the international portfolio and i is the local portfolio. The left-hand side term thus represents the gain from international diversification. In addition, δ represents the price of market covariance risk and p_i represents the correlation coefficient between the domestic and the global portfolio. t denotes time and Ω represents the set of available information. This equation shows that the power of portfolio diversification is magnified in segmented markets where $p_{i,w,t-1}$ tends towards 0. The CAPM indeed shows that in such markets, returns tend to be predominantly determined by the systematic risk of each security in the context of the national portfolio, as opposed to the world beta. By contrast, the gains from international diversification are equal to zero under perfect integration; i.e. when the domestic portfolio is perfectly positively correlated to the global portfolio ($p_{i,w,t-1}=1$). This suggests that the gains from international diversification to emerging markets can considerable in the aftermath of liberalisation episodes. However, these gains may disappear in the middle-run as international cross-market correlations increase. This phenomenon may lead to nonlinearities in the dynamics of capital flows.

3.2.2 Financial Contagion

The concept of 'financial contagion' is another important consequence of market integration and refers to the tendency of bear markets to move downwards in a synchronized fashion. The linkage between market integration and contagion has been formally described by Bekaert, Harvey and Ng (2005) within an empirical model. Their approach was to extend the traditional CAPM from a one-factor to a two-factor setting. To do so, they divided the world market into the United States (US) and a particular region (reg), and allowed for local factors to be priced. Letting i and j be two individual countries, and assuming that the idiosyncratic shocks to the US, regional and individual markets are non correlated, these authors have derived the following dynamic relation between covariances h, betas β and variances σ:

$$
\begin{cases}
h(i,us,t) = \beta_{i,US,t-1} \times \sigma^2_{US,t} \\
h(i,reg,t) = \left(\beta_{i,reg,t-1} \times \beta_{US,reg,t-1} \times \sigma^2_{US,t}\right) + \left(\beta_{i,reg,t-1} \times \sigma^2_{reg,t}\right) \\
h(i,j,t) = \left(\beta_{i,US,t-1} \times \beta_{j,US,t-1} \times \sigma^2_{US,t}\right) + \left(\beta_{i,reg,t-1} \times \beta_{j,reg,t-1} \times \sigma^2_{reg,t}\right)
\end{cases}
\tag{1}
$$

Equation (1) has three several important implications. *First*, a market's covariance with the U.S. (regional) market return is positively related to its country-specific beta with the U.S. (or region). *Second*, provided that the country specific beta parameter is positive, higher volatility in the U.S. market induces higher return covariance between the U.S. and market i. *Third*, the covariance with the regional market or any other national market j within the same region increases in times of high return volatility in the U.S. and/or the regional market. According to these authors, the direct implication of these relationships is the appearance of 'contagious bear markets' in times of financial turmoil.

3.2.3 Empirical Evidence

Related empirical studies have addressed the three following themes: (i) measuring equity market integration, (ii) analyzing portfolio allocations and the dynamics capital flows and (iii) investigating the issue of financial contagion.

3.2.3.1 Equity Market Integration

The existing empirical literature on equity market integration may be divided into two components. The first component gathers studies that test for static equity market integration. The second component gathers studies that account for the time-varying nature of equity market integration.

3.2.3.1.1 Static Estimates of Integration

One standard way to measure market integration is to derive a set of static measures based on time-series empirical models. Within this branch of the literature, a first type of study looked at integration through asset pricing models. For instance, one set of models directly tested for the hypothesis of perfect world equity market integration. Wheatley (1988) used an asset-pricing model in which a country level asset pricing line related a representative individual's expected real return on each asset to the covariance of this return with growth in the individual's real consumption. Using monthly data from January 1960 to December 1985, he was unable to reject the null hypothesis of equity market integration. Ferson and Harvey (1992) examined multifactor asset pricing models for real and expected returns on 18 national equity markets, in which multiple betas were chosen to represent global economic risks. Their results showed that multiple betas, as opposed to world market betas, are able to better explain cross-sectional differences in average returns. Bekaert and Hodrick (1992) followed a slightly different approach. They first estimated the predictable component in excess rates of returns for the equity markets of the US, Japan, the UK and Germany, using lagged excess returns, dividend yields, and forward premiums as instruments. They then implemented vector autoregressive regressions in which constraints were derived from dynamic asset pricing theory. Their estimates suggested mixed evidence in favour of financial integration. However, the main weakness of these studies is that they identify the source of asset risk purely with the covariance of the local returns with the world market portfolio. By doing so, these studies directly test for the hypothesis of perfect world integration by implementing a binary framework in which local markets are either perfectly segmented from the world market, or represent an adequate proxy to the world market. Neither of these assumptions is inherently plausible. Not surprisingly, these studies have performed unspectacularly overall in empirical tests (Kearney and Lucey, 2004).

An alternative approach is to consider the competing hypotheses of integration, mild segmentation and segmentation, in line with the theoretical model of Errunza and Losq (1985). Directly testing this hypothesis for a group of emerging markets, Errunza, Losq and Padmanabhan (1992) provided evidence in favour of a non-polar structure, showing that equity markets are neither fully integrated nor completely segmented. More recently, Akdogan (1997) investigated different degrees of market segmentation across twenty-six large countries for two sub-sample periods (1970's and 1980's) based on an international risk decomposition model. The originality of his approach was to provide a precise segmentation/integration score. The latter also constitutes an operational tool for portfolio managers, who may then identify portfolio diversification opportunities by ranking countries according to their level of international integration.

Checking for co-integration relationships is another way to assess the degree of international integration in equity markets. The Johansen and Juselius (1988) co-integration analysis constitutes the most common approach. Integrated stock markets are expected to have a common stochastic trend with stationary error terms when the data are examined by applying multivariate co-integration analysis to a system of nonstationary stock prices. According to Bernard (1991), the necessary condition for complete integration is that there be n-1 cointegrating vectors in a system of n indices. A voluminous number of studies are based on this approach.

For instance, Kasa (1992) found a single co-integrating vector between the US, Japanese, UK, German and Canadian equity markets over the 1974-1990 period. Chou, Ng and Pi (1994) found evidence of integration among G7 countries over the 1976-1987 period. De Fusco, Geppert and Tsetsekos (1996) suggested that emerging markets were not co-integrated with the US over the 1989-1993 period. Sheng and Tu (2000) examined the interrelationship of Asia-pacific markets around the Asian financial crisis and found evidence of pair-wise co-integration for South East Asia 'tiger' countries. Gallagher (1995) found no evidence of co-integration between Irish and either German or UK equity markets. Kanas (1988) examined the relationship between the U.S. and six large European equity markets pre and post October 1987, and found no evidence of co-integration. Serletis and King (1997) found that European markets did demonstrate integration over the 1971-1992 periods. Using the same methodology, Phylaktis (1999) found that the Pacific Basin countries are closely linked with world financial markets and more so with Japan than with the US. Finally, Arbelaez, Urrutia and Abbas (2001) found evidence of global integration in the Colombian equity market from the period ranging from January 2, 1988 through August 9, 1994.

3.2.3.1.2 Dynamic Estimates of Integration

However, one important line of criticism against static approaches is that they implicitly assume that the degree of integration remains constant over time (Kearney and Lucey, 2004). In doing so, they miss the important element of time variation in equity risk premiums. Taking this into account, a number of alternative approaches have been deployed over time.

In a seminal paper, Harvey (1989) presented strong evidence that conditional co-variances do change over time based on tests of asset pricing models that allow for time variation. Estimates of the expected excess return highlighted the standard Sharpe-Lintner CAPM's inability to capture the dynamic behaviour of asset returns. In an effort to improve existing results, Bekaert and Harvey (1995) investigated expected returns in countries that were segmented from world capital markets in one part of the sample and become integrated later in the sample. Using a measure of capital market integration arising from a conditional regime-switching model, they found that a number of emerging markets exhibited time-varying integration. In turn, Hardouvelis, Malliaroupoulos and Priestley (1999) examined the speed of integration among the EU equity markets by developing an explicit equilibrium asset-pricing model with a time-varying measure of integration. They found that the process of intra European equity market integration seems to have been completed by mid 1998. Along the same lines, Flood and Rose (2003) used an inter-temporal asset-pricing model, in which expected risk-free rates were allowed to vary freely over time, constrained only by the fact that they were equal across assets. Estimating and comparing expected risk-free rates across assets, they found that the S&P 500 and NASDAQ markets seemed to be well integrated, while the NASDAQ was poorly integrated with the S&P 500. Finally, Barari (2004) proposed a recursive version the Akdogan (1997) equity market integration score, thus providing a time-varying measure of equity market integration. Applying this extended methodology to a sample of six Latin American countries for the period of 1988-2001, she observed a trend towards increased regional integration relative to global integration until the mid-1990's, followed by a significant increase in global integration during the second half of the 1990's.

Parallel to these contributions is a branch of literature that examined the international integration of equity markets from the perspective of dynamic correlations between returns. The null hypothesis of no integration was rejected if the correlation matrix of international asset returns demonstrated instability over time. Early papers, such as Panton, Lessig, and Joy (1976) and Watson (1980) found stability. More recent work, however, indicated instability in the relationship. Koch and Koch (1991) estimated a simultaneous equation model over a number of contiguous sub-periods and found significant and increased linkages among world equity markets. Wahab and Lashgari (1993) implemented intertemporal stationarity tests of the variance-covariance matrix of monthly returns on seven international equity indices. Historical analysis revealed that pairwise covariances were invariably highly nonstationary over forecast intervals that varied in length between one month and five years, suggesting increasing integration. Longin and Solnik (1995) refined the analysis by estimating a multivariate general autoregressive conditional heteroskedasticity model with constant conditional correlation in order to capture the evolution in the conditional covariance structure. They studied the correlation of monthly excess returns for seven major countries over the period 1960-90 and also found that the international covariance and correlation matrices were unstable over time, indicating increasing integration. More recently, Steeley (2006) plugged the system of bi-variate equity market correlations into a smooth transition logistic trend model in order to establish how rapidly the countries of Eastern Europe were moving away from market segmentation. She found that Hungary was the most rapidly integrating country.

Recursive co-integration constitutes an alternative to the analysis of correlation coefficients. The idea is to plot the λ_{trace} statistic (which is a general test to determine whether there is one or more co-integrating vectors) and the λ_{max} statistic (which is a test to determine the precise number of co-integrating vectors) in order to examine how the nature of market integration changes over time. Rangvid (2001) used this approach, focusing on quarterly share indices for France, Germany and the UK over the 1960–1999 period. He found evidence of increasing convergence since 1982. Aggarwal, Lucey and Muckley (2004) also investigated the time-varying integration process within the EMU countries based on a recursive co-integration approach and highlighted increased integration through time with specific breaks around selected events. Another possibility is to use an alternative co-integration methodology that takes into account the dynamic component of the integration process. For instance, Voronkova (2004) investigated the existence of long-run relations between emerging Central European stock markets and the mature stock markets of Europe and the United States for the period ranging from September 7, 1993 through April 30, 2002. She implemented the Gregory and Hansen (1996) co-integration approach in an effort to consider the possibility of instability in long-run relations between time-series. She obtained evidence of increasing linkages and structural breaks between the Central European markets and between Central European and developed markets' indices.

In turn, Davies (2006) followed suggestions detailed in Gabriel et al. (2002) and considered the possibility of multiple switches in the long run co-integrating relationship by implementing a co-integration model based on Markov-switching residuals. He documented significant evidence to support a two-regime long-run equilibrium for the MSCI total return index data during the period ranging from 1969 to 2005. In the same spirit, Lucey and Voronkova (2006) used an extensive set of co-integration techniques including a stochastic co-integration test by Harris, McCabe and Leybourne (2002) and the non-parametric co-integration method of Breitung (2002). They focused on the Russian market and documented an increasing degree of co-movements of the Russian market with other developed markets in the aftermath of the Russian crisis of 1998, but not with Central European developing markets.

Finally, other dynamic studies were based on GARCH methodologies. For instance, Fratzscher (2001) used a multivariate GARCH framework to examine financial market integration in Europe and found that the move towards EMU contributed to an increasing integration of financial markets. However, he found that the degree of financial market integration in Europe has been very unstable and volatile over time. Gérard, Thanyalakpark and Batten (2003) modelled second moments and risk exposures using a bi-diagonal multivariate GARCH process and tested a conditional international asset pricing model with both world market and domestic risk included as independent pricing factors for five East Asian markets, the US and world markets. They found little evidence of market segmentation in East Asia over the 1985–1998 period. Kearney and Poti (2006) extended the multivariate dynamic conditional correlation (DCC-MV) GARCH model of Engle (2001) with the inclusion of a deterministic time trend. Their results confirmed a significant rise in the correlations amongst national stock market indexes, which they explained by a structural break shortly before the official adoption of the Euro.

Overall, there are a plethora of empirical studies investigating integration across international equity markets. This, in itself, is a good indicator of the importance of the phenomenon.

3.2.3.2 Portfolio Allocations and Capital Flows

Empirical studies analyzing portfolio allocations and the dynamics of capital flows can be divided into three main components. One type of studies attempted to measure the gains from diversification. Other studies emphasized the presence of specific risks when diversifying into emerging markets. Finally, macroeconomic investigations highlighted nonlinearities in the allocation of portfolio flows to emerging countries in the aftermath of equity market liberalization.

3.2.3.2.1 The Gains from Diversification

As discussed above, financial theory suggests that the net impact of equity market integration on portfolio flows is proportional to changes in time-varying international co-variances. This has given rise to many empirical studies. Investigating developed markets, Sinquefield (1996) argued that the integration of world markets has led to a significant decrease in diversification gains when mixing U.S. domestic portfolios with the MSCI World Index. Arouri (2003) investigated ex ante benefits from world market diversification in 8 markets: the world market, 4 developed markets and 3 emerging markets over the 1973 to 2003 period. His results confirmed the presence of significant benefits from international diversification; however, gains appeared considerably larger for investors from segmented markets. More recently, Timmermann and Blake (2005) analyzed international equity holdings of a large panel of U.K. pension funds over the 1991-1997 period and found that conditional co-variances were not quite as important as own-market volatility in Japan North America, and Europe. The evidence thus appears in line with theoretical models in the case of developed markets.

A considerable body of literature has also underlined the role of emerging market diversification as a return-enhancing strategy for private investors. In a seminal paper, Errunza (1977) investigated the mean-variance implications of including developing countries in a panel of 29 countries for the 1957-1971 period and found that the small correlation of the least developed markets justified their inclusion into the optimal portfolio. Divecha, Drach and Sefek (1992) carried out a similar analysis using a dataset of 23 emerging markets over the 1986-1991 period. Their results suggested that including emerging markets in a global portfolio (up to a 20% threshold) would significantly improve the ex post risk-to-return ratio. Sappenfield and Speidell (1992) used data for 18 emerging markets and 18 developed markets over the 1986-1991 period and suggested that emerging market diversification could be useful during periods of global turmoil such as the 1987 krach, or the 1990 Kuwait invasion. Along the same lines, Diwan, Errunza and Senbet (1994) divided world markets into three components: a developed portfolio, an emerging portfolio and a mixed emerging/developed portfolio. Their simulations were based on the 1989-1991 period and suggested that optimal strategies were, in increasing order, the developed portfolio, the emerging portfolio, and the combined portfolio. Harvey (1995), investigating the 1986-1992 period, showed that adding an emerging market component to a diversified developed portfolio would result in a reduction of six percentage points in the portfolio's total volatility while the expected returns would remain unchanged. More recently, Gilmore et.al (2005) constructed Eastern European portfolios for both US and German investors using various optimization models and several risk measures over the 1995-2003 period. Their results showed that diversification benefits were statistically significant for US investors, but not for German investors.

3.2.3.2.2 Specific Risks in Emerging Markets

There are, however, five specific risks associated with emerging market investment. Exchange risk constitutes the first category. It is related to the variability of cash flow generated in risky currencies. While studies have shown that the exchange risk decreases with firm size and export revenues (Kim and Sung, 2005), it is generally agreed that hedging strategies have partial results, so that conclusions drawn from an international capital asset pricing model that omits currency risk would be misguided (Madura, 1992; Phylaktis and Ravazzolo, 2002). In a seminal paper, Bailey and Chung (1995) suggested that currency fluctuations were a priced factor in cross-sections of emerging stock indexes converted in US dollars over the 1986-1994 period. Investigating the nature of the exchange risk premium in a sample of seven emerging markets for the 1976-2000 period, Carrieri, Errunza et.al (2006a) found that while exchange rate and domestic market risks were priced separately, the local currency risk was, on average, smaller than the domestic market risk but increased substantially during crisis periods, when it could be almost as large as the market risk. Exchange risk stemming from emerging market currencies also seems to be significantly priced in global equity returns, so that information about emerging market crisis episodes affects the prices of global risk factors (Carrieri, Errunza et.al, 2006b).

Political risk is another significant downside to emerging market investment. It includes various dimensions such as expropriation risk, firm nationalization, property seizing etc… There is growing consensus that political risk is a priced factor in emerging markets. For instance, Bilson et.al (2002) investigated the relation between political risk and stock returns within the context of 17 emerging markets and 18 developed markets over the 1984-1997 period. They highlighted the importance of political risk in explaining return variation in individual emerging markets, but not in developed markets. More particularly, they presented evidence to support a positive relation between political risk and ex-post returns in emerging markets. This echoes the conclusions of Perottu and Van Oijen (2001), who noted that political risk tends to have an effect on excess returns in emerging economies. Progress in privatization, however, is significantly correlated to improvements in perceived political risk. Finally, one important characteristic of political risk is that it can be considered 'binary': if it materializes, investors lose most of their expected gains. As a consequence, political risk is significantly associated with capital flights. Recently, Vu Le and Zaq (2006) estimated the equilibrium capital flight equation for a panel of 45 developing countries over 16 years. Their results highlighted that political instability, rather than economic risk, is the most important factor associated with capital flight from emerging markets.

Information asymmetries constitute another specific risk in emerging markets. This risk refers to potential difficulties in monitoring local managers due to cultural differences and inefficiencies in information systems (Lee and Kwok, 1988). Using a market microstructure framework, Krishnamurti et.al (2005) investigated whether there are cross-sectional differences in effective spread, depth and the adverse selection component of spread in a sample of 55 firms originating from 15 emerging markets over the January-June 2000 period. Their results suggested the existence of an information premium for firms with an inferior quality of disclosure. Al-Khouri (2005) also explored the identity and concentration of different block holders and firm value for 89 industrial and service firms listed at the Amman Stock Exchange (ASE) over the 1998–2001 period. His findings indicated a positive and significant relationship between ownership concentration and firm value. Existing studies also suggest that corporate governance and stock market development are associated with lower informational asymmetries. For instance, Bunkanwincha et.al (2006) used firm-level panel data from listed companies from Thailand and Indonesia to analyze the firm's corporate financing behaviours in connection with its corporate governance arrangements, and underlined that weaker corporate governance firms tend to have a higher debt level. Similarly, Black et.al (2006) found a strong correlation between governance and market value in Russia for the 1999-2006 period.

The global finance risk is another category of risk which refers to the transmission of financial crises into emerging markets. The period of financial turmoil that began with the Mexican 'tequila' crisis in January 1995, the Asian 'flu' crisis in August 1997 and the Russian default in 1998 have contributed both to an increase in return volatility and negative returns on the S&P/IFCI Composite Index over the 1994-2003 period (AIMR, 2005).

Finally, the 'self-fulfilling' risk refers to behavioural patterns among investors: by demanding higher returns from emerging markets investment, investors tend to automatically select projects with a higher degree of risk (Bancel and Perrotin, 2005). There are hence several risks associated with emerging market investment. However, the extent to which such risks may deter investors from entering emerging markets is difficult to measure. These risks may indeed be compensated by higher than average returns due to a faster rate of capital accumulation and faster economic growth than in developed countries (Bartram and Dunfey, 2001). They also need to be assessed on a case-by-case basis and depend on the country-context and on the investor's psychology. The 2005 AIMR report summarized the residual uncertainties associated with emerging market investment by arguing that in the last resort, investing in a particular market comes down to *'a bet on emergence'*.

3.2.3.2.3 Portfolio Allocations and Capital Flows

In line with theoretical models, empirical studies have shown that equity market liberalisation tends to be followed by a short-lived surge in capital flows. For instance, Bacchetta and Wincoop (1998) showed that aggregate portfolio flows rose from 0% to about 4% of emerging countries' GDPs during the 1980 to 1996 period. In a similar way, Bekaert and Harvey (2000) investigated a sample of 16 emerging markets and observed that American holdings increased on average from 6.2% to 9.4% of market capitalization from five years before liberalisation to five years after liberalisation. Empirical evidence also suggests that these capital flows are subject to sudden reversals. For instance, Bekaert and Harvey (2001) showed that equity capital flows to emerging markets increased by 1.4% of market capitalization on an annual basis after liberalisation, but were usually levelled out three years later.

The relationship between returns and capital flows can be traced back to Bohn and Tesar's (1995) empirical study. These authors indeed examined whether the expansion of US investment in foreign equities and the change in portfolio composition over time was consistent with models of international portfolio choice. Using monthly data on US equities and those of 22 countries over the 1980-1994 period, they found that foreign investors were mostly 'return chasers', i.e. that portfolio weights appeared to be mainly triggered by changing portfolio returns. Along the same lines, Froot, O'Connell and Seasholes (2001) explored the behavior of daily international portfolio flows into and out of 46 countries from 1994 through 1998. They found that flows increased following unexpectedly high returns in the host market. Turning to emerging markets, Nardari, Griffin and Stulz (2002), used daily data on net equity flows for nine emerging market countries over the 1996-2001 period, and confirmed the fact that a market experiences net equity inflow when its stocks earn unexpectedly high returns.

It has also been observed that capital flows simultaneously lead to higher returns by exerting pressure on local prices. For instance, Clark and Berko (1997) investigated the correlation between monthly foreign purchases of Mexican stocks and Mexican stock returns and found that a surprise foreign inflow equivalent to 1% of domestic market capitalization was associated with a 13% increase in Mexican stock prices. Along the same lines, L'Her and Suret (1997) defined the hyper-return period as a calendar year during which a cumulative geometric return in excess of 70% is observed. Analyzing hyper-return periods from 1976 to 1994 for 20 emerging stock markets, their results also suggested a positive impact of financial liberalization episodes on returns. Finally, Calvo, Leiderman and Reinhart (1996) also documented a significant increase in emerging markets share prices in the period following equity market liberalization: the Argentinean index posted an annual return of 400% in 1991, while Chile and Mexico offered returns of about 100%.

This phenomenon results in a mutually reinforcing dynamic between portfolio adjustment and price pressure within the context of a portfolio-optimizing framework. However, the inevitable opinion reversal among investors often leads to sudden capital outflows and a sharp adjustment in returns. The re-adjustment can be destabilizing for the recipient economy. For instance, Calvo and Mendoza (2000) attempted to measure the consequences of capital account liberalization in the context of informational inefficiencies and multiple equilibriums. They developed a theoretical model in which investors acquire country-specific expertise at a fixed cost and incur variable reputation costs, in a context where information asymmetries give rise to herding behaviour and sudden opinion reversals. They also implemented numerical simulations in the case of Mexico. According to their estimations, a rumour that reduced the expected return on Mexican equity from the equity market forecast (22.4 %) back to the level of the OECD mean return (15.3%) implied an outflow of about $20 billion, or a reduction in the share of the world portfolio invested in Mexico of 40%. The associated economic destabilization costs can be substantial in emerging countries which are often characterized by limited central bank foreign reserves. For instance, using a panel data set over 1975–1997 and covering 24 emerging-market economies, Hutchison and Noy (2006) found that the cumulative output loss of a sudden stop in capital flows amounts to around 13–15% of GDP over a 3-year period.

In line with this type of studies, Tobin (2000) underlined the speculative nature of financial globalization: according to his data, capital flows to emerging countries only represent US$150 billion a year, as opposed to US$1.5 trillion of overall foreign exchange transaction per business day, of which 90% are reversed within a week. The resulting international financial instability has led some authors to cast doubts on the usefulness of capital account liberalization for developing countries. Rodrik's (1998) empirical study is also widely cited. For a cross-section of East Asia, Latin America, and East Asian developing countries, and after controlling for per-capita income, education, institutional quality and regional dummies, he found no correlation between capital account liberalization and growth over the 1975-1989 period. In a recent paper, Jeanne and Gourinchas (2005) also put forward an 'allocation puzzle' in international capital flows: as opposed to neoclassical model assumptions, their theoretical model and estimates suggest that foreign investment has a tendency to flow 'upstream' from capital scarce to capital abundant countries.

3.2.3.3 Financial Contagion

The issue of financial contagion was placed at the forefront of academic debate following the repeated episodes of financial crises that hit emerging markets. These crises include the 1997-1998 Asian crisis, the 1998 Russian crisis, the 1999 Brazilian crisis, the 2001 Turkish crisis, and the 2002 Argentinean crisis. The particularity of these crises is that turmoil originating in a particular market tended to extend to other markets. As a consequence, the term 'contagion' became popular, both in the press and in academic literature, to refer to this phenomenon.

A myriad of studies have empirically tested for financial contagion by modelling shock spillovers among international equity markets. Three salient facts emerge from an investigation of this literature. *First*, financial contagion is common to a vast geographical area and many crisis episodes. *Second*, the nature of the findings cannot be separated from an ongoing methodological debate among empiricists. *Third*, financial contagion interacts with the dynamics international portfolio flows, and destabilizes domestic economies.

3.2.3.3.1 Fundamental or Shift-contagion?

Edwards (2000) underlined that, in the tradition of epidemiological studies, contagion reflects a situation where the effect of an external shock is larger that which was expected by experts and analysts. However, according to Marais and Bates (2006), two types of contagion may be distinguished. *Fundamental contagion* is a mechanic phenomenon resulting from normal interdependencies among economies, both in tranquil and crisis periods. Within this framework, 'monsoonal effects' refer to the cross-country transmission of aggregate shocks that hit different countries and lead to simultaneous negative co-movements. These shocks can be real or financial, and include an increase in international interest rates, a decrease in international demand, or sudden variations in the exchange rates of major currencies (Glick and Rose, 1999). Masson (1998) also argued that emerging market crises were triggered by major economic shifts in industrial countries, while Kaminsky and Reinhardt (2000) emphasized the role of real economic linkages, international bank lending, potential for cross-market hedging, and bilateral and third-party trade in the propagation of international financial shocks.

By contrast, *shift-contagion* is mainly a psychological phenomenon, which appears strongly related to behavioural patterns among investors in specific times of turmoil[3]. This phenomenon is usually explained by sudden opinion reversals among international investors in a situation characterized by informational asymmetries and the presence of multiple equilibriums (Chang and Velasco, 2001). The resulting *shift* in market expectations leads to a significant increase in cross-market linkages after a shock to an individual country or to a group of countries (Forbes and Rigobon, 2001). In other words, shift-contagion refers to the influence of excess returns in one country on the excess returns in another country *after* controlling for the effects of fundamentals. Shocks thus spread through a channel that does not exist during tranquil periods. Shift-contagion is thus a structural break producing both an intensification of relationships and discontinuities in the shock transmission mechanism during a period of turmoil.

This second definition has the advantage of emphasizing the important role played by indiscriminating investors and speculators during a crisis. It is thus a more restrictive definition than the "monsoonal effect", fundamental definition. The concept of shift contagion is also particularly appropriate for statistical analysis, as the structural break can be modelled as a shift in international linkages (AIMR, 2005). Finally, within this definition, *financial vulnerability* refers to the probability that a country will be affected by shift-contagion. Whereas shift-contagion deals with country-to-country crisis transmission within the framework of a specific crisis, vulnerability considers the broader financial interactions within a longer time period (Serwa and Bohl, 2005).

3.2.3.3.2 A Wide Geographical Coverage

Many empirical studies have revealed the wide spread nature of the contagion phenomenon. In developed markets, King and Wadhani (1990) modelled volatility spillovers between the US, the UK and Japan by estimating time-varying correlations between equity returns. They found a significant increase in correlations following the October 1987 stock market crash. Using a similar approach, Lee and Kim (1993) extended the analysis to 12 developed markets and documented further evidence of financial contagion.

Turning to Asian and Latin American emerging markets, Calvo and Reinhart (1995) indicated that the degree of co-movement across weekly equity and Brady bond returns for emerging markets in 11 Latin American countries increased in the wake of the Mexican crisis. Baig and Goldfajn (1998) also presented evidence of an increase in cross-market correlation after the 1997 Asian crisis among the financial markets of Thailand, Malaysia, Indonesia, Korea and the Philippines.

The debate surrounding the integration of Central and European Economies into the European Union has also drawn attention to the question of contagion in those countries. For instance, Serwa and Bohl (2005) investigated contagion in 17 Eastern and Western European stock markets in the wake of 7 big financial shocks between 1997 and 2002. Their results documented stronger evidence of structural breaks in cross-market linkages in Eastern Europe than in Western Europe. Darvas and Szapary (2000) examined the spillover effects of the global financial crises of 1997-1999 on the Czech Republic, Greece, Hungary, Israel and Poland. They found significant evidence of contagious spill-over. Likewise, Gelos and Sahay (2001) examined financial market co-movements across European transition economies and compared their experience to that of other regions using high-frequency data. Their results suggested that the pattern of high-frequency spillovers during the Russian crisis was similar to that observed in other regions during turbulent times.

Turning to Africa, Collins and Biekpe (2003) investigated financial contagion in eight frontier African equity markets during the Asian crisis and found evidence of contagion in the case of Egypt and South Africa. Finally, Alper and Yilmaz (2005) presented an empirical

---

[3] For instance, Eichengreen, Rose, and Wyplosz (1995) highlighted that the countries that came under speculative attack during the ERM crisis had heterogeneous macroeconomic fundamentals: only in some cases could the attack be justified by the degradation of fundamentals.

analysis of real stock return volatility transmission from emerging markets to the Turkish market since 1992, and documented clear evidence of volatility contagion in the aftermath of the Asian Crisis.

3.2.3.3.3 An Ongoing Methodological Debate

The analysis of financial contagion is also indissociable from the ongoing methodological debate on the appropriate means to estimate contagion spillovers. For instance, Forbes and Rigobon (2002) used daily data for stock indices of 28 developed and emerging countries to test for evidence of contagion during the 1987 U.S. stock market crash, the 1994 Mexican peso crisis, and the 1997 Asian crisis and found that most shocks were transmitted through non-crisis-contingent channels after addressing the problem of heteroscedasticity in correlation coefficients.

However, Favero and Giavazzi (2002) extended the measure to a full information framework capturing all nonlinearities in shock transmission and rejected the null of normal interdependency among seven European countries over the 1988-1992 periods. In a similar way, Pesaran and Pick (2002) developed a canonical model of contagion that allowed them to overcome the crisis identification bias inherent to correlation-based analysis. Their results suggested contagion in the European markets during the 1988–1992 period.

Using different assumptions for the variance of country-specific shocks, Corsetti et.al (2005) found contagion in five emerging markets out of a sample of 17 following the 1997 Hong Kong stock market crisis. Using an endogenous method based on a panel approach, Baur and Fry (2005) were able to identify contagion in 11 Asian equity markets during four distinct periods of the same crisis. Finally, modelling Australian equity prices in a structural VAR framework that distinguished between common shocks in international equity markets and domestic shocks in local financial and goods markets, Dungey, Fry and Martin (2004) uncovered additional contagion effects in Australian equity markets during the Asian financial crisis of 1997–1998 and the World Com crisis of 2000.

3.2.3.3.4. Contagion and International Portfolio Investment

The fundamental rationale for international portfolio diversification is that it expands investment opportunities beyond those available through domestic securities. However, the impact of financial contagion on international correlations could lead to a paradox: diversification works the least efficiently when it is most needed.

For instance, Gerlach et.al (2006) analyzed diversification benefits in four East Asian markets using weekly price returns from the 1993-2001 period. Their results showed the existence of significant linkages among these markets and highlighted that fund managers diversifying in East Asia should not ignore the impact of short-term turmoil on portfolio performance when examining the impact of globalization. Similarly, Butler and Joaqui (2002) assessed the benefits of international portfolio diversification by investigating correlations between US, UK, Japanese, Australian and European stock market indices and the corresponding MSCI world-ex-domestic index (that is, world market return excluding the domestic return) over the 372 months from January 1970 through December 2000. Their results suggested that equally weighted portfolio returns in the most extreme bear markets average about 2% less than predicted by a normal distribution. Finally, Schwebach et.el (2002) examined the correlations and volatility of 11 developed and emerging markets and revealed that potential diversification benefits changed dramatically following the devaluation of the baht in Thailand in July of 1997, causing the efficient portfolio set to shift downward and to the right in the Markowitz mean–standard deviation space. Overall, these empirical results echo Das and Uppal's (2004) theoretical model, which suggested that systemic risk reduces the gains from diversification and penalizes investors for holding levered positions.

In turn, the portfolio rebalancing process might also aggravate the contagion wave. Many authors have indeed sought to explain international financial contagion based on portfolio choice mechanisms. In a seminal paper, Schinasi and Smith (2000) argued that elementary portfolio theory offers key insights into financial contagion. They presented a model in which portfolio diversification explains why an investor would find it optimal to significantly reduce all risky asset positions when an adverse shock impacts on just one asset, thereby creating contagious spillovers through the 'contagious selling' of financial assets.

Kodres and Pritsker (2001) also showed how investors may respond to shocks in one market by optimally readjusting their international portfolios, thereby transmitting shocks and generating contagion. In this model, the extent of contagion is worsened in the presence of information asymmetries, which exaggerate price movements due to a bias in the information underlying the order flow.

In a similar vein, Lagunoff and Shreft (2001) developed a model in which agents hold diversified portfolios that link their financial positions to those of other agents in tranquil periods. Shocks at the initial crisis date cause some portfolio losses, to which agents who incur losses respond by reallocating their portfolios. Two related types of financial crisis occur in response: a gradual crisis, occurring as losses spread, and an instantaneous crisis, occurring when forward-looking agents pre-emptively shift to safer portfolios to avoid future losses resulting from contagion.

From an empirical point of view, Ang and Bekaert (2002) investigated the portfolio allocation consequences of increasing correlations and volatilities in bear markets. They modelled the time-varying investment opportunity set using a regime-switching process in which correlations and volatilities increased in bad times. Their results highlighted the significant impact of changing regimes on portfolio weights. More recently, Broner et.al (2006) argued that the impact of past gains and losses on international investors' risk aversion is an important factor in the propagation of financial shocks throughout countries. They examined the behaviour of international mutual funds by monitoring the geographic asset allocation of hundreds of equity funds with a focus on emerging markets, for the 1996-2000 period. Their results suggested that the tendency of mutual funds to respond to relative losses by moving closer to the average portfolio may exacerbate the effect of crises by creating both financial contagion and momentum trading at the country level. Overall, there appears to be a reciprocal relationship between portfolio rebalancing and waves of international contagion.

3.2.3.3.5 Contagion and Economic Instability

Finally, it should be underlined that the recent episodes of financial crisis have highlighted the economic costs associated with financial contagion: during the 1995-2003 periods, the return on the S&P/IFCI Composite Index (a widely used benchmark of emerging market returns) was negative and volatility increased (AIMR, 2005). Adelman and Yeldan (2000) investigated the impact of the East Asian contagion cycle on economic output in the developing world within the framework of an inter-temporal computable general equilibrium model. Their experiments suggested that the affected area's fixed investment declined by 7.9% while its GDP declined by 7.8% upon contagion impact, while the long term effects of the crisis were also felt severely as a consequence of deceleration in the rate of capital accumulation.

Not surprisingly, the issue of contagion vulnerability has become of particular concern for policy making in emerging countries. Some have wondered whether an optimum point between market segmentation and integration might exist, where countries could reap the benefits of financial integration without enduring the costs of contagion (Collins and Biekpe, 2002).

4. THE 'EQUITY MARKET DEVELOPMENT TRIANGLE'

Overall, this survey of the literature reveals that internal and external equity market developments exert separate economic effects. On the one hand, internal market development fosters the mobilization of financial resources and improves corporate governance, subject to satisfactory levels of informational efficiency. On the other hand, evidence highlights the ambiguous economic outcomes of equity market integration. The latter may indeed facilitate corporate financing, but impacts ambiguously on the dynamics of portfolio allocations, and increases the volatility of domestic financial systems. Overall, the optimal degree of international integration seems to depend on a trade-off between cheaper capital and financial stability

Two conclusions arise. *First*, policies seeking to maximize the growth-enhancing impact of equity markets should in priority reach and maintain adequate levels of institutional transparency. *Second*, the external equity market development process should be monitored very carefully. Potential nonlinearities in capital flows and the introduction of an external systemic risk component in domestic markets may indeed induce significant destabilization costs. In the worst possible configuration, premature financial integration would result in increased economic volatility, in a context where additional financial resources would be misallocated due to informational inefficiencies, thereby further increasing economic fragility. In other words, emerging countries may endure the costs of the market integration process without reaping its economic benefits. Taking this into account, policy makers should view institutional and corporate governance reforms as prerequisites for further market integration.

This conclusion appears in line with conventional wisdom. For instance, Aizenman and Powell (2003) suggested that legal and information-related problems explain why volatility has profound effects on emerging market economies. Similarly, Mishkin (1999) claimed that policy makers must put in place the proper institutional structures before liberalizing their financial systems. More generally, the importance of quality institutions for economic development has emerged as a central theme in economic thought. For instance, Rodrik et.al. (2002) have shown that institutional development tends to outperform geography and openness as explanations of real income per capita.

These mechanisms are summarized below using a simple heuristic device. From each side of this *'equity market development triangle'* runs a different axis representing a different facet of equity market development. The origins of these three axes are linked together to form a single triangle. This reflects the existing correlation between the different facets of equity market development.

From the top of this triangle runs a 'resource allocation' axis, which varies from 'institutional underdevelopment' to 'informational efficiency'. This axis represents the impact of market development and informational transparency levels on the allocation of internally and externally mobilized resources. From the right side of this triangle runs a 'resource mobilization' axis, which varies from 'market segmentation' to 'market integration'. This axis represents the impact of market development on the domestic financial sector, in which financing conditions vary from scarce and expensive capital to easier access to finance as equity markets develop and become integrated into global finance. Finally, from the left side runs a 'financial vulnerability' axis, which varies from 'financial repression' to 'financial vulnerability'. This axis represents the pervasive effects of international market integration, which may result in greater shock sensitivity, nonlinearities in capital inflows and a short-term bias in corporate governance. We suggest that the objective of market development policies is to approach the equilibrium point, which is represented by the intersection of these three axes. At this point, market development and market integration result in a slackening of financial constraint at the cost of a reasonable level of financial vulnerability, while the economic efficiency of the additional investments is ensured by an adequate level of market efficiency.

5. Suggestions for Future Research

This analysis allows us to identify at least three promising research ideas. *First*, the exact factors driving market efficiency are yet to be identified. Such an investigation would help policy makers to design an optimal sequencing of market development reforms. A possible research strategy could be to develop *de facto* and *de jure* institutional indicators reflecting market organizations, by-laws and market size, as well as composite indexes of market efficiency encompassing the various definitions of the concept. It could then be possible to assess the nature of the time-varying relationship between institutions and efficiency within a large panel of frontier, emerging and developed markets.

Second, theoretical models and empirical evidence suggest that equity market integration lowers the cost of capital, but increases financial volatility. Clarifying the relationship uniting market integration, financial vulnerability and the cost of capital, and identifying the main characteristics of firms affected by financial contagion would help policy makers to design appropriate responses. One possibility would be to measure the variations of the firm-level cost of capital within periods of externally induced financial stress and.

Third, the impact of financial integration and shareholder dominance on corporate governance and social, economic and environmental externalities in emerging countries could also be investigated. One possible approach might be to develop proxies for social, environmental and corporate governance, before assessing the impact of equity market development and international integration on these. Ethical funds and Islamic funds also constitute a burgeoning industry providing a new dataset for the traditional finance research agenda (efficiency studies, asset pricing, etc...).

To conclude, one might note that the complexity of the equity market development process may call for an interdisciplinary approach. Financial liberalization has implications for various social sciences including development economics, political science and law.

Increasing data availability and advances in econometric theory also permit researchers to obtain a very high degree of precision in empirical investigations. Taken together, these possible research angles seem to create the conditions for a vast research agenda.

Axis 1 : Resource allocation

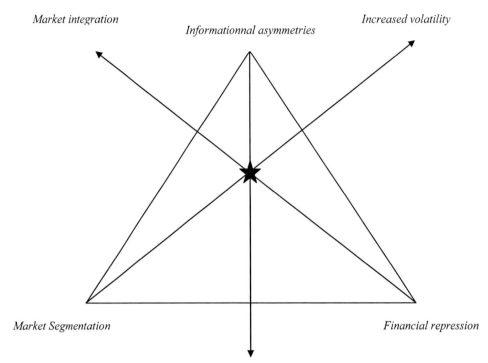

Figure 1. The equity market development triangle.

REFERENCES

Abraham, A., Seyyed, F.J, Alsakran, S.A, 2002. Testing the random walk behaviour and efficiency of Gulf Stock Market. *The Financial Review*, 37, 469-480.
Adelman, I., Yeldan, E., 2000. The minimal conditions for a financial crisis: A multiregional intertemporal CGE model of the Asian crisis. *World Development*, 28, 1087-1100.
Agenor, P.-R. 2003. Benefits and costs of international financial integration: theory and facts. *World Economy* 26, 1089-1118.
Aggarwal, R., B., Lucey, C., Muckley, 2004. Dynamics of equity market integration in Europe: evidence of changes over time and with events. *Institute of International Integration Studies Discussion paper*, DP 19.
Aggarwal, R., Rivoli, P., 1989. Seasonal and day of the week effects in four emerging stock markets. *Financial Review*, 24, 541-50.

Aglietta, M., 2001. Macroéconomie Financière 1. Repères, Editions La Découverte.

Aizenmann, J., Powell, A., 2003. Volatility and financial intermediation. *Journal of International Money and Finance* 22, 657-679.

Akdogan, H, 1997. International security selection under segmentation: theory and application. *Journal of Portfolio* 21, 33-40.

Akyüz Y., Boratav K., 2005. The making of the Turkish financial crisis. in *Financialization and the World Economy*, edited by Gerald Epstein of the Political Economy Research Institute.

Al-Khouri, R., 2005. Corporate governance and firms' value in emerging markets: the case of Jordan. *Advances in Financial Economics* 11, 31-50.

Al-Loughani, N., Chappell, D. Modelling the day-of-the-week effect in the Kuwait stock exchange. *Applied Financial Economics* 11, 353-359.

Al-Loughani, N.E, 1995. Random walk in thinly traded stock markets: the case of Kuwait. *Arab Journal of Administrative Science* 3, 198-209.

Aloui, C., 2003. Long-range dependence in daily volatility on Tunisian stock market. *Economic Research Forum*, Working Paper 40.

Alper, C. E., Yılmaz, K., 2004. Volatility and contagion: evidence from the Istanbul stock exchange. *Economic Systems* 28, 353-367.

Alper, C.E., 2001. The liquidity crisis of 2000: what went wrong? *Russian East Europe Finance Trade* 37, 54–75.

Al-Saad, K., Moosa, I.A., 2005. Seasonality in stock returns: evidence from an emerging market. *Applied Financial Economics* 15, 63-71.

American Institute for Management Research, 2005. Investing in Emerging Markets, *CFA Publications.*

Andrews, D.W.K., 1993. Tests for parameter instability and structural change with unknown change point. *Econometrica* 61, 821-856.

Ang, A., Bekaert, G., 2002. International asset allocation with regime shifts. *Review of Financial Studies*, Oxford University Press for Society for Financial Studies 15, 1137-1187.

Arbelaez H., Urrutia J., Abbas N., 2001. Short-term and long-term linkages among the Colombian capital market indexes. *International Review of Financial Analysis* 10, 237-273.

Arouri, M.E.H, 2003. Intégration financière et diversification internationale de portefeuilles : une analyse multivariée. *Working Paper, MODEM-CNRS*, Université Paris X-Nanterre.

Atje, R., Jovanovic, B., 1993. Stock markets and development. *European Economic Review*, 37, 632-640.

Bacchetta P., Wincoop, E.V., 2000. Capital flows to emerging markets. Liberalization, overshooting and volatility., in Edwards S.(Ed.) *Capital Inflows and the Emerging Economies*, University of Chicago Press and NBER, Cambridge, MA. 61-98.

Bae, K.-H., Karolyi, G.A., Stulz, R.M., 2003. A new approach to measuring financial contagion. *Review of Financial Studies* 16, 717–763.

Baig, T., Goldfajn, I., 1998. Financial market contagion in the Asian crisis. *IMF Staff Paper* 98-155.

Bailey, W., Chung, Y.P., 1995. Exchange rate fluctuations, political risk and stock returns: some evidence from an emerging market, *Journal of Financial and Quantitative Analysis* 30, 541–560.

Balaban, E., 1995. Day of the week effects: new evidence from an emerging stock market, *Applied Economics Letters* 2, 139-43.

Bancel, N., Perrotin, T., 2005. Le cout du capital dans les pays émergents. *ESCP-EAP Working Paper.*

Barari, M. 2004. Equity market integration in Latin America: A time-varying integration score analysis. *International Review of Financial Analysis* 13, 649-668.

Bartram, S. M., Dunfey, G., 2001. International portfolio investment: theory, evidence, and institutional framework. *Financial Markets, Institutions and Instruments* 10, 85-155.

Basher, S.A., Sadorsky, P. 2006. Day-of-the-week effects in emerging stock markets. *Applied Economics Letters* 13, 621-628.

Baur, D., Fry, R. 2005 Endogenous contagion – A panel analysis . *CAMA and EC Working Paper.*

Bekaert, G., Harvey C., 1998. Capital markets: an engine for economic growth. *Brown Journal of World Affairs* (Winter/Spring),.33-53.

Bekaert, G., Harvey, C. 1995. Time-varying world market integration. *Journal of Finance,* 50, 403-444.

Bekaert, G., Harvey, C., 1997. Emerging equity market volatility. *Journal of Financial Economics* 43, 29-78.

Bekaert, G., Harvey, C., 1998. Capital flows and the behavior of emerging market equity returns. *NBER Working Paper No. W6669.*

Bekaert, G., Harvey, C., 1998. Foreign speculators and emerging markets. *The Davidson Institute Working Paper Series*, Number 79.

Bekaert, G., Harvey, C., 2000. Foreign speculators and emerging equity markets. *Journal of Finance,* 55, 565-613.

Bekaert, G., Harvey, C., 2002. Research in emerging markets finance: looking to the future. *Emerging Markets Review* 3, 429–448.

Bekaert, G., Harvey, C., 2003. Emerging markets finance. *Journal of Empirical Finance* 10, 3–55.

Bekaert, G., Harvey, C., Lumsdaine, C., 2002. Dating the integration of world capital markets. *Journal of Financial Economics* 65, 203-249.

Bekaert, G., Harvey, C., Lundblad, C., 2001. *Does financial liberalization spur growth. Working Paper,* Columbia University and Duke University.

Bekaert, G., Harvey, C., Lundblad, C., 2001. Emerging equity markets and economic development. *Journal of Development Economics* 66, 465-504.

Bekaert, G., Harvey, C., Lundblad, C.T., 2000. Emerging Equity Markets and Economic Development. *NBER Working Paper No. W7763.*

Bekaert, G., Harvey, C., Ng, A., 2005. Market integration and contagion. *Journal of Business* 78, 39–70.

Bekaert, G., Hodrick, H., 1992. Characterizing predictable components in excess return on equity and foreign exchange markets. *Journal of Finance* 47, 467-509.

Bernard, A., 1991. Empirical implications of the convergence hypothesis. *CEPR Working Papers.* London.

Bessembinder, H., Chan, K., 1995. The profitability of technical trading rules in the Asian stock markets, *Pacific-Basin Finance Journal* 3, 257-284.

Bessembinder, H., Chan, K., 1998. Market efficiency and the returns to technical analysis. *Financial Management* 27, 5–17.

Bilson, C.M., Brailsford, T.J., Hooper, V.C., 2002. The explanatory power of political risk in emerging markets. *International Review of Financial Analysis* 11, 1-27.

Black F., 1972. Capital market equilibrium with restricted borrowing. *Journal of Business* 45, 444-454.

Black, B.S., Love, I., Rachinsky, A., 2006. Corporate governance indices and firms' market values: Time series evidence from Russia. *Emerging Markets Review* 7, 361-379.

Blavy, R. 2002. Changing volatility in emerging markets: a case study of two Middle Estern stock exchanges. *Revue Entente Cordiale* 02.

Bohn H., Tesar, L. 1996. US equity investment in foreign markets: portfolio rebalancing or return chasing? *American Economic Review* 86, 77-81.

Boubakri, N., Cosset, J.C., Guedhami, O., 2005. Liberalization, corporate governance and the performance of privatized firms in developing countries. *Journal of Corporate Finance* 11, 767–790.

Boyd, J. , Smith, B., 1996. The coevolution of the real and financial sectors in the growth process. *World Bank Economic Review*, Oxford University Press 10, 371-96.

Brock, W., Lakonishok, J., LeBaron, B., 1992. Simple technical trading rules and the stochastic properties of stock returns. *Journal of Finance* 47, 1731–1764.

Broner, F.A, Gelos, G., Reinhart, C.M, 2006. When in peril, retrench: Testing the portfolio channel of contagion. *Journal of International Economics* 69, 203-230.

Brown, D. P., Zhang, Z.M., 1997. Market orders and market efficiency. *Journal of Finance* 52, 277-308.

Bunkanwicha, P., Gupta, J., Rofikoh, R., 2006. Debt and entrenchment: Evidence from Thailand and Indonesia. *European Journal of Operational Research*, In Press, Corrected Proof, Available online 20 October 2006.

Butler, K.C., Joaqui, D.C., 2002. Are the gains from international portfolio diversification exaggerated? The influence of downside risk in bear markets. *Journal of International Money and Finance* 21, 981-1011. Cajueiro, D.O., Tabak, B.M., 2005. Possible causes of long-range dependence in the Brazilian stock market Physica A 345, 635-645.

Calvo, G. A, Leiderman, L., Reinhart, C.M., 1996. Inflows of capital to developing countries in the 1990s. *Journal of Economic Perspectives* 10, 123-139.

Calvo, G.A.,Mendoza, E. G., 1998. Rational herd behavior and the globalization of securities markets. *Duke Economics Working Paper* No. 97-26.

Calvo, G., Mendoza, E., 2000. Rational contagion and the globalization of securities markets. *Journal of International Economics* 51, 79-113.

Calvo, S., Reinhart, C., 1996. Capital flows to Latin America: Is there evidence of contagion effects? In G. Calvo, M. Goldstein, & E. Hochreiter (Eds.), Private capital flows to emerging markets after the Mexican crisis. Washington, D.C.: *Institute for International Economics.*

Capasso, S., 2004. Stock market development and economic growth: A matter of information dynamics. *CNR-ISSM Working Paper*, University of Salerno.

Caporale, G.M., Howells, P.G, Soliman, A.M, 2004. Stock market development and economic growth: the causal linkage. *Journal of Economic Development* 29, 156-178.

Carrieri, F., Errunza, V., Majerbi, B., 2006a. Does emerging market exchange risk affect global equity prices? *Journal of Financial and Quantitative Analysis*, in press.

Carrieri, F., Errunza, V., Majerbi, B., 2006b. Local risk factors in emerging markets: Are they separately priced? *Journal of Empirical Finance* 13, 444-461.

Cartapanis, A., 2004. Les marchés financiers internationaux. *Repères, Editions La Découverte.*

Chang R., Velasco, A., 2001. A model of financial crises in emerging markets: a canonical model. *Quarterly Journal of Economics* 116, 489-517.

Chang, E.J., Lima, E.J.A., Tabak, B.M., 2004. Testing for predictability in emerging equity markets. *Emerging Markets Review* 5, 295-316.

Chang, K.P., Ting, K.S., 2000. A variance ratio test of the random walk hypotheses for Taiwan's stock market. *Applied Financial Economics* 10, 525-532.

Chari, A., Henry, P.B., 2004. Risk sharing and asset prices: evidence from a natural experiment. *Journal of Finance* 59, 1295-1324.

Chelley-Steeley, P., 2004. Equity market integration in the Asia-Pacific region: A smooth transition analysis. *International Review of Financial Analysis* 13, 621-632.

Cheung K-C., Coutts J.A., 2001. A note on weak form market efficiency in security prices: evidence from the Hong Kong stock exchange. *Applied Economics Letters* 8, 407-410.

Cho Y.J., 1986. Inefficiencies from financial liberalization in the absence of well-functioning equity markets. *Journal of Money, Credit, and Banking* 18, 559-580.

Chordia, T., Roll, R., Subrahmanyam, A., 2005. Evidence on the speed of convergence to market efficiency. *Journal of Financial Economics* 76, 271-292.

Chou, R., Ng., V., Pi. L., 1994. Cointegration of international stock market indices. *IMF Working Papers.*

Chuah, H.L., 2004. Are international equity market co-movements driven by real or financial integration? *Duke University Durham Working Paper*, 2004.

Chuhan, P., 1992. Sources of portfolio investment in emerging markets. *Working Paper, International Economics Department, World Bank.*

Clark, J., Berko, E., 1997. Foreign investment fluctuations and emerging stock returns: the case of Mexico. Staff Report, 24, *Federal Reserve Bank of New-York*, New York, NY.

Collins, D., Biekpe, N. 2002. Contagion: A fear for African equity markets? *Journal of Economics and Business* 55, 285-297.

Corsetti, G., Pericoli, M., Sbracia, M., 2005. Some contagion, some interdependence: More pitfalls in tests of financial contagion. *Journal of International Money and Finance* 24, 1177-1199.

Dailami, M., Atkin, M., 1990. Stock markets in developing countries: key issues and a research agenda. PRE Working Paper Series, WPS 515. Washington D.C.: *International Finance Corporation & The World Bank.*

Darvas, Z., Szapáry, G., 2000. Financial contagion in five small open economies: does the exchange rate regime really matter? *International Finance* 3, 25–51.

Das, S. Uppal, R., 2004. Systemic Risk and International Portfolio Choice. *Journal of. Finance* 59, 2809-2834.

Davies, A., 2006. Testing for international equity market integration using regime switching cointegration techniques. *Review of Financial Economics* 15, 305-321.

De Fusco, R., Geppert, J., Tsetsekos, G., 1996. Long run diversification potential in emerging stock markets. *The Financial Review* 31, 343-363.

De Santis, G., Imrohoroglu, S., 1997. Stock returns and volatility in emerging financial markets, *Journal of International Money and Finance* 16, 561–579.

Dellas H., Hess M., 2005. Financial development and stock returns: A cross-country analysis. *Journal of International Money and Finance* 24, 891-912.

Demirguc-Kunt, A. Levine, R., 1996. Stock markets, corporate finance, and economic growth: an overview. *World Bank Economic Review* 10, 223-239.

Demirguc-Kunt, A., 1992. Developing country capital structures and emerging stock markets. Policy Research Working Paper Series 933, *The World Bank.*

Demirguc-Kunt, A., Levine, R. 1996. Stock market development and financial intermediaries: stylized facts. *World Bank Economic Review*,10, 291-321.

Demirguc-Kunt, A., Levine, R., 1995. Stock market development and financial intermediaries: stylized facts, Policy Research Working Paper Series 1462, *The World Bank.*

Demirgüç-Kunt, A., Maksimovic, V., 1998. Law, finance, and firm growth. *Journal of Finance* 53, 2107-2137.

Divecha, A.B., Drach, J., Sefek, D., 1992. Emerging markets. A quantitative perspective. *Journal of Portfolio Management.* Fall: 41-50.

Diwan, I., Errunza, V., Senbet, L., 1994. Diversification benefits of country funds. Investing in Emerging Markets, *Euromoney Books and the World Bank Working Paper.*

Dockery, E., Vergari, F., 1997. Testing the random walk hypothesis: evidence for the Budapest stock exchange. *Applied Economic Letters* 4, 627-629.

Dungey, M., Fry, R., Martin, V., González-Hermosillo, B., 2004. Empirical Modeling of Contagion: A Review of Methodologies. IMF Working Papers 04/78, *International Monetary Fund.*

Dyck, A., 2001. Privatization and corporate governance principles, evidence, and future challenges. *The World Bank Research Observer* 16, 59–84.

Edison, H.,Warnock, F., 2003. A simple measure of the intensity of capital controls. *Journal of Empirical Finance,* 10, 81-103.

Edwards, S., 2000 Contagion. *World Economy*, 23, pp. 873–900.

Ehling, P., Ramos, S.,B., 2005. Geographic Versus Industry Diversification: Constraints Matter. FAME Research Paper Series rp113, *International Center for Financial Asset Management and Engineering.*

Eichengreen B., Pempel T.J., 2002. Why has there been less financial integration in East Asia than in Europe? *Institute of East Asian Studies and the Institute of European Studies*, Working Paper.

Eichengreen, B., Rose, A.K., Wyplosz, C., 1996. Contagious currency crises. *NBER Working Paper No. 5681.*

El-Erian, M.A, Kumar M.S, 1995. Emerging equity markets in Middle Eastern countries, *IMF Staff Paper* 42, 313-343.

Engle, R., 2001. Financial econometrics – A new discipline with new methods. *Journal of Econometrics* 100, 53-56.

Erdal F., Gunduz L., 2001. An empirical investigation of the interdependence of Istanbul Stock Exchange with selected stock markets. An International Conference: *Economies and Business In Transition, Global Business and Technology Association,* Istanbul.

Errunza, V., 1977. Gains from portfolio diversification into less developed countries' securities. *Journal of International Business Studies* 8, 83-99.

Errunza, V., 1999. Foreign portfolio equity investments in economic development. Working paper available at SSRN: *http://ssrn.com/abstract=176939.*

Errunza, V., Losq, E., 1985. International asset pricing under mild segmentation: Theory and test. *Journal of Finance* 40, 105-124.

Errunza, V., Losq, E., Padmanabhan., P., 1992. Tests of integration, mild integration and segmentation hypotheses. *Journal of Banking and Finance* 16, 949-972.

Errunza, V., Miller, D., 1998, Market segmentation and the cost of capital in international equity markets, *McGill University Working Paper*.

Estrada, J., 2000. The cost of equity in emerging markets: a downside risk approach. *Emerging Market Quarterly* 56, 19–30.

Estrada, J., 2002. Systematic risk in emerging markets: the D-CAPM. *Emerging Markets Review* 3, 365–379.

Eun, C.S., Resnick, B.G., 1994. International Diversification of Investment Portfolios: U.S. and Japanese Perspectives, *Management Science* 40, p. 140-160.

Fama, E., 1970. Efficient capital markets: A review of theory and empirical work. *Journal of Finance* 25, 383–417.

Favero, C.A., Giavazzi, F., 2002. Is the international propagation of shocks non linear? Evidence from the ERM. *Journal of Financial Economics* 57, 231-246.

Fawson, R., 1996. The weak-form efficiency of the Taiwan share market. *Applied Economics Letters* 3, 663-67.

Fernandez-Arias, E., 1996. The new wave of private capital inflows: Push or pull?, *Journal of Development Economics* 48, 389–418.

Ferson, W.E., Harvey, C., 1992. Seasonality and consumption-based asset pricing. *Journal of Finance* 47, 511-552.

Fishburn, P.C., 1977. Mean-risk analysis with risk associated with below-target returns. *American Economic Review* 67, 116–126.

Flood, R.P.,Rose, A.K., 2005. Estimating the expected marginal rate of substitution: A systematic exploitation of idiosyncratic risk. *Journal of Monetary Economics* 52, 951-969.

Forbes, K.J., Rigobon, R., 2001. Measuring contagion: conceptual and empirical issues. In: Claessens, Stijn, Forbes, Kristin J. (Eds.), International Financial Contagion: How it Spreads and How it Can be Stopped. *Kluwer Academic Publishers*, Dordrecht, pp. 43–66.

Forbes, K.J., Rigobon, R., 2002. No contagion, only interdependence: measuring stock market co-movements. *Journal of Finance* 57, 2223–2261.

Franks, J., Mayer, C., 1990. Takeovers: capital markets and corporate control: a study of France, Germany and the UK. Economic Policy: *A European Forum* 10, 189-231.

Fratzscher, M. 2001. Financial market integration in Europe: on the effects of EMU on stock markets. Working Paper Series 48, *European Central Bank.*

Froot K.A., O'Connell, P.G.J., Seashole, M.S., 2001. The portfolio flows of international. investors. *Journal of Financial Economics* 59, 151-193.

Frost, P.A., Savarino, J.E., 1988. For better performance: constrain portfolio weights. *Journal of Portfolio Management*, 15, 29-34.

Füss, R., 2002. The financial characteristics between emerging and developed equity markets. Paper presented at the *ECOMOD conference*, 2002.

Gabriel, V.J., Sola, M., Psaradakis, Z., 2002. A simple method for testing for cointegration subject to multiple regime changes. *Economics Letters* 76, 213–221.

Gallagher, L. 1995. Interdependancies among the Irish, British and German Stock Markets. *Economic and Social Review* 26, 131-147.

Gębka, B., Serwa, D., 2006. Intra- and inter-regional spillovers between emerging capital markets around the world. Research in International Business and Finance, forthcoming. Gelos, G., Sahay, R., 2001. Financial spillovers in transition economies. *Economics of Transition* 9, 53–86.

Gérard, B., Thanyalakpark, K., Batten, J.A., 2003. Are the East Asian markets integrated? Evidence from the ICAPM. *Journal of Economics and Business*, Volume 55, 585-607 .

Gerlach, R., Wilson, P., Zurbruegg, R., 2006. Structural breaks and diversification: The impact of the 1997 Asian financial crisis on the integration of Asia-Pacific real estate markets. On line Working Paper.

Gilmore, C.G., McManus, G.M., Tezel, A., 2005. Portfolio allocations and the emerging equity markets of Central Europe. *Journal of Multinational Financial Management* 15, 2887-3000.

Glick, R., Rose, A.K., 1999. Contagion and trade: Why are currency crises regional? *Journal of International Money and Finance*, 18, 603-617.

Goldsmith, R. 1969. *Financial Structure and Development*, New Haven, CT, Yale University Press.

Gorkittisunthorn, M., Jumreornvong, S., Limpaphayom, P., 2006. Insider ownership, bid–ask spread, and stock splits: Evidence from the Stock Exchange of Thailand. *International Review of Financial Analysis* 15, 450-461.

Grieb, T., Reyes, M., 1999. Random walk tests for Latin American equity indexes and individual firms, *Journal of Financial Research* 22, 371-383.

Groenewold, N., Tang, S.H.K., Wu, Y., 2003. The efficiency of the Chinese stock market and the role of the banks. *Journal of Asian Economics* 14, 593-609.

Haber, S., 1991. Industrial concentration and the capital markets: A comparative study of Brazil, Mexico, and the United States, 1830-1930. *The Journal of Economic History* 19, 57-67.

Hardouvelis, G. A., Malliaropoulos, D., Priestley, R., 1999. EMU and European Stock Market Integration. *CEPR Discussion Papers* 2124, C.E.P.R. Discussion Papers.

Harvey, C., 1989. Time-varying conditional covariances in tests of asset pricing models. *Journal of Financial Economics* 24, 289-317.

Harvey, C., 1995. Predictable risk and returns in emerging markets. *Review of Financial Studies* 8, 773-816.

Harvey, C., 2000. Drivers of expected returns in international markets. *Emerging Market Quarterly* 4, 32–49.

Henry, C., Springborg, R., 2004. Globalization and the Politics of Development in the Middle-East. Cambridge, Mass, *Cambridge University Press*.

Hubbard, M., 2000. Money, the Financial System, and the Economy. Reading, MA: In Glenn Hubbard (Ed.) *Asymmetric Information, Corporate Finance and International Development* 11, 343-365.

Hutchison, M., Noy, I., 2006. Sudden stops and the Mexican wave: currency crises, capital flow reversals and output loss in emerging markets. *Journal of Development Economics*, 79, 225-248.

Ickes, B.W., Seabright, P., Yudaeva, K, 2004. Book Reviews. *Economics of Transition* 12, 801-809.

Jeanne, O., Gourinchas, P.O., 2005. Capital flows to developing countries: the allocation puzzle. Meeting Papers 240, *Society for Economic Dynamics*.

Jeffers, E., 2005. Corporate governance: towards converging models? *Global Finance Journal* 16, 221-232.

Jefferson, G. H., 2002. China's evolving (implicit) economic constitution *China Economic Review* 13, 394-401.

Jensen, M., Meckling, W., 1976.Theory of the firm: managerial behavior, agency costs, and capital structure. *Journal of Financial Economics* 3, 305-360.

Johansen, S., Juselius, K., 1990. Maximum likelihood estimation and inference on cointegration - with applications to the demand for money. *Oxford Bulletin of Economics and Statistics,* 52, 2.

Jones, C., 2001. A century of stock market liquidity and trading costs. Working paper, Columbia University. Available at: *www.columbia.edu/~cj88/papers/century.pdf.*

Kaminsky, G.L., Reinhart, C.M., 2000. On crises, contagion, and confusion. *Journal of International Economics,* Vol. 51, Issue 1, pp. 145-168.

Kanas, A., 1988. Linkages between the US and European equity markets: further evidence from cointegration tests. *Applied Financial Economics* 8, 607-614.

Karolyi, G.A., Stulz, R., 1996. Why do markets move together? An investigation of the US-Japan stock return comovements. *The Journal of Finance* 2, 951-986.

Kasa, K., 1992. Common stochastic trends in international stock markets. *Journal of Monetary Economics* 29, 95-124.

Kawakatsu, H., Morey, M., 1999. Financial liberalization and stock market efficiency: an empirical examination of nine emerging market countries. *Journal of Multinational Financial Management* 9, 353-371.

Kearney, C., Lucey, B. 2004. International equity market integration, *International Review of Financial Analysis Special Issue* 13-5 (eds).

Kearney, C., Poti, V., 2006. Correlation dynamics in European equity markets. *Research in International Business and Finance* 20, 305-321.

Kenny, C., Moss, T., 1998. Stock markets in Africa: emerging lions or white elephants? *World Development,* 26, 829-843.

Khwaja, A.I., Mian, A., 2005. Unchecked intermediaries: Price manipulation in an emerging stock market. *Journal of Financial Economics* 78, 203-241.

Kim, J., Wilson, J. 1997. Capital mobility and environmental standards: racing to the bottom with multiple tax instruments. *Japan and the World Economy* 9, 537-551.

Kim, W., Sung, T. What makes firms manage FX risk? *Emerging Markets Review* 6, 263-288.

King R., Levine, R., 1993. Finance, entrepreneurship, and growth. Paper presented at *World Bank Conference* on "How Do National Policies Affect Long-term Growth",Washington D.C., February, 1993.

King, M.A., Wadhwani, S., 1990. Transmission of volatility between stock markets, *Review of Financial Studies* 3, 5–33.

Koch, P.D., Koch, T.W., 1991. Evolution in Dynamic Linkages across National Stock Indexes. *Journal of International Money and Finance* 10, 231-251.

Kodres L.E., Pritsker M., 2001. A rational expectations model of financial contagion. *International Monetary Fund and the Board of Governors of the Federal Reserve System*, Working Paper.

Krishnamurti, C., Šević, A., Šević, Z., 2005. Voluntary disclosure, transparency, and market quality: Evidence from emerging market ADRs. *Journal of Multinational Financial Management* 15, 435-454.

Kumar, P. C., Tsetsekos, G.P., 1999. The differentiation of 'emerging' equity markets. *Applied Financial Economics* 9, 443-453.

L'Her, J.M., Suret, J.F., 1997. Liberalization, political risk and stock market returns in emerging markets. *CIRANO Working Paper*, 97s-15.

Lagunoff, R., Schreft, S., 2001. A model of financial fragility. *Journal of Economic Theory* 99, 220-264.

Lazonick, W., O'Sullivan, M., 1996. *Organisation, Finance and International Competition; Industrial and Corporate Change*, 5, 1.

Lee, S.B., Kim, K.J., 1993. Does the October 1987 crash strengthen the co-movements among national stock markets? *Review of Financial Economics* 3, 89–102.

Lee., K.C., Kwok., C.V., 1988. Multinational corporations versus domestic corporations: International environment factors and determinants of capital structure. *Journal of International Business Studies* 19, 195-217.

Lesmond, D.A., 2005. Liquidity of emerging markets. *Journal of Financial Economics* 77, 411-452.

Lesmond, D.A., Ogden, J., Trzcinka, C., 1999. A new estimate of transaction costs. *Review of Financial Studies* 12, 1113–1141.

Levine, R., Zervos, S., 1998. Stock markets, banks, and economic growth. *The American Economic Review* 88, 537-558.

Li, K., Sarkar, A., Wang, Z., 1999. Diversification benefits of emerging markets subject to portfolio constraints. Working Paper No. UBCFIN99-5

Lima, E.J.A, Tabak, B.M., 2004. Tests of the random walk hypothesis for equity markets: evidence from China, Hong Kong and Singapore, *Applied Economics Letters* 11, 255-258.

Lintner, J., 1965. The valuation of risk assets and the selection of risky investments in stock portfolios and capital budgets. *Review of Economics and Statistics* 47, 13-37.

Lo, A. W., Mackinlay, A.C, 1988. Stock market prices do not follow random walks. Evidence from a simple specification test. *Review of Financial Studies* 1, 41-66.

Lo, A. W., MacKinlay, A.C., 1989. The size and power of the variance ratio test in finite samples. *Journal of Econometrics* 40, 203-238.

Longin, F., Solnik, B., 1995. Is the correlation of international equity returns constant: 1960-1990? *Journal of International Money and Finance* 14, 3-26.

Lucey B., Voronkova, S., 2006. Linkages and relationships between emerging European and developed stock markets before and after the Russian crisis of 1997-1998. In *Emerging European Financial Markets: Independence and Integration Post-Enlargement*, Routledge.

Lucey, B., Voronkova, S., 2006. The relations between emerging european and developed stock markets before and after the Russian crisis of 1997–1998. *International Finance Review* 6, 383-413.

Madura, J., 1992. *International Financial Management*. New York : West Publishing Company.

Madura, J., Abernathy, G., 1985. Playing the international stock diversification game with an unmarked deck. *Journal of Business Research* 13, 465-71.

Marais, E., Bates, S., 2006. An empirical study to identify shift contagion during the Asian crisis. *Journal of International Financial Markets*, Institutions and Money 16, 468-479.

Markowitz, H., 1952. *Portfolio Selection :* Efficient Diversification of Investment, Yale University Press.

Markowitz, H., 1959. *Portfolio Selection*. John Wiley & Sons, New York.

Masson, P., 1998. Contagion-Monsoonal Effects, Spillovers, and Jumps Between Multiple Equilibria," IMF Working Papers 98/142, *International Monetary Fund.*

McKinnon, R., 1973. *Money and Capital in Economic Development*. Washington D.C., Brookings Institution.

Mishkin, F.S, White, E.N., 2003. U.S. Stock Market Crashes and Their Aftermath: Implications for Monetary Policy in William B. Hunter, George G. Kaufman and

Michael Pormerleano, eds., Asset Price Bubbles: The Implications for Monetary, Regulatory and International Policies, *MIT Press*, 53-79.

Mishkin, F.S., 1999. Lessons from the Tequila Crisis. *Journal of Banking and Finance* 23,1521-1533.

Mobarek, A., Keasey, K., 2000. Weak- form market efficiency of an emerging market: evidence from Dhaka stock market of Bangladesh. Presented at *ENBS Conference*, Oslo, 2000. Available online at: *http://www.bath.ac.uk/cds/enbs-papers-pdfs/mobarek-new.pdf*

Moosa, A., Al-Loughani, A., 2003. The role of fundamentalists and technicians in the foreign exchange market when the domestic currency is pegged to a basket. *Applied Financial Economics* 13, 79-84.

Myers, S., Majluf, N., 1984. Corporate financing and investment decisions when firms have information that investors do not have. *Journal of Financial Economics* 13, 187-221.

Nardai, F., Griffin, J.M., Stulz, R., 2002. Do Investors Trade More when Stocks have Performed Well? Evidence from 46 Countries. *Dice Center Working Paper* 13. Available at *SSRN: http://ssrn.com/abstract=567082*.

Nath, G.C., Dalvi, M., 2004. Day of the week effect and market efficiency – evidence from Indian equity market using high frequency data of national stock exchange. Working paper, CCIL, India.

Ndikumana, L., 2001. A study of capital account regimes in Africa. Paper prepared for the *UNCTAD workshop on "Management of capital flows: comparative experiences and implications for Africa"* held in Cairo on March 20- 21, 2001.

Oshikoya T.W., Osita O., 2003. Financial liberalization, emerging stock markets and economic developments in Africa. *In African Voices on Structural Adjustment*, Edited by Thandika Mkandawire and Charles C. Soludo, International Development Research Center.

Panton, D.B., Lessig, V.P., Joy, O.M., 1976. Comovement of international equity markets : a taxonomic approach. *The Journal of Financial and Quantitative Analysis* 11, 415-432.

Parisi, F., Vasquez, A., 2000. Simple technical trading rules of stock returns: evidence from 1987 to 1998 in Chile. *Emerging Markets Review* 1, 152–164.

Park Y.C., 2002. Financial liberalization and economic integration in East Asia. Unpublished manuscript, Korea University.

Patro, D.K., Wald, J.K., 2005. Firm characteristics and the impact of emerging market liberalizations. *Journal of Banking and Finance* 29, 1671-95.

Perotti, E., van Oijen, P., 2001. Privatization, market development and political risk in emerging economies. *Journal of International Money and Finance* 20, 43-69.

Pesaran H., Pick A., 2004. Econometric Issues in the Analysis of Contagion. *Cambridge Working Papers in Economics* 0402, Faculty of Economics, University of Cambridge.

Phylaktis, K., 1999. Capital market integration in the Pacific Basin region. An impulse response analysis. *Journal of International Money and Finance* 18, 287-91.

Phylaktis, K., Ravazzolo, F., 2002. Currency risk in emerging equity markets. *City University Business School, Finance Working Paper.*

Phylaktis, K., Xia, L., 2006. Sources of firms' industry and country effects in emerging markets. *Journal of International Money and Finance* 25, 459-475.

Piesse, J., Hearn, B., 2001. Integration and the asymmetric transmission of volatility: a study of equity market in sub-Saharan Africa. Paper presented at the *Financial Empowerment for Africa conference,* Cape Town, RSA.

Pollin, J.P, 2002. L'excessive volatilité des marchés financiers : quelles explications, quelles conséquences, quelles régulations ? *Chroniques Economiques, Le Cercle des Economistes.*

Rangvid, J., 2001. Increasing convergence among European stock markets? A recursive common stochastic trends analysis. *Economics Letters* 71, 383–389.

Ratner, M., Leal, R.P.C., 1999. Tests of technical trading strategies in the emerging equity markets of Latin America and Asia. *Journal of Banking and Finance* 23, 1887–1905.

Razin, S.E., Yuen, C.W., 1999. An information-based model of foreign direct investment: the gains from trade revisited. *NBER WP 6884.*

Rodrik, D. 1998. Who needs capital-account convertibility? In Should the IMF Pursue Capital Account Convertibility? *Essays in International Finance* no. 207, Department of Economics, Princeton University.

Rodrik, D., Subramanian, A., Trebbi, F., 2002. Institutions rule: the primacy of institutions over geography and integration in economic development. *CEPR Discussion Paper*, no. 3643. London: CEPR.

Santiso, J., 1997. Wall Street face à la crise mexicaine : Une analyse temporelle des marchés émergents. *Les Etudes du CERI*, 34. 12/97.

Sappenfield, R., Speidell, L., 1992. Global diversification in a shrinking world. *Journal of Portfolio Management* 19, 57-67.

Schinasi, G., Smith, T., 2000. Portfolio diversification, leverage, and financial contagion, *IMF Staff Papers* 47, 159–176.

Schwebach, R.G., Olienyk, J.P, Zumwalt, J.K., 2002. The impact of financial crises on international diversification. *Global Finance Journal* 13, 147-161.

Seddighi, H.R., Nian, W., 2004. The Chinese stock exchange market: operations and efficiency. *Applied Financial Economics* 14, 785-797.

Serletis, A., King, M., 1997. Common stochastic trends and convergence of European Union stock markets. *Manchester Business School Working Paper 65.*

Serwa, D., Bohl, M., 2005. Financial contagion vulnerability and resistance: a comparison of European capital markets. *Economic Systems* 29, 344-362.

Sharpe, W.F., 1964. Capital asset prices - A theory of market equilibrium under conditions of risk. *Journal of Finance* 1964, 425-442.

Shaw, E.S., 1973. Financial Deepening in Economic Development. New York, *Oxford University Press.*

Sheng, H.-C., Tu, A.H., 2000. A study of cointegration and variance decomposition among national equity indices before and during the period of the Asian financial crisis. *Journal of Multinational Financial Management* 10, 345-365.

Singh, A., 1997. Financial liberalization, stock markets and economic development. *The Economic Journal* 107, 771-782.

Sinquefield, R.A., 1996. *Where are the Gains from International Diversification?* On line working paper.

Smith, G., Jefferis, K., 2005. The changing efficiency of African stock markets. *South African Journal of Economics* 73, 54-67.

Solnik, B., 1974. An equilibrium model of the international capital market. *Journal of Economic Theory* 8, 500-524.

Steeley, J.M., 2006. Volatility transmission between stock and bond markets. *Journal of International Financial Markets, Institutions and Money* 16, 71-86.

Stein, C., 1955. Inadmissibility of the usual estimator for the mean of a multivariate normal distribution. Proceedings of the 3rd Berkeley Symposium on Probability and Statistics. Berkeley, *University of California Press*, 197-206.

Stevenson, S., 2000. Emerging markets, downside risk and the asset allocation decision. *Emerging Markets Review* 2, 50–66.

Stiglitz J.E., 1989. Financial markets and development. *Oxford Review of Economic Studies.*, 85, 156-79.

Stiglitz J.E., Weiss, A., 1981. Credit rationing in markets with imperfect information. *American Economic view* 71, 393-410.

Stulz, R.M., 1999. Globalization, corporate finance, and the cost of capital, Journal of *Applied Corporate Finance* 12, 8-25.

Taylor, M., Sarno, L., 1997. Capital flows to developing countries: Long- and short-term determinants. *The World Bank Economic Review* 11, 451–470.

Timmermann, A., Blake, D, 2005. International Asset Allocation with Time-Varying Investment Opportunities. *The Journal of Business* 78, 71–98.

Tobin, J. 2000. Financial globalization. *World Development* 28, 1100-1104.

Urrutia, J.L., 1995. Test of random walk and market efficiency for Latin American emerging equity markets, *The Journal of Financial Research* 18, 299-309.

Vinh Vo, X., 2005. Determinants of international financial integration. Australasian Financial Research Group - *University of Western Sydney Working Paper.*

Voronkova, S., 2004. Equity market integration in Central European emerging markets: A cointegration analysis with shifting regimes, *International Review of Financial Analysis, Special Issue,* 13-5.

Vu Le, Q., Zal, P.J., 2006. Political risk and capital flight. *Journal of International Money and Finance* 25, 308-329.

Wahab, M., Lashgari, M., 1993. Covariance stationarity of international equity markets returns: recent evidence. *Financial Review* 28, 239-260.

Wheatley, S. 1988. Some tests of international equity integration. *Journal of Financial Economics* 21, 177-212.

Yeldan, E., 2002. Behind the 2000/2001 Turkish crisis: stability, credibility, and governance for whom? Paper presented at the `1.

In: Economics of Emerging Markets
Editor: Lado Beridze, pp. 67-97

ISBN: 978-1-60021-850-7
© 2008 Nova Science Publishers, Inc.

Chapter 3

Dynamic Linkages between U.S. Portfolio Equity Flows and Equity Returns in China and India

Joseph J. French[*]

School of Finance and Quantitative Methods, Kenneth W. Monfort College of Business
University of Northern Colorado, Campus Box 128, Greely, CO 80639, USA

Atsuyuki Naka[†]

Department of Economics and Finance, College of Business Administration
University of New Orleans, Lakefront, New Orleans, LA70148, USA

Abstract

Asia presents one of the most vibrant economic environments in the world. China and India have emerged as the leaders in the Asian region due to their rapid growth and market size. Consequently, equity markets in both China and India have significantly developed following liberalization in the early 1990s. The rapid growth of these economies coupled with the development of their financial markets has attracted significant portfolio investment from U.S. investors. For example, U.S. equity portfolio flows have increased from 0.63 billion to 7.14 billion in China and from 0.5 to 11 billion in India between 1994 and 2005.

This research examines the dynamic nature of the relationship between U.S. portfolio equity flows and equity returns in China and India. To understand the linkages between equity flows, market returns, and other variables we dissect our empirical findings as follows: first, we examine the correlations between stock market returns and portfolio flows; second, we decompose flows into expected and unexpected components to analyze how returns are influenced by different flow components; and third, we explore the dynamic relationships among flows, returns, and related variables. Our findings show that flows are 'pulled' into China and India by returns greater than U.S. market returns.

[*] Email: joseph.french@unco.edu
[†] Email: anaka@uno.edu

Additionally, we find that the Indian equity index is influenced by U.S. investment activity and dividend yields, whereas the Chinese equity index is statistically unaffected by foreign investor behavior and fundamental determinates of value. This supports the ideas espoused in the popular press that the Chinese government still plays a major role in determining equity prices. A unique finding of this research is that the variance of the flow sequence in both China and India is better explained by shock to fundamentals vs. shocks to returns. This indicates that large American investors are making portfolio allocation decisions not simply on the basis of simple 'return chasing', but are at least partially informed about the markets of China and India. We anticipate that the strong relationship between equity flows and fundamentals should strengthen in the future as information asymmetries decline and U.S. investors continue to develop more sophisticated methods of assessing underlying value in these markets.

1. INTRODUCTION

China and India have recently emerged as the leaders in the Asian region due to their rapid growth and market size. China's economic growth in the past 20 years has been close to 8% per year, while India's annual GDP growth between 1999 and 2004 averaged approximately 6%. Consequently, equity markets in both China and India have significantly developed following liberalization in the early 1990s. The rapid growth of these economies, coupled with the development of their financial markets has attracted significant portfolio investment from U.S. investors. For example, U.S. institutional equity portfolio flows have increased from 0.63 billion to 7.14 billion in China and from 0.5 to 11 billion in India between 1994 and 2005.[1]

Portfolio flows have often been referred to as 'hot money', and are more volatile compared to other forms of capital flows (Kim and Ying, 2001). Investors have been known to reverse portfolio investments at the slightest hint of trouble in the host country or neighboring countries, often leading to disastrous economic consequences. Portfolio flows have been blamed for exacerbating small economic problems in a country by making large concentrated withdrawals at the first sign of economic weakness. Portfolio flows have also been held responsible for spreading financial crisis and causing contagion in international financial markets.[2]

This chapter examines the dynamic nature of the relationships between U.S. portfolio equity flows and equity returns in China and India. Equity flows represent cross-border portfolio flows of investors living abroad. These flows are comprised of inflows, the flows originating in the 'home' country and flowing into a foreign market; outflows, the flows originating in the 'foreign' country and flowing to the home market; and net flows (inflow-outflow). The broad purpose of this study is to understand the relationship between portfolio equity flows and equity returns in China and India. Do U.S. institutional flows affect asset returns? Do equity returns influence flows? These questions have been of recurrent interest to economists, investors, and policy makers, and are posed with greater urgency during times of financial upheaval or changes in the distribution of capital flows. The answers to the above

---

[1] Figures calculated using US treasury department data.
[2] Evidence is provided by the actions of portfolio investors in Malaysia during the 1997 Asian Financial Crisis. Maroney, Naka, and Wansi (2004) provide detailed discussion on the 1997 Asian Financial Crisis.

questions have often cast foreign investors in a negative light. It is often argued that foreign equity flows lead to price overreaction and can result in a contagion effect. An alternative efficient markets view is that equity flows are merely the process by which information is incorporated into asset prices

While there are numerous and strongly competing views, there is surprisingly little information on the behavior of international portfolio flows and their relation to asset returns, particularly in China and India. The large concentration of flows being channeled to China and India makes understanding the nature of the relationship between equity returns and flows in these countries of particular interest between equity flows and financial markets has not been extensively considered. The fact that China and India are special economies with huge market potentials and growth rates, coupled with the unique financial market in China, makes understanding how equity flows affect these financial markets particularly important.

International equity flows have emerged as an important policy issue in China and India (Tian, 2001). The danger of a 'Thailand-style' abrupt and sudden withdrawal of equity flows and the destabilizing effects on equity markets are of concern. While concerns about the negative impacts of sudden reversals of equity flows may have merits comparatively less attention has been paid to analyzing the actual equity flow data, to understand the key relationships between these flows and equity markets. A proper understanding of the influence of equity flows on equity markets and vice versa is essential to have a consequential debate about their effect.

To examine the dynamic relationship between U.S. cross-border equity flows of institutional investors and equity markets, we first look at the key features of equity flows, and then study the relationship between equity flows and stock markets with a key objective of determining causality or more generally forecastability. Secondly, we investigate the nature of the relationship between portfolio equity flows, equity markets, and related variables to uncover if U.S. portfolio investors act as informed investors. To address the emerging debate in the literature over the equality of information between foreign and domestic investors, we examine the response of U.S. equity flows to unexpected shocks in both market prices and fundamental determinants of equity prices. The majority of academic research argues that local (i.e., Chinese or Indian) investors in emerging markets naturally have an information advantage over foreigners (i.e., U.S.), while a new line of research suggests that foreign investors may perform better than domestic investors in their selection and timing of emerging market investments.[3]

The primary empirical method employed is vector autoregression (VAR) model. This method has been widely used by researchers to analyze the dynamic relationships as a reduced form of a system of simultaneous equations. The attractive feature of VAR is that the model allows for each variable in the system to be treated endogenously. The relationship between flows and returns is not well established, and neither variable is known to be exogenous. A VAR analysis allows for the estimation impulse response functions (IRF) and variance decompositions. IRFs provide the time path of the short-run dynamics that result from a shock in one variable to all of the variables in the system, while the variance decompositions provide the forecast error variance explained by variations in the variables in the system.

The findings of this chapter show that flows are 'pulled' into China by returns greater than U.S. market returns. Results in India are less conclusive, but indicate a similar influence of returns on flows. Overall, this result implies that U.S. investors funnel investment funds to foreign markets in an attempt to take advantage of higher returns. This finding is consistent with return chasing behavior, suggested by Bohn and Tesar (1996), and has been documented in other countries. There is stronger evidence of return chasing in China than in India. This suggests that agents are relying more on past return realizations to forecast future returns in China, and indicates that information asymmetries are larger for US investors in China than in India.

The second major finding of this research is that the variance of the Indian equity index is influenced by U.S. investment activity and dividend yields, whereas the Chinese equity index is statistically unaffected by U.S. investor behavior and fundamental determinates of value. This supports the ideas espoused in current academic literature that the Chinese government still plays a major role in determining equity prices.[4] The results indicate that the Chinese market does not view increases in U.S. equity purchases as signaling information because the time path of the market is unaffected by this behavior. On the other hand, Indian market participants consider changes in the purchasing behavior of large U.S. investors as signaling information. The variance of the Indian equity market is influenced by the investment decisions of U.S. portfolio investors. This finding provides evidence that U.S. institutional investors are playing a major role in the Indian market. Further, we find that when returns are decomposed, flows tend to be better explained by fundamental shocks as opposed to price shocks. These results indicate that U.S. investors are reacting to fundamentals in both the Chinese and Indian markets, which suggests that U.S. institutional investors are not informationally deficient.

The reminder of this chapter will be structured as follows: Section 2 discusses capital flows to China and India and the equity markets of these nations, Section 3 discusses the literature, Section 4 describes our methodology and data, Section 5 reports our empirical results and Section 6 concludes this chapter.

2. CAPITAL FLOWS AND EQUITY MARKETS

2.1. FDI and Portfolio Flows in China and India

Capital flows are comprised of foreign direct investment flows (FDI) and portfolio flows (bond flows and equity flows). International portfolio flows are, as opposed to foreign direct investment, liquid in nature and are motivated by international portfolio diversification benefits for individual and institutional investors. Institutional investors, such as pension funds and mutual funds, initiate the majority of cross-border equity flows and bond flows.[5] According to Table 1, there is a positive correlation between FDI and portfolio investment in both China and India. This indicates that many of the factors that make a country a desirable place to acquire fixed assets also make it a desirable place to invest portfolio monies. China has become a magnet for foreign direct investment, overtaking the United States in 2003 as the number one destination of FDI (Prasad and Shang-Jin, 2005). FDI makes up the majority of U.S. investment in China (www.bea.gov), while in India portfolio investments are equally important.

---

[3] See Brennan and Cao (1997), Seasholes (2004), Brennan, Cao, Strong and Wu (2005), Dvorak (2003).
[4] See Tian (2001) and Allen et al (2006).
[5] Treasury International Capital System Notes (TIC).

Table 1. Correlation between US Institutional Equity Flows and Foreign Direct Investment Flows (FDI)

	FDI (CHINA)	FDI (INDIA)	E(CHINA)	E(India)
FDI (CHINA)	1			
FDI (INDIA)	0.87	1		
Equity(CHINA)	0.63	0.39	1	
Equity(India)	0.57	0.54	0.66	1

Source: Bureau of Economic Analysis (BEA). Date from 1994-2005.

One of the primary theoretical reasons to invest in countries such as China and India is the diversification benefits. Erb, Harvey and Viskanta (1996) found that from 1985 to 1993, China had a correlation of 5% with the world market, and for the period from 1979 to 1993, India had a negative correlation of 5% with the world market. These findings imply that, at least theoretically, India and China are naturally attractive to international portfolio investors. Beginning in early 1992, the Chinese and Indian markets that were previously closed to foreign investors began to liberalize, making portfolio investments possible, and equity investments started to pour into the region. As the consequence, the correlation has increased. Chinese equity market return is now correlated with the U.S. market at 14.97% and India is correlated with the U.S. market at 24.72% for the period January 1994 to May 2006. Besides diversification benefits of investing in these markets, China and India's rapid growth, market size, and increasing global competitiveness make these two economies the leaders in the Asian region (Griffith-Jones, 2004). Table 2 presents net portfolio equity flows to emerging markets, including China and India, from the developed countries. As Table 2 illustrates, China and India are becoming the major destinations for portfolio investment, accounting for about 67% of total portfolio equity flows to developing countries in 2004.

Table 2. Net Equity Flows to Developing Countries: China and India

	1996	1997	1999	2000	2001	2002	2003	2004
Developing Countries	32.9	22.6	12.7	12.4	6.0	5.8	24.8	26.8
China	1.9	5.7	0.6	6.9	0.8	2.2	7.7	10.5
India	4.0	2.6	2.3	2.5	3.0	1.1	8.2	7.5
As a proportion of net equity flows to developing countries (%)								
China	5.8	25.2	4.7	55.6	13.3	37.9	31.0	39.2
India	12.2	11.5	18.1	20.2	50.0	19.0	33.0	28.0
China and India	18.0	36.7	22.8	75.8	63.3	56.9	64.0	67.2

Source: Global Development Finance 2005, all numbers in USD billions.

Graphs 1 and 2 show monthly portfolio equity inflows into China and India from the United States. The data, from the Treasury Department of the United States, provides further evidence of the importance of studying portfolio flows to China and India. As these pictures clearly illustrate, inflows to China and India from the United States have increased substantially from 2000 to 2005, and we expect that equity flows to the region should continue. Noteworthy spikes have occurred in both countries. In China, the spike in equity inflows occurred in the month immediately following the appreciation of the Chinese Yuan (RMB). In India, the spike in equity flows occurred around the time of increased public interest in Indian equities, evidenced by an investment of 100 million dollars by Goldman Sacs in the month the spike occurs and a corresponding visit by President George W. Bush on November 2005.

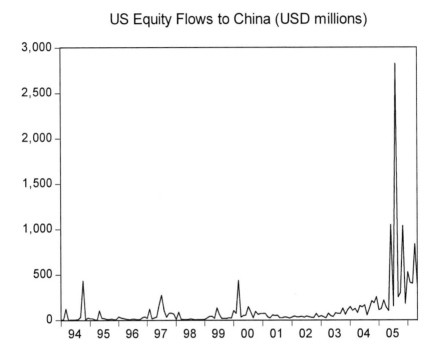

Graph 1. Monthly Equity Flows from the U.S. to China.

Another key aspect of the Chinese and Indian markets which makes them attractive to portfolio investors is the large reserve that both countries have built-up over the period of 2000 to 2004. These high reserves serve the purpose of protecting against instability in financial markets and help to mitigate undesirable appreciation of the Rupee and Yuan, which could undermine their international competitiveness (Griffith-Jones, 2004). Table 3 shows just how rapidly these two countries built-up foreign exchange reserves from 2000 to 2004. Most of these reserves have been invested in U.S. assets, and have helped to finance the U.S.'s large and growing current account deficit and Government debt (Rogoff, 2003).

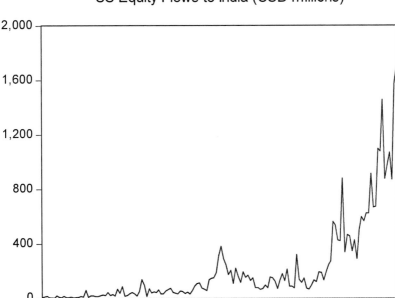

US Equity Flows to India (USD millions)

Graph 2. Monthly Equity Flows from the U.S. to India.

Table 3. Foreign Exchange Reserves of China and India

	2000	2001	2002	2003	2004
China	165.6	212.2	286.4	403.3	610.0
India	37.3	45.3	67.0	97.6	125.5

Source: Global Development Finance 2005. All number in USD billions.

Although China's trade surplus with the United States has been growing, its overall trade surplus is modest because it is running a growing trade deficit with Asia-Pacific countries; in large part offsetting its trade surplus with the U.S. China has accumulated substantial foreign exchange reserves that exceed its annual imports. There is little doubt that China's growing exports to countries outside of Asia has generated equally rapid growth in imports by China from other Asian and Pacific countries. According to Perez (2002), Japan's current economic recovery is being driven by a surge in exports to China. Australia's healthy economy is being kept that way by Chinese investments in liquid natural gas products. China is now also South Korea's largest trading partner. Although India is the largest market in South Asia, it has yet to have a major impact on the trade of its neighbors in South Asia despite of the creation of the South Asian Preferential Trade Area (SAPTA) in 1997. Prasad and Shang-Jin (2005) point out the recent increase in the pace of reserve accumulation in China is potentially related to "hot money' (i.e. bond and equity flows) rather than trade surplus or FDI flows. The evolution of Indian reserves is similar to what is occurring in China. India had reserves of around $98 billion at the end of 2003, exceeding by a substantial margin imports of $60 billion.

The issue of the appropriate level of reserves is unsettled (Griffith-Jones, 2004). Any attempt to determine the appropriate level of reserves has to be based on an analysis of the exchange rate regime for each country, and the related issue of whether the benefits from integration with the global financial markets outweigh the costs. Rogoff (2003) discusses these issues in the context of China and India, and concludes that for the most part China and India are getting to the point where the lost opportunity cost of building up reserves is beginning to outweigh the benefits of the reduction of the risk of exchange rate appreciation. The Indian exchange rate regime is one of managed float, and it does allow some flexibility. China, on the other hand, is maintaining a fixed exchange rate system. China also faces serious problems in the financial sector, in particular the overhang of nonperforming loans, and an immediate revaluation might worsen the problem.

2.2. Chinese Equity Markets

China's stock markets were not open to foreign equity portfolio investment until 1992, but since then the markets have been growing very rapidly. Despite the fast growth of the Chinese stock markets, they are not efficient in the traditional sense compared with more developed exchange markets (Tian, 2001). In general, prices and domestic investor's behavior do not reflect fundamental values of listed firms (Allen et al, 2006). Table 4 shows that the ranking of different exchange markets in terms of number of transactions. Shanghai Stock Exchange (SHSE) ranked fourth and the Shenzhen Stock Exchange (SZSE) ranked eighth in 2003 and 2004.

One distinctive characteristic of the Chinese equity markets is that the shares are of two primary types.[6] Class A and B shares are listed in either SHSE or SZSE. Class A shares are issued to domestic Chinese investors and class B shares to foreign investors, including who are overseas Chinese. The restriction on holding class A shares by foreigners was relaxed in 2002 (Lin et al, 2005). The A shares of each listed company are divided into three categories; state owned shares, legal person shares, and tradable shares. The first two types of shares are held by the government, government agencies, state owned enterprises, or other enterprises. They were not tradable on the stock exchanges until very recently when the government started the process of gradually making all shares tradable (Allen et al, 2006)

Shirai (2002) and Chen, Lee and Rui (2001) find a significant price discount for Class B shares held by foreigners, as compared to Class A shares held by Chinese. Tian (2001) finds that firm value is negatively affected by government ownership, and that B shares move more closely with fundamentals than A shares. Two major differences that academic literature has shown to be unique to the Chinese equity market are the separation of three types of shares (a non-tradable A tradable, and B tradable) and the dominant role of the government.[7] The separation of three different types of shares has its costs in terms of low market efficiency and corporate governance. When state owned shares are not tradable, the largest shareholder is

---

[6] Another issue associated with the Chinese equity markets is that many of the larger companies are listed overseas or in Hong Kong, which leave the domestic market with primarily small firms and has been blamed for the Chinese markets volatile first fifteen years.

[7] See Allen, Qian and Qian (2006) for a summary of this literature.

often the government. This gives the government the dominant position in the corporation. Even if the government prefers to reduce its dominant position, it cannot sell shares easily because they are not fully tradable on the stock market.

Table 4. Largest Exchanges by Number of Transactions

Index	2001	2002	2003	2004
NASDAQ	1	1	1	1
NYSE	2	2	2	2
NSE	4	3	3	3
SHSE	3	5	4	4
BSE	8	7	5	5
Korea	6	4	7	6
Taiwan	7	6	6	7
SZSE	5	8	8	8
Germany	9	9	9	9
London	14	12	11	10

Source: http:/indiabudget.nic.in

Another significant factor affecting the development of the Chinese equity market is the fact that there are very few stocks that would fit the definition of "blue-chip" trading on China's mainland exchanges (Gao, 2002). Whereas most developed markets are dominated by a limited number of large-cap stocks,[8] China's market has a disproportionate number of small-cap stocks. This feature allows for increased speculation and higher turnover. Another factor that has influenced speculation is that the Chinese market is a retail market, e.g., expansion through the issuance of new shares rather than the appreciation in value of existing stocks (Chen et al, 2003). There is also very stringent regulation of IPO's in China. The government sets the quota for new listings each year and selects the qualified companies based on provincial and sector allocations. Under current laws in China, no company is allowed to list without three years of continuous profitability, which has been cited as a law that favors state owned companies (Gao, 2002).

2.3. Indian Equity Markets

The Bombay Stock Exchange (BSE), established in 1875, has a long history. India hosts the largest number of listed companies after the United States and investors are increasing turning to India (Griffith-Jones, 2004). As of early 2006, there were about 3,500 Indian companies listed with the stock exchange, accounting for over 90% of the total market capitalization in India. The average value of transactions in India is small, but at the same time India has a very high volume of transactions that are required to be implemented by

---

[8] An example is Nokia in the Finnish market which accounts for roughly 70% of Finland's total market value. In China, the top fifteen companies account for only about 11% of market capitalization.

commensurately large, yet low-cost IT systems (Padmanabhan, 2005). The number of BSE transactions ranked among the world's top five in 2003 and 2004 (see Table 4). India officially opened its stock markets to foreign investors in September 1992 and has since received a considerable amount of portfolio investment in equities from Foreign Institutional Investors. In January of 1993, foreign brokerage firms were also allowed to begin operating in India. This has become one of the main channels of international portfolio investment in India for foreigners (Padmanabhan, 2005). During the liberalization period of 1992-1993, the gates to the Indian stock market was the scene of a series of major fraudulent transactions that resulted in regulators being blamed for inexperience, laxity, and outright corruption (Rao, 2002). However, as scandals have decreased, the number of registered foreign institutional investors has risen substantially. The total amount of foreign institutional investment in terms of market capitalization has steadily climbed to about 9% of the total market capitalization of the BSE with U.S.-based institutions accounting for over 41% of total equity flows (World Bank, 2005).

The growing sophistication of the market is evidenced by numerous and very large recent stock issues. The mean IPO size increased twenty fold over the period 2001-2004 (BSE). The success of these large issues has dispelled earlier doubts about the feasibility of billion-dollar offerings on the Indian market. Another major development is the introduction of the Indian primary market. It has been introduced as "screen based book building", where securities are auctioned through an anonymous screen-based system, and the price at which securities are sold is discovered on the screen. This eliminates the delays, risks, and implementation difficulties associated with traditional procedures. Despite considerable skepticism about the extent to which computers could replace the services of skilled investment bankers, it is reported that resource mobilization through book building rose steadily from 25 percent of public equity offerings in 2001 to 53 percent in 2002, 64 percent in 2003, and 99 percent in 2004 (Padmanabhan, 2005).

Just as in the case of China, the markets in India have unique structure of note. The Indian market, unlike the U.S., has widespread retail participation that spans the country. With households directly owing the bulk of securities, the shareholding pattern in India is not conducive to market to discipline. Given the high promoter stakes, hostile takeover bids are unlikely to succeed. In fact, there have been very few such bids in India, and even these turned out to be attempts at making fast money rather than seeking management control to improve performance of the target firm (Rao, 2002). There is also evidence that corporate governance may be improving, with insider trading laws have been enacted in 1992 and the first conviction under these laws occurring in 1998 (Rao, 2002).

3. LITERATURE REVIEW AND COMMON HYPOTHESES

Existing evidence indicates a strong relationship between inflows of foreign capital and market returns. Griffin, Nardari, and Stulz (2004) have confirmed this result in their studies on emerging Asian equity markets, although China and India were not included. What is unsettled is the interpretation of this relationship and implications for the role of foreign investors in emerging markets. There are several competing hypotheses to explain the relationship. One such hypothesis is that the participation of foreign investors in the market brings about a demand shift and hence a permanent price change.

In support of this hypothesis, Merton (1987) demonstrates that if investors were able to invest in all equities, the standard capital asset pricing model pricing relations would hold. However, with segmentation restrictions or a restricted investor base, the expected return on a market will be higher than its unrestricted return by a risk premium. Merton's model predicts that the greater the number of informed investors the lower the required rate of return. This hypothesis is often referred to as the base broadening hypothesis. Berkaert, Harvey and Lumsdaine (2002) apply this idea to show that equity flows should lower the cost of capital in many countries, and facilitate the flow of capital to firms and countries that have the best investment opportunities irrespective of their location. In their empirical work, Berkaert et al (2002) use dividend yield to proxy the cost of capital, and find a negative relationship between equity flows and dividend yields, implying that as investor base increases, the cost of capital declines, which in turn increases equity prices.

The converse of the base broadening theory was tested in the context of aggregate mutual fund flows by Warther (1995) and in the context of exchange rates by Hau, Massa and Peress (2005). Warther (1995) develops a theory in the context of aggregate mutual fund flows which is referred to as the price pressure hypothesis, suggesting that a rise in prices associated with inflow surges are due to temporary illiquidity. This theory then predicts that inflow induced price increases will be reversed. Shleifer (1986) presents evidence that increases in stock prices resulting from the announcement of inclusion of individual stocks in the Standard and Poor's 500 are at least partially reversed over the subsequent 30-60 trading days.

The most commonly found characteristic of the relationship between equity flows and returns is return chasing or the fact that U.S. purchases are positively correlated with both current and lagged stock returns. The seminal paper that developed the return chasing hypothesis in the context of equity flows was by Bohn and Tesar (1996). The return chasing hypothesis implies that investors chase high returns into equity markets. The empirical implication is that flows should be correlated with lagged returns, and therefore flows should be able to be predicted from lagged returns.

Froot, O'Connell and Seasholes (2001) find that the majority of co-movement of flows and returns is actually due to returns predicting future flows, which would be supportive of the return chasing behavior of international investors. They also find some ability for international inflows to forecast returns. A number of papers have documented a similar phenomenon, which has also been termed positive feedback trading. Choe, Kho and Stulz (1999) detect strong positive feedback activity in Korea before the Asian financial crisis, but not during the crisis. They find that foreign sales do not lead to negative abnormal returns, which implies that there is no evidence that foreign investment is destabilizing. Dahlquist and Robertsson (2004) also document a similar feedback trading behavior in the Swedish market, showing that such behavior may not be just a characteristic of emerging markets. However, the return chasing hypothesis is not without challenge. Portes and Rey (2005), for example, fail to find evidence of return chasing in a large panel study.

One consistent finding in the literature of equity flows is that foreign investors build up positions slowly, which leads to autocorrelation in equity flows. These results have been taken to suggest cross-border heterogeneity in information endowments because autocorrelation in equity flows reflects a learning process and may suggest informationally deficient foreign investors.[9] Brennan and Cao (1997) postulate that one reason for the autocorrelation of equity flows is that foreign investors are less informed about local markets than are domestic investors. The crux of their argument is that if domestic investors are better informed than foreign investors, they will hold more domestic shares on average. Foreign investors discount share prices relative to domestic investors since domestic investors tend to sell if they have adverse information that is not incorporated in asset prices. This implies that foreign investors do not take advantage of the complete benefits of diversification as they would if information were symmetric.

The home bias resulting from information asymmetries implies that the cost of capital in the domestic country is higher than it would be in the absence of these asymmetries. Therefore, as flows leave the country due to bad news, equity prices decline because domestic investors have to hold more domestic shares, and hence bear more risk (Brennan and Cao, 1997). Inflows have the opposite effect; prices should increase to reflect the lower risk bore by domestic investors. Kang and Stulz (1997) argue that the ideal setting to further test the hypothesis of information asymmetry would be to see if foreign investors favor large firms. Japan is one of the few countries besides the U.S. where the data on holdings of equity by foreign investors is easily available at the firm level. Kang and Stulz (1997) demonstrate that foreign investors have a considerable bias toward large firm stocks in Japan.

Dvorak (2003) and Seasholes (2004) suggest that there is a strong possibility that foreign investors may be well informed. If one assumes that foreign institutional investors are informed, this could explain the observed autocorrelation in flows. For example, if a US institution were able to gain an informational advantage, they would want to hide or conceal this informational advantage. The attempt to conceal this information would lead to rationing behavior in an attempt to minimize the price impact of their purchases.

Further motivation for the idea that U.S. investors may not have inferior information endowments reflects the nature of the economies of China and India. China and India are countries that export many products and services to the United States. Alfaro, Kalemali-Ozen and Volosovych (2005) mention that several factors tend to reduce information asymmetries between countries. The first one is the rapidly growing economy, i.e., as GDP increases, informational asymmetries decline. The second factor which reduces differences in information is an increase in trade between nations or regions. The fact that China and India are expanding, coupled with the increase in trade with the U.S., indicates that informational asymmetries have likely declined. The decline in information asymmetries combined with China and India's suboptimal financial systems makes it entirely possible that economists in the U.S. can be better at analyzing some companies in China and India than are Chinese and Indian economists.

Empirically, Seasholes (2004) finds evidence that foreign investors are better informed than domestic investors. He also finds that the amount that foreigners hold or trade in an underlying stock is a good proxy for profitability. Froot and Ramadori (2005) agree with Seasholds and find that foreign investors act informed. Hamao and Mei (2001) also argue that foreign investors are more sophisticated than domestic investors in Japan and tend to be long term contrarians; additionally Grinblatt and Keloharju (2000) suggest that foreign institutional investors are the most sophisticated investor class in Finland.

---

[9] See Brennan and Cao (1997), Griffen et al (2004), Brennan, Strong and Xu (2005), Kim and Ying (2001)

4. METHODOLOGY AND DATA

4.1. Motivations and Empirical Methods

To motivate for our variable selection, we begin with a simple model of stock prices given as:[10]

$$
P_{t+1} = E_t \left[\sum_{j=1}^{K} \left(\frac{1}{1+R_t} \right)^j D_{t+j} \right] + E_t \left[\left(\frac{1}{1+R_t} \right)^K P_{t+K} \right],
\tag{1}
$$

where P_{t+1} is the stock price level, D_{t+j} is the dividend, E_t is the conditional expectations operator based on information available to market participants, and K is the investor's time horizon. As K increases the second term on the right approaches zero, leaving the familiar Gordon growth model. R_t is the rate of return used by market participants to discount future value. R_t is a decreasing function of the number of foreign investors. To understand why R_t is decreasing in the number of foreign investors, we appeal to a model developed by Merton (1987), who present the base-broadening hypothesis in the context of capital market equilibrium with incomplete information.

The basic argument is best summarized by Merton's (1987) comparative statics, shown below:

$$
\frac{\partial V_k}{\partial q_k} = V_k \delta x_k \sigma_k^2 / q_k^2 > 0,
\tag{2}
$$

where V_k is market value of firm k (or market k), δ is a non-negative parameter in the utility function, q_k is the fraction of all investors who know about security k, x_k is the fraction of the market portfolio invested in security k, σ_k^2 is the standard deviation of security k. The result directly shows that as the number of investors increases, the value of the firm increases. His model has very appealing implications for studying the relationships between equity market prices and net equity flows. If one considers the q in Merton's model to be the number of foreign investors, then increases in purchases of foreign investors should increase the value of the market or firm. It has been empirically found that foreign portfolio flows as a percentage market capitalization will increase as relatively positive information is released about a foreign market (Henry, 2000).

Researchers have found that as markets are liberalized and more foreign investors enter the equity market, the cost of capital declines. Bekaert, Harvey and Lumsdaine (2002) find that the higher firm value is a result of a permanent reduction in the cost of capital by using dividend yield to proxy the cost of capital. This result could also be expected based on the nature of portfolio equity flows found in previous literature. Since portfolio equity flows are

---

[10] discussed by Campbell and Lo, MacKinlay (1997)

autocorrelated, after a positive shock to flows, rational foreign and domestic investors would expect greater demand from foreign investors in the future. This would cause prices to be bid higher following the flow shock.

A vector autoregression (VAR) model is useful for forecasting systems of interrelated time-series variables and testing causality among these endogenous variables. Let a VAR be expressed as:

$$Z_t = \mu + \Gamma_1 Z_{t-1} + \ldots + \Gamma_p Z_{t-p} + \varepsilon_t, \tag{3}$$

where $Z_t = [R_{it}, f_{it}]'$ and R_{it} and f_{it} are returns of market i and inflows from the U.S. to either China or India for a case of the bivariate VAR. μ is a parameter vector and Γ's are the matrices of the parameters estimated, and ε_t is the residual vector. The lag length is determined by the Akaike information criterion (AIC). VAR with an exogenous variables is also estimated (VARX), where the exogenous variable is a dummy variable for extreme observations on equity flows. Block exogeneity or Granger causality tests are used to examine whether or not the lagged values of other endogenous variables have forecasting power for a variable in the system. The variance decomposition and impulse response functions (IRF) are constructed to illustrate the responses of all variables given a shock in one variable. In order to control for other endogenous factors, we estimate a three variable and a four variable VAR. Griffen et al (2004) suggest the inclusion of industrial production as additional endogenous variable. Fama and French (1992) and Dvorak (2003) provide theoretical motivation for the consideration of dividend yields as endogenously related to equity returns and equity flows.

4.2. Data Description

The data for our empirical investigation consists of equity flows, industrial production, dividend yields, market capitalization, and returns on global market indices. The source for monthly data on equity flows is the U.S Treasury International Capital System (TIC) reporting system.[11] U.S. net purchases of securities are defined as gross purchases (inflows) of foreign securities by U.S. residents from the host country minus gross sales (outflows) of foreign securities from U.S. residents to the host country. We note that the data on equity flows is limited to bilateral portfolio flows into and out of the United States, and does not include other countries' investment in China and India. We use the International Financial Corporations Emerging Market Database (EMDB) for U.S. dollar returns for Global market indices, market capitalization, and dividend yields for China and India. Industrial production is taken from the International Financial Statistics database (IFS). Table 5 summarizes the definitions of the variables used in our empirical analysis.

---

[11] See Tesar and Werner (1994, 1995) for a complete description and analysis of this data.

Table 5. Variable Definitions

Variable	Definition
INFLOW	US purchases of Chinese/Indian equities
OUTFLOW	US sales of Chinese/Indian equities
NETFLOW	Inflows-Outflows
NIFLOWUS	Inflow divided by market capitalization in USD
NOFLOWUS	Outflow divided by market capitalization in USD
NNFLOWUS	Outflow divided by market capitalization in USD
EIFLOW	Expected inflows
UIFLOW	Unexpected inflows
FOREX	Exchange rate
DIV1	Log of dividend yield
INDEXUS, INDEXLC	Index level in USD and index level in local currency
LNIP	Log difference industrial production
RUSD, RLC	Return in USD and return in local currency
ERUSD	Indian or Chinese equity market return minus US equity market return in USD

Equity flow data is from the TIC database, equity prices, returns, market capitalization and dividends are from the EMDB, and industrial production is from IFS.

The sample period for this study is from January 1994 to May 2006 for both China and India. The reason this sample period is chosen is to allow for a significant time for the effects of liberalization to taper out. Henry (2000) and Berkaert et al (2002) show that equity flows follow a distinctively different pattern surrounding liberalization. Henry (2000) examines at the impact of stock market liberalization on 12 emerging markets. He finds that on average aggregate equity price index experiences a positive abnormal return of 3.3% after a country's government allows foreigners to purchase shares. Kim and Singal (2002) also find that emerging market stock returns are abnormally high in the months leading up to liberalization. Additionally, Berkaert and Harvey (2000) show that aggregate dividend yields decline after liberalization, which is evidence of a lower cost of capital after liberalization. The timeline that contains only post liberalization data with a significantly long time-series will make this research one of the first to look at the relationships between equity flows and returns for China and India without the contamination of liberalization.

Table 6 Panels A and B report the summary statistics for China and India, respectively. The average monthly inflow (INFLOW) from U.S. institutional investors into China over the sample period was about 109.5 million (USD), which represents approximately 0.1019% of market capitalization. While this number may seem insignificant, over the course of a year about 1.2% of the market capitalization of China flows to the country from the U.S. Net equity flows (NETFLOW) had a positive mean of 55.32 million over the sample period. This implies that U.S. institutional investors are increasing their portfolio weights in the Chinese equity market. In contrast, the average monthly equity flow from U.S. institutional investors to India was 268.72 million (USD), accounting for approximately 1% of market capitalization. Similar to China, India also had a positive mean net equity flow, indicating that

U.S. investors are building up portfolio investments in India.[12] Monthly returns (RUSD) in China averaged roughly 1% over the sample period, which is very close to the average return on the Indian market of 0.98%. Excess dollar returns (ERUSD) in both Chinese and Indian equity markets averaged above the U.S market by approximately 0.3% in China and 0.28% in India per month. [13]

Table 6. Summary Statistics

Panel A: China

	Obs	Mean	S.D	Min	Max
INFLOW	149	109.50	274.65	1.00	2823.00
OUTLFOW	149	54.17	70.44	0.00	395.00
NETFLOW	149	55.32	251.13	-265.00	2660.00
NIFLOWUS	149	0.0011	0.0023	0.0004	0.0210
NOFLOWUS	149	0.0005	0.0005	0.00	0.0041
NNFLOWUS	149	0.0006	0.0022	-0.0030	0.0208
LNIP	149	0.0081	0.5369	-0.2004	0.2148
DIV1	149	0.0022	0.0012	0.0002	0.0626
INDEXUS	149	134.15	43.99	37.59	218.91
ERUSD	149	0.0035	0.1174	-0.2361	0.9597
RUSD	149	0.0111	0.1161	-0.2046	0.9973

Panel B: India

	Obs	Mean	S.D	Min	Max
INFLOW	149	268.72	379.49	7.00	2962.00
OUTLFOW	149	220.88	330.03	2.00	1717.00
NETFLOW	149	47.85	156.21	-604.00	1245.00
NIFLOWUS	149	0.0102	0.0145	0.0003	0.1168
NOFLOWUS	149	0.0083	0.0124	0.0008	0.0677
NNFLOWUS	149	0.0019	0.0062	-0.0238	0.0491
LNIP	149	0.0050	0.0501	-0.1479	0.1141
DIV1	149	0.0162	0.0052	0.0063	0.0295
INDEXUS	149	525.66	259.37	281.40	1566.86
ERUSD	149	0.0022	0.0805	-0.1930	0.2198
RUSD	149	0.0099	0.0803	-0.1726	0.2267

Means, standard deviations and extreme values for data equity flow and return data are reported in the tables above for the period of January 1994 to June 2006.

---

[12] In equity flow, accounting inflows are reported as flows into a foreign country from the domestic country. Hence, an inflow would be a flow out of the US into to China or India. Accounting out flows are the exact opposite. Net flows are inflows minus outflows, where a positive net flow indicates that more equity has exited the US than entered.

[13] Following Bekaert, Harvey and Lumsdaine (2002), NIFLOWS, NOFLOWS and NNFLOWS are standardized by market capitalization.

Graph 3A. Chinese Global Index Level.

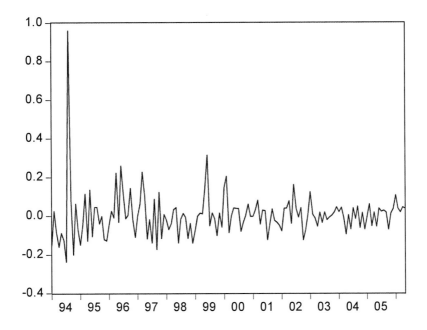

Graph 3B. Excess Return (Chinese return-U.S. return, in USD).

Graphs 3A and 3B illustrate the time series of the Chinese stock index and the excess returns over the U.S. returns. Also, Graphs 4A and 4B illustrate the Indian stock index and Indian excess returns. We observe that the Chinese stock index shows a steady upward trend over time, but that the Indian stock index remains relatively flat until 2002 when it then shows substantial upward movement.

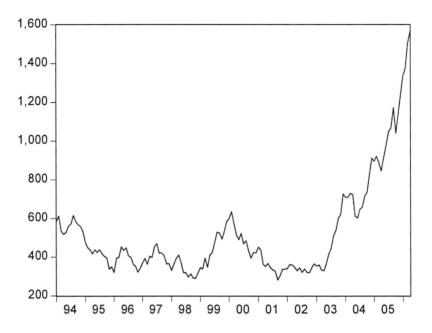

Graph 4A. Indian Global Index Level.

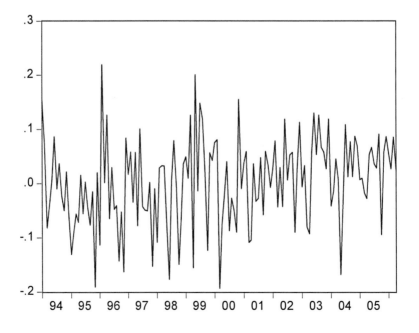

Graph 4B: Excess Return (Indian return-USA return, in USD).

Table 7 Panels A and B report the contemporaneous correlations between variables used in this study for China and India, respectively. The correlation between dividend yield and index level in both China and India are negative at -49% in China and at -34% in India. This finding is consistent with the notion that rapidly growing economies reinvest earnings rather than paying out dividends, and could indicate that future growth is expected. There is also a small negative correlation between equity flows and dividend yields, which is consistent with the base broadening hypothesis as adapted by Bekaert, Harvey and Lumsdaine (2002). If one uses dividend yield to proxy the cost of capital, then one would expect, according the base-broadening hypothesis that as inflows increase the cost capital should decline. There is a strongly positive correlation between inflows and outflows. Tesar and Werner (1995) first pointed out that international capital markets are characterized by large turnovers and show that turnover of foreign equity holdings is roughly twice that of domestic holdings.

Table 7. Correlation Matrixes of Variables

Panel A: China

	INDEXUS	RUSD	DIV1	IN-FLOW	OUT-FLOW	NET-FLOW	NI-FLOWUS	NO-FLOWUS
INDEXUS	1							
RUSD	0.071	1						
DIV1	-0.491	-0.020	1					
INFLOW	0.267	0.023	-0.004	1				
OUTFLOW	0.576	0.041	-0.142	0.448	1			
NETFLOW	0.127	0.013	0.036	0.968	0.209	1		
NIFLOWUS	0.009	-0.085	0.003	0.688	0.165	0.706	1	
NOFLOWUS	0.396	0.025	-0.187	0.254	0.784	0.058	0.131	1
NNFLOWUS	-0.070	-0.090	0.040	0.641	0.009	0.699	0.980	-0.069

Panel B: India

	INDEXUS	RUSD	DIV1	IN-FLOW	OUT-FLOW	NET-FLOW	NI-FLOWUS	NO-FLOWUS
INDEXUS	1							
RUSD	0.238	1						
DIV1	-0.344	-0.070	1					
INFLOW	0.891	0.104	-0.059	1				
OUTFLOW	0.860	0.147	-0.093	0.906	1			
NETFLOW	0.221	0.136	-0.098	0.108	0.520	1		
NIFLOWUS	0.860	0.147	-0.093	0.906	0.975	0.520	1	
NOFLOWUS	0.891	0.104	-0.059	0.894	0.906	0.108	0.906	1
NNFLOWUS	0.221	0.136	-0.098	0.108	0.520	0.933	0.520	0.108

Correlations between major variable used in this study are reported in the tables above for the period January, 1994 to June 2006.

If we measure excess flows as the difference between total flows (outflows + inflows) and the absolute value of net flows, then total flows are huge compared to net flows. In China net flows account for about 33% of total flows and in India net flows account for only about 10% of total flows on average. The large size of total flows compared to net flows, particularly in India, suggests that turnover is high and demonstrates that U.S. investors are constantly altering positions based on the changing investment environment. In China, the evidence is not so strong, with net flows being roughly equal to outflow. Further, gross inflows and outflows are positively correlated at over 45% in China and at 90% in India. This appears to indicate that investors, particularly in India, are adjusting or rebalancing their portfolios within a given month among different stocks. In India, the small positive correlation between flows and returns is consistent with the findings of previous literature (i.e., Froot et al, 2001). China, on the other hand, appears to demonstrate a small negative correlation between flows and returns.

5. EMPIRICAL RESULTS

5.1. Behavior of Portfolio Equity Flows

In this section we address the following questions: How are returns and flows related? Do flows forecast returns or vice versa? The first evidence is simply visual. As shown in Graphs 1, 2, 3 and 4 flows and prices move together at low frequencies. The co-movement could be ascribed to a variety of factors, including overreaction, information shocks, or demand shocks. Following the spirit of Froot et al (2001), we estimate correlations between flows and returns over four month lags and decompose the correlation structure between net and gross flows and returns. The correlation between lagged returns and flows may provide preliminary evidence of return chasing. The correlation between contemporaneous returns and flows will give some indication about the relevance of the information story of Brennan and Cao (1997). The correlation between future returns and flows will give us ideas about the predictability of returns from flows. For example, if future returns are positively correlated with contemporaneous flows, then flows could be a useful factor in predicting future equity returns. One the other hand, if returns are negatively correlated with contemporaneous flows, then this would provide preliminary evidence of the price pressure hypothesis.

Table 8 reports the results of correlation between excess returns and normalized net flows and inflows. Column 1 reports the correlation between flows and lagged excess returns (ERUSD) for four months. Column 2 reports the contemporaneous correlation between ERUSD and flows, and the final column reports the correlation between flows and four month future ERUSD. The correlation between lagged excess returns and flows is strongly positive in both countries indicating that flows appear to follow returns. If flows are correlated with lagged returns, then it indicates that excess returns have some predictive power as to the purchasing behavior of U.S. institutional investors. Contemporaneously, flows are positively correlated in India and negatively correlated in China. The model developed by Brennan and Cao (1997) demonstrates that if domestic investors have net information advantage, then flows and returns should be positively correlated. We find that this holds in the case of India, but in the case of China, we see the opposite effect. This could be because of a number of reasons related to the degree of regulation in the Chinese market. As far as the predictability of future returns from current flows, again we find opposite results in China and India. In China, flows are negatively correlated with future returns, but in India, inflows are positively correlated with future returns. The result indicate that price pressure is be present in India, as U.S. investors make up 41% of foreign equity flows to the nation.

Table 8. Monthly Correlation Structure

	Flows and lagged returns (4 months)	Contemporaneous correlation	Flows and future returns (4 months)
China (net flows)	0.405	-0.113	-0.188
China (inflows)	0.403	-0.106	-0.194
India (net flows)	0.204	0.180	-0.093
India (inflows)	0.754	0.144	0.581

Reported are correlations between monthly Chinese and Indian stock market index returns (in USD) and inflows and net flows from the US to China and India.

Table 9 presents the results of the correlations between unexpected inflows (UIFLOW) and ERUSD. Following Warther (1995), we estimate an autoregressive model to predict one-step-ahead values of inflows and to obtain both an expected and an unexpected inflow series, where the unanticipated flows are based on the residuals. The results show that lagged ERUSD appear to be positively correlated to unexpected inflows. This is consistent with the logic of Warther (1995) and Clark and Berko (1997). For example, our findings imply that after the Chinese or Indian equity market outperforms the U.S. markets, U.S. institutional investors increase their purchases of equities in China and India more than anticipated. Contemporaneously, there is also a positive relationship between excess returns and flows in the case of India and only a slightly negative correlation in China. Also in China, high unexpected flows are negatively correlated with future excess returns, and in India future excess returns are positively correlated with unexpected flows.

Table 9. Monthly Correlation Structure: Unanticipated Inflows

	Flows and lagged returns (4 months)	Contemporaneous correlation	Flows and future returns (4 months)
China (uiflows)	0.280	-0.023	-0.230
India (uiflows)	0.256	0.128	-0.194

Unanticipated inflows are calculated as the residual of an AR(2) model similar to Warther (1995).

5.2. Causality and Impulse Response Functions

We estimated several sets of the bivariate VARs with excess returns and different measures of equity flows (i.e., inflows, outflows, net flow, and unexpected inflows, etc) in order to check the robustness of the results. The results are similar for each, mostly likely due to most likely the high correlation between different flow components in both countries.

Additionally we note that the results of our VAR estimation are generally unaffected by the ordering of variables, which is consistent with the findings by Bekarert et al (2002) and Dahlquist and Robertsson (2004). We select the lag length of two based on the AIC for all VARs estimated.

Table 10 reports the summary of the Granger causality tests for three different VAR configurations. The first column of Table 10 reports the results of the causality between excess returns (ERUSD) and normalized inflows (NIFLOWUS). From Panel A, we find that lagged excess returns are statistically significant in predicting future inflows, but inflows do not have statistically significant predictive power on ERUD in China. It appears that the results support the return chasing behavior in China.[14] There is no significant causality between excess returns and flows in India from Panel B. These results indicate that foreign investors are involved in positive feedback trading in China but not in India.

The second VAR model are estimated is a bivariant model of unexpected inflows (UIFLOW) and ERUSD, and the results are reported in Column 2. Excess returns are found to cause unexpected flows in China but not visa versa, and there is no significant causality for India as found in the first column. The contrasting results between China and India with respect to unanticipated inflows and returns can be partially explained by the fact that 41% of portfolio equity inflow to India is from the U.S., while only about 1% of portfolio flows to China are from American institutional investors.

Column 3 of Table 10 reports the results of Granger causality tests of VARX, including an exogenous dummy variable to control for extreme values.[15] The motivation for including a dummy variable for extreme observations can be given in, for example, Graphs 1A and 2A. It is clearly evident that there are a few significant outliners in both countries, and in order to uncover the general nature of the relationship between flows and returns, spikes should be controlled out. Panel A reports the results of the causality test for China, and they are consistent with results found in Column 1 and 2. This provides further support for the ERUSD as a predictive factor in equity flows for China. According to Panel B, lagged returns are now significant in predicting flows at the 5% significant level.

Graphs 5A and 5B illustrate the impulse response functions constructed with ERUSD and NIFLOWUS in China and India, respectively. We observe that in China, one standard deviation shock to excess returns causes a significant increase in inflows over the next two to four months but returns do not respond to a shock in inflows.[16] We observe that in Inida, neither inflows nor returns respond to a shock in another variable. The impulse response functions basically agree with the results found in Table 10. Graphs 6A and 6B present the IRFs with ERUSD and UIFLOW in China and India. In both China and India, a shock to unexpected flows negatively predicts future unexpected flows after an initial increase. This pattern indicates that temporary distortions to the unexpected inflow series are transient and then partially reversed over a short forecasting period. U.S. investors may incorporate information on equity flows quickly into their future purchasing behavior. The response of UFLOWS to an unexpected ERUSD shock is significant in China, where one standard deviation shock to ERUSD leads to a 1.2% increase in equity inflows by the third month. Again the results in India do not show any clear relationships between ERUSD and UIFLOW.

---

[14] Similar Granger causality results are found with net flows (not reported).

[15] Extreme values are observations two standard deviations or more from the mean.

[16] Standard errors for impulse response functions are calculated using Monte Carlo Simulation and the bands represent 90% confidence levels. Note that the lower bound of 90% confidence crosses the middle line.

Table 10. Summary of Granger Causality Tests

	VAR 1	VAR 2	VARX
Panel A: China			
Flows Causing Returns	0.58	1.06	0.23
Returns Causing Flows	55.95***	60.14***	42.84***
Panel B: India			
Flows Causing Returns	3.30	3.82	3.33
Returns Causing Flows	3.21	1.00	8.38**

The table above summarizes the results of the Granger causality tests for three different VAR specifications. VAR1 is based on ERUSD and INFLOWUS. VAR2 is based on ERUSD and UIFOW. VARX is based on ERUSD, INFLOWUS with an exogenous dummy for extreme observations of inflows. Test statistics are distributed as a Chi-square with two degrees of freedom. *** indicates significance at 1% and ** indicates significance at 5%. Significance levels are calculated using Chi-square statistics with 2 degrees of freedom.

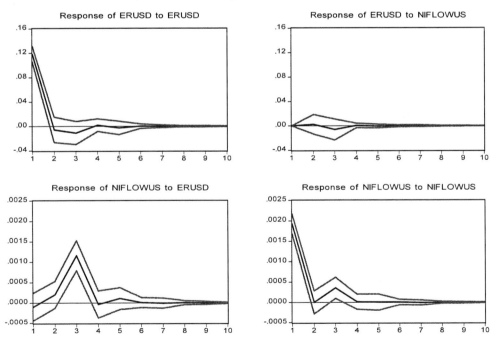

Graph 5A. Impulse Response Functions of China: VAR [ERUSD, NIFLOWUS].

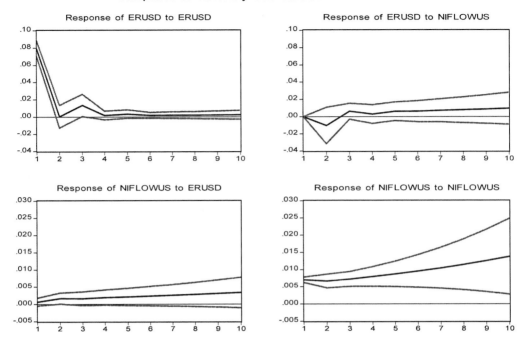

Graph 5B. Impulse response functions in India: VAR [ERUSD, NIFLOWUS].

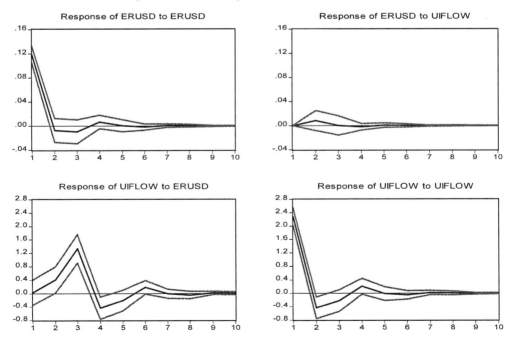

Graph 6A. Impulse response functions in China: VAR [ERUSD, UIFLOW].

Response to Cholesky One S.D. Innovations ± 2 S.E.

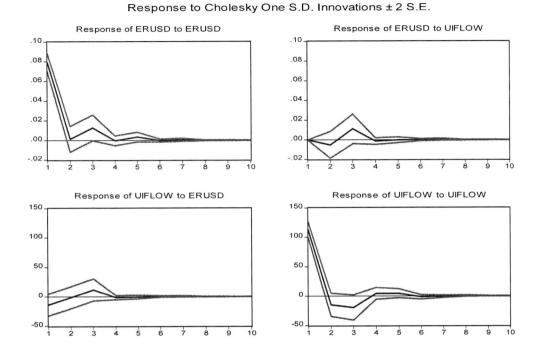

Graph 6B. Impulse response functions in India: VAR [ERUSD, UIFLOW].

In sum, it appears that there is strong evidence of returns forecasting flows positively in China, but the evidence of returns forecasting flows is rather ambiguous in India. Froot et al (2001) find positive forecastability of capital flows from returns in emerging markets. However, in more developed markets the forecastablity of flows from returns is ambiguous, as our findings suggest for India. If we interpret these findings in terms of relative information asymmetry between the U.S. and China, and the U.S. and India, it could be conjectured that information asymmetry is more acute in China due to two possible reasons. First, equity flows to India are over two times greater than flows to China, and this relatively larger amount of equity flowing to India implies that U.S. investors are likely more informed about the Indian equity market than the Chinese market. As Alfaro et al (2005) point out, information asymmetries decline as trade increases. The second evidence for relatively greater information asymmetry between the U.S. and China comes from the strong relationship between returns and flows in China. The strong relationship could be a result of the U.S. investors relying on previous realizations of the return sequence to forecast future returns due to lack of detailed information on fundamentals. On the other hand, there is relatively more information available for investors to forecast future market performance in India as developed countries, and hence returns may not be as important in forecasting future purchases.

5.3. Additional Variables in VAR and Variance Decompositions

We investigate the trivariate and four-variable VAR for China and India to see if the previous findings hold after adding other endogenous variables in a VAR. For example, there may be a positive relationship between current equity flows and lagged equity returns, but part of this correlation may come indirectly through the effect of industrial production and other fundamental variable such as dividend on equity returns. In the literature, dividend yield is frequently hypothesized to be an important factor in determining equity prices, and possibly the investor decision making process. Panel A and Panel B of Table 11 report the results of the block exogeneity tests (Granger causality for more than two variables) in China and India, respectively. We find that returns are causing inflows in China but not for India. The results are consistent with the previous findings in Table 10. Interestingly, there is no causality running between dividend yields and returns in China. This is in contrast to the case of India shown in Panel B. In India, dividends appear to have predictive power for forecasting returns and this is consistent with the finding of developed markets. These contrasting findings in the cases of China and India further lend credence to the idea that the Chinese market is not operating efficiently (Tian, 2001). We also observe that returns on the Indian market as well as dividend yields are significant for forecasting future industrial production. This, again, is consistent with the findings in developed markets that equity markets lead real markets. Since expectations are built into equity market and returns, firms make dividend policy decisions based on estimated future productivity.

Table 11. Summary of Granger Causality Tests

	ERUSD	Inflows	DIV	IP
Panel A: China				
ERUSD causing	n/a	74.34***	0.04	1.02
Inflows causing	0.45	n/a	0.8	0.04
Dividends Causing	0.55	0.12	n/a	0.33
IP causing	0.42	0.11	0.07	n/a
Panel B: India				
ERUSD causing	n/a	1.43	1.61	7.83**
Inflows causing	3.49	n/a	0.34	0.16
Dividends Causing	6.84**	2.66	n/a	6.45**
IP causing	0.34	0.01	1.04	n/a

The table above summarizes the results of the Granger causality tests for a VAR that includes ERUSD, INFLOWUS, DIV, and IP. *** indicates significance at 1% and ** indicates significance at 5%. Significance levels are calculated using Chi-square statistics with 6 degrees of freedom.

Panels A and B of Table 12 report variance decompositions based on shocks in returns, dividends and inflows over ten periods for China and India, respectively. In China, the contribution of dividend shocks to the variance of returns is negligible at only 0.28% and the results support the notion that equity markets in China are basically controlled by the government. In contrast, between 20% and 24% of the variance in the return sequence is explained by shocks to dividends for India. A particularly interesting finding in the context of this study comes from the decomposition of the flows sequences. We observe that between about 27% and 21% of the variance in the flows sequences are explained by dividend shocks in China and India, respectively. These results indicate that the behavior of U.S. institutional investors might be influenced more by fundamental determinants (i.e., dividend shocks) than price shocks or flow shocks. The findings support a model developed by Dvorak (2003).

Table 12. Variance decomposition [ERUSD, dividend, Inflow]

	ERUSD Shock	Div. Shock	Flow Shock
		Panel A: China	
Variance Decomposition RUSD			
Period			
1	100	0	0
2	99.67	0.29	0.04
3	99.42	0.28	0.3
4	99.41	0.28	0.3
5	99.41	0.28	0.3
6	99.41	0.28	0.3
7	99.41	0.28	0.3
8	99.41	0.28	0.3
9	99.41	0.28	0.3
10	99.41	0.28	0.3
Variance Decomposition Dividend			
Period			
1	0.12	99.88	0
2	0.06	99.94	0
3	0.05	99.58	0.37
4	0.04	99.37	0.59
5	0.15	99.05	0.79
6	0.23	98.84	0.93
7	0.3	98.68	1.02
8	0.34	98.58	1.08
9	0.37	98.51	1.12
10	0.39	98.46	1.15
Variance Decomposition Flows			
1	20.05	0.24	79.72
2	20.19	1.33	78.48
3	20.14	26.63	53.22
4	20.2	26.63	53.17
5	20.2	26.8	53.01
6	20.2	26.8	53
7	20.2	26.8	53
8	20.2	26.8	53
9	20.2	26.8	53
10	20.2	26.8	53

Table 12. Variance decomposition [ERUSD, dividend, Inflow] (Continued)

Panel B: India

Variance Decomposition RUSD

Period			
1	100	0	0
2	69.22	20.16	10.62
3	68.39	20.93	10.68
4	67.66	21.62	10.72
5	66.99	22.3	10.71
6	66.46	22.83	10.71
7	66.02	23.27	10.71
8	65.68	23.61	10.71
9	65.41	23.88	10.7
10	65.2	24.1	10.7
	ERUSD Shock	Div. Shock	Flow Shock

Variance Decomposition Dividend

Period			
1	17.79	82.21	0
2	16.12	83.55	0.32
3	18.19	81.3	0.52
4	18.93	80.14	0.92
5	19.52	79.12	1.36
6	19.77	78.31	1.91
7	19.85	77.58	2.57
8	19.78	76.85	3.38
9	19.58	76.07	4.35
10	19.29	75.19	5.52

Variance Decomposition Flows

Period			
1	0.31	20.03	79.66
2	2.1	20.5	77.41
3	7.23	20.8	71.96
4	7.83	20.99	71.18
5	8.35	21.05	70.6
6	8.42	21.08	70.5
7	8.46	21.09	70.45
8	8.46	21.1	70.44
9	8.47	21.1	70.43
10	8.47	21.1	70.43

Table 12 presents the variance decomposition based on VAR with ERUSD, Dividend and NIFLOWUS. Each value indicates how much each shock affects others in percentage over 10 future periods.

To gauge the stability of the relationship found in the previous section, we estimate the VAR using sub-samples, and the results (not reported) are basically similar to those reported in Tables 10 and 11. The results for China appear to be consistent for periods before 2003, but they differ somewhat after 2003. This could be due in part to the fact that foreign investors were allowed to invest in both A and B shares after 2002.

6. CONCLUSION

This research has uncovered several important aspects of the Chinese and Indian equity markets and the influences of U.S. institutional equity portfolio investment on these two emerging giants. The results indicate that U.S. institutional investors are chasing returns into China, but that similar results are not found in India. Some evidence is found that U.S. investors' behavior might be influencing the Indian equity market, while no evidence supports U.S. equity flows influencing the Chinese market. In China, returns appear to forecast future inflows positively; in India, the results are more ambiguous. The results of the variance decomposition demonstrate that the variance of the Indian equity market is influenced by foreign activity and dividend yields, whereas the Chinese equity markets is unaffected by foreign investor behavior and fundamental determinates of value. This supports the ideas espoused in the financial press that the Chinese government still plays a major role in determining the markets. In both markets, fundamental shocks have a stronger influence than excess return shocks. This finding points toward the conclusion that foreign investors are responding to real information rather than simply to returns, which are likely noisy proxies for underlying value, and demonstrates that U.S. investors are reacting more strongly to shocks in fundamentals in both markets. These findings are in contrast to much of the literature that assumes that domestic investors are better informed than foreign investors.

REFERENCES

Alfaro, L., & Kalemli-Ozcan, S., & Volosovych, V. (2005). Capital Flows in a Globalized World: The Role of Policies and Institutions. *NBER Working Papers.*

Allen, F., & Quin, J., & Quin, M., (2006). Law, Finance and Economic Growth in China. *Financial Institutions Center of Wharton School of Business Working Paper,* University of Pennsylvania.

Bekaert, G., & Harvey, C. (2000). Foreign Speculators and Emerging Equity Markets. *Journal of Finance, 55,* 565-613.

Bekaert, G., & Harvey, C., & Lumsdaine, C. (2002). The Dynamics of Emerging Market Equity Flows. *Journal of International Money and Finance, 21,* 295-350.

Bohn, H., & Tesar, L.L. (1996). US equity investment in foreign markets: Portfolio rebalancing or return chasing? *American Economic Review 86,* 77–81.

Brennan, M.J., & Cao, H., & Strong, N., & Xu, X. (2005). The dynamics of international equity expectations. *Journal of Financial Economics, 77,* 257-288.

Brennan, M. J., & Cao, H., (1997). International Portfolio Flows. *Journal of Finance, 52,* 1851–1880.

Campbell, J., & Andrew W. Lo., & MacKinlay, A. (1997), *The Econometrics of Financial Markets.* Princeton University Press.

Chen, G., & Lee, B., & Rui, O. (2001). Foreign ownership restriction and market segmentation in China's stock markets. *Journal of Financial Research*, *24*, 133-155.

Chen, G., & Lee, B., & Rui, O., & Wu, W. (2003). Revisiting B-share Discounts in the Chinese Stock Market. *Working Paper,* University of Houston.

Choe, H., & Kho, B.-C., & Stulz, R. (1999). Do foreign investors destabilize stock markets? The Korean experience in 1997. *Journal of Financial Economics, 54*, 227-264.

Clark, J., & Berko, E. (1997). Foreign investment fluctuations and emerging market stock returns: The case of Mexico. *Sta. report 24, Federal Reserve Bank,* New York, NY.

Dahlquist, M., & Robertsson, G. (2004). A note on foreigners' trading and price effects across firms. *Journal of Banking and Finance, 28*, 615-632.

Dvorak, T. (2003). Gross Capital Flows and asymmetric information. *Journal of International Money and Finance, 22*, 835-864.

Erb, C., & Harvey, C., & Viskanta, T. (1996). Expected Returns and Volatility in 135 Countries. *Journal of Portfolio Management, 22*, 46-58.

Fama, Eugene F., & French, K. (1992). The cross-section of expected stock returns. *Journal of Finance, 47*, 427-465.

Froot, K., & O'Connell, P., & Seasholes, M. (2001). The Portfolio Flows of International Investors. *Journal of Financial Economics, 59*, 151-193.

Froot, K., & Ramadorai, T. (2005). Currency Returns, Intrinsic Value, and Institutional Investor Flows. *Journal of Finance, 60*, 03, 1535-1566.

Gao, S. (2002). China Stock Market in a Global Perspective. *Dow Jones Indexes.*

Global Development Finance. (2005). *Statistical Appendix.*

Grinblatt, M., & Keloharj. M. (2000). The Investment Behavior and Performance of Various Investor Types: A Study of Finland's Unique Data Set. *Journal of Financial Economics, 55*, 43-67.

Griffith-Jones. S. (2004). Asian Drivers: international financial and macro-economic implications globally and for developing countries. Paper prepared for the First Asian Drivers' workshop held in November 2004 at IDS, Sussex.

Griffin J., & Nardari, F., & Stulz, R., (2004). Daily Cross-Border Equity Flows: Pushed or Pulled? *Review of Economics and Statistics*, *86*, 641-657.

Hamao, Y. & Mei, J. (2001). Living with the "enemy": An analysis of foreign investment in the Japanese equity market. *Journal of International Money and* Finance, *20*, 715–735.

Hau, H., & Massa, M., & Peress, J. (2005). Do Demand Curves for Currencies Slope Down? Evidence from the MSCI Global Index Change. *CEPR Discussion Papers* 4862, C.E.P.R. Discussion Papers.

Henry, P.B. (2000b). Stock market liberalization, economic reform, and emerging market equity prices. *Journal of Finance, 55*, 529–564.

Kang, J., & . Stulz, R., (1997). Why is there home bias? An analysis of foreign portfolio equity ownership in Japan. *Journal of Financial Economics.*

Kim, E. H., & Singal, V. (2002). Stock market openings: Experience of emerging economies. *Journal of Business, 73*, 25-66.

Kim, Y. & Ying, T. (2001). An Empirical Analysis on Capital Flows: The Case of Korea and Mexico. *Southern Economic Journal*, *67*, No4, 954-968.

Lin, K., & Menkveld, A., & Yang, Z. (2005). China and the World Equity Markets: A Review of the First Decade. *Working paper,* Portland State University.

Maroney, N., & Naka., A., & Wansi, T. (2004). Changing Risk, Return, and Leverage: The 1997 Asian Financial Crisis. *Journal of Financial and Quantitative Analysis, 39*,143-66.

Merton, R, C. (1987). A Simple Model of Capital Market Equilibrium with Incomplete Information. *Journal of Finance, 42*,483-510.

Padmanabhan, P. (2005). Operationalising Capital Account Liberalization: The Indian Experience. *BIS paper, 15*.

Perez, C. (2002). *Technological Revolutions and Financial Capital: The Dynamics of Bubbles and Golden Ages.* Cheltenham:Edward Elgar.

Portes R., & Rey, H. (2005). The Determinants of Cross-Border Equity Flows. *Journal of International Economics, 65*, 269-296.

Prasad, E., & Shang-Jin, W., (2005). The Chinese approach to Capital Inflows: Patterns and Possible Explanations. *NBER Working Paper.*

Rao, K.S., & Chalapati. (2002). An Overview of the Indian Stock Market with Emphasis on Ownership Pattern of Listed Companies. *Alternative Economic Survey.*

Rogoff, K. (2003). Globalization and Global Disinflation. *Federal Reserve Bank of Kansas City, Monetary Policy and Uncertainty: Adapting to a Changing Economy*, 2003. (Paper presented at a symposium sponsored by the Federal Reserve Bank of Kansas City, at Jackson Hole, WY, August 28-30.

Seasholes, M. S. (2004). Smart foreign traders in emerging markets. *Working paper, Harvard University*, Cambridge, MA.

Shirai., S. (2002). Is the Equity market really developed in the People republic of China? *Working Paper*, Keio University.

Shleifer, A. (1986). Do demand curves for stocks slope down? *Journal of Finance* 41, 579-590.

Tesar, L., & Werner, I.. (1994). International equity transactions and U.S. portfolio choice. *In: Frankel, J. (Ed.), The Internationalization of Equity Markets.* University of Chicago Press, Chicago, IL, 185–215.

Tesar, L., & Werner, I. (1995). U.S. equity investment in emerging stock markets. *World Bank Economic Review, 9*, 109–130.

Tian., G. L. (2001). State Shareholding and the Value of Chin's firms. *Working paper*, London Business School.

Warther, V.A.(1995). Aggregate mutual fund flows and security returns. *Journal of Financial Economics, 39*, 209–235.

World Bank. (2005). *Private Capital flows to Developing Countries.*

In: Economics of Emerging Markets
Editor: Lado Beridze, pp. 99-113

ISBN: 978-1-60021-850-7
© 2008 Nova Science Publishers, Inc.

Chapter 4

ON THE LINKAGES BETWEEN MONETARY POLICY, INFLATION, OUTPUT AND UNEMPLOYMENT IN THE EURO ZONE

Priti Verma[*]

College of Business, Texas A&M University, Kingsville
Kingsville, TX 78363, USA

Rahul Verma[†]

College of Business, University of Houston-Downtown
One Main Street, Houston, TX 77002, USA

ABSTRACT

This paper examines whether monetary policy shocks have any varying degrees of effect on the inflation, output and unemployment indicators of the European Union member countries. We hypothesize that a positive monetary policy shock increases the output and the price levels causing a decrease in unemployment. The results show that a one standard deviation positive shock in monetary policy positively affects inflation in France and Italy. Also there is negative response of unemployment to the monetary base in the case of Germany, France and Italy. We do not find any such significant relationship between output and monetary policy. Overall, monetary policy shocks have asymmetric effect on inflation and unemployment.

JEL classification codes: E5, E52, E58
Keywords: European Monetary Union, Monetary Policy, VAR model

---

[*] Tel : 361 593 2355 Fax: 361 593 3912; E-mail: priti.verma@tamuk.edu
[†] Tel: 713 221 8590 Fax: 713 226 5238; E-mail: vermar@uhd.edu

1. INTRODUCTION

The conception of the European Economic and Monetary Union (EMU) has invoked doubts on whether the common monetary policy is going to have the same effect on all member countries. This in turn has prompted several studies (such as Ramaswamy and Slok, 1998; Gerlach and Smets, 1995, Barran, Coudert and Mojon, 1996; Keiler and Saarenheimo, 1998; Dornbusch et al., 1998; Clausen and Hayo, 2002; Britton and Whitley, 1997; Taylor, 1993; BIS, 1994 and BIS, 1995) to examine the international transmission mechanism of monetary policy across the European Union (EU). This issue is particularly important in the case of the euro zone, because of the following two reasons: first, there exists heterogeneous financial and economic structures between the member countries; and second, differences in transmission mechanisms may lead to asymmetric business cycles and adjustment problems which may hamper the decision making process of the European Central Banks (ECBs).

Dornbusch et al. (1998) suggests three conditions which pre-EMU era empirical studies must account for in order to analyze the effects of monetary policy transmission on the post-EMU era. First, the direct effects on prices and output due to monetary policy changes must be separated from the indirect effect through the exchange rates. Second, the empirical set-up must be modeled allowing for simultaneous change in monetary policy for all the EMU countries. Third, empirical analysis should be able to test the statistical significance of the cross-country differences in prices and output due to changes in monetary policy. However, most of the previous studies examining the potential asymmetric effects of monetary policy transmission across the EU countries do not account for the aforesaid conditions and as such may be misspecified. As such these studies provide inconclusive results as to whether the common monetary policy will have an asymmetric impact on different countries in the EMU.

Macroeconomic models by Mundell (1968), Calvo and Rodrigues (1968) and Frenkel and Rodriguez (1977), suggests that a positive monetary policy shock leads to an increase in output and prices causing is a decrease in the unemployment. The purpose of this paper is to empirically test these predictions and assess the extent of asymmetry in international transmission of monetary policy in the European Union member countries. Specifically, this paper examines whether monetary policy shocks have any varying degrees of effect on the prices, output and unemployment of Germany, France and Italy.

This study extends prior research by using post-EMU data from January 1999 to October 2003[1]. We use the impulse response functions from a vector auto regressions (VAR) and monthly data on money supply, prices, output and unemployment to examine the postulated relationships. Consistent with the theoretical predictions, we find significant positive effect of the Euro zone monetary base on inflation in the case of France and Italy. However, there are insignificant effects of monetary policy on the output of these European countries. Lastly, there are significant negative responses of unemployment to monetary policy shocks in the case of France, Germany and Italy. Overall, a one unit standard deviation positive shock in monetary base increases inflation in Italy and France and decreases unemployment in Germany, France and Italy.

---

[1] The advantage of using post-EMU data is twofold. First, we eliminate the direct and indirect effects of monetary policy shocks on prices, output and unemployment. Second, the monetary policy we analyze is the common monetary policy by the European Central Bank. Further, unlike previous studies using interest rates, this study uses monetary base as the monetary policy variable. Monetary base includes all tangible money i.e. currency in circulation, required reserves and the excess reserves and is a better measure of monetary policy.

The balance of the paper is organized as follows: section 2 highlights the econometric methodology and data. Section 3 discusses the empirical results, followed by the concluding remarks in Section 4.

2. DATA AND METHODOLOGY

The three countries included in our study are Germany, France and Italy as these are the most important EMU countries. These countries have been chosen in this study for two reasons: First, Germany, France and Italy are relatively more open economies than other European countries and more open than the US economy also. Second, they have participated in the EMU since its inception in 1979. Furthermore, Germany, France and Italy account for almost three quarters of the aggregate European output.

The sample period spans January 1999 through October 2003. We obtain all data in monthly interval from DataStream. Our analysis includes the following variables: monetary base, which is calculated as the sum of currency in circulation, excess reserves and required reserves, as the monetary policy variable, output measured by the industrial production, inflation measured by consumer price index and unemployment rate.

To investigate the response of the exchange rates and the trade balance to monetary policy innovations we employ a vector auto regression (VAR) model. This model is useful in estimating unrestricted, reduced–form equations with uniform set of dependent variables as regressors (Sims 1980; Hamilton, 1994). The model does not impose a priori restrictions on the structure of the relationship among variables and can be viewed as a flexible approximation to the reduced form of the correctly specified but unknown model of true economic nature. The VAR model series can be expressed as:

$$Z_t = \gamma_0 + \sum_{s=1}^{m} \gamma_s Z_{t-s} + e_t \tag{1}$$

where Z_t is a column vector of variables under consideration, $\square_0$ is the deterministic component comprised of a constant, $\square_s$ is a matrix of coefficients, m is the lag length and et is a vector of random error terms.

The response of the output, inflation and unemployment to monetary policy shocks is analyzed by computing and plotting the impulse response functions (IRFs). In particular the IRFs trace the response of one variable to a one standard deviation, once and for all shock to another variable in the system and can be thought as a type of dynamic multiplier. The "pure effects" of these shocks can then be captured using Choleski orthogonalization. However, reporting IRFs without standard errors or confidence intervals is equivalent to reporting regression coefficient without t-statistics (Runkle, 1987). For statistical inference purposes the confidence bands around the mean responses is based on Doan and Litterman's (1986) Monte Carlo simulation technique. Accordingly, the responses are considered statistically significant at the 95% confidence level, when the upper and lower bands carry the same sign.

Table 1 reports the descriptive statistics for the continuously compounded monthly series of the variables employed in this study. Italy has the highest mean inflation and unemployment followed by France and Germany. The standard deviation of inflation and unemployment are higher in Italy and France than in Germany signaling higher volatility.

Unit root tests are performed to analyze the time series properties of the data to avoid the possibility of finding spurious relationships. Table 2 reports the result of unit root tests in log levels and log first differences for Germany, Italy and France using Augmented Dickey Fuller (ADF) test (Dickey and Fuller, 1979, 1981, Enders 1995). For the ADF test, we fail to reject the null hypothesis of non-stationarity in log levels of most of the series. Given that most of the series are stationary in levels, we take first differences wherever necessary.

Table 1. Descriptive Statistics

	MB	P	U	Y
Mean	0.3771			
France		0.1598	-0.2523	0.0747
Germany		0.1137	-0.2659	0.0782
Italy		0.2140	-0.5663	0.0436
Median	0.6175			
France		0.1800	0.0000	0.0858
Germany		0.0934	-0.9217	0.0000
Italy		0.1838	-0.8811	0.0000
Maximum	10.9653			
France		0.7143	1.1561	1.9911
Germany		1.3896	10.1470	2.5586
Italy		1.2505	1.1173	1.9398
Minimum	-7.8867			
France		-0.4666	-2.2728	-2.1669
Germany		-0.8439	-8.8553	-2.9612
Italy		-0.5286	-1.9608	-1.4903
Std. Dev.	2.4915			
France		0.2514	0.9417	0.7064
Germany		0.3686	4.0241	1.3119
Italy		0.3505	0.6079	0.7629
Skewness	0.3428			
France		-0.0522	-0.1656	-0.3159
Germany		0.7682	0.6478	-0.3422
Italy		0.4061	0.1114	0.0640
Kurtosis	9.1667			
France		2.8461	2.3380	4.2129
Germany		4.9758	3.4990	2.7612
Italy		3.6922	2.4874	2.6097

Variables are monetary base (MB), inflation (P), unemployment (U) and output (Y).

Table 2. Unit root tests

	Augmented Dickey Fuller	
	Log Level	Log 1st difference
MB	-7.9246	-
Germany		
Y	-11.6258	-
P	-8.8908	-
U	-2.2057	-7.5907
France		
Y	-8.5182	-
P	-6.3252	-
U	-1.0079	-9.7340
Italy		
Y	-8.1336	-
P	-3.1993	-5.6853
U	-6.2633	-
Critical Values		
1%	-3.5527	-3.5575
5%	-2.9145	-2.9166
10%	-2.5950	-2.5961

Variables are monetary base (MB), inflation (P), unemployment (U) and output (Y).

3. EMPIRICAL RESULTS

We estimate three VAR models by including two countries in each model to examine the effect monetary shocks on output, inflation and unemployment. Each VAR model contains 7 variables i.e. three for each country and one monetary base. Based on the AIC and SBC criteria, consistency and considering the degrees of freedom we decide to keep the lag length as two for each model. Table 3 reports the coefficient estimates and diagnostic statistics for the VAR model for Germany and France, table 4 reports the VAR model for Germany and Italy and table 5 reports the VAR estimates for France and Italy.

We generate impulse response functions from the respective VAR models to analyze the effect of one standard positive artificial shock in monetary base on each output, inflation and unemployment of Germany, France and Italy. We only report the relevant and significant IRFs generated from the VAR model. Figure 1a and 1b show the response of France and Italy inflation respectively to monetary base shock. In both cases, monetary base shock affects inflation with a lag. In case of France, the effect is significant and positive from the second month and increases till about the fourth month and thereafter dies out. In case of Italy, we see that the effect is again significant and positive and increases from the second month to about the third month and then starts to decline and dies out after the fifth month. Overall, a one standard deviation positive shock in monetary base increases inflation in Italy and France.

Table 3. Vector Auto regression Estimates for Germany and France

	MB	P_GER	P_FR	UN_GER	UN_FR	Y_GER	Y_FR
MB(-1)	0.213884	0.003271	-0.0334**	-0.045908	0.007331	0.169064	0.024969
	(0.1554)	(0.0264)	(0.0162)	(0.0487)	(0.0435)	(0.0692)	(0.0476)
MB(-2)	-0.3414**	-0.003712	0.020349	-0.059861	-0.028352	0.015681	0.070071
	(0.1398)	(0.0238)	(0.0146)	(0.0438)	(0.0392)	(0.0622)	(0.0428)
P_GER(-1)	2.4790***	-0.124256	0.076904	0.542589	-0.134682	0.466167	0.198858
	(0.9264)	(0.1575)	(0.0968)	(0.2902)	(0.2595)	(0.4124)	(0.2838)
P_GER(-2)	-3.3720***	-0.077305	0.2392**	-0.072891	-0.7434**	-0.076095	0.043378
	(1.1266)	(0.1915)	(0.1178)	(0.3528)	(0.3155)	(0.5015)	(0.3451)
P_FR(-1)	-1.163429	0.087247	0.228803	-0.066145	0.301628	-0.120583	0.062927
	(1.4306)	(0.2432)	(0.1495)	(0.4481)	(0.4007)	(0.6368)	(0.4383)
P_FR(-2)	1.328242	-0.072487	-0.3689***	-0.230489	0.356778	0.498051	0.071206
	(1.3472)	(0.2291)	(0.1408)	(0.4219)	(0.3773)	(0.5997)	(0.4127)
UN_GER(-1)	0.240186	-0.137367	-0.038798	0.4037***	0.178518	-0.312015	-0.012255
	(0.4797)	(0.0816)	(0.0501)	(0.1502)	(0.1344)	(0.2135)	(0.1469)
UN_GER(-2)	-0.076822	0.066734	0.082681	0.334384	-0.097744	-0.024326	-0.3534**
	(0.4881)	(0.0830)	(0.0510)	(0.1529)	(0.1367)	(0.2173)	(0.1495)
UN_FR(-1)	-0.618652	0.039787	-0.000802	-0.058747	-1.1326***	-0.6716***	-0.118695
	(0.5392)	(0.0917)	(0.0564)	(0.1689)	(0.1510)	(0.2400)	(0.1652)
UN_FR(-2)	-0.485277	0.15187	0.027551	-0.031341	-0.3511**	-0.7035***	-0.187903
	(0.5280)	(0.0898)	(0.0552)	(0.1654)	(0.1479)	(0.2351)	(0.1618)
Y_GER(-1)	0.526878	0.014029	-0.017566	-0.092666	-0.013051	-0.7096***	-0.124949
	(0.3389)	(0.0576)	(0.0354)	(0.1061)	(0.0949)	(0.1509)	(0.1038)
Y_GER(-2)	-0.146841	-0.028877	-0.00403	-0.047596	-0.057056	-0.364448	-0.074932

	(0.3195)	(0.0543)	(0.0334)	(0.1001)	(0.0895)	(0.1423)	(0.0979)
Y_FR(-1)	0.27035	0.042583	0.071691	0.3137*	0.2384*	0.5297**	-0.204933
	(0.5273)	(0.0897)	(0.0551)	(0.1651)	(0.1477)	(0.2347)	(0.1615)
Y_FR(-2)	0.516103	-0.071216	-0.00049	-0.021433	0.033972	0.3246	-0.13119
	(0.5352)	(0.0910)	(0.0559)	(0.1676)	(0.1499)	(0.2382)	(0.1640)
C	0.004321	0.001424	0.0013***	0.000764	0.000252	0.000358	0.000758
	-0.00436	-0.00074	-0.00046	-0.00137	-0.00122	-0.00194	-0.00134
R-squared	0.431736	0.241645	0.375537	0.501005	0.751442	0.543039	0.331177
Adj. R-squared	0.227744	-0.030585	0.151371	0.321878	0.662216	0.379002	0.091087
Sum sq. resids	0.019724	0.00057	0.000216	0.001935	0.001547	0.003909	0.001851
S.E. equation	0.022489	0.003824	0.002351	0.007043	0.006299	0.010011	0.006889
F-statistic	2.116437	0.887651	1.675262	2.796935	8.421794	3.310464	1.379386
Log likelihood	137.0799	232.7574	259.0276	199.7698	205.8025	180.7822	200.9636
Akaike AIC	-4.521477	-8.065088	-9.038061	-6.843327	-7.066761	-6.140083	-6.887542
Schwarz SC	-3.968982	-7.512592	-8.485565	-6.290831	-6.514265	-5.587587	-6.335046
Mean dependent	0.003683	0.001057	0.001509	0.001666	0.000166	0.000998	0.000674
S.D. dependent	0.025591	0.003766	0.002552	0.008553	0.010838	0.012704	0.007226

Variables in the VAR model are: monetary base (MB), inflation of Germany (P_GER), inflation of France (P_FR), unemployment in Germany (UN_GER), unemployment in France (UN_FR), output in Germany (Y_GER) and output in France (Y_FR).

The estimate and standard errors are shown in the table.

*, ** and *** denote significance levels at the 10%, 5% and 1% respectively.

Table 4. Vector Auto regression Estimates for Germany and Italy

	MB	P_GER	P_IT	UN_GER	UN_IT	Y_GER	Y_IT
MB(-1)	0.153793	0.000521	-0.0554***	-0.055512	0.1032***	0.052815	0.045536
	(0.1456)	(0.0257)	(0.0202)	(0.0444)	(0.0362)	(0.0756)	(0.0537)
MB(-2)	-0.158244	-0.014594	0.0353*	-0.1053**	-0.052341	0.012795	0.014101
	(0.1513)	(0.0267)	(0.0209)	(0.0462)	(0.0377)	(0.0785)	(0.0558)
P_GER(-1)	2.3188**	-0.216015	0.086633	0.25289	0.073836	0.468496	0.07523
	(0.8977)	(0.1586)	(0.1242)	(0.2739)	(0.2233)	(0.4656)	(0.3311)
P_GER(-2)	-3.1363**	-0.011865	0.019521	-0.012138	-0.8081**	0.34446	-0.079042
	(0.9778)	(0.1728)	(0.1353)	(0.2984)	(0.2433)	(0.5072)	(0.3607)
P_IT(-1)	1.8746*	-0.050743	0.152024	-0.192288	0.5050*	-0.230627	-0.052158
	(1.0503)	(0.1856)	(0.1453)	(0.3205)	(0.2613)	(0.5448)	(0.3875)
P_IT(-2)	0.722711	0.148857	-0.3037**	-0.187969	0.324702	0.168873	0.382068
	(0.9251)	(0.1635)	(0.1280)	(0.2823)	(0.2301)	(0.4799)	(0.3413)
UN_GER(-1)	0.356707	-0.1736**	0.035132	0.2598*	0.070589	-0.3942*	-0.169462
	(0.4220)	(0.0746)	(0.0584)	(0.1288)	(0.1050)	(0.2189)	(0.1557)
UN_GER(-2)	-0.135421	0.045026	0.010195	0.2499*	0.103134	-0.084721	-0.094994
	(0.4541)	(0.0803)	(0.0628)	(0.1386)	(0.1130)	(0.2356)	(0.1675)
UN_IT(-1)	-0.214048	0.035987	-0.096024	0.144074	0.009621	-0.037447	-0.230589
	(0.5765)	(0.1019)	(0.0798)	(0.1759)	(0.1434)	(0.2991)	(0.2127)
UN_IT(-2)	0.130618	0.129688	-0.1557*	0.2765*	0.3184**	0.155097	-0.024596
	(0.5622)	(0.0994)	(0.0778)	(0.1716)	(0.1399)	(0.2916)	(0.2074)
Y_GER(-1)	0.5689*	0.020211	-0.005272	-0.029188	0.08043	-0.7126***	0.121598
	(0.3233)	(0.0571)	(0.0447)	(0.0986)	(0.0804)	(0.1677)	(0.1193)
Y_GER(-2)	-0.029416	0.003194	0.039785	-0.017358	0.036667	-0.3840**	-0.048784

	(0.2952)	(0.0522)	(0.0408)	(0.0901)	(0.0734)	(0.1531)	(0.1089)
Y_IT(-1)	0.594014	-0.092845	-0.060701	-0.016374	0.159421	0.310309	-0.196223
	(0.4432)	(0.0783)	(0.0613)	(0.1352)	(0.1103)	(0.2299)	(0.1635)
Y_IT(-2)	0.133552	-0.077021	-0.031762	-0.3134***	-0.005674	0.172495	0.034547
	(0.4421)	(0.0781)	(0.0612)	(0.1349)	(0.1100)	(0.2293)	(0.1631)
C	-0.002105	0.0024**	0.000955	0.0045**	-0.0051***	0.002044	-0.001486
	(0.0068)	(0.0012)	(0.0009)	(0.0021)	(0.0017)	(0.0035)	(0.0025)
R-squared	0.467266	0.239408	0.484988	0.556127	0.441734	0.426548	0.216908
Adj. R-squared	0.280809	-0.0268	0.304734	0.400771	0.246341	0.22584	-0.057174
Sum sq. resids	0.018497	0.000578	0.000354	0.001722	0.001145	0.004977	0.002517
S.E. equation	0.021504	0.0038	0.002975	0.006562	0.00535	0.011154	0.007933
F-statistic	2.506029	0.899328	2.69058	3.579698	2.260746	2.125217	0.791398
Log likelihood	141.8889	237.211	250.6723	207.1736	218.4049	177.9911	196.7374
Akaike AIC	-4.614141	-8.080401	-8.569901	-6.988131	-7.396542	-5.926949	-6.608631
Schwarz SC	-4.066687	-7.532946	-8.022446	-6.440677	-6.849087	-5.379495	-6.061177
Mean dependent	0.003747	0.001107	0.002151	0.001635	-0.005552	0.001204	0.000433
S.D. dependent	0.025357	0.003751	0.003568	0.008477	0.006162	0.012678	0.007715

Variables in the VAR model are: monetary base (MB), inflation of Germany (P_GER), inflation of Italy (P_IT), unemployment in Germany (UN_GER), unemployment in Italy (UN_IT), output in Germany (Y_GER) and output in Italy (Y_IT).

The estimate and standard errors are shown in the table.

*, ** and *** denote significance levels at the 10%, 5% and 1% respectively.

Table 5. Vector Auto regression Estimates for France and Italy

	MB	P_FR	P_IT	UN_FR	UN_IT	Y_FR	Y_IT
MB(-1)	-0.066873	-0.016024	-0.0599**	-0.03457	0.044197	-0.016806	0.067916
	(0.1632)	(0.0157)	(0.0165)	(0.0424)	(0.0393)	(0.0448)	(0.0476)
MB(-2)	-0.140823	0.022852	0.0437**	-0.007575	-0.037225	0.00997	0.001703
	(0.1949)	(0.0187)	(0.0197)	(0.0507)	(0.0470)	(0.0536)	(0.0569)
P_FR(-1)	-0.696144	0.2828*	0.43908	0.109596	0.191573	0.526167	0.597067
	(1.6312)	(0.1567)	(0.1653)	(0.4240)	(0.3932)	(0.4483)	(0.4759)
P_FR(-2)	-2.18981	-0.224421	0.151068	0.053695	-0.078926	-0.039032	-0.481418
	(1.7178)	(0.1651)	(0.1740)	(0.4465)	(0.4141)	(0.4721)	(0.5011)
PH_IT(-1)	1.874724	-0.023019	0.056531	0.06474	0.339626	-0.412477	-0.197756
	(1.4101)	(0.1355)	(0.1429)	(0.3665)	(0.3399)	(0.3875)	(0.4114)
PH_IT(-2)	1.25977	0.011086	-0.2895**	0.199036	0.447838	0.193205	0.6493*
	(1.1716)	(0.1126)	(0.1187)	(0.3045)	(0.2824)	(0.3220)	(0.3418)
UN_FR(-1)	-0.571566	0.016908	0.1304**	-1.0223***	0.09088	-0.332374	-0.4833**
	(0.6678)	(0.0642)	(0.0677)	(0.1736)	(0.1610)	(0.1835)	(0.1948)
UN_FR(-2)	-0.613246	0.048267	0.08542	-0.266052	0.066038	-0.3947**	-0.248461
	(0.6581)	(0.0632)	(0.0667)	(0.1711)	(0.1586)	(0.1809)	(0.1920)
UN_IT(-1)	0.487253	-0.076869	-0.124612	-0.16686	0.058787	0.3444**	-0.115908
	(0.7156)	(0.0688)	(0.0725)	(0.1860)	(0.1725)	(0.1967)	(0.2088)
UN_IT(-2)	-0.465153	0.048311	-0.066381	-0.018459	0.2791**	-0.106976	-0.276728
	(0.7070)	(0.0679)	(0.0716)	(0.1838)	(0.1704)	(0.1943)	(0.2063)
Y_FR(-1)	0.103796	0.081893	-0.062249	0.129673	-0.038574	-0.160165	0.3591**
	(0.5700)	(0.0548)	(0.0578)	(0.1482)	(0.1374)	(0.1566)	(0.1663)

Y_FR(-2)	0.718488	-0.017997	-0.018599	0.068746	-0.024478	-0.189281	0.005205
	(0.5864)	(0.0563)	(0.0594)	(0.1524)	(0.1413)	(0.1611)	(0.1711)
Y_IT(-1)	0.682784	-0.030394	-0.038024	-0.076943	0.145206	0.047524	-0.125211
	(0.5338)	(0.0513)	(0.0541)	(0.1387)	(0.1287)	(0.1467)	(0.1557)
Y_IT(-2)	-0.32615	-0.010057	0.000667	-0.081053	-0.03571	0.2515*	-0.011494
	(0.5225)	(0.0502)	(0.0529)	(0.1358)	(0.1260)	(0.1436)	(0.1524)
C	0.001983	0.0012*	0.000745	-0.001319	-0.0055***	0.001805	-0.003076
	(0.0076)	(0.0007)	(0.0008)	(0.0020)	(0.0018)	(0.0021)	(0.0022)
R-squared	0.256069	0.309268	0.614352	0.719784	0.256991	0.295424	0.31167
Adj. R-squared	-0.010983	0.061314	0.475914	0.619194	-0.00973	0.0425	0.064577
Sum sq. resids	0.025821	0.000238	0.000265	0.001744	0.0015	0.00195	0.002197
S.E. equation	0.025731	0.002472	0.002607	0.006688	0.006202	0.007071	0.007506
F-statistic	0.958874	1.247277	4.437742	7.155612	0.963521	1.168032	1.261347
Log likelihood	129.8071	256.3044	253.4435	202.5657	206.6366	199.5576	196.3318
Akaike AIC	-4.252115	-8.937202	-8.831239	-6.946878	-7.09765	-6.835465	-6.715992
Schwarz SC	-3.699619	-8.384706	-8.278744	-6.394382	-6.545155	-6.282969	-6.163497
Mean dependent	0.003683	0.001509	0.00214	0.000166	-0.005655	0.000674	0.000519
S.D. dependent	0.025591	0.002552	0.003601	0.010838	0.006172	0.007226	0.007761

Variables in the VAR model are: monetary base (MB), inflation of France (P_FR), inflation of Italy (P_IT), unemployment in France (UN_FR), unemployment in Italy (UN_IT), output in France (Y_FR) and output in Italy (Y_IT).

The estimate and standard errors are shown in the table.

*, ** and *** denote significance levels at the 10%, 5% and 1% respectively.

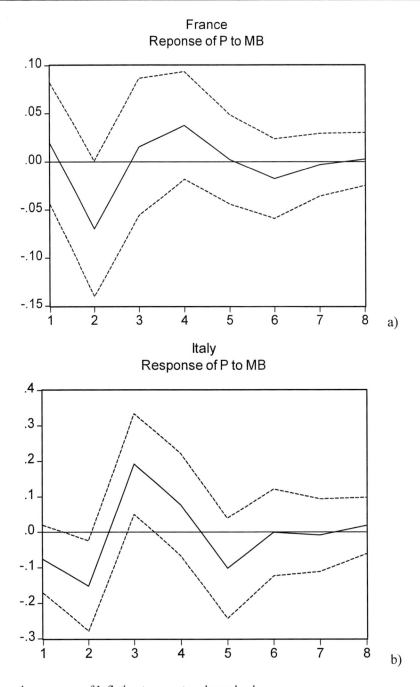

Figure 1. Impulse response of Inflation to monetary base shock.

Figure 2a, 2b and 2c show the response of unemployment indicators in Germany, France and Italy respectively to monetary base shock. In case of Germany we find that unemployment is significant and decreases till about the third month and then dies out. In case of France, we find the effect to be significant and negative till the second month. In case of Italy the effect is significant and negative and dies out after about three months. This suggests that a one standard deviation positive shock in monetary base leads to a decrease in unemployment in Germany, France and Italy.

In all the three countries, we find no significance in the case of a one standard deviation positive shock in monetary base on output.

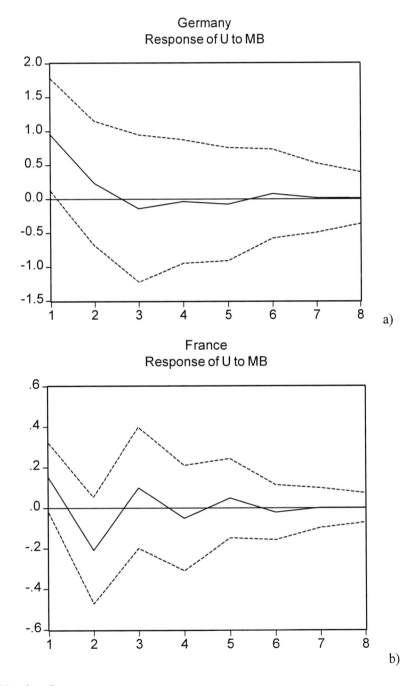

Figure 2. (Continued)

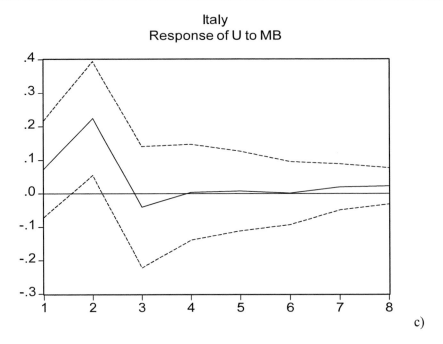

Figure 2. Impulse response of Inflation to monetary base shock.

4. CONCLUSIONS

This paper examines whether monetary policy shocks have any varying degrees of asymmetric effect on the prices, output and unemployment of the European Union member countries of Germany, France and Italy.

Results show that monetary base affects inflation with a lag in France and Italy. In case of France, the effect is significant and positive from the second month and increases till about the fourth month. In case of Italy, we see that the effect is again significant and positive and increases from the second month to about the third month and then starts to decline. In case of Germany we find that unemployment is significant and decreases till about the third month and then dies out. In case of France, we find the effect to be significant and negative till the second month. In case of Italy the effect is significant and negative and dies out after about three months. Overall, a one standard deviation positive shock in monetary base increases inflation in Italy and France and decreases unemployment in Germany, France and Italy. Overall, we see that monetary policy shocks have asymmetric effect on inflation and output. However, in all the three countries, we find no significance in the case of a one standard deviation positive shock in monetary base on output.

REFERENCES

Bank for International Settlements, 1994, *National differences in Interest rate transmission,* Basel.

Bank for International Settlements, 1995, *Financial Structure and the Monetary Policy Transmission Mechanism,* Basel, Switzerland, March, No. C.B. 394.

Barran, F., V. Coudert, and B. Mojon, 1996. The transmission of monetary policy in the European countries, London School of Economics, *Financial Markets Group,* special paper, No. 86.

Britton, E., and J. Whitley, 1997. Comparing the monetary transmission mechanism in France, Germany and the United Kingdom: Some issues and results, Bank of England, *Quarterly Bulletin,* May, pp. 152-162.

Calvo, G.A., Rodriguez C.A., 1977. A model of exchange rate determination under currency substitution and rational expectations. *Journal of Political Economy* 85(3), 617-625.

Clausen, V., and Hayo, B. (2002). Monetary policy in the Euro Area – Lessons from the first years, *ZEI working paper.*

Doan, T., Litterman, R., 1986. *User's manual RATS: Version 2.0.* VAR Econometrics: Evanston, IL.

Dornbusch, R., C. Favero, and F. Giavazzi, 1998. Immediate challenges for the European Central Bank. NBER Working, No. 6369 (Cambridge, Massachusetts: National Bureau for Economic Research, January).

Dickey, D. A., Fuller, W. A.,1981. Likelihood ratio statistics for autoregressive time series with unit root. *Econometrica,* 49: 1057 - 1072

Enders, W.,1995. *Applied econometrics time series.* John Wiley and Sons Inc.

Frenkel, J.A., Rodriguez C.A., 1982. Exchange rate dynamics and overshooting hypothesis. *IMF Staff papers* 29(1), 1-30.

Hamilton, J. D.,1994. Time series analysis. *Princeton University Press,* Princeton, NJ.

Gerlach, S., and F. Smets, 1995. The monetary transmission mechanism: Evidence from the G-7 countries, in *Financial Structure and the Monetary Policy Transmission Mechanism,* Basel, Switzerland: Bank for International Settlements, March, No. C.B. 394.

Kieler M., and T. Saarenheimo, 1998. Differences in monetary policy transmission? A case not closed, European Commission, economic paper, No. 132.

Runkle, D. E., 1987. Vector auto regressions and reality. *Journal of Business and Economics Statistics,* 5: 437 - 442.

Ramaswamy, R., and T. Slok, 1998. The real effects of monetary policy in the European Union: What are the differences? *IMF Staff Papers,* Vol. 45, No. 2, pp. 374-396.

Sims, C. A.,1980. Macroeconomics and reality. *Econometrica,* 48: 1 - 49.

In: Economics of Emerging Markets
Editor: Lado Beridze, pp. 115-129

Chapter 5

EXPANSION OF MEAN-VARIANCE ANALYSIS IN EMERGING EQUITY MARKETS

Yasuaki Watanabe[*]

Stanford University Graduate School of Business,
Visiting Scholar and the Japan Research Institute

ABSTRACT

We examine how the precision of asset allocation increases when considering the higher order moments such as skewness and kurtosis. This is because the normality of equity returns are dubious as documented in the finance literature. Thus, we execute an empirical analysis of emerging equity markets by considering skewness and kurtosis. We believe that this is the first paper which considers until kurtosis in the empirical analysis of asset allocation. In the analysis, it is subject to the sequential quadratic programming based on a quasi-Newton updating method. As the covariance affects the asset allocation in the mean-variance model, it seems that the coskewness and cokurtosis affect the asset allocation in the mean-variance-skewness-kurtosis model. We find that if the investors' amounts are relatively small, the traditional mean-variance approach of asset allocation is acceptable. However, when considering large investments, we note a small but significant percentage change in investor satisfaction when using skewness and kurtosis.

JEL Classification: C61, G11, G12
Keywords: Normality Test, Skewness, Kurtosis, Sequential Quadratic Programming, Mean-Variance-Skewness-Kurtosis Model

The mean-variance approach, the traditional analytical method that is used in rate-of-return market projections, is based on the premise that the rate of return is normally distributed. Therefore, mean-variance analysis can't fully grasp the characteristics of returns

[*] Mailing Address : 350 Sharon Park Drive, #C-23, Menlo Park, CA, 94025 U.S.A. E-mail Address : TUmanaayuhaku@hotmail.comUT; Home Phone No. : (650) 233-9153; Fax No.: (650) 233-9153.

when normality is dubious. However, by introducing the concepts of skewness and kurtosis in higher order moments, we can make clear the characteristic of the rate of return in emerging equity markets.

In the first part of this paper, we examine how the normality test can be executed in both the emerging equity markets and in the advanced equity markets by utilizing skewness and kurtosis. According to the normality test of Bekaert and Harvey (1997), returns are not normally distributed in many emerging markets using a U.S. dollar base. The results reported in this paper using a Japanese yen base coincide with that observation.

In the latter part of this paper, the implications for change of investment policy through consideration of skewness and kurtosis are analyzed by using non-linear programming method.

1. NORMALITY TEST OF SKEWNESS AND KURTOSIS

In this first analysis, we test normality[1] utilizing skewness and kurtosis by applying the standardized skewness and standardized kurtosis to the EM-Composite[2] and each of ten selected emerging equity markets. The details of our results are summarized in Table 1.

Table 1. Normality Tests of Skewness and Kurtosis
(Jan. 1980-Dec.1999; Simple Interest)

Market	Annualized Mean	Annualized Std. dev.	Skewness	Standardized Skewness	Kurtosis	Standardized Kurtosis	Bera-Jarque	Kolmogorov Smirnov
EM-Comp.	0.2102	0.2558	0.0839	0.5309	4.5460	4.8889	24.1831	0.4351
Argentina	0.3301	0.8448	2.7153	17.1728	18.2711	48.2915	2626.9710	0.3562
Brazil	0.2911	0.6071	0.3114	1.9886	3.6139	1.9413	7.7233	0.3639
Chile	0.1458	0.3248	0.0328	0.2075	3.3529	1.1159	1.2883	0.4138
Mexico	0.1948	0.4648	-0.7064	-4.4679	6.1794	10.0542	121.0491	0.3857
India	0.1190	0.3083	0.4630	2.9285	4.3622	4.3076	27.1314	0.4250
Korea	0.1213	0.3882	1.2002	7.5909	8.1966	16.4332	327.6706	0.4069
Thailand	0.1113	0.3785	-0.0007	-0.0047	4.7058	5.3943	29.0981	0.3887
Greece	0.1221	0.3829	1.4372	9.0897	8.0532	15.9796	337.9699	0.4168
Jordan	0.0474	0.1982	0.2034	1.2865	3.7166	2.2662	6.7909	0.4417
Zimbabwe	0.0848	0.3799	-0.1711	-1.0818	4.8896	5.9753	36.8750	0.3988

* Normality Tests are based on at 5 percent significant level.
** Shadow cells mean that the normalilties are not rejected.

---

[1] These tests are based on the monthly percentage change in Japanese Yen by modifying the original data from S&P/IFCG total return indices.

[2] This is an original composite made by the author and is constituted from the ten emerging equity markets described in Table 1.

Table 2. Normality Tests of Skewness and Kurtosis
(Jan. 1980 - Dec. 1999; Simple Interest)

Market	Annualized Mean	Annualized Std. dev.	Skewness	Standardized Skewness	Kurtosis	Standardized Kurtosis	Bera-Jarque	Kolmogorov Smirnov
Japan	0.0998	0.1988	-0.0642	-0.4061	4.1992	3.7923	14.5466	0.4366
U.S.A.	0.1432	0.1946	-0.5184	-3.2787	4.5795	4.9950	35.6997	0.4426
U.K.	0.1332	0.2019	-0.6016	-3.8046	4.4281	4.5160	34.8692	0.4436
Germany	0.1210	0.2257	-0.2182	-1.3802	4.2605	3.9861	17.7937	0.4248
France	0.1264	0.2183	-0.4266	-2.6978	4.1985	3.7899	21.6413	0.4348

* Normality Tests are based on at 5 percent significant level.
** Shadow cells mean that the normalilties are not rejected.

These results show us that the normality test of standardized skewness can not be rejected at five percent significant level in the EM-Composite or the emerging markets of Chile, Thailand, Jordan, and Zimbabwe.

In addition, we accept the hypothesis of normality using the standardized kurtosis test at the five percent significant level in the markets of Brazil and Chile. While normality using the Bera-Jarque test[3] can not be rejected in Chile's market, the normality using the Kolmogorov-Smirnov test[4] can be rejected in all the sample markets. In short, except for the Kolmogorov-Smirnov test, the Chilean market is the only one where normality can not be rejected. From these results, we can surmise that the assumption of normality in emerging equity markets is dubious.

At this point, it is important for us to investigate the normality of the more advanced markets for sake of comparison. Table 2 reports that using similar tests, we find normality utilizing the standardized skewness test can not be rejected at the five percent significant level in the markets of Japan and Germany. The hypothesis of normality is rejected for all of the other advanced markets using any of the normality tests. We can therefore also surmise that the assumption of normality in advanced markets is, like emerging equity markets, erroneous.

2. INVESTMENT POLICY IN CASE OF
CONSIDERING SKEWNESS AND KURTOSIS

Most modern portfolio theory only considers the first and second moments concerning the stochastic distribution of future returns, as first demonstrated by the mean-variance approach in Markowitz (1952). The assumption that returns are normally distributed underlies this mean-variance approach. We can surmise that the normality of emerging equity markets is dubious from the reported analytical results. Thus, we need to consider the impact of higher order moments on utility functions. If investors' utility functions are not quadratic, maximization of investors' expected utility functions with respect to mean and variance will not coincide with their utility maximizing asset allocation.

---

[3] The Bera-Jarque test is subject to the chi-square distribution with freedom two under the null hypothesis of normal distribution.
[4] For example, Kolmogorov-Smirnov test is to compare the values in data vector X with a normal distribution having mean 0 and variance 1. The cutoff value is 0.0869 in this case.

We can use the HARA type utility function to consider skewness and kurtosis. In this case, taking into account the skewness of the return distribution can increase the precision of asset allocation. We present this as a mean-variance-skewness model. In addition, we can get even more precise about agents' optimal asset allocation by considering kurtosis. The importance of precision in asset allocation can be confirmed by the empirical anlysis of Brinson, et al. (1986). According to their mean-variance analysis, more than 90 percent of the performance of a portfolio is determined by asset allocation.

Theoretically, Samuelson (1970) points out that if variance is close enough to zero, then mean-variance analysis yields results that are a good approximation of agents' optimal portfolio holdings. In contrast, Merton (1971) points out that if the utility function is locally quadratic and the return distribution is locally normal, then the mean-variance model is valid for a broad range of utility functions and a broad range of probability distributions. Rubinstein (1973) succeeded in creating a three moment capital asset pricing model under the assumption that investors have cubic utility functions.

Arditti (1967), Kraus and Litzenberger (1976), Konno, Shirakawa, and Yamazaki (1993) and Konno and Suzuki (1995), Wang and Xia (2002) all do empirical studies of the mean-variance-skewness model. Arditti analyzes the importance of the third moment by using regression analysis. He regresses returns on variance, skewness, and the correlation of each firm's returns with the market. Kraus and Lizenberger construct a three moment capital asset pricing model and find that investors have an aversion to variance and a preference for positive skewness. The validity of quadratic utility as a basis for positive valuation theory is dubious in this case. In addition, they find out that a regression of return on beta and gamma (systematic skewness) is much better than a regression of return on beta in terms of average R-square (the mean of the R-squared values from the cross-sectional regressions).

Konno, Shirakawa, and Yamazaki, and Konno and Suzuki contribute to the literature by converting the non-linear programming problem into a linear programming problem by using a piecewise linear approximation of the quadratic constraint and the cubic objective function for a large number of assets. They find that the fourth order moment (kurtosis) is negligible in determining utility maximization.

Finally, Wang and Xia propose a mean-variance-skewness model for portfolio selection with transaction costs. They use a transformation to convert, the non-convex and non-smooth programming problem into a linear programming problem.

The paper examines optimal asset allocation using a non-linear programming method in a mean-variance-skewness model. We find different results from previous papers that have examined the mean-variance-skewness-kurtosis model. We find that optimal asset allocation changes marginally from a mean-variance model when considering the skewness and kurtosis of returns.

3. NON-LINEAR PROGRAMMING MODELS

Denote expected rate of return and the actual returns of asset j as r_j and R_j and let the covariance between R_j and R_k be defined as σ_{jk}, then

$$E[R(x)] = E\left[\sum_{j=1}^{n} R_j x_j\right] = \sum_{j=1}^{n} E[R_j] x_j = \sum_{j=1}^{n} r_j x_j \tag{1}$$

$$V[R(x)] = E[R(x) - E[R(x)]]^2 = E\left[\sum_{j=1}^{n} R_j x_j - \sum_{j=1}^{n} r_j x_j\right]^2 = E\left[\sum_{j=1}^{n}\sum_{k=1}^{n}(R_j - r_j)(R_k - r_k)x_j x_k\right]$$

$$= \sum_{j=1}^{n}\sum_{k=1}^{n} E[(R_j - r_j)(R_k - r_k)]x_j x_k = \sum_{j=1}^{n}\sum_{k=1}^{n} \sigma_{jk} x_j x_k \tag{2}$$

Thus, the optimal portfolio is determined by the point that minimize (2) under a given constraint. For example, if we put $E[R(x)]$ as ρ, and don't admit short sales, the quadratic programming as follows.

Minimize ; $\displaystyle\sum_{j=1}^{n}\sum_{k=1}^{n} \sigma_{jk} x_j x_k$

Subject to ; $\displaystyle\sum_{j=1}^{n} r_j x_j = \rho, \sum_{j=1}^{n} x_j = 1, x_j \geq 0, j = 1,...,n$ $\tag{3}$

Now, suppose that the vector of rates of return; $(R_1,..., R_n)$ is subject to the discrete distribution of the realized value $(r_{1t},...,r_{nt})$ and it's probability is given as

$$f_t = \Pr\{(R_1,..., R_n) = (r_{1t},...,r_{nt})\}, t = 1,...,T \tag{4}$$

In addition, the expected rate of return and correlated coefficient are represented as follows from their definitions.

$$r_j = E[R_j] = \sum_{t=1}^{T} f_t r_{jt}, j = 1,...,n \tag{5}$$

$$\sigma_{jk} = \sum_{t=1}^{T} f_t (r_{jt} - r_j)(r_{kt} - r_k), j, k = 1,...,n \tag{6}$$

Then, the variance of $R(x)$ becomes

$$\sum_{j=1}^{n}\sum_{k=1}^{n} \sigma_{jk} x_j x_k = \sum_{j=1}^{n}\sum_{k=1}^{n}\sum_{t=1}^{T} f_t (r_{jt} - r_j)(r_{kt} - r_k)x_j x_k = \sum_{t=1}^{T} f_t \left\{\sum_{j=1}^{n}(r_{jt} - r_j)x_j\right\}^2 \tag{7}$$

Put $z_t = \sum_{j=1}^{n} (r_{jt} - r_j) x_j, t = 1,...,T$ (8), and substitute equation (7) and equation (8) for

equation (3), this quadratic programming can be shown as follows:

$$Minimize ; \sum_{t=1}^{T} f_t z_t^2$$

$$Subject\ to ; \sum_{j=1}^{n} r_j x_j = \rho, \sum_{j=1}^{n} x_j = 1, x_j \geq 0, j = 1,...,n \qquad (9)$$

This method is called compact decomposition and is generally faster to solve than the common equation (3).

Now, cubic programming which considers skewness in the mean-variance model is as follows:

$$Maximize ; S(x)$$

$$Subject\ to ; V(x) = v, \sum_{j=1}^{n} r_j x_j = \rho, \sum_{j=1}^{n} x_j = 1, x_j \geq 0, j = 1,...,n \qquad (10)$$

$$Where,\ S(x) = \sum_{t=1}^{T} f_t \left(\sum_{j=1}^{n} (r_{jt} - r_j) x_j \right)^3 \qquad (11)$$

The introduction of skewness is justified by Scott and Horvath (1980). These results follow from the relationship between the preference of higher order moments and the sign of a differentiable utility function where $U^{(1)}(\mu_w) > 0$, $U^{(2)}(\mu_w) < 0$ (the utility function of a risk-averse, not satiated investor).

The proposition is that "investors exhibiting positive marginal utility of wealth for all wealth levels, consistent risk aversion at all wealth levels, and strict consistency of moment preference will have positive preference for positive skewness (negative preference for negative skewness)," (Scott and Horvath, (1980)). That is, an increase in the skewness of the distribution of future return, will increase expected utility. Then, $U^{(3)}(\mu_w) > 0$ and it follows that one should consider skewness when solving for optimal asset allocation. This is most easily demonstrated by doing a Taylor series expansion of the utility function,

$$U(\widetilde{W}_1) = \sum_{n=0}^{\infty} \frac{1}{n!} U^{(n)}(\mu_w)(\widetilde{W}_1 - \mu_w)^n,\ \text{where, } \mu_w \text{ is an average of random variable: } \widetilde{W}_1.$$

And $\widetilde{W}_1$ is an uncertain future return. (12)

Here, if we take the expectation of both sides of equation (12), we have

$$E\left(U\left(\tilde{W}_1\right)\right)=\sum_{n=0}^{\infty}\frac{1}{n!}U^{(n)}\left(\mu_w\right)m_w^{(n)} \tag{13}$$

$\left(\because m_w^{(n)}=E\left[\left(\tilde{W}_1-\mu_w\right)^n\right]\right)$, $m_w^{(n)}$ is n-th central moment of m_w).

In addition, if we let the third moment $m_w^{(3)}=s_w^{\ 3}$ (skewness) and the fourth moment $m_w^{(4)}=k_w^{\ 4}$ (kurtosis), equation (13) becomes

$$E\left[U\left(\tilde{W}_1\right)\right]=U\left(\mu_w\right)+\frac{1}{2}U^{(2)}\left(\mu_w\right)\sigma_w^{\ 2}+\frac{1}{6}U^{(3)}\left(\mu_w\right)s_w^{\ 3}+\frac{1}{24}U^{(4)}\left(\mu_w\right)k_w^{\ 4}+\sum_{n=5}^{\infty}\frac{1}{n!}U^{(n)}\left(\mu_w\right)m_w^{(n)} \tag{14}$$

Thus, when we substitute equation (10), equation (8), and equation (11) into

$V(x)=\sum_{t=1}^{T}f_t\left(\sum_{j=1}^{n}\left(r_{jt}-r_j\right)x_j\right)^2$ (15), the cubic programming problem can be represented as follows:

Maximize ; $\sum_{t=1}^{T}f_t z_t^3$

Subject to ; $\sum_{t=1}^{T}f_t z_t^2 \le v, \sum_{j=1}^{n}r_j x_j=\rho, \sum_{j=1}^{n}x_j=1, x_j\ge 0, j=1,...,n \tag{16}$

While, $\sum_{t=1}^{T}f_t z_t^2=V(x)=v$ can be expressed as $\sum_{t=1}^{T}f_t z_t^2=V(x)\le v$.

This follows from the fact that $U^{(2)}\left(\mu_w\right)<0$, and that expected utility increases when $V(x)=\sigma_w^{\ 2}$ decreases. Using this method it is possible to maximize the expected utility under a HARA type utility function. Moreover, biquadratic programming that considers kurtosis can be expressed as follows:

Minimize ; $K(x)$

Subject to ; $S(x)=s, V(x)=v, \sum_{j=1}^{n}r_j x_j=\rho, \sum_{j=1}^{n}x_j=1, x_j\ge 0, j=1,...,n \tag{17}$

While, $K(x)=\sum_{t=1}^{T}f_t\left(\sum_{j=1}^{n}\left(r_{jt}-r_j\right)x_j\right)^4 \tag{18}$

Here, the kurtosis is minimized for similar reasons as skewness is maximaized. The proposition that "investors exhibiting positive marginal utility of wealth for all wealth levels, consistent risk aversion at all wealth levels and strict consistency of moment preference will have positive preference for negative kurtosis (negative preference for positive kurtosis)" (Scott and Horvath, (1980)). That is, an increase in kurtosis in the distribution of future returns, will decrease expected utility. Then, $U^{(4)}(\mu_w) < 0$ and we must minimize kurtosis. This is also confirmed by equation (14), and likewise in the case of skewness. When we substitute equation (8), equation (11), and equation (15) into (18), the biquadratic programming is:

$$Minimize \; ; \; \sum_{t=1}^{T} f_t z_t^4$$

$$Subject \; to \; ; \; \sum_{t=1}^{T} f_t z_t^3 \geq s, \sum_{t=1}^{T} f_t z_t^2 \leq v, \sum_{j=1}^{n} r_j x_j = \rho,$$

$$\sum_{j=1}^{n} x_j = 1, x_j \geq 0, j = 1,...,n \qquad (19)$$

where, $\sum_{t=1}^{T} f_t z_t^3 = S(x) = s$ can be replaced by $\sum_{t=1}^{T} f_t z_t^3 = S(x) \geq s$.

The reason is that the expected utility $U^{(3)}(\mu_w) > 0$, and that expected utility increase when the $S(x) = s_w^3$ decreases. This is, in essence, the mean-variance-skewness-kurtosis model.

4. EMPIRICAL ANALYSIS

The following empirical analysis[5] is executed based on the models already presented. Initially the allotted assets are J-Mix (Domestic Securities)[6], where the domestic CB is excluded for only one percentage occupation, and EM-Composite. Therefore, there are n=4 total returns securities used. Next, the term is set at 20 years on a monthly basis, thus k=240 and $ft = 1/240$ when we use historical data. Normally skewness is defined as s_w^3 / σ_w^3 and kurtosis is defined as k_w^4 / σ_w^4. However, the mean-variance-skewness model and the mean-variance-skewness-kurtosis model use skewness and kurtosis that are not standardized. Thus, we use non-standardized skewness and kurtosis in the following analysis to coincide with our models.

---

[5] The Software used for analysis here is MATLAB. The algorithm is subject to the sequential quadratic programming. At each major iteration an approximation is made of the Hessian of the Lagrangian function using a quasi-Newton updating method. For further details, see Appendix.

[6] This index is a balanced-type benchmark developed by Nikko Security. It includes short-term financial assets, domestic bonds, domestic CB, and domestic equities.

The analytical results[7] are reported in Table 3. We note that the range of expected rates of returns that are from six to nine percent have a tendency to be subject to the marginal effect of skewness and kurtosis. As a general tendency, the marginal effect of skewness exceeds the marginal effect of kurtosis. Short-term financial assets, domestic bonds and domestic equities with seven percent expected rates of return are taken as exceptions. In addition, no marginal effect can be detected in expected rates of return of eight, ten, and eleven percent.

For example, if we consider skewness in the case of a six percent expected rate of return, the EM-Composite will decrease by about 0.71 percent. This figure can't be ignored if the investment amount is large enough. The same thing holds true for the other assets. Concerning kurtosis, it seems that a seven percent expected rate of return will give the largest decrease of 0.38 percent in domestic bonds.

When we consider asset allocation, covariance is a factor in the traditional mean-variance approach. Likewise, coskewness[8] and cokurtosis[9] will affect the asset allocation when considering higher order moments. We must note here that partial problems equivalent to the quadratic programming of iterations are solved, and we find optimal solutions to these (or approximate solutions). This method is called sequential quadratic programming and it is described in the footnotes. The problem here is that the rounding error will become large as an increase in the number of figures below the decimal point.

As a next step, variance, skewness, and kurtosis of the portfolio in each model are calculated . Then, a comparison is made by calculating below four decimal points (rounding up below five decimal points) to see how they change in each model.

As a result, all the models at each expected rate of return meet the constraints. In addition, variance, skewness, and kurtosis in each model are equal under the same expected rate of return.

Concerning the EM-Composite, as mentioned before, skewness changes asset allocation the most, by about minus 0.71 percent at the six percent expected rate of return. In addition, as the EM-Composite shows higher mean and variance in comparison with other assets, the higher the expected rate of return the investor desire, the larger the portion allocated in the portfolio becomes.

Thus, the significance of adding EM-Composite exists in the risk diversification effect and the offer of new investment opportunity from the low correlated coefficients with other assets from the mean-variance approach. However, this holds true to the more precise asset allocation results that consider skewness and kurtosis.

---

[7] Initial value is set up at 0.25 in each asset in solving the optimization problem.
[8] Concerning the conceptual explanation, see Appendix.
[9] Concerning the conceptual explanation, see Appendix.

Table 3. Affection of higher Order Moments to Asset Allocation (Period Annualized , Annualized Data, January 1980-December 1999)

	Mean	Variance	Skewness	Kurtosis
Short-Term Financial Assets	0.0444	0.0001	0.0000	0.0000
Domestic Bond	0.0695	0.0021	0.0000	0.0000
Domestic Equity	0.0961	0.0370	-0.0001	0.0005
EM-Composite	0.1112	0.0640	-0.0023	0.0019

Correlation Coefficients

Short-Term Financial Assets	1			
Domestic Bond	0.1360	1		
Domestic Equity	0.0060	0.1164	1	
EM-Composite	-0.0430	-0.1667	0.2417	1

i) 5 percent of expected rate of return

	Variance	Skewness	Kurtosis	Short-Term Financial Assets	Domestic Bond	Domestic Equity	EM-Composite	Total
Mean-Variance Model	0.0002	0.0000	0.0000	0.7594	0.2405	0.0000	0.0000	1.0000
Change Rate	0.0000%	0.0000%	0.0000%	0.0000%	0.0416%	0.0000%	0.0000%	N/A
Mean-Variance-Skewness Model	0.0002	0.0000	0.0000	0.7594	0.2406	0.0000	0.0000	1.0000
Change Rate	0.0000%	0.0000%	0.0000%	0.0000%	0.0000%	0.0000%	0.0000%	N/A
Mean-Variance-Skewness-Kurtosis Model	0.0002	0.0000	0.0000	0.7594	0.2406	0.0000	0.0000	1.0000

ii) 6 percent of expected rate of return

	Variance	Skewness	Kurtosis	Short-Term Financial Assets	Domestic Bond	Domestic Equity	EM-Composite	Total
Mean-Variance Model	0.0010	0.0000	0.0000	0.5240	0.3331	0.1288	0.0141	1.0000
Change Rate	0.0000%	0.0000%	0.0000%	0.0763%	-0.2402%	0.3882%	-0.7092%	N/A
Mean-Variance-Skewness Model	0.0010	0.0000	0.0000	0.5244	0.3323	0.1293	0.0140	1.0000
Change Rate	0.0000%	0.0000%	0.0000%	0.0000%	0.0000%	0.0000%	0.0000%	N/A
Mean-Variance-Skewness-Kurtosis Model	0.0010	0.0000	0.0000	0.5244	0.3323	0.1293	0.0140	1.0000

iii) 7 percent of expected rate of return

	Variance	Skewness	Kurtosis	Short-Term Financial Assets	Domestic Bond	Domestic Equity	EM-Composite	Total
Mean-Variance Model	0.0032	0.0000	0.0000	0.3871	0.2925	0.1891	0.1313	1.0000
Change Rate	0.0000%	0.0000%	0.0000%	0.0517%	-0.0342%	-0.1586%	0.1523%	N/A
Mean-Variance-Skewness Model	0.0032	0.0000	0.0000	0.3873	0.2924	0.1888	0.1315	1.0000
Change Rate	0.0000%	0.0000%	0.0000%	0.1291%	-0.3762%	0.3178%	0.0000%	N/A
Mean-Variance-Skewness-Kurtosis Model	0.0032	0.0000	0.0000	0.3878	0.2913	0.1894	0.1315	1.0000

iv) 8 percent of expected rate of return

	Variance	Skewness	Kurtosis	Short-Term Financial Assets	Domestic Bond	Domestic Equity	EM-Composite	Total
Mean-Variance Model	0.0077	0.0001	0.0000	0.2501	0.2520	0.2495	0.2484	1.0000
Change Rate	0.0000%	0.0000%	0.0000%	0.0000%	0.0000%	0.0000%	0.0000%	N/A
Mean-Variance-Skewness Model	0.0077	0.0001	0.0000	0.2501	0.2520	0.2495	0.2484	1.0000
Change Rate	0.0000%	0.0000%	0.0000%	0.0000%	0.0000%	0.0000%	0.0000%	N/A
Mean-Variance-Skewness-Kurtosis Model	0.0077	0.0001	0.0000	0.2501	0.2520	0.2495	0.2484	1.0000

v)9percent of expected rate of return

	Variance	Skewness	Kurtosis	Short-Term Financial Assets	Domestic Bond	Domestic Equity	EM-Composite	Total
Mean-Variance Model	0.0147	0.0003	0.0001	0.1134	0.2111	0.3098	0.3657	1.0000
Change Rate	0.0000%	0.0000%	0.0000%	0.0000%	-0.0474%	0.0646%	-0.0273%	N/A
Mean-Variance-Skewness Model	0.0147	0.0003	0.0001	0.1134	0.2110	0.3100	0.3656	1.0000
Change Rate	0.0000%	0.0000%	0.0000%	0.0000%	0.0000%	0.0000%	0.0000%	N/A
Mean-Variance-Skewness-Kurtosis Model	0.0147	0.0003	0.0001	0.1134	0.2110	0.3100	0.3656	1.0000

vi)10percent of expected rate of return

	Variance	Skewness	Kurtosis	Short-Term Financial Assets	Domestic Bond	Domestic Equity	EM-Composite	Total
Mean-Variance Model	0.0251	0.0006	0.0003	0.0000	0.1338	0.3672	0.4990	1.0000
Change Rate	0.0000%	0.0000%	0.0000%	0.0000%	0.0000%	0.0000%	0.0000%	N/A
Mean-Variance-Skewness Model	0.0251	0.0006	0.0003	0.0000	0.1338	0.3672	0.4990	1.0000
Change Rate	0.0000%	0.0000%	0.0000%	0.0000%	0.0000%	0.0000%	0.0000%	N/A
Mean-Variance-Skewness-Kurtosis Model	0.0251	0.0006	0.0003	0.0000	0.1338	0.3672	0.4990	1.0000

vi)11percent of expected rate of return

	Variance	Skewness	Kurtosis	Short-Term Financial Assets	Domestic Bond	Domestic Equity	EM-Composite	Total
Mean-Variance Model	0.0563	0.0020	0.0015	0.0000	0.0000	0.0784	0.9216	1.0000
Change Rate	0.0000%	0.0000%	0.0000%	0.0000%	0.0000%	0.0000%	0.0000%	N/A
Mean-Variance-Skewness Model	0.0563	0.0020	0.0015	0.0000	0.0000	0.0784	0.9216	1.0000
Change Rate	0.0000%	0.0000%	0.0000%	0.0000%	0.0000%	0.0000%	0.0000%	N/A
Mean-Variance-Skewness-Kurtosis Model	0.0563	0.0020	0.0015	0.0000	0.0000	0.0784	0.9216	1.0000

5. Conclusion

When investors' risk tolerance is moderate (desired expected rate of return in the range of six to nine percent) and the investment amount is small, optimal investment policy decisions can be made by considering skewness (kurtosis has marginal impact). However, if the scale of investment amount is extremely large, optimal portfolio allocation can be made much more precise by considering the kurtosis of future returns. In contrast, if the scale of investment amount is extremely small, the traditional mean-variance approach is acceptable.

In addition, if the mean-variance-skewness-kurtosis approach is 100 percent correct from the view of precision in the portfolio, it has been shown that the traditional mean-variance approach of solving for optimal portfolio weights is about 99.29 percent accurate and the mean-variance-skewness approach of investment policy is about 99.62 percent accurate.

Appendix

1. Sequential Quadratic Programming

At each major iteration a positive definite quasi-Newton approximation of the Hessian of the Lagrangian function, H, is calculated by using BFGS method where λ_i ($i = 1,.....,m$) is an estimate of the Lagrange multipliers. Here, quasi-Newton methods build up curvature information at each iteration to formulate a quadratic model problem of the form

$$\min_x \frac{1}{2} x^T H x + c^T x + b$$

where the Hessian matrix, H, is a positive definite symmetric matrix, c is a constant vector, and b is a constant. The optimal solution for this problem occurs when the partial derivatives of x go to zero, for example,

$$\nabla f(x^*) = Hx^* + c = 0$$

The optimal solution point, x^*, can be written as $x^* = -H^{-1}c$

Quasi-Newton methods avoid Newton-type methods by using the observed behavior of $f(x)$ and $\nabla f(x)$ to build up curvature information to make an approximation to H using an appropriate updating technique.

H_k must well approximate $\nabla^2 f(x_x)$ to make a superlinearlity like Newton-type methods in this case. This condition is called the Quasi-Newton condition, that is,

$$\nabla f(x_{k+1}) - \nabla f(x_k) = H_{k+1}(x_{k+1} - x_k)$$

Generally, the formula of Broyden [1970], Fletcher [1970], Goldfarb [1970] and Shanno [1970] (BFGS), is thought to be the most effective for use in a general purpose method. This is because the BFGS formula achieves global convergence and local superlinearlity. Thus, the BFGS formula is the best of the Quasi-Newton methods.

The formula given by BFGS is $H_{k+1} = H_k + \dfrac{q_k q_k^T}{q_k^T s_k} - \dfrac{H_k^T s_k s_k^T H_k}{s_k^T H_k s_k}$

where $s_k = x_{k+1} - x_k$, $q_k = \nabla f(x_{k+1}) - \nabla f(x_k)$, while,

$$q_k = \nabla f(x_{k+1}) + \sum_{i=1}^{n} \lambda_i \nabla g_i(x_{k+1}) - \left[\nabla f(x_k) + \sum_{i=1}^{n} \lambda_i \nabla g_i(x_k) \right]$$

$$\left(\because L(x,\lambda) = f(x) + \sum_{i=1}^{m} \lambda_i g_i(x) \right)$$

2. Coskewness

Suppose investors have a third moment utility function.

Let the rate of return of an investor's optimal portfolio be given by $\tilde{R}_e$. We call this as the agent's efficient portfolio.

Consider another portfolio that is made up of an arbitrary asset; j and the efficient portfolio. The investment ratio between the two assets is x and $(1-x)$ respectively.

Thus, the new portfolio can be expressed as; $\tilde{R}_p = x \bar{R}_j + (1-x) \bar{R}_e$

The third central moment is shown as follows.

$$s_p^3 = E[\{x(\tilde{R}_j - \mu_j) + (1-x)(\tilde{R}_e - \mu_e)\}^3]$$

$$= x^3 E[(\tilde{R} - \mu_j)^3] + 3x^2(1-x) E[(\tilde{R}_j - \mu_j)^2(\tilde{R}_e - \mu_e)]$$

$$+ 3x(1-x)^2 E[(\tilde{R}_j - \mu_j)(\tilde{R}_e - \mu_e)^2] + (1-x)^3 E[(\tilde{R}_e - \mu_e)^3]$$

$$= x^3 s_j^3 + 3x^2(1-x)s_{jje} + 3x(1-x)^2 s_{jee} + (1-x)^3 s_e^3$$

Here, we can express coskewness as $s_{hij} \equiv E[(\tilde{R}_h - \mu_h)(\tilde{R}_i - \mu_i)(\tilde{R}_j - \mu_j)]$

(Note: Skewness usually means the third central moment divided by the cube of the standard deviation; here skewness is the unnormalized third central moment.)

3. Cokurtosis

Likewise, suppose that investors have a fourth moment utility function.
The fourth central moment is shown as follows.

$$k_p^4 = E[\{x(\tilde{R}_J - \mu_j) + (1-x)(\tilde{R}_e - \mu_e)\}^4]$$

$$= x^4 E[(\tilde{R}_J - \mu_j)^4] + 4x^3(1-x)E[(\tilde{R}_J - \mu_j)^3(\tilde{R}_e - \mu_e)]$$

$$+ 6x^2(1-x)^2 E[(\tilde{R}_J - \mu_j)^2(\tilde{R}_e - \mu_e)^2] + 4x(1-x)^3 E[(\tilde{R}_J - \mu_j)(\tilde{R}_e - \mu_e)^3]$$

$$+ (1-x)^4 E[(\tilde{R}_e - \mu_e)^4]$$

$$= x^4 k_j^4 + 4x^3(1-x)k_{jjje} + 6x^2(1-x)^2 k_{jjee} + 4x(1-x)^3 k_{jeee} + (1-x)^4 k_e^4$$

Here, we can express cokurtosis as $k_{hijk} \equiv E[(\tilde{R}_h - \mu_h)(\tilde{R}_i - \mu_i)(\tilde{R}_j - \mu_j)(\tilde{R}_k - \mu_k)]$

(Note: Kurtosis usually means the fourth central moment divided by the biquadrate of the standard deviation; here kurtosis is the unnormalized fourth central moment.)

ACKNOWLEDGEMENTS

I am grateful to Mark Rubinstein, Richard Grinold, Robert Stambaugh, Philipe Jorion, Frank Fabozzi, Ryan Steve, Yoshio Kanazaki, Ken-ichi Suzuki and Masayuki Ikeda for thoughtful comments and suggestions. This original earlier version was presented at the 2003 JAFEE (The Japanese Association of Financial Econometrics & Engineering).

REFERENCES

Arditti, F.D., 1967 , Risk and Required Return on Equity, *Journal of Finance Vol.22,* 19-36.

Arditti, F.D., 1971, Another look at mutual fund performance, *Journal of Financial and Quantitative Analysis Vol.6,* 909-912.

Bekaert, Geert, Claude B. Erb, Campbell R. Harvey, and Tadas E. Viskanta, 1997, *The Cross-Sectional Determinants of Emerging Equity Market Returns; Quantitative Investing for the Global Markets,* Glenlake Publishing Company.

Brinson,G.P., L.R. Hood, and G.L. Beebower, 1986, Determinants of Portfolio Performance, Financial Analysts Journal July/August.

Broyden,C.G.., 1970 , The Convergence of a Class of Double–rank Minimization Algorithms, *Journal Institute of Mathematics and its Applications,* Vol.6, 76-90.

Fletcher,R., 1970, A New Approach to Variable Metric Algorithms, *Computer Journal,* Vol.13, 317-322.

Goldfarb,D., 1970, A Family of Variable Metric Updates Derived by Variational Means, *Mathematics of Computing,* Vol.24, 23-26.

Ikeda, Masayuki, 2000, *Fundamentals of Financial Economics* (Asakurashoten).

Kariya, Takeaki, and NobuhikoTerui, 1997, *Non-linear Economic Time Series Analyses and their applied methods* (Iwanamishoten).

Konno, Hiroshi, 1995, *Financial Engineering I* (Asakurashoten).

Konno, H. and K. Suzuki, 1995, A mean-variance-skewness optimization model, *Journal of the Operations Research Society of Japan,* Vol.38, No.2 June, 137-187.

Konno, H., H. Shirakawa, and Hiroaki Yamazaki, 1993, A mean-absolute deviation-skewness portfolio optimization model, *Annals of Operations Research,* Vol.45, 205-220.

Kraus, A. and R. H. Litzenberger, 1976, Skewness Preference and the Valuation of Risk Assets, *Journal of Finance* vol.38, no.4 September, 1085-1100.

Markowitz, H., 1952, Portfolio Selection, *Journal of Finance,* Vol.7, No.1 March, 77-91.

Merton, R.C., 1971, Optimum Consumption and Portfolio Rules in a Continuous Time Model, *Journal of Economic Theory3,* 373-413.

Owen, J. and R. Rabinovitch, 1983, On the Class of Elliptical Distributions and Their Applications to the Theory of Portfolio Choice, *Journal of Finance,* vol.38, No.3 June, 745-752.

Rubinstein, M., 1973, The Fundamental Theorem of Parameter-Preference Security Valuation, *Journal of Financial and Quantitative Analysis* vol.8, No.1 January, 61-69.

Samuelson, P., 1970, The Fundamental Approximation Theorem of Portfolio Analysis in terms of Means, Variances and Higher Moments, *The Review of Economic Studies* vol.37 (4), 537-542.

Shanno, D.F., 1970, Conditioning of Quasi-Newton Methods for Function Minimization, *Mathematics of Computing,* Vol.24, 647-656.

Scott, R. C. and P. A. Horvath, 1980, On the Direction of Preference for Moments of Higher Order than Variance, *Journal of Finance,* vol.38, No.4 September, 915-919.

Wang, Shouyang. and Yusen Xia, 2002, *Portfolio Selection and Asset Pricing,* Springer.

In: Economics of Emerging Markets
Editor: Lado Beridze, pp. 131-168

Chapter 6

AN EMPIRICAL TEST OF THE CONSUMPTION-BASED ASSET PRICING MODEL (CCAPM) IN LATIN AMERICA

Guilherme Kirch[*]
FEEVALE University College, Institute of Applied Social Sciences
RS239 #2755, Novo Hamburgo RS 93352-000, Brazil

Paulo Renato Soares Terra[†]
UFRGS University, Universidade Federal do Rio Grande do Sul, School of Management
Rua Washington Luís 855, Office 321, Porto Alegre RS 90010-460, Brazil

Tiago Wickstrom Alves[‡]
UNISINOS University, Universidade do Vale do Rio dos Sinos, Graduate Program in
Economics, Avenida Unisinos 950, São Leopoldo RS 93022-000, Brazil

ABSTRACT

This study investigates whether the Consumption-based Capital Asset Pricing Model (CCAPM) is consistent with the data from four Latin-American countries: Brazil, Chile, Colombia, and Mexico. Empirical results showed that there is a statistically significant relationship between mean excess returns and consumption betas in the countries cited above, with the exception of Mexico. Such results are, in part, similar to the results reported in previous studies for the United States of America.

Keywords: Capital Markets; Assets Pricing Models; CCAPM; Latin America; Two-Stage Cross-Sectional Regressions.
JEL Classification: G12, C21

---

[*] Tel: +55 51 99 59 37 55, guilherme.kirch@terra.com.br
[†] Tel: +55 51 33 08 35 36, Fax: +55 51 33 08 39 91, prsterra@ea.ufrgs.br
[‡] Tel: +55 51 35 90 81 86, Fax: +55 51 35 90 84 47, twa@unisinos.br

1. INTRODUCTION

According to Mehra and Prescott (1985), historically, the average return on stock market shares in the United States has exceeded the average return on the short-term virtually default-free bond. Analyzing the period from 1889 to 1978, they found that the real average annual return of the Standard and Poor's 500 Index is 6.98%, while that of the United States Government risk-free debt bond is 0.8%, resulting in an equity premium of 6.18% per year.

In principle, according to asset pricing theory, an equity premium of this magnitude could only be explained by the risk inherent in the stock market, that is, the stocks, as they carry a higher risk than near-risk-free bonds, would need to compensate investors with higher average rates of return, which, in equilibrium, would be sufficient to balance the demand and the supply of these bonds. According to Abel (1991), this basic principle underpins the Capital Asset Pricing Model (CAPM), initially developed in the 1960s and enhanced since then.

However, as demonstrated by Mehra and Prescott (1985), the equity premium observed in the North American financial market, in the period from 1889 to 1978, can not be explained by an intertemporal equilibrium model, more specifically the Consumption-Based Capital Asset Pricing Model (CCAPM), which, according to Abel (1991), is perhaps one of the most important advances of the CAPM. This empirical inconsistency of the model proposed by the modern neoclassical theory of asset pricing has been denominated by Mehra and Prescott (1985) the equity premium puzzle.

According to Kocherlakota (1996), in order to better understand why the equity premium seen in the North American economy constitutes a puzzle, it is useful to review the bases of modern neoclassic theory of asset pricing. According to this theory, the differences between the average returns of the various financial securities are attributed to the level at which the return of these securities would covary with the consumption of the typical investor.

Kocherlakota (1996) asserts that, for the CAPM, the consumption flow of the typical investor is perfectly correlated with the return of the stock market and, thus, the risk of a given asset can be measured by the covariance of its returns with the return of the stock market. In the CCAPM, an intertemporal equilibrium model based on the 'representative agent', the consumption flow of the typical investor is perfectly correlated with the per capita consumption and, consequently, the risk of an asset can be measured by the covariance of its returns with the rate of growth of per capita consumption.

Based on these considerations, it is possible to clearly specify what Mehra and Prescott (1985) define as the equity premium puzzle: within a reasonable interval of risk aversion on the part of the representative agent, the covariance of the real average return of the stock market and of the real average rate of the risk-free asset with the real rate of growth of consumption are not sufficiently different to explain the average equity premium of 6.18% per annum seen in the North American data for the period 1889 to 1978. In other words, stocks do not display high enough risk in comparison to the short-term U.S. T-Bill to justify such the higher excess returns.

Prior to Mehra and Prescott (1985) identifying this empirical inconsistency, Grossman and Shiller (1981) and Hansen and Singleton (1983) had already empirically tested the representative agent model and, in both cases, the estimated parameters led to the rejection of the CCAPM for the data from the North American economy. Other empirical studies based on the North American economy have also demonstrated that the CCAPM is inconsistent, particularly the studies of Mankiw and Shapiro (1986) and Grossman, Melino and Shiller (1987). The only evidence found to be favorable to the CCAPM in the North American setting is presented by Breeden, Gibbons and Litzenberger (1989), which reported the existence of a statistically significant relationship between expected returns and the consumption beta, although the expected linear relationship between the variables had been rejected.

In the international economy, Campbell (1996) tested the CCAPM in several developing countries and his results revealed the existence of the equity premium puzzle in almost all the countries – of the twelve countries tested only one failed to present the phenomenon – showing that the puzzle is an internationally robust phenomenon.

In Latin America, especially in those countries included in the present study, the findings are mixed. In Brazil, the studies of Issler and Piqueira (2000), Sampaio (2002), Bonomo and Domingues (2002) among others, point to the inexistence of the puzzle, hence corroborating with the CCAPM. However, evidence recently presented by Cysne (2005) indicates that the equity premium puzzle is to be found in Brazil. Opazo (1998) and Bravo and Oyarzún (2001) tested the existence of the puzzle in the Chilean economy and confirmed the phenomenon there. In Colombia, Osorio and Puerta (2004) estimate the relative risk aversion coefficient close to zero, corroborating with the CCAPM.

The equity premium puzzle and all the studies that have demonstrated empirical inconsistencies when testing the CCAPM imply serious restrictions to the representative agent models. Therefore, testing the model in other countries, mainly among the emerging economies, becomes of great importance for the modern neoclassical theory of asset pricing, as favorable evidence for the model, in emerging countries, could shed new light on this theory and could provide the better understanding of the causes of its rejection in other countries; while the rejection of the model in these countries could lead academics to reformulate the theoretical bases supporting the model, incorporating new characteristics, in a way that the model becomes more compatible with the observed behavior of the individuals.

Given this situation, the aim of the present study is to empirically test whether the Consumption-Based Capital Assets Pricing Model (CCAPM) is consistent with the economic data from four Latin American countries: Brazil, Chile, Colombia and Mexico. More specifically, it intends to: 1) verify whether the theoretical implications associated with the CCAPM are confirmed by the empirical test proposed in this study; 2) demonstrate whether the CCAPM is capable of adequately explaining the differences between the returns on financial assets (stocks) in each country analyzed; and 3) compare the empirical results of the tests in this study of Latin American countries with previous studies in the literature.

According to Cochrane (2005, p.41), "the consumption-based model is, in principle, the complete answer to all asset pricing questions, but works poorly in practice", that is, despite being insightful from the theoretical point of view, in practice, there are difficulties with the CCAPM that are made evident by the large number of studies that reject the model at the international level. In spite of the empirical rejections, the author emphasizes that instead of inventing, testing and rejecting new models, studies such as those of Mehra and Prescott (1985) and Hansen and Jagannathan (1991), for example, have offered new insights into the characteristics of the model, thus, opening the door to improvements of the model that may allow it to adjust to economic data more easily.

The present study can further the understanding of the CCAPM by testing it in the emerging countries of Latin America, contributing towards the theoretical enhancement of the model and advancing the understanding of the factors that lead to its rejection at an international level.

Furthermore, it should be pointed out that, to the best knowledge of the authors, empirical tests of the nature intended in the present study have not yet been carried out in relation to the CCAPM in Latin American countries. To date, the studies performed in these countries have focused on the estimation of some parameters of the model, such as the risk aversion coefficient and the stochastic discount factor, but have not carried out cross-sectional regressions in order to verify the capacity of the CCAPM to explain the differences between the returns obtained from a certain class of financial assets, as the present study aims to do. Therefore, the findings obtained from the research can be considered original and it is hoped that they will contribute towards improving the understanding of the behavior of the model in these countries.

This study is structured as follows: in section 2, the CCAPM is presented; the research method is detailed in section 3, where the econometric model, the hypotheses, the data collection and treatment are all dealt with; in section 4, the results of the empirical test are shown for each country analyzed and finally, in the last section, the conclusions drawn in relation to the study are put forward.

2. THE INTERTEMPORAL MODEL OF CAPITAL ASSET PRICING CCAPM[1]

According to Varian (1992), the study of asset markets requires the general equilibrium approach, given that the value of a particular risky asset depends on the presence or absence of other risky assets that might serve as complements to, or substitute for that asset; and, as will be seen, the equilibrium price of a given asset, in an environment of uncertainty and intertemporal optimization of utility, will depend on its covariance with aggregated consumption.

For Duffie (2001), there are three pillars underpinning the theory of asset pricing: arbitrage, optimization and equilibrium. Arbitrage, according to this author, can be represented by a portfolio with a non-positive market value that offers a positive payment at some future date, that is, arbitrage is a portfolio that offers 'something for nothing'. In a competitive market, the opportunity for arbitrage should naturally be eliminated and, consequently, asset pricing should be based on the 'absence of arbitrage'. Optimization requires that individuals have well-behaved preferences and, thus, maximize their expected

---

[1] Intertemporal asset pricing models originated in the work of Merton (1973). He developed an equilibrium model consistent with the maximization of the expected utility, in an economy where individuals can trade continually in time and the investment opportunities are stochastic. According to Breeden (1979), in Merton's model the excess return of any asset is given by a 'multi-beta' version of the CAPM, the number of betas being defined by one plus the number of state variables necessary to describe the modifications in the set of investment opportunities. With the aim of making Merton's model more empirically treatable, Breeden (1979) demonstrated that the multiple betas could be concentrated in a single beta: the consumption beta. In this case, the expected return of any asset should be determined by its covariance with aggregate consumption, since the latter is perfect and negatively correlated to the marginal utility of an additional monetary unit of wealth. Grossman and Shiller (1982) show that the Breeden's results are obtained even after some assumptions are relaxed.

utility. Lastly, the condition of equilibrium determines that the prices of diverse assets should lead to an equilibrium allocation, that is, an allocation that satisfies the budgetary restrictions of individuals and that maximizes their utility given their endowments, so achieving a Pareto-efficient distribution.

In the paragraphs below, the intertemporal model of consumption-based capital asset pricing model is formally presented, beginning with the problem of intertemporal maximization of utility by the representative agent and the first order condition for the optimal consumption decision and portfolio formation.

Assuming that there is a representative agent in the economy, it is possible to model this typical investor, according to Cochrane (2005, p. 4), by the utility function defined on the current and future values of consumption:

$$U(c_t, c_{t+1}) = u(c_t) + \delta E_t[u(c_{t+1})],$$ (1)

where:

 u is the utility function defined on the consumption in each period;

 c_t denotes the consumption in the period t;

 c_{t+1} denotes the consumption in the period $t+1$, a random variable, since the investor does not know her/his wealth in the following period and, therefore, does not know how much he will decide to consume in the period in question;

 δ is the subjective discount factor and its theoretical limits are: $0 < \delta < 1$;

 E_t is the expectations operator conditioned by the information available in the period t.

The utility function is restricted to the class of Constant Relative Risk Aversion (CRRA), a convenient and frequent form employed in real business cycle theory (MEHRA and PRESCOTT, 2003):

$$u(c_t) = \frac{c_t^{1-\gamma}}{1-\gamma},$$ (2)

where:

 γ is the Arrow-Pratt relative risk aversion coefficient.

This utility function (2), according to Cochrane (2005), is increasing, reflecting the desire for greater consumption in each period, and concave, denoting the decreasing marginal utility, that is, each additional monetary unit of consumption produces less satisfaction than the previous monetary unit of consumption.

By means of this modeling, given by (1) and (2), the impatience as well as the aversion to risk of the typical investor is captured. The subjective discount factor, δ, is the value by which the future utility is discounted and represents the impatience of the investor. The lower its value, the greater the impatience, that is, the greater is the preference for present consumption in relation to future consumption. The relative risk aversion coefficient, γ, measures the concavity of the utility function and the greater its value, the greater the aversion to risk on the part of the investor. Moreover, the form of the utility function (2) restricts the elasticity of the intertemporal substitution from being the inverse of the relative risk aversion coefficient, hence, the greater the aversion to risk the lesser the desire for intertemporal substitution of consumption. Therefore, the risk averse investor prefers a flow of consumption that is stable throughout states of nature and over time (Mehra and Prescott, 2003; Cochrane, 2005).

Denoting the price of an asset by p_t and its expected future payoff by x_{t+1}, it is possible, using the above defined framework, to determine the present value (p_t) of the future cash flow (x_{t+1}), that is, how much the investor will be willing to pay today for an asset that provides an expected future payoff of the order of x_{t+1}. In the case of a share of stock, the expected future payoff is the price of the stock plus the dividend to be received in the following period, that is, $x_{t+1} = p_{t+1} + d_{t+1}$. According to Cochrane (2005), x_{t+1} is a random variable, given that the investor does not know exactly what she/he will receive in the future for the investment made in the present, but she/he can assess the probability of several possible outcomes and determine the expected value of the investment.

Assuming that the investor can freely buy or sell any quantity of the future expected payoff x_{t+1} at the price p_t, denoting the original level of consumption (prior to making any investment) by e and denoting by ω the amount of a given stock that the investor wishes to buy, her/his intertemporal choice problem is given by (COCHRANE, 2005, p. 5):

$$\max_{\omega} u(c_t) + E_t[\delta u(c_{t+1})], \text{ subject to:}$$

$$c_t = e_t - p_t \omega,$$

$$c_{t+1} = e_{t+1} + x_{t+1} \omega$$

The first-order condition for the optimal consumption decision and portfolio formation is obtained by substituting the restrictions above in the objective function and setting the derivative with respect to ω to zero (COCHRANE, 2005, p. 5):

$$p_t u'(c_t) = E_t[\delta u'(c_{t+1}) x_{t+1}], \tag{3}$$

This equation, according to Mehra and Prescott (2003), expresses the condition for intertemporal optimization of consumption: the loss in the present utility ($p_t u'(c_t)$), due to the reduction in consumption in favor of the purchase of an additional unit of a determined asset at the price p_t, should be equal to the expected gain in the discounted future utility ($E_t[\delta u'(c_{t+1}) x_{t+1}]$), resulting from the expected increase in the future consumption due to the sale of the asset for p_{t+1} and the receipt of dividends at the value d_{t+1} (in the case that the asset is a stock). According to Cochrane (2005), the investor will buy more or less of a determined asset until the equation (3) is satisfied, that is, until the loss in the present utility equals the expected gains in the future utility.

Rearranging (3) the central asset pricing formula is obtained (COCHRANE, 2005, p. 6):

$$p_t = E_t \left[\delta \frac{u'(c_{t+1})}{u'(c_t)} x_{t+1} \right] \tag{4}$$

According to Cochrane (2005), the expression $\delta \frac{u'(c_{t+1})}{u'(c_t)}$ is known as the stochastic discount factor, that is, the random value by which the expected future payoff of each asset is discounted in order to determine its present value (p_t). This factor is also denominated the marginal rate of substitution, that is, the rate at which the investor would be willing to substitute future consumption for present consumption.

Asset pricing theory requires that the expected future payoff of an asset be discounted by a factor adjusted to the specific systematic risk. Although the stochastic discount factor is unique for all assets, equation (4) incorporates a correction for the specific systematic risk of each stock, as demonstrated below.

By denoting the stochastic discount factor as m_{t+1}, the basic asset pricing equation (4) can be expressed in the following form:

$$p_t = E_t(m_{t+1} x_{t+1}) \tag{5}$$

When both sides of (5) are divided by p_t the basic pricing equation in terms of expected returns is obtained instead of that of expected future payoffs:

$$1 = E_t(m_{t+1} R_{t+1}), \tag{6}$$

where:

$R_{t+1} = \dfrac{x_{t+1}}{p_t}$ is the gross expected return.

According to Cochrane (2005), the gross return can be thought as a payoff with a price equal to 1 (one), as demonstrated by equation (6).

Given that the expectation of the product of two variables is equal to the product of its expectations plus the covariance between them, it is possible to rewrite (5) as:

$$p_t = E_t(m_{t+1})E_t(x_{t+1}) + Cov(m_{t+1}, x_{t+1}), \tag{7}$$

In general, this equation (7), shows that the price of any asset is a function of three factors:

1) The stochastic discount factor: the greater this value the greater the desire of the investor to transfer present consumption to the future, as in this case the discounted marginal utility of the future consumption is high in relation to the marginal utility of the present consumption, and, consequently, the greater the price of any asset that permits the transference of income intertemporally;
2) Expected future payoff: maintaining the discount rate constant, the greater the future payoff of an asset the greater its present value will be; and,
3) Covariance between the stochastic discount factor and the expected future payoff: assets whose payoffs covary positively with the stochastic discount factor tend to pay more when the marginal utility of consumption is high and less when the marginal utility of consumption is low. Therefore, assets so characterized should be sold at the highest price, as they smooth the investor's flow of consumption.

From equation (6), it can be seen that the gross return of a risk-free asset is equal to the inverse of the stochastic discount factor:

$$R_{f,t+1} = \frac{1}{E_t(m_{t+1})},\qquad(8)$$

where:

$R_{f,t+1}$ is the gross return of the risk-free asset in the next period, definitely known in the period t and, therefore, expectations-free, as shown below:

$$1 = E_t(m_{t+1}R_{f,t+1}) = E_t(m_{t+1})R_{f,t+1}$$

Substituting the stochastic discount factor in (7) by (8) leaves:

$$p_t = \frac{E_t(x_{t+1})}{R_{f,t+1}} + Cov(m_{t+1}, x_{t+1})\qquad(9)$$

According to Cochrane (2005, p. 13), the first term on the right side of (9) is the standard formula of the discounted present value and represents the price of an asset when the investors are risk neutral. The second term is an adjustment for the specific systematic risk of the asset in question, given by the covariance of its payoffs with the stochastic discount factor.

In order to better understand this risk adjustment, substitute m_{t+1} in (9) by $\delta \frac{u'(c_{t+1})}{u'(c_t)}$ to obtain:

$$p_t = \frac{E_t(x_{t+1})}{R_{f,t+1}} + \frac{\text{cov}\left[\delta u'(c_{t+1}), x_{t+1}\right]}{u'(c_t)} \tag{10}$$

Assets whose payoffs covary negatively with consumption (positively with marginal utility) smooth the investor's consumption flow, while those assets whose payoffs covary positively with consumption (negatively with marginal utility) make the investor's consumption flow more volatile. As previously defined, risk averse investors prefer a stable consumption flow over time and throughout the states of nature, therefore such investors attribute greater value to those assets that offer stability in the consumption flow, as shown in equation (10). Assets whose payoffs covary positively with consumption (negatively with marginal utility) are considered risky assets, as they increase the consumption volatility, and, consequently, *ceteris-paribus*, in equilibrium would have to be traded at lower prices.

In the vast majority of studies about asset pricing models, returns are used instead of prices in order to test the implications of such models, since returns are typically stationary over time, which is a characteristic required in studies based on time series (Gujarati, 2003). Accordingly, it is considered opportune to derive the pricing formulas in terms of expected gross returns.

Based on equation (6) and applying the definition of the expectation of the product of two variables, the following is obtained:

$$1 = E_t(m_{t+1})E_t(R_{t+1}) + Cov(m_{t+1}, R_{t+1}) \tag{11}$$

Following Cochrane (2005), knowing that the gross return of the risk-free asset is given in (8), it is possible to rewrite (11) as:

$$E_t(R_{t+1}) - R_{f,t+1} = -R_{f,t+1}Cov(m_{t+1}, R_{t+1}), \tag{12}$$

or

$$E_t(R_{t+1}) - R_{f,t+1} = -\frac{Cov\left[u'(c_{t+1}), R_{t+1}\right]}{E_t\left[u'(c_{t+1})\right]} \tag{13}$$

Equations (12) and (13) show that the risk premium of any asset is a function of the covariance of its returns with the stochastic discount factor (marginal utility). Assets whose returns covary positively with the stochastic discount factor (marginal utility) will have a negative risk premium, while assets whose returns covary negatively with the stochastic discount factor (marginal utility) will have a positive risk premium.

According to Cochrane (2005), it is convenient to express equation (12), for the purposes of the empirical tests, in the following form:

$$E_t(R_{i,t+1}) = R_{f,t+1} + \left(\frac{Cov(m_{t+1}, R_{i,t+1})}{Var(m_{t+1})}\right)\left(-\frac{Var(m_{t+1})}{E_t(m_{t+1})}\right) \tag{14}$$

or

$$E_t\left(R_{i,t+1}\right)= R_{f,t+1} + \beta_{i,m}\lambda_m, \tag{15}$$

where:

$E_t\left(R_{i,t+1}\right)$ is the expected return of the asset i, $i = 1, ..., $ N;

$\beta_{i,m}$ is the slope coefficient of the regression of returns of the asset i on the stochastic discount factor and, hence, is a measure of the sensibility of the returns of the asset i to changes to the stochastic discount factor;

λ_m is the premium for exposure to the risk factor or simply the risk premium.

Equations (14) and (15) show that there is a linear relationship between the expected return and the slope coefficient (beta) of the assets. The risk premium, λ_m, is strictly negative, is unique for all assets and its value depends on the volatility of the stochastic discount factor. The slope coefficient (beta), a measure of the systematic risk, varies throughout the assets in accordance with the exposure of each to the risk factor. In general, the betas will be negative, since most assets are characterized by returns that covary negatively with the stochastic discount factor (marginal utility – COCHRANE, 2005; JAGANNATHAN and WANG, 2005).

According to Cochrane (2005), given that $u'(c)= c^{-\gamma}$ and, hence, $m_{t+1} = \delta\left(c_{t+1}/c_t\right)^{-\gamma}$, it is possible to perform a Taylor approximation of equation (14) in order to express the betas in terms of the growth rate of consumption instead of the stochastic discount factor. Jagannathan and Wang (2005) show that this approximation reduces the effects of the measurement errors in the aggregate consumption and, therefore, there are advantages in their use in empirical tests. The result of this approximation is illustrated below:

$$E_t\left(R_{i,t+1}\right)= R_{f,t+1} + \beta_{i,\Delta c}\lambda_{\Delta c}, \tag{16}$$

where:

$\beta_{i,\Delta c}$ is the slope coefficient of the regression of returns on asset i on the consumption growth rate, which is commonly referred to as the 'consumption beta';

$\lambda_{\Delta c} = \gamma\, \text{var}(\Delta c)$ is the premium for exposure to the risk factor 'consumption growth rate'.

Equation (16) implies a linear relationship between the expected return and the consumption beta of an asset and is known as the Consumption-Based Capital Asset Pricing Model (CCAPM). The consumption beta is an individual measure of exposure to the risk factor 'consumption growth rate' and, for the vast majority of assets, its value is strictly positive. The premium for exposure to risk is strictly positive and, according to Cochrane (2005), it is determined by (absolute) aversion to risk and by the volatility of consumption, that is, the more averse individuals are to risk, or the greater the environmental risk, the greater the risk premium demanded.

Lastly, it is important to point out that the CCAPM, according to Jagannathan and Wang (2005, p. 4), "has the advantage that its validity can be evaluated using sample analogues of means, variances and covariances of returns and per capita consumption growth rates without the need for specifying how these moments change over time in some systematic stochastic fashion". It should also be highlighted that, according to Cochrane (2005, p. 41), the use of the pricing equation (16) "do not require us to take any stand on exogeneity or endogeneity, or general equilibrium. This is the condition that must hold for any asset, for any production technology".

3. METHOD, HYPOTHESES, SAMPLING, DATA COLLECTION AND TREATMENT

3.1. Estimation Process

According to the CCAPM, given by equation (16), there is a positive relationship between the expected return and the consumption beta of the assets. In the present study, we test this relationship by using cross-sectional regression of the risk premiums on the consumption betas of a given set of assets (shares traded on the stock exchange). In the following paragraphs more details are given regarding to the process of estimating the parameters of the model.

The theoretical model given by equation (16) is based on expected returns (*ex-ante*), nevertheless, such values are not observable and, thus, make estimation of the model unfeasible. To get round this problem, Huang and Litzenberger (1988, p. 304) suggest adopting the assumption of *rational expectations*,[2] as "under rational expectations, the realized rates of return on assets in the given time period are drawings from the *ex ante* probability distributions of returns on those assets". Therefore, based on this assumption, the use of realized returns (*ex-post*) in the estimation of the empirical model can be justified.

Besides using realized returns, it is convenient to set model (16) in terms of risk premium of the assets over the risk-free asset, which gives the following cross-sectional regression model:

$$R_i^e = \lambda_0 + \lambda_1 \beta_{i,\Delta c} + u_i, \, i = 1, ..., N, \tag{17}$$

where:

$R_i^e = R_{i,t} - R_{f,t}$ is the risk premium of asset i, $i = 1, ..., N$;

$\beta_{i,\Delta c}$ is the consumption beta of asset i, $i = 1, ..., N$;

---

[2] For more details on the assumption of rational expectations, see Muth (1961), Lucas (1978, p. 1431), and Huang and Litzenberger (1988, p. 304), among others.

λ_0 and λ_1 are parameters to be freely estimated by the regression model (17). The theoretical expectation is that the parameter λ_0, the regression constant, equals zero, as the risk premium of an asset whose covariance with the growth rate of per capita consumption is null, theoretically, should be equal to zero. With regard the parameter λ_1, the slope coefficient, the expectation is that it will be positive and statistically significant, given that it should represent the premium for exposure to the risk factor 'consumption growth rate'.

u_i is the stochastic error term of the asset i, $i = 1, ..., N$, and it is expected to present the usual properties of white noise.[3]

In the econometric model (17) the explanatory variable is the consumption beta of asset i, a variable that can not be directly observed, but can be estimated from time series regressions. This way, the two-stage cross-sectional regression method proposed by Black, Jensen and Scholes (1972) and Fama and MacBeth (1973) is employed. In short, this method consists in estimating, in the first stage, the consumption beta for each asset by means of time series regressions and, in the second stage, performing cross-sectional regression of the econometric model (17) using the consumption betas obtained in the previous stage as the explanatory variable.

The choice of this method of regression is made, primarily, because of its extensive use in tests of capital asset pricing models, such as the CAPM and the CCAPM.[4] According to Jagannathan and Wang (1998, p. 1285), although there are more sophisticated methods for testing linear beta-pricing models, the method proposed by Black, Jensen and Scholes (1972) and Fama and MacBeth (1973) has been preferred in many empirical studies. Furthermore, according to the same authors, this method allows a clear interpretation of the results in economic terms, while with more sophisticated methods there is greater difficulty in interpreting the results obtained.

Another relevant aspect in the choice of this method, according to Lettau and Ludvigson (2001, p.1254), concerns the advantages in applying the cross-sectional regression method from Fama and MacBeth (1973) in samples characterized by a small number of time series observations and by a reasonable number of cross-sectional observations, as is the case with the sample studied in the present study. According to these authors, in samples where the number of time series observations is small relative to the number of cross-sectional observations, the use of the Generalized Method of Moments (GMM) with estimation of the weighted matrix is not appropriate, since, in small samples, this form of estimation will result in a poor estimation of that matrix.

This argument can naturally be extended to the maximum likelihood estimation (MLE), since, according to Gujarati (2003, p. 91), the maximum likelihood estimator of the variance

---

[3] For more details on such properties, see Gujarati (2003) and Maddala (2001).

[4] Of particular interest among the empirical studies that adopt the two-stage cross-sectional regression method for testing CCAPM are: Mankiw and Shapiro (1986), Elyasiani and Nasseh (2000), Lettau and Ludvigson (2001) and Jagannathan and Wang (2005). With regard the tests of the CAPM model, the following empirical studies can be highlighted: Black, Jensen and Scholes (1972), Fama and MacBeth (1973), Blume and Friend (1973), Mankiw and Shapiro (1986), Fama and French (1992), Jagannathan and Wang (1996), Elyasiani and Nasseh (2000), Lettau and Ludvigson (2001) and Jagannathan and Wang (2005).

of the error terms (σ^2) can only be considered unbiased in the case that the sample size (n) increase indefinitely, that is, the maximum likelihood estimator of σ^2 is asymptotically unbiased. Corroborating with this limitation, Maddala (2001, p. 64) asserts that "the MLE method is an estimation method for large samples". Therefore, considering the limited size of our sample, it is understood that the MLE method is not the most appropriate method for the empirical tests to be carried out in the present study.

Given these considerations, the estimation of the parameters in (17) by the two-stage cross-sectional regression method is convenient and suitable, and, therefore, will be the method adopted in the empirical tests in the present study.

3.1.1. Details of the Two-stage Cross-sectional Regression Method

As previously mentioned, the first stage consists in estimating the consumption beta of each asset i by means of a time series regression for each asset in the sample. According to the CCAPM, estimation of this parameter can be performed by employing the following econometric model, which relates the risk premium of a given asset with the growth rate of per capita consumption:

$$R^e_{i,t} = \alpha_i + \beta_{i,\Delta c}\Delta c_t + \varepsilon_{i,t}, \, t = 1, ..., \text{T for each } i, i = 1, ..., N, \tag{18}$$

where:

$R^e_{i,t}$ is the risk premium of the asset i in the period t.

Δc_t is the growth rate of per capita consumption in the period t.

α_i is the intercept of the asset i to be estimated by the regression model (18). According to Cochrane (2005), these intercepts are equal to the pricing errors of the model and the theoretical expectation is that they be equal to zero.

$\beta_{i,\Delta c}$ is the slope coefficient to be estimated by the time series regression of $R^e_{i,t}$ on Δc_t and corresponds to the consumption beta of the asset i. This estimated parameter will be the explanatory variable in the cross-sectional regressions in the second stage of the method.

$\varepsilon_{i,t}$ is the stochastic error term of the asset i in the period t.

To conclude the first stage, the average risk premiums of each asset i are computed throughout the sample and these will be the dependent variables in the cross-sectional regressions in the second stage. Therefore, at the end of the first stage, an N x 1 vector of the average risk premiums, whose typical element is $\bar{R}^e_i$, and an N x 1 vector of the consumption betas, whose typical element is $\hat{B}_{i,\Delta c}$, are obtained.

The second stage of the method consists in estimating the λ_0 and λ_1 parameters of the econometric model (17). As this model is not expressed in terms of estimated average risk premiums and consumption betas, it is modified in order to meet the necessities of the study, as follows:

$$\bar{R}_i^e = \lambda_0 + \lambda_1 \hat{\beta}_{i,\Delta c} + u_i, \; i = 1, \, ..., \, N, \tag{19}$$

where:

$\bar{R}_i^e$ is the average risk premium of the asset i, $i = 1, \, ..., \, N$, obtained in the first stage.

$\hat{\beta}_{i,\Delta c}$ is the consumption beta of the asset i, $i = 1, \, ..., \, N$, estimated in the first stage.

Also, it is intended to extend the econometric model (19) in order to test another implication suggested by the CCAPM. According to this pricing model, the consumption beta is the only measure of the systematic risk of an asset and, therefore, no other variable could explain the risk premium of the assets. In order to test this implication, in the same way that Lintner (1965) and Levy (1978), it is verified whether the residual variances present a statistically significant risk premium in the cross-sectional regression. This variable is formed by the variances of the residuals of the time series regressions for estimation of the consumption betas of each asset. Therefore, when the intention is to test this latter implication, the econometric model (19) is extended as shown below:

$$\bar{R}_i^e = \lambda_0 + \lambda_1 \hat{\beta}_{i,\Delta c} + \lambda_2 VR_i + u_i, \; i = 1, \, ..., \, N, \tag{20}$$

where:

VR_i is the variance of the residuals of the time series regression for estimation of the consumption beta of the asset i.

3.1.2. Limitations of the Two-stage Cross-sectional Regression Method

As previously stated, the 'true' consumption betas are not directly measurable and, hence, are estimated by time series regressions. Nevertheless, the use of estimated betas instead of the 'true' consumption betas represents a measurement error in the explanatory variable, a problem known as the *errors-in-variables problem* or *EIV problem*.

According to Gujarati (2003), measurement errors in the explanatory variable cause the violation of a crucial hypothesis of the classical linear regression model: the hypothesis that there is no correlation between the explanatory variable and the stochastic error term. If this hypothesis is violated the estimators by ordinary least squares (OLS) will be biased and inconsistent, even asymptotically.

According to Gujarati (2003) and Maddala (2001), when there are measurement errors in the explanatory variable the estimation of the parameters of the model behave in the following manner: I) the slope coefficient will not converge to its true value and, admitting that its true value is positive, will be underestimated, that is, biased towards zero; and, II) the intercept, given the underestimation of the slope coefficient, will be overestimated, that is, will be biased away from zero. Therefore, in the case that the problem of the errors in variables is not corrected the consequences for the estimation of the linear model derived from the CCAPM will be the following:

- underestimation of the risk premium, which could lead to the rejection of the relationship implied by the model; and,
- overestimation of the intercept, which could lead to the conclusion that this parameter is greater than zero when in fact it is not.

One of the most frequently used approaches for correcting the problem of errors in variables, when testing capital asset pricing models, is the formation of portfolios (HUANG and LITZENBERGER, 1988).[5] According to these authors, if the measurement errors are not correlated with the criterion used to group the assets, the variance of the measurement errors associated to the portfolio betas approximates zero, the closer the number of assets in each portfolio tends towards infinite, eliminating the bias in the estimations of the parameters.

Besides the possibility of eliminating the problem of errors in variables, Cochrane (2005, p. 436) suggests some other motives from the formation of portfolios:

- Individual stock betas vary over time as the size, leverage, and risk of the business change. Portfolio betas may be more stable over time, and hence easier to measure accurately.
- Individual stock returns are so volatile that you cannot reject the hypothesis that all average returns are the same... By grouping stocks into portfolios based on some characteristic (other than firm name) related to average returns, you reduce the portfolio variance and thus make it possible to see average return deferences (sic).

Therefore, the formation of portfolios allows part of the excessive volatility that characterizes individual returns to be eliminated and gives plausibility to the assumption that the betas are stationary (when such assumption is made).

Despite these positive aspects, the formation of portfolios has not been recommended in the specialized literature on econometrics (COCHRANE, 2005). Thus, in the following paragraphs some of the negative aspects related to this procedure will be discussed and assessed in order to arrive at a decision regarding its adoption or otherwise.

According to Roll (1977, p. 131), in his critique of asset pricing theory tests, the formation of portfolios can lend support to the theory even when it is false. This would occur because individual assets deviations from exact linearity can cancel out in the formation of portfolios. That is, as the number of assets in each portfolio tends to infinity, the individual assets deviations from exact linearity tend to be cancelled out. It leads the expected deviation of the portfolio to be equal to zero, and, as a consequence, to support the model even though it may be false. This criticism naturally extends to the CCAPM, since it establishes a linear relationship between the returns of the assets and their respective consumption betas.

For Kim (1995, p. 1609), the construction of a finite set of well-diversified portfolios is difficult in practice and, accordingly, the grouping of assets within portfolios does not fulfill its initial purpose of eliminate, asymptotically, the bias in the estimations of the parameters.

---

[5] For instance, such procedure has been adopted in the following empirical tests of the CCAPM and/or CAPM: Black, Jensen and Scholes (1972), Fama and MacBeth (1973), Blume and Friend (1973), Fama and French (1992), Jagannathan and Wang (1996), Elyasiani and Nasseh (2000), Lettau and Ludvigson (2001), Jagannathan and Wang (2005), among others.

Kim (1997, p. 464) points to three advantages arising from the use of individual assets instead of portfolios in the cross-sectional regressions: I) it ensures the full use of the information about the cross-sectional behavior of the individual stocks, which can be lost with the formation of portfolios; II) it avoids bias arising from *data-snooping*;[6] and, III) it avoids arbitrary formation of portfolios, as the allocation criteria and/or the number of portfolios can influence the estimations of the parameters.[7]

Given these arguments concerning the formation of portfolios, it becomes apparent that there are some disadvantages[8] that should be weighed against the possible benefits arising from the use of this procedure. Only then can the decision be made on whether to use the procedure or otherwise. It is important to note that the benefits of the formation of portfolios depend, to a great extent, on the characteristics of the sample used in the study and, therefore, in the following paragraphs, it will be discussed whether or not such benefits can be obtained with the sample that we used.

The sample used in the present study is characterized by a relatively small number of assets, in each analyzed country, when compared with samples used in other countries, such as the United States of America, for example. There are on average around 80 assets in each of the four countries included in the study, varying from 27 assets in the case of Colombia to 141 assets in the case of Brazil, while in empirical tests of CAPM and/or CCAPM carried out in the United States this number frequently exceeds 2,000 assets.

As previously stated, the bias arising from the problem of errors in variables can only be eliminated by the formation of portfolios if the number of assets in each portfolio tends towards infinity, this presupposes a sample, in terms of number of assets, large enough to form a reasonable number of well-diversified portfolios. The sample obtained in the present study does not appear to fulfill this presupposition and, thus, may make the formation of portfolios unfeasible in terms of the number and size desired.

According to Kim (1995), there is a trade-off between bias and efficiency of the estimates that depends on the number of portfolios. As the number of portfolios increases and, consequently, the number of assets in each portfolio diminishes, the magnitude of the bias resulting from the errors in variables increases while the variance in the estimations decreases (enhancing their efficiency), and vice-versa. Given the aforementioned characteristics of the sample in the present study, it is understood that the number of assets available is not sufficiently large to produce unbiased estimates together with efficient parameters.

With regard the difficulties on the formation of well-diversified portfolios, pointed out by Kim (1995) in a reality where the number of assets is relatively large, it is believed that this difficulties are even greater in countries characterized by a relatively small number of assets, as is the case of the Latin American countries. This being the case, it is believed that the benefits arising from the grouping of assets into portfolios can not be obtained from the sample used in the present study.

---

[6] According to Lo and MacKinlay (1990), the data-snooping bias, regarding portfolio formation in tests of asset pricing models, derives from the clustering of assets in portfolios according to a criteria that is not theoretically related to the return of the assets but that presents an empirical relation derived from the same data set used to implement the tests. These authors show that such bias may lead to the rejection of the model with unit probability even when it is true.

[7] For evidence on the sensibility of parameter estimates to the portfolio formation criteria see, for instance, Kothari, Shanken and Sloan (1995) and Lo (2004), among others.

[8] Other implications of the portfolio formation procedure, not directly related to the research method used, can be found in Berk (2000) and Grauer and Janmmat (2004).

A possible method of enlarging the number and size of the portfolios to the desired levels would be the random formation of portfolios, based on a resampling method such as *bootstrapping*. According to this method, from the sample, *n* portfolios, composed of *m* *assets*, would be randomly withdrawn, so that each asset could be part of several portfolios. However, according to Huang and Litzenberger (1988), the random formation of portfolios can maximize the variance of the estimates and, as a consequence of this, lead to inefficient estimation of the parameters.

It can, therefore, be concluded that in the present study the formation of portfolios will not achieve its main purpose: the elimination of the bias resulting from the problem of errors in variables. Given this situation and the fact that the procedure is subject to arbitrariness, biases, and other limitations, it is decided that an alternative approach is needed to correct the problem. In the following paragraphs, the approach adopted in the present study, together with its limitations will be discussed.

According to Huang and Litzenberger (1988), the problem of errors in variables can be corrected through estimators that incorporate the impact of the measurement errors in the explanatory variable. According to Campbell, Lo and MacKinlay (1997), this approach to the problem of errors in variables is first developed by Litzenberger and Ramaswamy (1979) and refined by Shanken (1992).

Shanken (1992) notices that even though the measurement errors decline in the proportion that the time series size increases and, thus, lead to *T*-consistent estimators of the second-stage parameters, the effects on the inference can not be ignored, not even in large samples. In order to solve this problem, the aforementioned author derives the corrected asymptotic variances.

Cochrane (2005, p. 240) suggests that Shanken's (1992) corrected asymptotic variances can be derived by assuming that the stochastic errors (ε_{it}) of the time series regressions, used in the estimation of the consumption betas, are independent and identically distributed (i.i.d.) over time and independent of the factors. Based on these suppositions, the following corrected formula for the calculation of the variance–covariance matrix of the parameters of the *cross-sectional* regression is obtained:

$$\sigma^2\left(\hat{\lambda}\right) = \frac{1}{T}\left[(X'X)^{-1} X'\Sigma X (X'X)^{-1}\left(1 + \Gamma'\Sigma_f^{-1}\Gamma\right) + \begin{bmatrix} 0 & 0 \\ 0 & \Sigma_f \end{bmatrix} \right], \tag{21}$$

where:

$\sigma^2\left(\hat{\lambda}\right)$ is the 2 x 2 variance–covariance matrix of the estimated coefficients in the *cross-sectional* regression;

T is the size of time series used for the estimation of the consumption betas, that is, number of years, quarters or months in the sample;

X is a matrix N x 2 of data, N being the number of assets used in the *cross-sectional* regression. The first column of this matrix is formed by 1s (a vector N x 1 of ones), representing the intercept term, and the second column contains the consumption betas of the assets;

Σ is the N x N matrix of variance-covariance of the residues from the time series regressions used for the estimation of the consumption betas;

Γ is a vector of the estimated slope coefficients in the *cross-sectional* regression; and

Σ_f is the population variance of the growth rate of per capita consumption.

Note that this formula requires that the model presents the intercept term and that this is only applicable to the variances of the intercept and of the slope coefficient of the consumption beta variable. In this way, the correction given by (21) is only applied to the *cross-sectional* regressions of the average risk premiums on the consumption betas (19). Regarding the regression of the average risk premiums on the consumption betas and the residual variances (20) traditional statistical inferences are used, emphasizing that in this case, when the two explanatory variables are measured with error, both are biased[9] and, therefore, caution should be adopted when interpreting the results.

It should also be pointed out that the correction proposed in the present study has some limitations, which are: it makes suppositions concerning the distribution of the residues that may not be confirmed by the data; and it is an asymptotic correction, that is, it is only valid in large samples. The latter limitation is of particular concern and demands that caution should be used in interpreting the results. Nonetheless, there is a need for a correction from the econometric perspective and, it should be applied with the aim of obtaining tests of hypotheses more reliable.

Another possible econometric problem related to the method adopted in the present study, according to Shanken (1992), arises from the fact that the cross-sectional regressions employ average risk premiums and betas estimated throughout the entire period of the sample. According to the author, this could have an undesired spurious cross-sectional relation as a result of the statistical dependence between such risk premiums and betas, since both are estimated with data from the same period.

According to Shanken (1992, p.9), under assumptions typically made in the literature, average returns (or risk premiums) and betas estimated throughout the entire period of the sample are not correlated and, assuming joint normality of the asset returns and factors, such variables are statistically independent. So, the spurious cross-sectional relation is avoided. The assumptions necessary in order to obtain such results are formally described in Shanken (1992, p.7) and, put briefly, consist in:

- The stochastic error terms of the time series regressions should be independently and identically distributed (i.i.d.) over time;
- The factors should be generated by a stationary process such that the first and second sample moments converge in probability, as $T \rightarrow \infty$, to the true moments;
- The factors are asymptotically normally distributed.

Additionally, it is important to note that, according to Shanken (1992), the estimation of a single beta for each asset throughout the entire time period of the sample can reduce the

---

[9] See Maddala (2001).

measurement errors of the consumption betas, since the errors decline in proportion to the increase in the extension of the estimation period. However, it should be pointed out that this approach assumes that the consumption betas are stationary, thus ignoring the findings of Cornell (1981) regarding their non-stationarity. It should also be noted that this approach, besides being used in the present study has also been adopted in the studies of Mankiw and Shapiro (1986) and Lettau and Ludvigson (2001).

3.2. Formulation of Hypotheses

In order to ascertain the adherence of the CCAPM to the data from four Latin American countries (Brazil, Chile, Colombia and Mexico), it is examined whether the theoretical implications derived from the model can be confirmed by the empirical test proposed in this study. In this section, the theoretical implications of the model are defined, and those implications give rise to the research hypotheses.

According to the CCAPM, the differences between assets returns are determined by the differences between their consumption betas, the latter being a measure of exposure of the returns from an asset to the risk factor 'growth rate of per capita consumption'. The greater the consumption beta of an asset, the greater its risk and, consequently, the greater its expected return should be. Therefore, the CCAPM implies a positive linear relation between the average returns (or average risk premiums) and the consumption betas. This implication is central to the CCAPM and gives rise to the primary hypothesis:

Primary Null Hypothesis (H_0): There is not a positive and statistically significant relation between the average risk premiums and the consumption betas of the assets, that is:

$$H_0 : \lambda_1 = 0,$$

where:

λ_1 is the slope coefficient of the cross-sectional regression of the average risk premiums on the consumption betas.

Primary Alternative Hypothesis (H_1): There is a positive and statistically significant relation between the average risk premiums and the consumption betas of the assets, that is:

$$H_1 : \lambda_1 > 0$$

In the CCAPM, the consumption beta appears as the only measure of systematic risk of the asset, that is, nothing apart from exposure to the risk factor 'growth rate of per capita consumption' should systematically affect the expected returns of the assets. Thus, the consumption beta is a complete measure of the risk of any asset. This implication results in the following secondary hypothesis to be tested:

Secondary Null Hypothesis (H_0'): the consumption beta of an asset is a complete measure of its systematic risk. Thus, it is that:

$$H_0': \lambda_2 = 0,$$

where:

λ_2 is the slope coefficient of the residual variances variable in the cross-sectional regression determined by the econometric model (20).

Secondary Alternative Hypothesis (H_1'): the consumption beta of an asset is not a complete measure of its systematic risk, that is:

$$H_1': \lambda_2 > 0.$$

Lastly, a specification test of the econometric model (19) is carried out. According to the CCAPM, if all individuals are able to invest or borrow at the risk-free interest rate, the intercept of the regression of the average risk premiums on the consumption betas should be equal to zero (Sharpe-Lintner's hypothesis). However, if this interest rate does not exist, it can be assumed that an asset exists in the economy whose covariance with the growth rate of per capita consumption is equal to zero (zero-beta) and, hence, the intercept need not necessarily be equal to zero (Black's hypothesis). It is important to note that the rejection of the Sharpe-Lintner's hypothesis favors the specification given by Black (1972), while the acceptance of that hypothesis does not imply the rejection of the latter. Thus, the third pair of hypotheses to be tested is:

Third Null Hypothesis (H_0''): There is a risk-free interest rate in the economy at which all individuals are able to invest and borrow, that is:

$$H_0'': \lambda_0 = 0,$$

where:

λ_0 is the intercept of the cross-sectional regression of the average risk premiums on the consumption betas – econometric model (19).

Third Alternative Hypothesis (H_1''): There is not a risk-free interest rate in the economy in which all individuals are able to invest and borrow, that is:

$$H_1'': \lambda_0 \neq 0.$$

Table 1. Period of Study for Each Country

Country	Initial Quarter	Final Quarter	Number of Quarters
Brazil	1991:Q2	2004:Q4	55
Chile	1996:Q2	2005:Q2	37
Colombia	1994:Q2	2005:Q2	45
Mexico	1993:Q2	2005:Q3	50

It should be noted that only the primary and secondary hypotheses can lead to the rejection of the CCAPM, given that they both test the theoretical implications of the model, while the third hypothesis is merely a test of the specification and, therefore, does not have the power to reject the pricing model subjected to the empirical tests.

3.3. Description of the Sample

The frequency of the data used in the present study is quarterly and this choice is based, fundamentally, on three important aspects related to empirical tests of the CCAPM: i) According to Breeden, Gibbons and Litzenberger (1989), the longer the time interval in which the consumption is reported, the less affected the data are by temporary fluctuations and measurement errors in this variable; ii) Furthermore, according to these authors, in the proportion that the time interval decreases, non-durable consumer goods become "more durable"; and iii) According to Jagannathan and Wang (2005, p.2), "working with a longer horizon attenuates the errors that may arise due to ignoring the effect of habit formation on preferences".

As can be seen, the use of longer time intervals is preferable when performing tests of the CCAPM. Annual series would be the most recommended. However, in the present study, characterized by a consumption series whose publication only began in the 1990s, the use of a series at such a frequency would result in a very small number of observations.

The period covered by the research in each of the countries (Brazil, Chile, Colombia and Mexico) is determined by the availability of the series of growth in aggregated consumption. Thus, Table 1 shows the period in which these series are available, as well as the number of quarters covered in each country in the present study.

The initial sample of firms, in each country, refers to all the traded stocks whose quotes are available in the database of Economática®. The criteria for firm selection, in the present study, must fulfill two purposes: i) generate a sample of the most traded stocks in each country; and, ii) generate samples with a considerable number of stocks, in such a way as to obtain significant and representative results for each economy in the study.

In the present study, quarterly returns of the financial assets are computed by aggregating the monthly returns into quarters by means of capitalization of these returns. Given that returns are necessary at a monthly frequency, the selection criteria basically refer to the quantity of months, within a determined period, in which the stocks have been quoted. Hence, in order to be included in the sample of their respective country, the stocks must obey the following selection criteria: present one (1) quotes in at least "X" months and "Y" quotes in at least "Z" months, in which "X", "Y" and "Z" are numbers to be defined for each country according to the number of months available and observing the objective of including a significant number of stocks in the sample. This method of selection is also used by Mellone Junior (1999) when testing the CAPM in Brazil.

Table 2 shows the "X", "Y" and "Z" values for each country in the study. The period shown in Table 2, includes, besides the monthly frequency, an extra quarter at the beginning of the period in relation to the previous table (Table 1). This occurs because it is necessary to have quotes lagged in one period to calculate the returns of financial assets. Considering the information contained in Table 2 as a whole, it should be clear that the criteria are more restrictive in the cases of Brazil and Chile, requiring one (1) quote in 67% of the months and

11 quotes in 50% of the months, while in Colombia and Mexico these criteria are less restrictive, so that the two aforementioned objectives are fulfilled satisfactorily.

Applying the above defined selection criteria, we get the set of stocks that makes up the sample of each of the countries under analysis. Table 3 shows the number of stocks initially collected from the Economática® database, the number of stocks that are selected according to the previously described criteria, the number of stocks excluded, the number of stocks that constitutes the final sample and the percentage of the final sample in relation to the initial one, for each country in the study.

Observing Table 3, it can be noticed that the selection criteria significantly reduced the number of stocks in comparison with the initial sample. This is necessary because the objective is to obtain a sample with the most traded stocks from each country. It is important to bear in mind that liquidity is an important factor when testing pricing models, as Ribenboim (2002) states when testing the CAPM with Brazilian data. However, as Rodrigues (2000) notes, upon selecting the most traded firms some degree of bias in terms of survival could be imputed. Nonetheless, it is believed that this bias should not influence the results, as *a priori*, in an efficient market, there should be no difference in the pricing of "winning" and "losing" assets.

Regarding the exclusions shown in Table 3, these refer to the stocks that underwent extraordinary alterations in their prices overnight (possibly a recording mistake in the Economática® database). It is understood that these exclusions are necessary, given that the average returns of these stocks are clearly influenced by the return on a single day.

Table 2. "X", "Y" And "Z" Values of the Selection Criteria for Each Country

Country	Period	Total Months	Number of Months ≥ 1 Quote ("X")	% of Total	Number of Quotes ("Y")	Number of Months ≥ "Y" Quotes ("Z")	% Total
Brazil	1991:M1-2004:M12	168	112	67%	11	84	50%
Chile	1996:M1-2005:M6	114	76	67%	11	57	50%
Colombia	1994:M1-2005:M6	138	69	50%	5	46	33%
Mexico	1993:M1-2005:M9	153	77	50%	8	51	33%

Table 3. Initial and Final Sample for Each Country

Country	Initial Sample	Firms Selected	Exclusions	Final Sample	% Total
Brazil	860	142	1	141	16%
Chile	259	75	1	74	29%
Colombia	77	28	1	27	35%
Mexico	185	80	1	79	43%

It is noteworthy that the final Brazilian sample is the one that has the largest number of stocks, although it is the least representative in relation to the initial sample. Despite this, the sample is composed of the largest Brazilian firms and in terms of market value can be considered representative.

3.4. Data Collection

In order to carry out the empirical tests on the CCAPM the following data are necessary: a) returns on stocks; b) aggregate consumption of non-durable goods and services; c) rates of return on risk-free assets; d) consumer price index; e) resident population.

The series of daily stock quotes, adjusted for inflation and dividends, from each of the countries are collected from the Economática® database. The deflator used to adjust the prices in real terms is the Consumer Price Index (CPI) of each country.

With regard the quarterly consumption of non-durable goods and services,[10] in Brazil, this series, is provided by Pessoa (2006). This series is available for the period 1991:Q1 to 2004:Q4. For the remaining Latin American countries, the series of quarterly consumption of non-durable goods and services is collected as shown in Table 4.

As proxy for the returns on risk-free assets, the interest rates from each country in the analysis are used. In Brazil, the Selic (*Sistema Especial de Liquidação e Custódia*) rate is used, which is the basic rate of interest of the economy, serves as a reference for other rates of interest in the country. The nominal monthly series of this rate is collected from the website of the Instituto de Pesquisa Econômica Aplicada (IPEADATA).

**Table 4. Sources for the Series Consumption of Non-Durable Goods and Services:
Chile, Colombia and Mexico**

Country	Source	Availability
Chile	Banco Central de Chile	1996:Q1-2005:Q2
Colombia	Departamento Administrativo Nacional de Estadística (DANE)	1994:Q1-2005:Q2
Mexico	Instituto Nacional de Estadística Geografia e Informática (INEGI)	1993:Q1-2005:Q3

---

[10] In the CCAPM model, the risk factor is the rate of growth of per capita consumption. Nevertheless, there is no effective direct measure of individual consumption, but only a measure of the expenditures with consumption. According to Breeden, Gibbons and Litzenberger (1989) this difference between consumption in theory and its measurement in the real world leads to the following problem: goods and services are not necessarily consumed at the same time that they are purchased. In order to minimize this problem, the empirical test involving CCAPM make use of the expenditures with non-durable goods and services of individuals, excluding the expenditures with durable goods, since the consumption flow of this kind of good is much more difficult to estimate. As only a fraction of the effective consumption is used in empirical tests of the CCAPM, it becomes subject to the same problem reported by Roll (1977) in testing of the CAPM model: the non-observable true market portfolio. However, like Breeden (1979, p. 292), it is believed that the consumption of non-durable goods and services represents a much larger fraction of the true consumption flow of individuals when compared with the fraction that the stock market occupies in the true market portfolio.

Table 5. Sources for the Series Consumer Price Index for Each Country

Country	Source	Unit
Brazil	Instituto de Pesquisa Econômica Aplicada (IPEADATA)	Monthly Percent
Chile	IMF's International Financial Statistics (IFS)	Index
Colombia	IMF's International Financial Statistics (IFS)	Index
Mexico	Banco Central de Mexico	Index

In the case of Chile[11] and Colombia,[12] the interest rates available from the International Financial Statistics (IFS) database of the International Monetary Fund (IMF) are used. Of those available, the '*Lending Rate*' is chosen, as it presents the lowest volatility in relation to the other rates of interest. The nominal annualized series of this interest rate is collected on a monthly basis.

In Mexico, the 91-day Cetes (*Certificados de la Tesorería de la Federación*) are used as proxy for the returns on the risk-free assets. According to Castellanos and Oviedo (2004), these certificates are credit bonds issued by the Mexican Federal Government and liquidated on their maturity. According to the same authors, the yield from these public debt bonds serve as a base for determining the other rates of interest in the Mexican economy, which warrants the use of this bond as a proxy for risk-free asset. The series of nominal monthly yields of the 91-day Cetes are collected from the website of the Banco Central do Mexico.

As the interest rates in Latin American countries are expressed in nominal terms, including those collected from the IMF database, it is necessary to deflate them in order to obtain real series. To ensure coherence regarding the deflator used to adjust the series of stock prices in real terms, the Broad Consumer Price Index (IPCA) for the Brazilian series and the Consumer Price Index (CPI) for the other Latin American countries are used. These price indexes are collected on a monthly basis, as shown in Table 5.

Data regarding the resident population in each quarter is necessary to compute the per capita consumption series. In Brazil the consumption series obtained is already expressed in per capita terms, therefore data is not collected regarding the resident population for this country. In the other Latin American countries the annual estimated population series are collected from the following databases: Chile – Instituto Nacional de Estadísticas (INE); Colombia – Departamento Administrativo Nacional de Estadística (DANE); and Mexico – Comissão Econômica para America Latina and Caribe (CEPAL).

In order to make a comparison with the Latin American countries in the study, data is also collected from the United States. A series of real monthly returns on 25 weight-valued portfolios of Fama and French and the interest rate of the one-month U.S. Treasury Bill are obtained from Kenneth R. French's website.[13] The series necessary for the formation of the

---

[11] In Chile a number of different interest rates could be used as proxies for risk-free asset, for example: the interest rate of the 90-day securities offered by the Chilean Central Bank – PRBC (*Tasas de interés de los pagarés y bonos licitados por el Banco Central de Chile*), the interest rate of the 90-day bonds and certificates offered by the Chilean Central Bank – PDBC, and the monetary policy rate. However, it was not possible to use these in the present study, due to the unavailability of data covering the entire research period as well as the various structural breaks.

[12] The interest rate series of the 90-day term deposits (*Tasa de Interés de los Certificados de Depósito a Término a 90 días*), which would represent a good proxy for the risk-free asset in Colombia, underwent a change in its methodology in July 1993. As this change occurred during the period covered by the research in Colombia we decided not to use this series.

[13] http://mba.tuck.dartmouth.edu/pages/faculty/ken.french/data_library.html

growth rate of per capita consumption of non-durable goods and services are collected from the website of the Bureau of Economic Analysis, Division: National Income and Product Accounts (NIPA).[14]

3.5. Data Treatment

The data collected is the base for the construction of the time series necessary for application of the empirical test proposed in the present study. The series used in the regressions detailed below, are multiplied by 100 in order to obtain their percentage values. The remaining aspects related to the construction of the series are described below.

Beginning with the daily stock quotes traded on the stock exchange in each of the countries, the simple mean of the prices of each of the stocks in each of the months is obtained. These series of average monthly prices are then used in calculating the monthly return of each stock. This process of calculating the monthly returns is used by Mellone Junior (1999) and Ribenboin (2002) when testing the CAPM in Brazil. This is believed to be the most suitable procedure of all those available, as it takes into consideration all the quotes of a determined month in order to calculate the monthly return, instead of being based on only an initial and final quote, for example. The real quarterly series of stock returns are computed by capitalizing the monthly stock returns.

By the capitalization of the monthly interest rates within each quarter, the nominal quarterly series of interest rates from each one of the countries is obtained. For Chile and Colombia, where the interest rates are annualized, the rates are converted to a monthly base from which the capitalization within each quarter is obtained. The interest rate series from each one of the countries are then deflated by their respective Consumer Price Index, which resulted in quarterly series of real interest rates.

The quarterly risk premiums are formed from the difference between the series of real quarterly returns on stocks and the series of real quarterly returns on the risk-free asset of each country. The risk premiums are the dependent variables in the time series regressions for estimation of the consumption betas of each asset (1st stage of the regression method). The average risk premium of each stock is calculated from these time series, based on the simple arithmetic average of the quarterly risk premiums. These average values are the dependent variables in the cross-sectional regressions carried out in the present study (2nd stage of the regression method).

Given that not all the stocks presented returns in all the quarters of the sample,[15] for the purposes of statistical inference and estimation, the missing observations are substituted by estimates. These estimates are obtained in the following manner:

1) Using the available information for each stock, the intercepts and consumption betas are estimated by means of the econometric model (18);

---

[14] http://www.bea.gov/national/index.htm
[15] In Brazil, a total of 7,755 (55 x 141) observations, 439 (5.66% of the total) are estimated. In Chile, a total of 2,738 (37 x 74) observations, 66 (2.41% of the total) are estimated. In Colombia, of a total of 1,215 (45 x 27) observations, 239 (19.67% of the total) are estimated. In Mexico, of a total of 3,950 (50 x 79) observations, 585 (14.81% of the total) are estimated.

2) Based on these coefficients and in the growth rate of consumption series, whose observations are available for the entire sample, the missing risk premiums are calculated using the following equation:

$$R_{i,t}^e = \alpha_i + \beta_{i,\Delta c}\Delta c_t$$

According to Greene (1997, p. 430), this method of estimating the missing data is widely known as first-order regression. For this author, the method maintains the non-tendentious property of the estimators and apparently produces a gain in efficiency, given that the errors of the model in the formerly missing observations equal to zero. However, the author emphasizes "the gain in efficiency from using these fitted values may be illusory" and that "the overall conclusion seems to be that in the single-equation regression context, filling in missing values of y is not a good idea". Despite these warnings, estimates are made of the missing values, as the corrected variance estimates require complete time series of the returns. It should be pointed out that the results do not appear to be sensitive to the use of these estimates.

In order to maintain the comparability of the CCAPM, as suggested in the literature, the series of consumption of non-durable goods and services are adjusted for seasonality. The method chosen for this is the 'ratio to moving average' of the E-views statistical software. The Brazilian, Colombian and North-American series are already adjusted for seasonality. The per capita series[16] are constructed based on the series adjusted for seasonality, by dividing them by the quarterly population of each country. The quarterly population series are obtained from the geometric interpolation of the annual series. Lastly, the growth rate of per capita consumption is obtained by dividing the per capita consumption of one quarter by the per capita consumption of the previous quarter and subtracting one.

For the purposes of analyzing the stock market behavior in each country over time, an equally weighted portfolio is formed of all the stocks contained in the final sample. Hence, time series are obtained with the real quarterly returns of the stock portfolio of each one of the countries in the study, including the United States. For the same purposes, a series of the excess returns (risk premium) of the stock portfolio is constructed by the difference between the series of real quarterly returns on the stock portfolio and the series of real quarterly returns on the risk-free asset of each country.

4. ANALYSIS OF THE RESULTS

Table 6 shows some statistical descriptions of the main time series used in carrying out the empirical tests. For the benefit of comparison, the statistics from the North-American series for the period 1991:Q1-2005:Q2 have also been included. The analysis of this data shows that the average risk premium (equity premium) is positive for all the countries with the exception of Colombia. Brazil has the highest average risk premium, with a value of 4.78% per quarter, followed by the United States, Mexico, and Chile, where the risk premiums are respectively 3.16%, 1.51% and 0.60% per quarter. According to the theory

---

[16] This procedure is not necessary in the case of Brazil, since the Brazilian series obtained is already expressed in per capita terms.

outlined above, the higher the risk premium, the greater the risk aversion of the individuals and/or the greater the risk of the environment (variability of consumption). With regard to Colombia, the existence of a negative risk premium (-2.37% per quarter) suggests that the stock portfolio is less risky than the asset considered to be risk free, an assumption that will be confirmed in the following analysis.

It can be seen that Brazil, Mexico, and the United States have very similar average growth rates of per capita consumption, varying from 0.39% per quarter for Brazil to 0.47% per quarter for the United States. At the extremes is Colombia, with an average growth rate of per capita consumption of 0.05% per quarter, and Chile, whose average growth rate of per capita consumption is 0.72% per quarter.

Looking at the volatility of the stock portfolio and the growth rate of per capita consumption, it can be seen that there are great differences in these figures between Chile and the United States, the stock portfolios being much more volatile than the growth rate of per capita consumption.[17] The greater this difference, the greater the level of risk aversion necessary to explain the variations in the prices in stock market given a variation in the per capita consumption. In the other countries, Brazil, Colombia, and Mexico, the growth rate of per capita consumption is seen to be slightly more volatile than the stocks portfolio, suggesting that the level of risk aversion on the part of individuals is lower in these countries, *ceteris paribus*. Colombia can be seen to have the greatest volatility in the per capita consumption series (15.60) among the countries in the sample, followed by Mexico (5.10), Brazil (3.46), Chile (1.65), and the United States (0.74). It is important to point out that, according to the theory, the greater the volatility in this series the greater the risk in the environment.

Table 6. Time Series Descriptive Statistics

Country	Risk Premium	ΔC	Market Volatility	ΔC Volatility	Cov (Market, ΔC)	Cov (RF, ΔC)	Covariance Difference
Brazil	4.78%	0.39%	2.48	3.46	7.8147	-1.1685	8.9832
Chile	0.60%	0.72%	4.15	1.65	-1.1179	-0.3253	-0.7926
Colombia	-2.37%	0.05%	13.00	15.60	0.7165	-0.3258	1.0423
Mexico	1.51%	0.42%	4.76	5.10	2.5491	1.1280	1.4211
E.U.A.	3.16%	0.47%	2.20	0.74	0.2265	-0.0162	0.2427

Risk Premium = mean sample risk premium; ΔC = average rate of growth of per capita consumption; Market Volatility = Coefficient of variation (ratio between the standard deviation and the sample mean) of the return on the stock portfolio; Volatility ΔC = Coefficient of variation (ratio between the standard deviation and the sample mean) of the rate of growth of per capita consumption; Cov(Market, ΔC) = Covariance of returns on stock portfolio and the rate of growth of per capita consumption; Cov(RF, ΔC) = Covariance of the return on risk-free asset and the rate of growth of per capita consumption; Covariance Difference = Difference between Cov(Market, ΔC) and Cov(RF, ΔC). The mean values are expressed in percentage points per quarter; The covariances are obtained from the data expressed in this measurement unit.

---

[17] This corroborates the evidence reported in previous studies regarding the excessive variability in the North American share market. See, for example, Grossman and Shiller (1981) and the review made at an international level by Campbell (1996).

When analyzing the covariance between the return and consumption series, it can be seen that in all the countries, with the exception of Chile, the covariance of the returns of the stock portfolio with the growth rate of consumption is greater than the covariance of the returns of the risk-free asset with the growth rate of consumption. In these countries, therefore, the returns of the stock portfolio are shown to be of greater risk than the returns of the asset that is considered risk-free, suggesting that there is a positive risk premium among these assets. In Brazil, Mexico, and the United States there is a positive risk premium (equity premium), corroborating the theory. In Colombia, as highlighted previously, the stock portfolio had a negative risk premium,[18] in contrast to the prediction of the theory which suggests that the greater exposure of this portfolio to risk should lead to a positive risk premium in relation to the risk-free asset. With regard to Chile, in the period under analysis, the opposite behavior to that seen in the other countries is found, that is, the returns of the stock portfolio present less risk than the returns of the asset considered risk-free. This fact is really quite intriguing and leads to the following question: how can be explained the positive risk premiums of these assets in the Chilean economy?

Another important aspect to be noted is the magnitude of the differences between these covariances. According to the CCAPM, the greater this difference, the greater the risk of the stock portfolio in relation to the risk-free asset and, so, the lower the level of risk aversion necessary to explain the risk premium among these assets. This relationship between the risk premium, the covariance, and the relative risk aversion coefficient is demonstrated by the equation of the determination of the risk premium of the stocks given by Grossman, Melino and Shiller (1987, p. 316):

$$E_t\left(R_i^e\right) = \gamma \operatorname{cov}\left(R_i^e, \Delta c\right),$$

where: $\operatorname{cov}(R_i^e, \Delta c) = \operatorname{cov}(R_i, \Delta c) - \operatorname{cov}(R_f, \Delta c)$.

Analysis of these differences, shown in Table 6, reveals that Brazil has the greatest difference between the risk levels of the stock portfolio and the risk-free asset, while among the other countries this distinction is relatively small.

Before proceeding with the analysis of the cross-sectional regressions it is important to verify the stationarity of the series of growth rates of per capita consumption of each country, since this is a property required in the time series regressions necessary for the estimation of the consumption betas. To this end, the Augmented Dickey-Fuller Unit Root Test is performed, in which the null hypothesis is that the time series has a unit root, that is, it is non-stationary. The results reject the null hypothesis at the 1% significance level for the consumption series of Brazil, Chile, and Colombia, and at a significance level of 5.31% for the consumption series of Mexico.

Similarly, it is important to investigate whether or not the model satisfies the main classical hypotheses of the linear regression model, since the desirable properties of the

---

[18] It is important to note that this negative risk premium is highly influenced by the frequent negative returns presented by this portfolio at the start of the period covered by the sample. By limiting the sample to the period 2000:Q1 to 2005:Q2 a positive risk premium in the range of 3.51% per quarter is obtained.

estimators (absence of bias and minimal variance) and the validity of the significance tests depend on their confirmation.[19]

Regarding the homoskedasticity of the residuals, the White test shows that the null hypothesis that the residuals are homoskedastic in the regressions carried out for Brazil and Chile cannot be rejected. In the regressions carried out in Colombia and Mexico, the White test points to the rejection of the null hypothesis at a significance level of 5% and 10%, respectively. The presence of heteroskedasticity, according to Gujarati (2003), does not destroy the properties of non-tendentiousness and of consistency of the OLS estimators, but they do lose efficiency, even in large samples. Therefore, in such cases, caution should be used when interpreting the results obtained.

The Durbin-Watson test points to the absence of first-order serial correlation of the residuals and the Breusch-Godfrey test suggests that the null hypothesis of absence of second-order serial correlation cannot be rejected. These findings are present in all regressions performed.

The normality of the residuals is not rejected in the regressions carried out for Brazil, Chile, and Colombia.[20] In the regression for Mexico, this hypothesis is rejected at the level of significance of 5% for all the applied tests. According to Gujarati (2003), the hypothesis of normality is not essential if the aim is only to obtain an estimate, as the estimators of ordinary least squared are the best linear unbiased estimators (BLUE) whether the residuals are normally distributed or otherwise. However, according to the same author, the usual *t*-statistics may not follow the Student-*t* distributions, that is, such statistics may not be valid in small samples, affecting the tests of the hypotheses. In this case, therefore, greater caution should be applied to the results obtained with the cross-sectional regression carried out on the Mexican financial assets.

Table 7. Results of the Cross-sectional Regressions of the Average Risk Premiums on the Consumption Betas

Country	Constant		Consumption Betas		R^2	Adj. R^2	F-Stat	Durbin-Watson
Brazil	2.7176		0.3522		0.1183	0.112	18.6513	1.88145
	0.98848		1.35215	*				
Chile	0.8861		0.43499		0.141	0.129	11.8141	2.09442
	0.47923		1.4942	*				
Colombia	-3.1677		0.3312		0.2048	0.173	6.4389	1.71532
	-2.02802	*	1.92362	**				
Mexico	0.7059		0.0738		0.002	-0.011	0.1547	2.12198
	0.46705		0.17122					

These results refer to the cross-sectional regression of model (19). Coefficient estimates (first line) and Shanken (1992) corrected t-statistics (second line) are reported for each country, alongside the coefficients of determination, F-statistic, and Durbin-Watson statistic for the regressions.

* Significant at the 10% level; ** Significant at the 5% level.

---

[19] The quantitative results of the tests for heteroskedasticity, autocorrelation of higher order, and non-normality of the residues are not reported here. However, such results can be requested from the authors.

[20] The normality tests applied are: Jarque-Bera (assimptotic), Lilliefors (D), Cramer-von Mises (W2), Watson (U2), and Anderson-Darling (A2).

Table 7 shows the results of the cross-sectional regression of the average risk premiums on the consumption betas in each country analyzed: Brazil, Chile, Colombia, and Mexico. The main purpose of the regression is to verify whether the central implication of the pricing model in question can be confirmed, that is, whether there is a statistically significant relationship between the average risk premiums and the consumption betas.

Based on the corrected t-statistics, it can be seen that the constant is statistically different from zero only in Colombia, with a significance level of 10%, thus rejecting the third null hypothesis and suggesting that the specification zero-beta, proposed by Black (1972), is more suitable in the Colombian case. In the other countries, this hypothesis cannot be rejected at the usual levels of significance. Therefore, the hypothesis of Sharpe-Lintner, that there is a risk-free asset being freely traded in the economies of Brazil, Chile, and Mexico cannot be rejected.

The slope coefficient of the variable 'consumption beta' is shown to be positive and statistically significant in the cross-sectional regressions carried out in Brazil, Chile, and Colombia, rejecting the primary null hypothesis and showing that there is a statistically significant relationship between the average risk premiums and the consumption betas in these countries. These findings corroborate the CCAPM in the above mentioned countries, since the principal implication derived from the model is confirmed by the empirical test. It is of particular note that the level of significance necessary for the rejection of the primary null hypothesis is 10% in Brazil and Chile and 5% in Colombia. In Mexico the value of the slope coefficient is at 0.0738, although statistically insignificant at the usual levels of significance, failing to reject the primary null hypothesis. The non-rejection of this hypothesis implies the rejection of the CCAPM in Mexico, as there is no positive and statistically significant relationship between the average risk premiums and the consumption betas in that country. It is important to point out that the Shanken (1992) adjusted t-statistics would be based on an asymptotic correction and, therefore, should be analyzed with caution.

By assessing the adjusted R^2 and R^2, it is possible to get some idea of how well the CCAPM explains the differences between the average risk premiums of the assets in the countries under study. The adjusted R^2 values vary from a minimum of -0.011 (Mexico) to a maximum of 0.173 (Colombia), indicating that, taking into account the degrees of freedom, only a small fraction (-1.1% in Mexico and 17.3% in Colombia, for example) of the cross-sectional variations of the average risk premiums are explained by the CCAPM. Coefficients of determination of this magnitude indicate that the model explains poorly the differences between the returns of the diverse financial assets (stocks). Therefore, this finding restricts the practical use of the model in most actual financial decisions, such as: cost of capital, determining expected returns, resource allocation, etc.

The results of the regression of the average risk premiums on the consumption betas and the residual variance, the purpose of which is to test the secondary null hypothesis that the consumption beta is a complete measure of the risk of an asset, are presented in Table 8. In Brazil and Mexico the slope coefficient of the variable 'residual variance' is shown to be positive and statistically significant at the levels of 1% and 10%, respectively, rejecting the secondary null hypothesis. These findings show that the consumption beta may not be a complete measure of asset risk and imply the rejection of the CCAPM in these countries. In the other countries, Chile and Colombia, the slope coefficient of this variable is not significantly different from zero at the usual levels of significance, corroborating the secondary null hypothesis and suggesting that the consumption beta could be used as a complete measure of asset risk in these countries. Lastly, it is appropriate to point out that these regressions are susceptible to the problem of measurement errors in variables and, therefore, their results should be interpreted with caution.

Table 9 presents a summary of the results of the hypotheses tests performed in the four Latin American countries, as well as the benchmark, i.e. the United States. For the United States, the results obtained by Lettau and Ludvigson (2001) based on quarterly data covering the period 1963:3 to 1998:3 are used, which can be found in Table 8 of their paper. In that study, the authors run a cross-sectional regression of the returns of the 25 Fama and French portfolios on the consumption betas of these portfolios.

The primary null hypothesis states that the slope coefficient of the consumption betas is equal to zero. This hypothesis is considered the most important as it refers to the central idea of the model, that is, the existence of positive and statistically significant relationship between the average risk premiums and the consumption betas, consequently its non-rejection would imply the empirical inconsistency of the CCAPM. Analysis of Table 9 shows that the hypothesis is rejected in Brazil, Chile, and Colombia. The rejection of the CCAPM, according to this hypothesis, is verified only for Mexico and the United States (benchmark).

Table 8. Results of the Cross-Sectional Regressions of the Average Risk Premiums on the Consumption Betas and Residual Variances

Country	Constant		Consumption Betas		Residual Variances	
Brazil	0.4641		0.2336	***	0.0020	***
	0.78221		3.16688		6.54439	
Chile	0.5069		0.4144	***	0.0011	
	1.08739		3.23547		1.03306	
Colombia	-4.1689	**	0.3147	**	0.0031	
	-2.67914		2.36084		0.77365	
Mexico	0.2537		-0.0177		0.0009	
	0.52486		-0.08976		1.39997	*

These results refer to the cross-sectional regression of model (20). Coefficient estimates (first line) and usual t-statistics (second line) are reported for each country.
* Significant at the 10% level; ** Significant at the 5% level; and *** Significant at the 1% level.

Table 9. Summary of the Tests of the Hypotheses in Each Country

Country	Primary H_0	Secondary H_0'	Tertiary H_0''	R^2
Brazil	Reject	Reject	Cannot Reject	0.11196
Chile	Reject	Cannot Reject	Cannot Reject	0.12903
Colombia	Reject	Cannot Reject	Reject	0.17300
Mexico	Cannot Reject	Reject	Cannot Reject	-0.01096
USA[#]	Cannot Reject	*	*	0.13000

[#] Source: Lettau and Ludvigson (2001); * Hypothesis not tested explicitly.

The secondary null hypothesis states that the consumption beta is a complete measure of the risk of an asset, that is, there is no other risk factor, apart from the covariance of the returns with the growth rate of per capita consumption, that systematically affects the returns of the assets. This hypothesis, like the first, can lead to the rejection of the CCAPM. In observing Table 9 it can be seen that this hypothesis is rejected in Brazil and Mexico, suggesting the rejection of the model in these countries. In contrast, in Chile and Colombia there is no such rejection of this hypothesis, thus demonstrating that these countries are the only ones that corroborate all the theoretical implications derived from the model.

The coefficients of determination, represented by the adjusted R^2 of the cross-sectional regressions in each country, demonstrate that the explanatory power of the CCAPM is very small in the countries under study and also in the North-American benchmark. Even in those countries where there appears to be a positive and statistically significant relationship between the average risk premiums and the consumption betas, the explanatory power of the model is at best 17.3% of the cross-sectional variation of the returns of the assets in the financial market (Colombia).

These combined results suggest that the adherence of the CCAPM to the data from Latin American economies is very weak. Although the data from Chile and Colombia do not reject the CCAPM outright, the explanatory power of the model in relation to these countries, as in the remaining countries, is unsatisfactory. In the cases of Brazil and México, the findings are even more unfavorable to the CCAPM. In the former, though there is a statistically significant relationship between the average risk premiums and the consumption betas, the residual variance is shown to be statistically significant in the cross-sectional regressions, in contrast to the theoretical prediction of the model. In the latter, besides the variable residual variances being statistically significant, there appears to be no statistically significant relationship between the average risk premiums and the consumption betas, thus leading to the rejection of the CCAPM. Given these restrictions to the model and considering the fact that several studies indicate the rejection of the model at an international level,[21] we conclude that this is a worldwide phenomenon, affecting both developed and developing countries.

As mentioned before, the third null hypothesis is more a specification test than a test of the implications of the CCAPM. It requires a statistically insignificant intercept in the cross-sectional regression. This hypothesis does not have the power to reject the model and its only purpose is to verify which of the alternate specifications is correct (Sharpe-Lintner's risk-free asset or Black's zero-beta asset). Based on the results in Table 9, it can be seen that the third null hypothesis is rejected only in Colombia, suggesting that Black's zero-beta specification (1972) is the most suitable in that country, while Sharpe-Lintner's more restrictive specification appears to be more consistent with the data from the other Latin American economies.

In summary, the weak performance of the CCAPM in the Latin American countries analyzed in the present study is quite evident. The model is not capable of satisfactorily explaining the realized returns of the assets in these countries and the theoretical implications of the model are only fully confirmed in Chile and Colombia. Considering the evidence from other studies at an international level, it is understood that some assumptions that form the base of the model need to be modified, which represents the main implication of the present

---

[21] See, for instance, the results from Campbell (1996) and Carmichael and Samson (2005).

study, as well as those of other studies that highlight the inconsistencies of the CCAPM, for the modern neoclassic theory of asset pricing.

At this point, it is pertinent to reflect on the statement made by Mankiw and Shapiro (1986, p. 458) that "the apparent rejection of the consumption CAPM is potentially attributable to failure of one of the many auxiliary assumptions". According to these authors, the weak explanatory power of the CCAPM could be explained by, among other aspects, non-stable preferences, costs of adjustment in consumption, durability of non-durable goods, and so on.

Nonetheless, it should be borne in mind that, as Cochrane (2005, p. 455) emphasizes, the point of departure for understanding which risks affect the prices and expected returns of assets is: the individual's first order conditions for saving and portfolio formation, that is, the consumption-based model. Accordingly, models with more restrictive assumptions regarding the investor behavior and the stochastic discount factor could be of help in better understanding the demand for financial assets.

Following this line of thought, it is worth highlighting three studies carried out in the United States that offer encouraging results regarding the CCAPM: the study from Lettau and Ludvigson (2001) that uses a conditional model of CCAPM to explain the differences between asset returns; the study by Parker and Julliard (2005) that defines the risk of an asset as the covariance of its returns with the accumulated growth in consumption over various quarters following the occurrence of returns; and Jagannathan and Wang (2005) study in which they begin with the assumption that the investors revise their consumption and portfolio decisions in the fourth quarter of each year.

Besides proposing modifications to the original model, these three studies also offer evidence that the CCAPM can explain a significant part of the variations in the average returns of the financial assets. In our opinion, the test of these models in the countries of Latin America is the next step to be taken in attempting to increase the understanding of the factors that affect asset risk in financial markets.

5. CONCLUSION

The objective of this study is to verify whether the Consumption-Based Capital Asset Pricing Model (CCAPM) is consistent with the economic data from the following Latin American countries: Brazil, Chile, Colombia, and Mexico. To this end, the theoretical implications of the model in question are checked against the data from those countries and, moreover, the capacity of the model to explain the differences between the returns of assets (stocks) in the financial markets of each country is assessed.

In summary, the tests of the hypotheses and the explanatory capacity of the CCAPM suggest the rejection of the model in Brazil and Mexico, while in Chile and Colombia the model only offered unsatisfactory power of explanation of the average risk premiums of the assets. In the United States, the rejection of the model is demonstrated by the study by Lettau and Ludvigson (2001), whose results are reproduced in Table 9.

However, in the same way as Faff (1998), these results need to be seen in the context of several empirical problems and assumptions made in order to make the testing of the CCAPM viable. Thus, it is important to question up to what point the results are influenced by: non-stable betas, durability of the non-durable goods, failure to observe the true flow of individual consumption, asymptotic correction for the problem of errors in variables, etc.

With regard to the objectives of the present study, it is believed that they have been fully achieved, since it is shown to be possible to assess the explanatory capacity of the model and test the implications derived from it. Furthermore, comparisons are made with data previously obtained relating to the United States, whose results are very similar to those found in this study.

The present study has contributed towards increasing the understanding of the behavior of the CCAPM in the Latin American countries under study. The empirical evidence of this study corroborates with the evidence reported for other countries, such as the United States, and suggests that modifications to the original model, such as those proposed by Lettau and Ludvigson (2001), Parker and Julliard (2005), and Jagannathan and Wang (2005), might be implemented in the future in order to allow a better understanding of the CCAPM and of the factors determining risk in Latin American financial markets.

This study has also contributed to the empirical literature in proposing tests with individual assets, instead of the formation of portfolios, in countries characterized by a relatively small number of assets. The use of portfolios is very common in tests of asset pricing models, and they are constructed with the objective of mitigating the problem of errors in variables and reducing the volatility of individual assets. However, as underscored previously, there are some inconveniences associated with the formation of portfolios, mainly in countries characterized by a small number of financial assets, as is the case of the Latin American countries. Hence, the use of individual assets with a correction for the problem of errors in variables is recommended in the tests.

As a potential theme for future studies in Latin American countries, the application of the conditional CCAPM as proposed by Lettau and Ludvigson (2001) is suggested. With regard to the studies of Parker and Julliard (2005) and Jagannathan and Wang (2005), it is of particular interest that they both require extended time series in order to achieve more reliable results. The execution of studies of such a nature is also recommended with the purpose of correcting the problem of errors in variables aimed at finite samples.

ACKNOWLEDGEMENTS

This research is largely based on the M.Sc. thesis of Guilherme Kirch, who is grateful to CAPES for financial support. A substantial part of this research is developed while Paulo R. S. Terra was affiliated with Universidade do Vale do Rio dos Sinos. The authors are thankful to Marcelo de Sales Pessoa for providing part of the data for this study, and to the overall help of Felipe Kirch, Magda M. B. L. Donia and Tim Donovan. The authors are indebted to Ricardo P. C. Leal, Roberto C. Moraes, and Rodrigo O. Soares for their comments and suggestions on an earlier draft. The authors are also thankful to referees, discussants, and participants of the VI Brazilian Finance Meeting (Vitória, 2006) for their input on an earlier version of this paper. All remaining errors are the authors' sole responsibility.

REFERENCES

Abel, Andrew B., 1991, The equity premium puzzle, *Business Review* Sept/Oct, 3-14.

Araújo, Eurilton, 2004, Avaliando três especificações para o fator de desconto estocástico através da fronteira de volatilidade de Hansen and Jagannathan: Um estudo empírico para o Brasil, *Working Paper*, Ibmec Business School.

Araújo, Eurilton, Josis Fajardo Barbachan, and Leonardo C. di Tavani, 2004, CAPM usando uma carteira sintética do PIB brasileiro, In: IV Encontro Brasileiro de Finanças, *Annals...*, Rio de Janeiro.

Berk, Jonathan B., 2000, Sorting out sorts, *The Journal of Finance* 55, 407-427.

Black, Fischer, 1972, Capital market equilibrium with restricted borrowing, *The Journal of Business* 45, 444-455.

Black, Fischer, Michael C. Jensen, and Myron S. Scholes, 1972, The capital asset pricing model: Some empirical tests, In: Michael C. Jensen, Org., *Studies in the Theory of Capital Markets* (Praeger, New York, 79-121).

Blume, Marshall E., and Irwin Friend, 1973, A new look at the capital asset pricing model, *The Journal of Finance* 28, 19-33.

Bonomo, Marco, and Gabriela Bertol Domingues, 2002, Os puzzles invertidos no mercado brasileiro de ativos, In: Marco Bonomo, Org., *Finanças Aplicadas ao Brasil* (FGV, São Paulo, 105-120).

Bravo, Karin, and Carlos Oyarzún, 2001, Consumption and asset return dynamics in the Chilean economy. In: Encuentro de Economistas, *Banco de Papers*, Punta de Tralca, Universidad de Chile, Faculdad de Ciências Económicas y Administrativas, available at: http://econ.facea.uchile.cl/encuentro/Consumption%20and%20Assets%20Return%20Dynamics%20EE.pdf

Breeden, Douglas T., 1979, An intertemporal asset pricing model with stochastic consumption and investment opportunities, *Journal of Financial Economics* 7, 265-296.

Breeden, Douglas T., Michael R. Gibbons, and Robert H. Litzenberger, 1989, Empirical tests of the consumption-oriented CAPM, *The Journal of Finance* 46, 231-262.

Campbell, John Y., 1996, Consumption and the stock market: Interpreting international experience, *Working Paper*, NBER 5610.

Campbell, John Y., Andrew W. Lo, and A. Craig MacKinlay, 1997, *The Econometrics of Financial Markets* (Princeton University Press, New Jersey).

Campbell, John Y., and John H. Cochrane, 1999, By force of habit: the consumption-based explanation of aggregate stock market behavior, *Journal of Political Economy* 107, 205-251.

Campbell, John Y., and John H. Cochrane, 2000, Explaining the poor performance of consumption-based asset pricing models, *The Journal of Finance* 55, 2863-2878.

Carmichael, Benoît, and Lucie Samson, 2005, Consumption growth as the risk factor? Evidence from Canadian financial markets, *Journal of International Money and Finance* 24, 83-101.

Castellanos, Sara G., and Marco A. Oviedo, 2004, Análisis de las posturas óptimas en las subastas primarias de títulos gubernamentales: Resultados de un enfoque econométrico estructural, *Documento de Investigación nº 2004-7*, Dirección General de Investigación Económica, Banco de Mexico.

Cochrane, John H., 2005, *Asset Pricing: Revised Edition* (Princeton University Press, New Jersey).

Constantinides, George M., 1982, Intertemporal asset pricing with heterogeneous consumers and without demand aggregation, *Journal of Business* 55, 253-267.

Cornell, Bradford, 1981, The consumption based asset pricing model: A note on potential tests and applications, *Journal of Financial Economics* 9, 103-108.

Cysne, Rubens Penha, 2005, Equity premium puzzle: Evidence from Brazilian data, *Ensaios Econômicos EPGE* nº 586, Fundação Getúlio Vargas.

Duffie, Darrell, 2001, *Dynamic Asset Pricing Theory* (Princeton University Press, New Jersey).

Elyasiani, Elyas, and Alireza Nasseh, 2000, Non nested procedures in econometric tests of asset pricing theories, *The Journal of Financial Research* 23, 103-128.

Faff, Robert W., 1998, The empirical relationship between aggregate consumption and security prices in Australia. *Pacific-Basin Finance Journal* 6, 213-224.

Fama, Eugene F., and James D. Macbeth, 1973, Risk, return, and equilibrium: Empirical tests, *Journal of Political Economy* 71, 607-636.

Fama, Eugene F., and Kenneth R. French, 1992, The cross-section of expected stock returns, *The Journal of Finance* 47, 427-465.

Ferson, Wayne E., and John J. Merrick Jr., 1987, Non-stationarity and stage-of-the-business-cycle effects in consumption-based asset pricing relations, *Journal of Financial Economics* 18, 127-146.

Grauer, Robert R., and Johannus A. Janmaat, 2004, The unintended consequences of grouping in tests of asset pricing models, *Journal of Banking & Finance* 28, 2889-2914.

Greene, William H., 1997, *Econometric Analysis* (Prentice Hall, New Jersey).

Grossman, Sanford J., and Robert J. Shiller, 1981, The determinants of the variability of stock market prices, *The American Economic Review* 71, 222-227.

Grossman, Sanford J., Ângelo Melino, and Robert J. Shiller, 1987, Estimating the continuous-time consumption-based asset-pricing model, *Journal of Business & Economic Statistics* 5, 315-327.

Gujarati, Damodar N., 2003, *Basic Econometrics* (McGraw-Hill, New York).

Hansen, Lars Peter, and Kenneth J. Singleton, 1983, Stochastic consumption, risk aversion, and the temporal behavior of asset returns, *Journal of Political Economy* 91, 249-265.

Hansen, Lars Peter, and Ravi Jagannathan, 1991, Implications of security market data for models of dynamic economies, *Journal of Political Economy* 99, 225-262.

Huang, Chi-fu, and Robert H. Litzenberger, 1988, *Foundations for Financial Economics* (Prentice Hall, New Jersey).

Issler, João Victor, and Natalia Scotto Piqueira, 2001, Estimando a aversão ao risco, a taxa de desconto intertemporal, e a substutibilidade intertemporal do consumo no Brasil usando três tipos de função utilidade, *Ensaios Econômicos EPGE* nº 424, Fundação Getúlio Vargas.

Jagannathan, Ravi, and Zhenyu Wang, 1996, The conditional CAPM and the cross-sectional of expected returns, *The Journal of Finance* 51, 3-53.

Jagannathan, Ravi, and Zhenyu Wang, 1998, An asymptotic theory for estimating beta-pricing models using cross-sectional regression, *The Journal of Finance* 53, 1285-1309.

Jagannathan, Ravi, and Yong Wang, 2005, Consumption risk and the cost of equity capital, *Working Paper*, NBER 11026.

Kim, Dongcheol, 1995, The errors in the variables problem in the cross-section of expected stock returns, *The Journal of Finance* 50, 1605-1634.

Kim, Dongcheol, 1997, A reexamination of firm size, book-to-market, and earnings price in the cross-section of expected stock returns, *Journal of Financial and Quantitative Analysis* 32, 463-489.

Kocherlakota, Narayana R., 1996, The equity premium: It's still the puzzle, *Journal of Economic Literature* 34, 42-71.

Kothari, S. P., Jay Shanken, and Richard G. Sloan, 1995, Another look at the cross-section of expected stock returns, *The Journal of Finance* 50, 185-224.

Lettau, Martin, and Sydney Ludvigson, 2001, Resurrecting the (C)CAPM: the cross-sectional test when risk premia are time-varying, *Journal of Political Economy* 109, 1238-1287.

Levy, Haim, 1978, Equilibrium in an imperfect market: a constraint on the number of securities in the portfolio, *The American Economic Review* 68, 643-658.

Liang, Bing, 2000, Portfolio formation, measurement errors, and beta shifts: a random sampling approach, *The Journal of Financial Research* 23, 261-284.

Lintner, John, 1965, Security prices, risk, and maximal gains from diversification, *The Journal of Finance* 20, 587-615.

Litzenberger, Robert H., and Krishna Ramaswamy, 1979, The effect of personal taxes and dividends on capital asset prices: Theory and empirical evidence, *Journal of Financial Economics* 7, 163-195.

Lo, Andrew W., and A. Craig MacKinlay, 1990, Data-snooping biases in tests of financial asset pricing models, *Review of Financial Studies* 3, 431-467.

Lo, Ingrid, 2004, Portfolio formation can affect asset pricing tests, *Journal of Asset Management* 5, 203-216.

Lucas, Robert E., 1978, Asset prices in an exchange economy, *Econometrica* 46, 1429-1445.

Maddala, G. S., 2001, *Introduction to Econometrics* (Wiley, Chichester).

Mankiw, N. Gregory, and Matthew D. Shapiro, 1986, Risk and return: consumption beta versus market beta, *Review of Economics and Statistics* 68, 452-459.

Mehra, Rajnish, and Edward C. Prescott, 1985, The equity premium: the puzzle, *Journal of Monetary Economics* 15, 145-161.

Mehra, Rajnish, and Edward C. Prescott, 2003, The equity premium in retrospect, *Working Paper*, NBER 9525.

Mellone Junior, Geraldo, 1999, Evidência empírica da relação cross-section entre retornos e earnings to price ratio e book to market ratio no Mercado de Ações do Brasil no Período de 1995 a 1998, In: XXIII Encontro Nacional de Programas de Pós-Graduação em Administração, *Annals...* , Foz do Iguaçu.

Merton, Robert C., 1973, An intertemporal capital asset pricing model, *Econometrica* 41, 867-887.

Muth, John F., 1961, Rational expectations and the theory of price movements, *Econometrica* 29, 315-335.

Opazo R., Luis A., 1998, Evaluación comparada de modelos de valoración de activos: el caso del premio accionario en Chile, *Revista de Análisis Económico* 13, 53-80.

Osorio, Isabel Cristina Montoya, and Juan Manuel Restrepo Puerta, 2004, Existe el enigma de la prima de riesgo en el mercado bursátil colombiano? 1993-2002. *Ecos de Economía*, No. 19, 31-58.

Parker, Jonathan A., and Christian Julliard, 2005, Consumption risk and the cross section of expected returns, *Journal of Political Economy* 113, 185-222.

Pessoa, Marcelo de Sales, 2006, *Reproduzindo os momentos dos retornos dos ativos Brasileiros com aversão a desapontamento generalizada*, Doctoral dissertation, Escola de Pós-Graduação em Economia (EPGE), Fundação Getúlio Vargas, Rio de Janeiro.

Ribenboim, Guilherme, 2002, Testes de versões do modelo CAPM no Brasil, In: Marco Bonomo, Org., *Finanças Aplicadas ao Brasil* (FGV, São Paulo, 17-40).

Rodrigues, Murilo Ramos Alambert, 2000, O efeito valor, o efeito tamanho e o modelo multifatorial: Evidências do caso brasileiro, In: XXIV Encontro Nacional de Programas de Pós-Graduação em Administração, *Annals...* , Florianópolis.

Roll, Richard, 1977, The critique of the asset pricing theory's tests part I: On past and potential testability of the theory, *Journal of Financial Economics* 4, 129-176.

Sampaio, Frederico Santana, 2002, Existe equity premium puzzle no Brazil?, In: Marco Bonomo, Org., *Finanças Aplicadas ao Brasil* (FGV, São Paulo, 87-104).

Shanken, Jay, 1992, On the estimation of beta-pricing models. *The Review of Financial Studies* 5, 1-33.

Sharpe, William F., 1964, Capital asset prices: the theory of market equilibrium under conditions of risk. *The Journal of Finance* 19, 425-442.

Varian, Hal R., 1992, *Microeconomic Analysis* (Norton & Company, New York).

In: Economics of Emerging Markets
Editor: Lado Beridze, pp. 169-202

Chapter 7

RATIONAL BUBBLES IN ISTANBUL STOCK EXCHANGE: LINEAR AND NONLINEAR UNIT ROOT TESTS[*]

Erdinç Altay
Istanbul University, Faculty of Economics,
Department of Business Administration, Turkey

ABSTRACT

We analyzed the presence of rational bubbles in Istanbul Stock Exchange (ISE) between 1998-2006 period by implementing linear and nonlinear unit root tests to 7 different indices. The first analysis is based on implementing augmented Dickey-Fuller unit root and KPSS stationary tests to the price-dividend ratios of the indices. The results are in favor of the presence of rational bubbles in the indices. We implemented a further test which enables time-varying discount rates. Generally the results of the loglinear model also support the previous results. The potential weaknesses of linear test methods as well as the advantages of nonlinear models motivated to use the bilinear test method. The evidence from the nonlinear test is in favor of the existence of rational bubbles in all indices in the sample period of 2nd March 1998–29th December 2006. But the results of the subperiods are contradictory for some indices. In the first and second subperiods we cannot accept unit root bilinearity for ISE National-Services index. The results also reject the significance of the bilinear term for ISE National-Industrials and ISE Investment Trusts indices in the second subperiod. As a result, we can conclude that as a general structure, the rational bubbles present in ISE.

---

[*] The present work was supported by the Research Fund of Istanbul University: Project No:581/14082006.

1. INTRODUCTION

The stock market efficiency and the rational behavior of investors are two of the most important hypotheses in explaining investor behavior and stock price formation in the finance literature. The efficient markets hypothesis depends on the immediate flow of the news to the market participants and instantaneous reflection of all relevant information to the stock prices. Such an efficient market environment with rationally behaving market participants result in ensuring the market prices of stocks equal to their fundamental values. However, since 1980's there is a continuous academic interest on a phenomenon which is called as the stock price bubble: deviation of the market prices from the fundamentals.

The models developed in the neoclassical finance framework ensure the absence of stock price bubbles by the assumption of transversality condition in infinite horizon models and backwards induction argument in finite horizon models. According to the theory, all market participants need not to be rational in order to keep the market prices equal to fundamentals. Any deviation, because of the irrational behavior of noise traders can be offset in a short time by the arbitrage procedure which will be started by the sufficient number of rational market participants. Although the market efficiency and the rational behavior hypotheses prevent the presence of the bubbles in the theory, empirical analysis of capital markets and the evidence of various market anomalies show that the strong form of efficient market hypothesis does not always hold. On the other hand, recent studies of behavioral finance present serious evidence of irrational or boundedly rational behavior, which causes significant effects on the stock pricing process. A brief glance to the history of capital markets also provides interesting examples of sharp increases without market justification, which are followed by abrupt market collapses. Among the others, some of the classical examples of bubbles can be given as Tulip mania of the 1630's, South Sea bubble of 1710-1720, Mississippi bubble of 1718-1720 and the internet bubble of 1992-2000. Such sharp increases in the market prices unrelated with the fundamentals are followed by market crashes causing deep problems in the economy.

Properly functioning capital markets have critical roles not only for financial sector but also for the overall economy. Taipalus (2006) states four different channels of how stock prices affect whole economy. These are the effects of stock markets on investments, firms' balance-sheets, household wealth and household liquidity. The close relationship between stock prices and overall economy shows the importance of correct formation of the market prices and hence the potential problems that may occur because of a bubble process. This relation between the overall economy and the capital markets are especially important for emerging markets with their instable and vulnerable economic structures. In order to understand why bubbles occur in capital markets it may be a good starting point to analyze previous bubbles' driving forces. Taipalus (2006) stated detailed information about these driving forces under five titles: 1) breaks or major changes in the regulatory environment, 2) growth prospects within a sector or a country, 3) policy changes concerning taxation, monetary operations, financial liberalization etc, 4) market infrastructure, and 5) overtrading as a result of speculation for profit.

The above stated first three issues generally create optimistic effects on traders and push stock prices upward. But on the other hand they are hard to be correctly evaluated and reflected to the stock prices by the supply and demand process of the market. The difficulty in correctly evaluating the changes in the regulatory environment, growth prospects and policy changes can result in the overreaction of traders and stimulates a bubble process in the market. Abreu and Brunnermeier (2003) also define one of the driving forces of bubbles as the structural change which causes productivity increase and give the examples of the railway, electricity, internet and telecommunication booms. Over-optimistic traders' lack of understanding the fact that the implementation of structural changes and thus the returns of productivity increase may take a long time and may be on the benefit of only a small number of firms, incorrectly increase the stock prices over their fundamental values.

While the stock price bubble is generally defined as the deviation of market prices from the fundamentals, the question arises from how one can estimate the fundamental value. If the model which is used for the estimation of the fundamental value omits some of the revelant variables, it becomes impossible to argue whether the difference between the observed market price and the estimated fundamental price is because of the bubble or the omited variables (Dezhbakhsh and Demirguc-Kunt, 1990). Related with the specification problem in detecting the bubbles, Siegel (2003) make an operational definition of the bubble. This definition is based on the explanation of Rosser (2000): the fundamental value is the long run equilibrium price level. To which extend the expected cash flows and discount factor are correctly estimated and the length of the estimation period has a critical importance. According to the operational definition of Siegel (2003), the estimation period for expected return is the duration of the stock and in order to decide on the existence of the bubble, the realized rate of return of the stock should be two standard deviations greater than its expected return.

In this research we investigated the existence of the rational bubbles in Istanbul Stock Exchange (ISE) by implementing linear and bilinear unit root test procedures to ISE National-All, ISE National-100, ISE National-30, ISE National-Industrials, ISE National-Services, ISE National-Financials and ISE Investment Trusts indices data. The results are consistent with the existence of rational bubbles in ISE. The chapter is organized as follows. The following section briefly defines the types of the stock price bubbles. The third section presents the present value model and rational bubbles. In section four, various empirical tests of rational bubbles are explained. The fifth section presents the linear and bilinear unit root test methodologies that are implemented in order to test existence of the rational bubbles in ISE. The section six summarizes the empirical findings. The last section contains the conclusion.

2. TYPES OF STOCK PRICE BUBBLES

Boucher (2003) defines three types of bubbles according to the behavior of traders and informational efficiency. These are 1) non rational bubbles, 2) rational bubbles and 3) inefficiencies due to imperfect and heterogeneous information.

2.1. Non Rational Bubbles

The non rational bubbles occur in the markets that are not fully rational so their existence can be attributed to the presence of the irrational traders. The possible reasons of non rational bubbles can be explained in the framework of two different models: the two-traders model and the investor psychology.

2.1.1. Two-traders Model

According to the two-traders model (see Shleifer and Summers, 1990; De Long et al., 1990a; De Long et al., 1990b and De Long et al., 1991) there are two different types of traders in the market: the rational investors and the irrational noise traders. The rational investors base their trading decisions on the economic fundamentals and their motivation is to earn profit by detecting the stocks which are incorrectly priced relative to their risk levels. On the other hand, the noise traders have systematically wrong evaluations about the stock prices and base their trading decisions on the erroneous beliefs and signals which donot carry revelant information. According to the model, such a violation of the homogeneous agents assumption may cause deviation of market prices from fundamentals and the stock price bubbles arise from the interaction of these two kinds of traders.

The presence of noise traders in the maket increases the risk of stocks by their systematic biases in pricing the stocks and cause bubbles. On the other hand, if the rational arbitragers' investment horizons are infinite, they invest according to their expectations about future dividends. But if their investment horizons are not infinite and noise traders exist in the market then the rational traders also trade irrationally. Because when a non-rational bubble occurs because of the presence of the irrational trading of noise traders, as a first reaction rational arbitragers start an arbitrage process in order to profit from the misevaluation of the stocks by the noise traders. But a shorter investment horizon of rational arbitragers protects the adjustment of the over priced stocks to their fundamental level because when the investment horizon of the noise traders is longer they persist in the market and able keep the stock prices over their fundamental levels even for a longer period then the arbitragers liquidate their positions. As a result, arbitrage position becomes far away from a profitable strategy. Under these conditions, spotting market trends and benefiting from the increasing market by trying to liquidate the investments before the bubble bursts, that is trading like a noise trader becomes the real "rational" strategy for the rational investors and feeds the irrational bubble.

2.1.2. Investor Psychology

Another source of non rational bubbles is related with investor psychology and behavior. Overconfidence, incorrect weighting of information, entrapment, overreaction and herding behaviour are some of the phenomena that are related with investor psychology which may start a bubble processes.

The overconfidence is the self-deception of investors that they make the right decision among the other. The overconfidence leads the investors to over assess their information, under estimate their risks and exaggerate their ability to control the happenings. Once an overconfident irrational investor enters into the market, he thinks that his decision of investment is right, his investment is profitable and less risky. This kind of a market wide speculation which is based on overconfident behavior of investors can result in stimulating a non rational bubble.

The incorrect weighting of information can be described as the bias in estimating the probability distribution of information. The irrational investors often overweight some rarely probable happenings and underweight highly probable ones leading to the bias in expectations. If incorrect weighting of information is common in the market, this can cause a deviation of market prices from their fundamental values. This kind of a psychologic bias in the market may increase the overpriced stock's demand by creating the expectation of a further increase in its market price and may result in a non rational bubble.

The entrapment is also another kind of psychological bias which is based on the past mistakes of irrational investors. These past mistakes may affect the future decisions although they are irrelevant information. A decrease in the price of the stock of the irrational trader may result in a further demand of that stock in order to decrease the average cost of the investment, ignoring its risk and expected return.

Investor reactions to information may be different from what is stated by the efficient market hypothesis. According to the efficient market hypothesis, rational investors correctly assess the full information set and reflect it to the market prices. On the other hand, empirical findings of De Bondt and Thaler (1985) support the evidence that the investors violate bayesian rationality, overreact to the unexpected news and overweight the last information.

Another psychological phenomenon is herding. Brunnermeier (2001) describes the herding as the behaviour of people blindly following the decisions of others. The herding behavior, combined with the other psychological biases may drive market prices above their fundamental values and cause non rational stock price bubbles.

2.2. Rational Bubbles

Bubbles donot arise only because of market biases and non rational behavior of market participants. A kind of stock price bubble, rational bubble, may be consistent with the rational behavior of the investors when they expect capital gains from stock trading. Even if all the investors are rational, the presence of finite investment horizon, non limited number of investors and/or non limited number of stocks may start a rational bubble process. Rational bubbles occur if the investors are willing to pay for the stock higher than its fundamental value with the expectation of selling it at an even higher price to another investor.

If the investors are rational and have infinite investment horizons, they buy the stocks and hold them for an infinite period. One result of such a situation is the no trade structure of the market. In this case all stocks will be priced at the present value of their infinite number of future dividends and nobody would pay higher than the fundamental values of these stocks. As a result, there would be no bubble in the stock prices. Tirole (1982) shows the nonexistence of bubbles under the condition of the presence of finite number of infinite lived rational investors in a general equilibrium framework. While the arbitragers play the role of precluding the bubbles in the economy of finite number of investors with infinite investment horizons, higher interest rates than the growth rate of the economy also avoids the existence of the bubbles in an overlapping-generations economy with infinite number of investors that have finite investment horizons (Tirole, 1985). But if the number of investors increase and their investment horizons are not infinite, rational bubbles may arise.

If the investors are rational, they increase in number and their invesment horizons are finite, the only way of buying a stock for the new investors becomes to offer a price which is higher than its fundamental value. Because the previous owner of the stock would not sell it lower than its fundamental price and prefer holding it until the end of investment horizon. Thus trading in the market may result in a rational bubble. In this case the important point for an investor becomes whether the price of the stock at the end of the investment horizon will be above than its cost or not, rather than whether the market price is deviated from fundamental value or not. If the investor expects to sell his/her stocks higher than their costs, which are higher than the fundamental value, rational bubbles may continue to exist in the market. This is a kind of self-fullfiling expectations about future increases in market prices. Under these conditions, the rational strategy for an investor becomes to hold the stocks as long as the prices increase and sell them just before the bubble bursts. The motivation of such an investor is the anticipation that the stock can be resold at a higher price to another investor who has the same anticipation. This is called as the "greater fool theory". Brooks and Katsaris (2003) define this as the inclusion of the expectation of stock's future price into the information set of investors. The expectation of the stock's future price becomes a more important factor on its supply and demand than the comparison of its market price with the fundamental value.

According to Koustas and Serletis (2005), the rational bubbles may be initially started by exogeneous shocks or rumors and continued by self-fulfilling expectations of market participants. Such a bubble structure arising from the investor expectations about the possibility of reselling the stocks which are bought higher than their fundamental values must continuously expand in order to survive. Because the expectation is based on reselling the stocks at a higher price to some other investors who also expect to sell them even at a higher price in the future.

Diba and Grossman (1988b) points out two problems about this kind of continuously diverging rational bubbles: 1) a negative bubble cannot exist, and 2) it can never disappear and reappear. But previous observations of stock markets show that bubbles are followed by crashes and new bubbles may start and burst. These critisms, cause generation of new models of rational bubbles which are consistent with the reality of their periodically diminishing charateristics. Two of these rational bubble versions are the intrinsic bubbles[1] and the periodically collapsing bubbles.[2] (Boucher, 2003: 2)

2.3. Inefficiencies due to Imperfect and Heterogeneous Information

The third group of the explanation of stock price bubbles can be considered in the class of inefficiencies due to imperfect and heterogeneous information. According to this explanation, the main reason of the bubbles is the informational asymmetricies among market participants.

3. PRESENT VALUE MODEL AND RATIONAL BUBBLES

While one of the basic questions about bubbles is why market prices deviate from fundamentals, the other question is how can the fundamental value correctly calculated in order to understand whether there is a deviation or not. The finance theory explains this problem by the present value model of Lucas (1978).

---

[1] See Froot and Obsfeld (1991), and Ikeda and Shibata (1992).
[2] See Evans (1991), and van Norden and Schaller (1993).

According to the present value model, the fundamental value of a stock for a rational investor is the present value of all its cash flows, namely the dividends and future market price:[3]

$$P_t^* = E_t \left[\sum_{i=1}^{k} \beta^i D_{t+i} \right] + E_t \left[\beta^k P_{t+k} \right] \tag{1}$$

where P_t^* is the fundamental value of the stock at time t, P_{t+k} is the market price of the stock at time $t+k$, D_{t+i} is dividend of the stock paid between time t and time $t+i$, β^i coefficient is the discount factor and $E[\cdot]$ is the expectation operator conditional to the information available at time t.

In order to have a unique solution from the equation (1), expected present value of the price has to converge to zero while it is going to infinity. This is called as the transversality condition and it can be expressed as follows:

$$Lim_{k \to \infty} E_t \left[\beta^k P_{t+k} \right] = 0 \tag{2}$$

Another condition for calculating the fundamental value is the requirement of a lower growth rate of prices and dividends than the discount rate. Otherwise the stock price goes to infinity in the case of infinite investment horizon. When the transversality condition holds and the discount rate is sufficiently low (lower than the dividend growth rate), the fundamental value which has a unique solution can be written as follows:

$$P_t^* = \sum_{i=1}^{\infty} \beta^i E_t \left[D_{t+i} \right] \tag{3}$$

If the transversality condition does not hold, we get infinite number of solutions of the equation (1) which lead to the differences between market prices and the fundamental value. The difference or the stock price bubble can be shown as follows:

$$P_t = P_t^* + B_t \tag{4}$$

where, B_t is the bubble at time t. This kind of a formulation shows two components of asset prices. The first companent is the fundamental value and the second component is the bubble term. The bubble process satisfies the following equation:

$$B_t = \beta^i E_t \left[B_{t+i} \right] \tag{5}$$

---

[3] We utilized heavily from Campbell, Lo and MacKinlay (1997), Koustas and Serletis (2005), and Cajueiro and Tabak (2005) for explaining the present value model and the rational bubble model.

The above stated bubble process is called as the rational bubble, because it is only one solution of the present value model which is compatible with the rational behavior among the other possible solutions. Thus the presence of rational bubbles is not contradictory to the rational expectations model. (Lardic and Priso, 2004: 560) In other words, the reason of the presence of the bubble term in the model is the expectation of its presence in the next period. Such an expectation of a difference between the fundamental value and the market price of the stock in the future motivates the rational investor to continue to demand the stock at a higher price then its fundamental value. This behavior contains the aim of profiting by reselling the stock even at a higher price to another one so it can be described as a rational behavior.

4. EMPIRICAL TESTS OF RATIONAL BUBBLES

The tests of Shiller (1981), Blanchard and Watson (1982), and West (1987) provide some of the first bubble tests which investigate the consistency between dividends and market prices. There is still a growing number of research to detect rational bubbles in the finance literature. Brooks and Katsaris (2003) categorize the bubble tests into three groups: 1) bubble premium tests, 2) excess volatility tests, and 3) stationary (unit root) and cointegration tests.

4.1. Bubble Premium Tests

Hardouvelis (1988), and Rappoport and White (1993) implemented bubble premium tests in their research. According to this test methodology, the bubble premium is defined as the excess return above the fundamental return which is demanded by the investors in the presence of a bubble. In this definition, fundamental return can be explained by the sum of three components: risk free rate, risk premium which is related with the undertaking of a risky investment and a random disturbance. The method depends on the calculation of the difference between the excess returns of bubble period and no bubble period and detecting the bubble premium. However there are two critical problems in the implementation of such a methodology. First, how can one be sure that the period which is assumed as bubble free is really a bubble free period? Second, in the prediction of excess returns, the slope coefficients are assumed to be equal in order to subtract the excess returns of bubble and bubble free periods but this assumption may also not be true. (Brooks and Katsaris, 2003: 327)

4.2. Excess Volatility Tests

Another method of testing the rational bubbles depends on the comparison between the volatilities of fundamental value and market price of the stocks. The research of Flood and Garber (1980), Shiller (1981), LeRoy and Porter (1981), Hart and Kreps (1986), Kleidon (1986), West (1987), and Dezhbakhsh and Demirguc-Kunt (1990) are the examples of excess volatility or variance bounds tests. According to this methodology, a higher market price volatility relative the volatility of fundamental value is accepted as indicative of stock price bubbles.

Excess volatility test is previously developed by Shiller (1981) and Grossman and Shiller (1981) in order to critize the present value model. Following the initial results that present the evidence of violation of the present value model, Tirole (1985) and Blanchard and Watson (1982) presented another perspective to the model. This perspective depends on the idea of the higher variance of the asset prices may be due to the existence bubbles. According to the excess volatility tests, the asset price under the no bubble condition can be shown as the present value model as follows (Gurkaynak, 2005):

$$P_t = \sum_{i=1}^{\infty} \beta^i E_t \left(D_{t+i} \right) \qquad (6)$$

On the other hand the ex-post rational price is the present value of actual dividends:

$$P_t^* = \sum_{i=1}^{\infty} \beta^i D_{t+i} \qquad (7)$$

The difference between actual and expected dividends, forecast error (ε) is zero mean and unforecastable:

$$P_t^* = \sum_{i=1}^{\infty} \beta^i \left[E_t \left(D_{t+i} \right) + \varepsilon_i \right] \qquad (8)$$

$$P_t^* = P_t + \sum_{i=1}^{\infty} \beta^i \varepsilon_{t+i} \qquad (9)$$

The variance of the ex-post rational price can be written as:

$$\sigma \left(P_t^* \right) = \sigma \left(P_t \right) + \varphi \sigma \left(\varepsilon_t \right) \qquad (10)$$

thus; $\sigma \left(P_t^* \right) \geq \sigma \left(P_t \right)$ \qquad (11)

where, $\sigma \left(P_t^* \right)$ is the variance of the ex-post rational price, $\sigma \left(P_t \right)$ is the variance of the market price and $\sigma \left(\varepsilon_t \right)$ is the variance of the diffecence between actual and expected dividends. Such a framework presents an upper bound for the volatility of asset prices: variance of ex-post rational prices should be equal or greater than the variance of the observed market prices.

However one of the basic problems in such a variance bound test methodology is the sensitivity of the test results to the assumptions in the estimation of the dividends for calculating the fundamental value. Inappropriate assumptions may seriously decrease the dependability of the test results and conclusions about the presence of the bubbles. For example if the dividends are generated from a non-stationary process and if the discount rate which is used in the construction of the fundamental price is assumed to be unrealistically constant, the test results can lead to the wrong conclusions. Unless the assumptions and information set used in the modelling of the fundamental value cover the real information set of the investors, it would be very hard to talk about the robustness of the test methodology. Another critique about the volatility test is the possibility of a bubble effect in the proxy of the fundamental value because the cut off prices are used as the proxy of the present value of future dividends. The critique of Kleidon (1986) is also another important point to consider. Kleidon points out the possibility of the irrationality of the investors and the misspecification of the model used in the construction of the fundamental value as the reasons of excess volatility. (Brooks and Katsaris, 2003: 328-330)

4.3. Unit Root and Cointegration Tests

Among the others, Campbell and Shiller (1987, 1988), Diba and Grossman (1988a), Froot and Obstfeld (1991), Craine (1993), Timmermann (1995), Horvath and Watson (1995), Lamont (1998), Bohl (2003), and Cunado, Gil-Alana and Gracia (2005) implemented unit root and cointegration tests in order to investigate the rational bubbles in stock markets. In this test methodology, the non stationarity in the logarithm of the dividend price ratio time series is consistent with the presence of rational bubbles. Because Diba and Grossman (1988a) show that if the stock prices are exclusively depend on future dividends, if there is no rational bubble in the stock market and if the dividend time series is stationary in the mean, then the price series should also be stationary.

In the literature, another kind of rational bubble test is the cointegration test between dividend and market price data. A cointegration between dividend and market price implies that fundamental value and market price cannot drift apart indefinitely. A nonstationary deviation between these two time series indicates nonexistence of a long-run equilibrium condition in the market which is an evidence of the presence of rational bubbles. (Koustas and Serletis, 2005: 2524)

If the fundamental value is equal to the market price, then market price and dividend series are cointegrated. This means, although the market price and dividend time series are nonstationary, their linear combination should be stationary. In order to test the existence of the bubbles, unit root tests are implemented to the price and dividend time series. Non rejection of unit root hypothesis for both series is followed by a cointegrating regression between these two series for implementing another unit root test on the residual process. The presence of a unit root in the residual process is considered as the evidence of no cointegration relation between market prices and dividends which results to the conclusion that there is a rational bubble in the stock prices. (Boucher, 2003: 5-6)

Campbell and Shiller (1987) also implement such a cointegration test to the annual data of Standart and Poor's 500 index. The test period is 1871-1986 and the results are in favor of the presence of rational bubbles but they find that the results are sensitive to the discount factor which is used in the present value model. On the other hand, Froot and Obsfeld (1991) also implement a unit root test procedure to the price-dividend ratio of Standart and Poor's index and find the evidence of the existence of rational bubbles due to the lack of cointegration relationship between these two variables.

However Diba (1990) and Evans (1991) think that in finite samples, the nonstationarity can be masked and cointegration tests cannot detect all kinds of bubbles. The exclusion of significant variables in the fundamental value model may also result in wrong conclusions. Another pitfall of such a linear stationarity procedure is that it is only capable of detecting the bubble in the expanding phase. However periodically collapsing bubbles have both expanding and collapsing phases. Therefore the bubble structure becomes hard to be detected by a linear unit root procedure.

The test procedures like unit root and cointegration are inadequate especially in detecting the periodically collapsing bubbles and may result in incorrect conclusions. This is also true for not only periodically collapsing bubbles but also for the non-negative rational bubbles and intrinsic bubbles, which contain linear fundamental value and nonlinear bubble terms. Another weakness of these linear stationarity test procedures is their assumption of a linear discount rate in the fundamental value modeling. In his research in Japan Stock Market, Fukuta (2002) points out this problem. He argues that the discount factor which is employed in determining the present value of future dividends should not be constant but rather it should be a stochastic process, so a time-varying cointegration vector should be employed in the model. Boucher (2003) also employs time-varying risk premium in rational bubble tests. Referring to the no necessary reason of assuming the economic systems as linear as well as the nonlinear dependencies of financial time series, Chang et al. (2005) implemented a nonparametric cointegration test to Taiwan Stock Market data and rejected the presence of rational bubbles.

In order to overcome the above stated problems of linear unit root and cointegration tests, various nonlinear test procedures are started to be employed. Among the others, Bohl (2003) employed MTAR (Momentum Threshold Autoregressive) model for testing the periodically collapsing bubbles and Charemza, Lifshits and Makarova (2005) employed bilinear stochastic unit root procedure for testing the rational bubbles.

Peel and Davidson (1998) state that bilinear unit root test has advantages in capturing the sudden and unexpected changes in the time series relative to the TAR (Threshold Autoregressive) models such as SETAR (Self-Exciting Threshold Autoregressive) and MTAR models. Thus in this research, we also employed a bilinear unit root test in investigating the rational bubble in Istanbul Stock Exchange.

5. TESTING RATIONAL BUBBLES IN ISTANBUL STOCK EXCHANGE

In order to test the presence of rational bubbles in ISE, we implemented linear and nonlinear unit root test methodologies to daily and monthly data of 7 indices of ISE in March 1998- December 2006 period.

5.1. Linear Unit Root Test Methodology

Linear unit root test methodology is based on the stationarity of the price-dividend ratio. If the discount factor and the dividend growth rate are stationary, than the price-dividend ratio is also stationary under no rational bubble conditions. The equations through (12) to (16) show the derivation of price-dividend ratio (Lardic and Priso, 2004: 564-565):

$$P_t^* = \sum_{i=1}^{\infty} \beta^i E_t \left[D_{t+i} \right] \tag{12}$$

$$P_t = P_t^* + B_t \tag{13}$$

$$B_t = \beta^i E_t \left[B_{t+i} \right] \tag{14}$$

$$\frac{P_t}{D_t} = E_t \left(\sum_{i=1}^{\infty} \beta^i \frac{D_{t+i}}{D_{t+i-1}} \right) + E_t \left(\beta^i \frac{B_{t+i}}{D_{t+i-1}} \right) \tag{15}$$

$$\frac{P_t^*}{D_t} = \left(\sum_{i=1}^{\infty} \beta^i \frac{D_{t+i}}{D_{t+i-1}} \right) + \left(\beta^i \frac{B_{t+i}}{D_{t+i-1}} \right) + \varepsilon_t \tag{16}$$

where, ε_t is the error term. Lardic and Priso (2004) indicate two basic advantages of this famework. The first advantage is the inclusion of the error term in the model. The error term in the equation (16) enables to compansate the specification errors by including the forgotten or the excluded but significant variables in the pricing model. The second advantage of the model is stated as the importance in the implementation of the unit root tests to the left hand side of the model $\left(P_t / D_t \right)$. This is indeed an important advantage because the right hand side of the model is closely related with the specification of the utility function of the representative agent and testing the left hand side of the model may cause specification problems.

The implementation of unit root tests like augmented Dickey-Fuller or KPSS tests on the above price-dividend ratio provide evidence about the existence or nonexistence of rational bubbles in the stock markets. The null hypothesis of augmented Dickey-Fuller test is the price-dividend ratio time series is unit root, thus the rejection of the null hypothesis is indicative of the non existence of stock price bubbles. On the other hand, the null hypothesis of KPSS test is the stationary price-dividend ratio time series, therefore the rejection of null hypothesis is a sign of the presence of stock price bubbles.

One pitfall of the linear unit root test arises from the assumption of constant discount rate which is contradictory to the reality. Campbell and Shiller (1988) implement a methodology in order to allow for the time-varying discount factor in the model. The methodology is based on the following loglinear approximation:[4]

$$r_{t+1} \approx k + \rho p_{t+1} + (1-\rho) d_{t+1} - p_t \qquad (17)$$

where, r_{t+1} is the first logarithmic difference of market price at time $t+1$, p_{t+1} is the market price at time $t+1$, d_{t+1} is the dividend at time $t+1$, $k \equiv -\log(\rho) - (1-\rho)\log\left[\dfrac{1}{\rho-1}\right]$

and $\rho \equiv \dfrac{1}{[1+\exp(d-p)]}$. Imposing no rational bubble to equation (17) yields to the following equation:

$$p_t = \frac{k}{1-\rho} + \sum_{i=0}^{\infty} \rho^i \left[(1-\rho) d_{t+1+i} - r_{t+1+i} \right] \qquad (18)$$

Taking the expectations of the equation (18), we obtain the following equation which is the dynamic generalization of the Gordon model:

$$p_t = \frac{k}{1-\rho} + E_t \left[\sum_{i=0}^{\infty} \rho^i \left[(1-\rho) d_{t+1+i} - r_{t+1+i} \right] \right] \qquad (19)$$

We can derive the logarithmic dividend price ratio from the equation (19) as follows:

$$d_t - p_t = -\frac{k}{1-\rho} + E_t \left[\sum_{i=0}^{\infty} \rho^i \left[-\Delta d_{t+1+i} + r_{t+1+i} \right] \right] \qquad (20)$$

where, Δ is the first difference. Craine (1993) states that if Δd_t and r_t are stationary processes and the no rational bubble condition holds, then the logarithmic dividend price ratio $(d_t - p_t)$ should also be stationary. Thus the rational bubble test has a two stage process. At the first stage the stationary of Δd_t and r_t are tested, then in the second stage, the stationary of logarithmic dividend price ratio $(d_t - p_t)$ is tested. If the Δd_t and r_t are stationary and $(d_t - p_t)$ is unit root, then this is consistent with the presence of the rational bubbles in the market. (Taipalus, 2006: 40)

---

[4] We utilized from Taipalus (2006; 39-40) for the loglinear model.

5.2. Bilinear Unit Root Test Methodology

Recent developments in the bubble test methodology document that linear unit root test procedures may fail to conclude about the existence of the rational bubbles especially which are collapsing periodically. The problems due to the linear test procedures lead to the utilization of nonlinear models in order to get stronger evidence.

According to the model of Diba and Grossman (1988a), the object of the household is to maximize the utility of the comsumpion over an infinite horizon (Cajueiro and Tabak, 2005: 4-5):

$$C_t = P_t(S_{t+1} - S_t) \le Y_t + D_t S_t \tag{21}$$

where, C_t is the consumption at time t, P_t is the market price of the stock at time t, S_t is the amount of the stock bought at time t, Y_t is the periodic income, and D_t is the dividend at time t. The object of the individuals is to choose the amount of stocks (S_t) that maximizes their utility. If we assume that the statistical distribution of stock prices and consumption are independend, we get the following equilibrium:

$$P_t U'(C_t) = \beta E_t \left[(P_{t+1} + D_{t+1}) \right] E_t \left[U'(C_{t+1}) \right] \tag{22}$$

If we use dividend adjusted stock prices, the equation (22) can be rewritten as follows:

$$P_t U'(C_t) = \beta E_t [P_{t+1}] E_t \left[U'(C_{t+1}) \right] \tag{23}$$

The ratio of the discounted marginal utility of the future consumption and the marginal utility of current consumption is the preference of the investor between current consumption and expected future consumption. Diba and Grossman (1988a) and Charemza, Lifshits and Makarova (2005) define this ratio as a random variable that is affected by the mistakes in stock pricing which are made in the previous periods. This ratio can be shown as follows:

$$\frac{\beta E_t \left[U'(C_{t+1}) \right]}{U'(C_t)} = 1 + \psi \left(P_t - E_{t-1}[P_t] \right) \tag{24}$$

where, ψ is the adjustment coefficient and indicates to which extend investors are affected by their previous pricing mistakes. Charemza, Lifshits and Makarova (2005) show that the following bilinear unit root test procedure can be utilized in order to test whether the adjustment coefficient is statistically equal to zero:

$$p_t = (a + b\varepsilon_{t-1}) p_{t-1} + \varepsilon_t \tag{25}$$

where, p_t is the logarithm of the price of the stock at time t, a is the constant and b is the adjustment factor.

Considering the well known problem of unit root in financial time series, when a is assumed as equal to 1, the equation (25) can be rewritten as follows in order to test the significance of b (Charemza, Lifshits and Makarova, 2005: 63-93):

$$\Delta p_t = b p_{t-1} \Delta p_{t-1} + \varepsilon_t \qquad (26)$$

where, Δ is the first difference, p_t is the logarithmic stock prices and Δp_{t-1} is the return of the stock. The test statistic which is utilized in order to test the significance of the adjustment coefficient (b) can be shown as follows:

$$t_{\hat{b}} = \frac{\sum_{t=2}^{T} p_{t-1} \Delta p_{t-1} \Delta p_t}{\hat{\sigma}_e \sqrt{\sum_{t=2}^{T} p_{t-1}^2 \Delta p_{t-1}^2}} \qquad (27)$$

In this research we employ the two stage test procedure of bilinear unit root test of Charemza, Lifshits and Makarova (2005) in order to investigate the rational bubble in Istanbul Stock Exchange. In the first stage augmented Dickey-Fuller and KPSS (Kwiatkowski, Philips, Schmidt, and Shin) tests are implemented. The condition for passing through the second stage is rejection of the stationarity hypothesis. In the second stage, the model in equation (26) is utilized for testing a statistically significant and positive b coefficient. A positive and statistically significant adjustment coefficient is accepted as an evidence of nonlinear property of the unit root.

6. EMPIRICAL FINDINGS

6.1. Empirical Findings of Linear Unit Root Model

In this part of the research, we analyzed the presence of rational bubbles in ISE by employing the linear unit root test procedures to the data of ISE National-All, ISE National-100, ISE National-30 and 4 different sector indices. The daily data of indices cover the period between 1st March 1998-29th December 2006. The data are provided by the Istanbul Stock Exchange. The codes and the names of the indices are presented in Table 1.

Classical examples of rational bubble tests implement linear unit root test procedures as it is mentioned above. Thus we also utilized linear unit root tests to the price-dividend ratio in order to implement the classical bubble tests to the indices of ISE as initial analyses.

Following the methodology of Taipalus (2006), the price-dividend ratio is derived from the daily total return index and price index series. According to the methodology, return of the index is the sum of dividend return and capital gains return:

$$\frac{TRI_t}{TRI_{t-1}} = \frac{D_t}{P_{t-1}} + \frac{P_t}{P_{t-1}} \tag{28}$$

where, TRI_t is the value of total return index at time t, D_t is the dividend at time t and P_t is the value of price index at time t. Thus the daily dividend (D_t) can be approximately derived from the following equation:

$$D_t = P_{t-1} \cdot \left[\frac{TRI_t}{TRI_{t-1}} - \frac{P_t}{P_{t-1}} \right] \tag{29}$$

Considering the fact that in ISE dividends are not paid evenly in whole year and usually accrue over a one-year period, the monthly dividends can be derived by the sum of rolling previous 364 days dividends for the end of each month.[5] Similarly the dividend yield (DY_t) can also be calculated as the sum of rolling previous 364 days dividends and dividing by end of the month value of the price index as follows:

$$DY_t = \frac{\sum\limits_{t}^{t-364} D_t}{P_t} \tag{30}$$

Table 1. List of Indices

Code	Index
N-All	ISE NATIONAL - ALL SHARES
N-100	ISE NATIONAL - 100
N-30	ISE NATIONAL - 30
N-Ind	ISE NATIONAL - INDUSTRIALS
N-Serv	ISE NATIONAL - SERVICES
N-Fin	ISE NATIONAL - FINANCIALS
InvTrst	ISE INVESTMENT TRUSTS

---

[5] See Taipalus (2006) for the same monthly dividend time series generating method for the Finnish stock market.

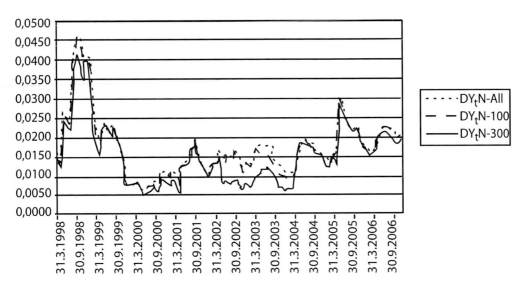

Figure 1. Dividend Yields of N-All, N-100 and N-30 Indices (March 1998–December 2006).

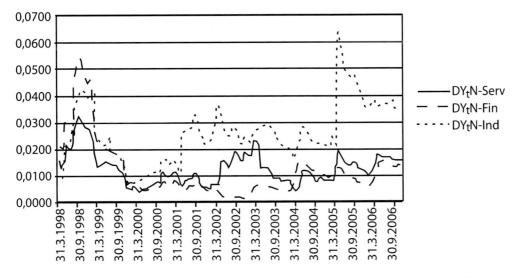

Figure 2. Dividend Yields of N-Serv, N-Fin and N-Ind Indices (March 1998–December 2006).

The dividend yields of the indices between March 1998 – December 2006 are shown in Figure 1, Figure 2 and Figure 3.

We also produced the monthly data of P_t and D_t from the daily data of total return and price indices. Although the total sample period of monthly data is decided between March 1998-December 2006, we considered the possible effects of two economic crises on the Turkish economy for our analysis. These crises are experienced in November 2000 and February 2001. Considering the sensitivity of unit root tests to the structural breaks, we divided the total sample period into two subperiods: March 1998-October 2000 and March 2001-December 2006. Summary statistics of monthly price indices, dividends and price-dividend ratios are presented in Table 2.

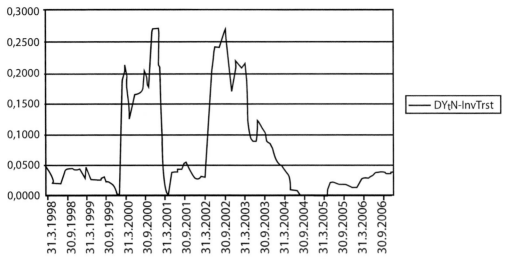

Figure 3. Dividend Yield of InvTrst Index (March 1998 – December 2006).

When we look at the summary statistics presented in Table 2, it is seen that the variables are not normally distributed in the full sample period of March 1998 – December 2006, and the second subperiod of March 2001-December 2006. However this is not the same for the first subperiod.

Referring to the equation (16), we implemented augmented Dickey-Fuller unit root tests and KPSS stationary tests to the dividend-price ratios of indices in order to test the stationarity of ISE indices. The evidence of a nonstationary price-dividend ratio of the index is considered as an indication of the rational bubble.

While implementing the augmented Dickey-Fuller unit root test, we investigated three different models of price-dividend ratio time series for all indices. The first model donot have a constant term, the second model has a constant term and the last model has both constant and linear trend terms. On the other hand we also implemented two models for the KPSS test: model with constant term and the model with constant term and linear trend. The results of the models are summarized in Table 3.

The augmented Dickey-Fuller test results presented in Table 3 show that the null hypothesis of unit root in price-dividend ratio cannot be rejected for all indices except InvTrst index for the models without a constant term and with a constant term and linear trend in the full sample period. On the other hand, the null hypothesis of unit root is rejected for the N-All, N-100, N-30 N-Serv and InvTrst indices when we implement the model with a constant term. This result is also supported by the KPSS test. Considering the robustness of the KPSS test relative to the augmented Dickey-Fuller test, the results of the KPSS model with a constant and linear trend becomes important with the rejection of the stationarity in most of the indices. The nonstationary price-dividend ratios of N-All, N-100, N-30 and N-Fin are indicative for the existence of rational bubbles in ISE.

The analysis results of the first subperiod are stronger. The null hypothesis of unit root in price-dividend ratios cannot be rejected in all indices except InvTrst index in all three models. The results of the KPSS tests are also consistent with the augmented Dickey-Fuller tests when the model with constant term is applied. The rejection of stationarity in all indices, except InvTrst index, can be considered as the evidence of the presence of rational bubbles in March 1998 – October 2000.

Table 2. Summary Statistics of Monthly P_t, D_t, and P_t/D_t Data

Variables	Index	March 1998 – December 2006			March 1998 – October 2000			March 2001 – December 2006		
		Mean	Standard Deviation	JB p-value	Mean	Standard Deviation	JB p-value	Mean	Standard Deviation	JB p-value
Monthly Close Level of Price Index P_t	N-All	15992.48	11241.97	0.0001	7608.37	5081.86	0.1295	20243.85	11236.10	0.0156
	N-100	16617.27	11550.52	0.0002	8013.83	5397.88	0.1323	20972.29	11520.56	0.0177
	N-30	21023.86	14703.02	0.0003	9930.28	6776.53	0.1392	26626.95	14615.83	0.0203
	N-Ind	13568.35	8976.21	0.0039	5854.25	3832.73	0.1277	17485.95	8360.18	0.0345
	N-Serv	10113.20	5180.01	0.0018	7857.84	4169.38	0.0925	11411.48	5262.81	0.0207
	N-Fin	23855.48	18737.63	0.0000	10712.40	7470.64	0.1306	30500.07	19394.18	0.0102
	InvTrst	9701.55	6287.18	0.0085	4935.75	3617.92	0.1023	12121.57	6045.22	0.0333
Dividends D_t	N-All	261.66	231.85	0.0000	100.30	14.20	0.0000	344.98	246.92	0.0052
	N-100	268.62	244.17	0.0000	103.17	15.74	0.0041	354.02	262.35	0.0056
	N-30	319.41	314.06	0.0000	120.22	28.58	0.8833	422.65	343.32	0.0068
	N-Ind	387.67	386.74	0.0000	81.24	16.04	0.0245	544.02	392.97	0.0029
	N-Serv	122.64	81.42	0.0000	83.57	13.71	0.4387	143.28	93.38	0.0039
	N-Fin	227.75	215.64	0.0000	139.89	39.87	0.2232	275.08	251.46	0.0111
	InvTrst	561.60	535.84	0.0005	557.26	738.01	0.0446	536.31	381.72	0.0979
Price – Dividend ratio P_t/D_t	N-All	70.48	30.81	0.0000	75.67	48.18	0.1302	66.88	17.53	0.0000
	N-100	72.84	32.00	0.0004	76.63	48.00	0.1344	69.88	20.93	0.0000
	N-30	84.87	41.95	0.0073	82.32	53.00	0.1505	84.52	36.21	0.0019
	N-Ind	48.90	29.36	0.0000	69.74	41.89	0.0651	38.44	12.98	0.0000
	N-Serv	95.80	46.52	0.0000	98.49	63.62	0.0477	94.50	37.53	0.0014
	N-Fin	157.21	128.47	0.0000	86.49	69.42	0.0994	190.92	139.00	0.0000
	InvTrst	19538.14	200550.1	0.0000	29.31	28.71	0.0000	29572.12	246787.5	0.0000

Table 3. Unit Root and Stationary Test Results of Price-Dividend Ratio

| Index | Augmented Dickey-Fuller Test[a] | | | | | | KPSS Test[b] | | | |
| | Model with no constant term | | Model with constant term | | Model with constant term and linear trend | | Model with constant term | | Model with constant term and linear trend | |
	t-Statistic	L[c]	t-Statistic	L[c]	t-Statistic	L[c]	LM statistic[d]	B[f]	LM statistic[e]	B[f]
					PANEL A: March 1998 – December 2006					
N-All	-1.0527	0	-2.6382*	0	-2.7161	0	0.1893	8	0.1392*	8
N-100	-1.0811	0	-2.7180*	0	-2.8030	0	0.2023	8	0.1535**	8
N-30	-1.0997	1	-3.0733**	0	-3.1270	0	0.2288	8	0.1993**	8
N-Ind	-1.3284	0	-2.4217	0	-2.7892	0	0.3926*	8	0.0825	8
N-Serv	-1.1930	0	-2.8701*	0	-2.8888	0	0.1252	8	0.1126	8
N-Fin	-1.5253	0	-2.4817	0	-2.4250	0	0.2400	8	0.2247***	8
InvTrst	-10.1977***	0	-10.2472***	0	-10.2247***	0	0.1065	1	0.0705	2
					PANEL B: March 1998 – October 2000					
N-All	-0.3151	0	-1.1109	0	-1.7778	0	0.4908**	5	0.1227*	4
N-100	-0.3253	0	-1.1638	0	-1.8594	0	0.4963**	5	0.1220*	4
N-30	-0.3942	0	-1.2445	0	-2.2895	0	0.5011**	5	0.1415*	4
N-Ind	-0.5429	0	-1.3391	0	-1.4227	0	0.4679**	4	0.0920	4
N-Serv	-0.6286	0	-1.4022	0	-2.4528	8	0.4432*	5	0.0902	4
N-Fin	-0.5882	0	-2.1126	0	-2.1430	5	0.5589**	4	0.1618**	4
InvTrst	-2.1276**	0	-3.2061**	0	-3.2942*	0	0.1464	3	0.1218*	2
					PANEL C: March 2001 – December 2006					
N-All	-1.1261	1	-3.6468***	0	-4.5994***	0	0.7548***	5	0.0625	4
N-100	-1.1289	1	-3.2589***	0	-4.1577***	0	0.7266**	5	0.0835	5
N-30	-1.2094	1	-3.0428**	0	-3.8858**	0	0.6637**	6	0.1254*	5
N-Ind	-1.3504	1	-4.0098***	0	-4.6033***	0	0.5845**	5	0.1141	4
N-Serv	-0.8739	2	-3.3437**	1	-3.6964**	1	0.2596	5	0.0878	5
N-Fin	-1.2907	0	-2.1011	0	-2.7205	0	0.4853**	6	0.1047	6
InvTrst	-8.3063***	0	-8.3669***	0	-8.6609***	0	0.3165	0	0.1233*	1

[a] Null hypothesis of augmented Dickey-Fuller unit root test: Ho = price-dividend ratio of the index has a unit root,

[b] Null hypothesis of KPSS test: Ho = price-dividend ratio is stationary,

[c] L=Lag length is based on Schwartz info criterion,

[d] Asymptotic critical values: 1% level = 0.739 , 5% level = 0.463, 10% level = 0.347,

[e] Asymptotic critical values: 1% level = 0.216 , 5% level = 0.146, 10% level = 0.119,

[f] B=Bandwidth:Newey-West using Barlett kernel,

* Null hypothesis is rejected at 1% level,

** Null hypothesis is rejected at 5% level,

*** Null hypothesis is rejected at 1% level.

Table 4. Summary Statistics of Monthly Δd_t, r_t and $(d_t - p_t)$ Data

Variables	Index	March 1998 – December 2006			March 1998 – October 2000			March 2001 – December 2006		
		Mean	Standard Deviation	JB p-value	Mean	Standard Deviation	JB p-value	Mean	Standard Deviation	JB p-value
Panel A: First logarithmic difference of dividends Δd_t	N-All	0.0245	0.1285	0.0000	0.0141	0.1237	0.0000	0.0302	0.1337	0.0000
	N-100	0.0243	0.1323	0.0000	0.0139	0.1255	0.0000	0.0302	0.1385	0.0000
	N-30	0.0258	0.1862	0.0000	0.0158	0.1653	0.0000	0.0316	0.1996	0.0000
	N-Ind	0.0275	0.1701	0.0000	0.0196	0.0641	0.0000	0.0322	0.2042	0.0000
	N-Serv	0.0156	0.1751	0.0000	0.0025	0.1322	0.0000	0.0223	0.1955	0.0000
	N-Fin	0.0237	0.2174	0.0000	0.0091	0.2694	0.0000	0.0314	0.1961	0.0000
	InvTrst	0.0143	1.5600	0.0000	0.0755	0.5720	0.0000	0.0151	1.8607	0.0000
Panel B: Logarithm of total return index r_t	N-All	0.0252	0.1496	0.0000	0.0311	0.2053	0.2420	0.0237	0.1165	0.0687
	N-100	0.0249	0.1530	0.0000	0.0314	0.2096	0.3366	0.0229	0.1197	0.0843
	N-30	0.0254	0.1554	0.0000	0.0329	0.2132	0.4622	0.0221	0.1214	0.0902
	N-Ind	0.0261	0.1381	0.0000	0.0330	0.1948	0.1220	0.0250	0.1048	0.0025
	N-Serv	0.0183	0.1422	0.0000	0.0166	0.1894	0.3550	0.0196	0.1152	0.0304
	N-Fin	0.0260	0.1666	0.0002	0.0322	0.2209	0.4158	0.0239	0.1342	0.2592
	InvTrst	0.0243	0.1781	0.0001	0.0358	0.2486	0.7915	0.0240	0.1350	0.0442
Panel C: Dividend return $d_t - p_t$	N-All	-4.1656	0.4293	0.7481	-4.1163	0.6703	0.2784	-4.1713	0.2516	0.7331
	N-100	-4.1953	0.4389	0.7961	-4.1358	0.6595	0.2883	-4.2057	0.2864	0.8270
	N-30	-4.3186	0.5054	0.2679	-4.2023	0.6631	0.2849	-4.3531	0.4087	0.3002
	N-Ind	-3.7640	0.4737	0.0015	-4.0794	0.5837	0.5373	-3.5987	0.3185	0.3254
	N-Serv	-4.4551	0.4636	0.6616	-4.3987	0.6267	0.4326	-4.4769	0.3770	0.3040
	N-Fin	-4.7595	0.8003	0.6369	-4.1374	0.8251	0.2573	-5.0426	0.6241	0.0746
	InvTrst	-3.2897	1.6477	0.0000	-2.9794	0.9498	0.5827	-3.4972	1.8727	0.0000

Table 5. Augmented Dickey-Fuller Unit Root Test Results of Loglinear Model

Index	Model with no constant						Model with constant term						Model with constant term and linear trend					
	Δd_t		r_t		$d_t - p_t$		Δd_t		r_t		$d_t - p_t$		Δd_t		r_t		$d_t - p_t$	
	t-Statistic	Lag[a]	t-Statistic	Lag[a]	t-Statistic	Lag[a]	t-Statistic	Lag[a]	t-Statistic	Lag[a]	t-Statistic	Lag[a]	t-Statistic	Lag[a]	t-Statistic	Lag[a]	t-Statistic	Lag[a]
PANEL A: March 1998 – December 2006																		
N-All	-11.9160***	0	-10.0240***	0	-0.2812	0	-12.4296***	0	-10.2591***	0	-2.4275	0	-12.3712***	0	-10.2157***	0	-2.4150	0
N-100	-12.0207***	0	-10.1740***	0	-0.2826	0	-12.5081***	0	-10.4019***	0	-2.4684	0	-12.4535***	0	-10.3599***	0	-2.4640	0
N-30	-11.7639***	0	-10.3772***	0	-0.3489	0	-11.9931***	0	-10.6193***	0	-2.5314	0	-11.9359***	0	-10.5834***	0	-2.5293	0
N-Ind	-12.8783***	0	-9.8759***	0	-0.5144	1	-13.2343***	0	-10.1562***	0	-2.3646	0	-13.1726***	0	-10.1146***	0	-2.8053	0
N-Serv	-10.6738***	0	-10.5770***	0	-0.2157	0	-10.7305***	0	-10.6968***	0	-2.5819*	0	-10.7089***	0	-10.6450***	0	-2.5486	0
N-Fin	-10.0334***	0	-10.0408***	0	-0.2403	0	-10.1519***	0	-10.2506***	0	-1.9076	0	-10.1053***	0	-10.2072***	0	-1.7787	0
InvTrst	-15.3412***	0	-9.5211***	0	-1.5062	1	-15.2692***	0	-9.6327***	0	-5.6775***	0	-15.1942***	0	-9.5958***	0	-5.7565***	0
PANEL B: March 1998 – October 2000																		
N-All	-7.8538***	1	-4.3358***	1	0.1980	0	-7.5592***	1	-4.3293***	0	-0.9622	0	-7.3001***	1	-4.2552**	0	-2.1204	0
N-100	-6.1593***	0	-4.4664***	0	0.2069	0	-6.1855***	0	-4.4685***	0	-1.0190	0	-6.5242***	0	-4.3932***	1	-2.1518	0
N-30	-5.9194***	0	-4.6274***	0	0.1698	0	-5.8976***	0	-4.6479***	0	-1.0812	0	-6.4917***	0	-4.5800***	0	-2.4975	0
N-Ind	-3.1273***	1	-4.3266***	1	0.1140	0	-3.1079**	1	-4.3176***	0	-1.0446	0	-5.5076***	0	-4.2240**	0	-1.3540	0
N-Serv	-6.8869***	0	-4.0259***	0	0.0854	0	-6.7915***	0	-3.9376***	0	-1.1496	0	-7.1672***	0	-4.0101**	0	-1.5097	0
N-Fin	-7.2860***	0	-4.5220***	0	0.1532	0	-7.2176***	0	-4.5369***	0	-1.0854	0	-8.2455***	0	-4.4547***	0	-2.6371	0
InvTrst	-5.5200***	0	-4.5771***	0	-0.8592	0	-5.5513***	0	-4.5567***	0	-1.6320	0	-5.5743***	9	-4.4529***	9	-2.6195	0
PANEL C: March 2001 – December 2006																		
N-All	-9.9408***	0	-9.5399***	0	-0.5590	0	-10.5208***	0	-9.9041***	0	-3.1653**	0	-10.4428***	0	-9.8267**	0	-4.0834**	0
N-100	-10.0246***	0	-9.5610***	0	-0.5768	0	-10.5665***	0	-9.8769***	0	-2.8551*	0	-10.4912***	0	-9.8021***	0	-3.8339**	0
N-30	-9.8378***	0	-9.5665***	0	-0.6937	1	-10.0707***	0	-9.8506***	0	-2.4756	0	-9.9988***	0	-9.7761***	0	-3.3445*	0
N-Ind	-10.6810***	0	-9.9059***	0	-0.7406	1	-10.9690***	0	-10.5115***	0	-3.3253**	0	-10.9249***	0	-10.4409***	0	-3.8626**	0
N-Serv	-8.4323***	0	-10.2434***	0	-0.3439	0	-8.4835***	0	-6.5872***	4	-2.4657	0	-8.4674***	0	-6.8294***	4	-2.7032	0
N-Fin	-6.4327***	0	-8.9313***	0	-0.4545	0	-6.5197***	0	-9.1538***	0	-1.4855	0	-6.5644***	0	-9.0860***	0	-2.4433	0
InvTrst	-12.9274***	0	-8.7524***	0	-1.2861	1	-12.8329***	0	-8.9623***	0	-4.9316***	0	-12.7400***	0	-8.9472***	0	-4.9564***	0

[a] Lag length is based on Schwartz info criterion.

* Null hypothesis of augmented Dickey-Fuller unit root test: Ho = variable has a unit root is rejected at 10% level.

** Null hypothesis of augmented Dickey-Fuller unit root test: Ho = variable has a unit root is rejected at 5% level.

*** Null hypothesis of augmented Dickey-Fuller unit root test: Ho = variable has a unit root is rejected at 1% level.

Table 6. KPSS Test Results of Loglinear Model

Index	Model with constant term						Model with constant term and linear trend					
	Δd_t		r_t		$d_t - p_t$		Δd_t		r_t		$d_t - p_t$	
	LM statistic	Bandwidth[c]	LM statistic	Bandwidth[c]	LM statistic	Bandwidth[c]	LM statistic	Bandwidth[c]	LM statistic	Bandwidth[c]	LM statistic	Bandwidth[c]
PANEL A: March 1998 – December 2006												
N-All	0.0954	5	0.0533	1	0.1689	8	0.0707	6	0.0491	1	0.1684**	8
N-100	0.1005	4	0.0546	1	0.1867	8	0.0656	4	0.0495	1	0.1837**	8
N-30	0.0830	3	0.0611	1	0.2234	8	0.0687	3	0.0516	1	0.2200***	8
N-Ind	0.0493	7	0.0532	2	0.4602*	8	0.0483	7	0.0409	2	0.0966	8
N-Serv	0.1314	3	0.0584	4	0.1254	8	0.0498	5	0.0579	4	0.1264*	8
N-Fin	0.1677	2	0.0537	1	0.3453	8	0.0964	1	0.0520	1	0.2602***	8
InvTrst	0.1252	26	0.0565	3	0.2059	7	0.1255*	26	0.0436	3	0.1023	7
PANEL B: March 1998 – October 2000												
N-All	0.3478*	3	0.1467	2	0.4909**	5	0.1468**	9	0.1289*	3	0.1199*	4
N-100	0.3168	3	0.1477	2	0.4965**	5	0.1620**	10	0.1297*	3	0.1171	4
N-30	0.3295	3	0.1560	2	0.4991**	5	0.1359*	9	0.1442*	2	0.1284*	4
N-Ind	0.1143	2	0.1234	2	0.4472*	5	0.1117	2	0.1246*	3	0.1002	4
N-Serv	0.2224	4	0.1967	3	0.4845**	5	0.1242*	6	0.1313*	3	0.0969	4
N-Fin	0.3294	4	0.1479	2	0.4917**	5	0.2656***	15	0.1411*	2	0.1456*	4
InvTrst	0.1951	1	0.1220	3	0.4089*	4	0.0746	3	0.1171	3	0.1471**	4
PANEL C: March 2001 – December 2006												
N-All	0.0700	5	0.0877	7	0.741***	5	0.0689	5	0.0818	7	0.0725	4
N-100	0.0741	3	0.0918	7	0.973***	5	0.0681	3	0.0836	7	0.0960	5
N-30	0.0816	2	0.0897	6	0.183**	6	0.0759	2	0.0824	6	0.1446*	5
N-Ind	0.0864	6	0.0806	8	0.6008**	5	0.0780	7	0.0723	8	0.1230*	5
N-Serv	0.1088	8	0.2100	14	0.2115	6	0.0632	9	0.1088	15	0.0952	5
N-Fin	0.1790	3	0.0826	4	0.6190**	6	0.0999	2	0.0783	5	0.1040	6
InvTrst	0.2224	33	0.1131	3	0.2294	5	0.2193***	33	0.0669	3	0.1463**	5

[a] Asymptotic critical values: 1% level = 0.739 , 5% level = 0.463, 10% level = 0.347.
[b] Asymptotic critical values: 1% level = 0.216 , 5% level = 0.146, 10% level = 0.119.
[c] Bandwidth:Newey-West using Barlett kernel.
* Null hypothesis of KPSS test: Ho = price-dividend ratio of the index is stationary is rejected at 10% level.
** Null hypothesis of KPSS test: Ho = price-dividend ratio of the index is stationary is rejected at 5% level.
*** Null hypothesis of KPSS test: Ho = price-dividend ratio of the index is stationary is rejected at 1% level.

Table 7. Results of Linear Rational Bubble Tests

Methodology	Augmented Dickey-Fuller Unit Root test of P_t/D_t			KPSS Stationary test of P_t/D_t		Augmented Dickey-Fuller Unit Root test of Δd_t, r_t and $(d_t - p_t)$			KPSS Stationary test of Δd_t, r_t and $(d_t - p_t)$	
Model	no constant	constant term	constant and linear trends	constant term	constant and linear trends	no constant	constant term	constant and linear trends	constant term	constant and linear trends
Index	**PANEL A: March 1998 – December 2006**									
N-All	B	□	B	□	B	B	B	B	□	B
N-100	B	□	B	□	B	B	B	B	□	B
N-30	B	□	B	□	B	B	B	B	□	B
N-Ind	B	B	B	B	□	B	B	B	B	□
N-Serv	B	□	B	□	□	B	□	B	□	B
N-Fin	B	B	B	□	B	B	B	B	□	B
InvTrst	□	□	□	□	□	B	B	□	□	.
	PANEL B: March 1998 – October 2000									
N-All	B	B	B	B	B	B	B	B	.	.
N-100	B	B	B	B	B	B	B	B	B	.
N-30	B	B	B	B	B	B	B	B	B	.
N-Ind	B	B	B	B	□	B	B	B	B	.
N-Serv	B	B	B	B	□	B	B	B	B	.
N-Fin	B	B	B	B	B	B	B	B	B	.
InvTrst	B	□	□	□	B	B	B	B	B	B
	PANEL C: March 2001 – December 2006									
N-All	B	□	□	B	□	B	□	□	B	□
N-100	B	□	□	B	□	B	□	□	B	□
N-30	B	□	□	B	B	B	B	□	B	B
N-Ind	B	□	□	B	□	B	B	□	B	B
N-Serv	B	□	□	□	□	B	B	B	□	□
N-Fin	B	B	B	B	□	B	B	B	B	□
InvTrst	□	□	□	□	B	B	□	□	□	.

□: Evidence of the presence of the nonexistence of rational bubbles,
B: Evidence of the presence of the existence of rational bubbles.

∴ The condition of stationary Δd_t and stationary r_t does not hold.

The results got from the second subperiod are harder to be interpreted. When we implement the augmented Dickey-Fuller test to the models with a constant term, and a constant term and linear trend, the null hypothesis of unit root in price-dividend ratios are rejected for all indices except N-Fin index. However the results of the model without constant term cannot reject the null hypothesis of all indices except InvTrst. The results of the KPSS tests are also controversial in March 2001 – December 2006 subperiod. It can be seen that the null hypothesis of stationary price-divided time series is rejected for all indices except for N-Serv and InvTrst indices when we implement the model with constant term. On the other hand, when we include the linear trend, stationarity is rejected for only N-30 and InvTrst indices. As an overall result, we can say that there is the evidence of unit root and nonstationarity in all indices in at least one model. So we can conclude that there is some evidence of the existence of rational bubbles also in the second subperiod.

Lardic and Priso (2004) also implemented unit root tests to the price-dividend ratios of the stock market indices of France, Italy, UK, Belgium, Spain, Canada, Australia and Germany. The results are in favor of accepting the existence of rational bubbles for most of the countries. Our results are also parallel to their findings.

The possibility of time-varying discount rates requires another methodology of rational bubble testing for getting more dependable evidence. We also tested the loglinear model of Craine (1993) which is described in the equation (20) for this purpose. The summary statistics of the variables which are tested in loglinear methodology is presented in Table 4.

The test results of the loglinear model are summarized in Table 5 and Table 6. According to the test methodology, if the Δd_t and r_t are stationary and $(d_t - p_t)$ is unit root, then this is consistent with the presence of the rational bubbles in the market.

The augmented Dickey-Fuller test results in the full period present the evidence of the existence of rational bubbles in all indices when the model with no constant term is employed. The Δd_t and r_t series of all indices reject the null hypothesis of unit root at 1% significance level. However the null hypothesis cannot be rejected for $(d_t - p_t)$ time series of all indices, indicating the dividend returns are not stationary, therefore the rational bubbles are present in all indices. On the other hand, the models which implement constant terms, also support the existence of rational bubbles in all indices except N-Serv and InvTrst indices. When the model with constant term and linear trend is implemented, we cannot reach the evidence of rational bubbles for only InvTrst index.

The first subperiod of March 1998 – October 2000 presents strong evidence of the existence of rational bubbles in all indices when we employ augmented Dickey-Fuller test. The Δd_t and r_t series of all indices reject the null hypothesis of unit root at 1% significance level for all models. On the other hand the null hypothesis cannot be rejected for $(d_t - p_t)$ time series of all indices. However the results reject the existence of rational bubbles for N-All, N-100, N-Ind and InvTrst indices when the model with constant term, and constant term and linear trend are implemented in March 2001 – December 2006.

On the other hand, when we implement KPSS test, we get the evidence of the existence of rational bubbles in all indices except InvTrst index in full period. The presence of the rational bubbles is also supported by the KPSS tests in the first subperiod for all indices except for N-All index. The general structure of the existence of the rational bubbles continued to be accepted in the second subperiod for all indices except for N-Serv and InvTrst indices.

The results of both tests which implement different models are summarized in Table 7. As a general result, it can be seen that there is the evidence of the presence of rational bubbles in all indices in at least one model. We also have the evidence of the existence of rational bubbles in both subperiods. The evidence of the presence of rational bubbles in the indices is stronger when the loglinear model test results are analysed. This difference can be attributed to the time-varying discount rates.

6.2. Empirical Findings of Bilinear Unit Root Model

Following Charemza, Lifshits and Makarova (2005) we also implemented a two stage test procedure in testing rational bubbles by bilinear unit root methodology. In the first stage we implemented the Leybourne type augmented Dickey-Fuller unit root and KPSS stationary tests and in the second stage the unit root bilinearity is tested. We utilized Gauss 7.0 package program and Blini 1.03 software[58] for performing the Leybourne type augmented Dickey-Fuller, KPSS and Bilineer unit root tests.

Daily returns of the indices of full period (2nd March 1998-29th December 2006) and two subperiods (2nd March 1998–31st October 2000 and 1st March 2001–29th December 2006) are computed by taking the first logarithmic differences of dividend adjusted daily close values of the indices. All index returns are further adjusted according to their best convenient generalized autoregressive conditional heteroscdasticity (GARCH) models in order to eliminate the GARCH effects on the bilinear test procedure. The adjustment process is implemented as follows. In the first step, the conditional variance series of each index are generated by implementing the most significant GARCH model to the index return data. In the second step, conditional variance series are utilized for computing the correction coefficients of each index. In the third step, logarithmic returns of each index are divided into their correction factors and adjusted returns are generated. The correction factor is computed by using the following formula (see Cajueiro and Tabak, 2005 and Charemza, Lifshits and Makarova, 2005):

$$CF_t = {h_t^{1/2}} \Big/ {mean\left[h_t^{1/2}\right]} \tag{31}$$

where, CF_t is the correction factor, h_t is the conditional variance, $mean[\cdot]$ is the average operator. We utilized E-views 4 in order to estimate the GARCH models and generate the adjusted returns. The summary statistics of the adjusted returns are presented in Table 8.

The logarithmic price levels that are used to perform the linear unit root and linear stationarity tests are derived by the inclusion of the GARCH adjusted returns on the previous index values starting from the first day index value of $log100 = 4.6052$.

---

[58] See Charemza and Makarova (2002) for Bilini software.

Table 8. Summary Statistics of Daily Adjusted Returns

Index	Mean	Standard Deviation	Skewness	Kurtosis	JB	JB p-value	GARCH(p,q)*
PANEL A: 2nd March 1998 – 29th December 2006							
N-All	0.0013	0.0266	-0.2884	4.6623	281.0824	0.0000	GARCH(2,2)
N-100	0.0012	0.0276	-0.2424	4.5583	241.8154	0.0000	GARCH(2,2)
N-30	0.0012	0.0289	-0.1249	4.4226	189.4100	0.0000	GARCH(2,2)
N-Ind	0.0013	0.0241	-0.4847	4.9135	417.7506	0.0000	GARCH(3,3)
N-Serv	0.0009	0.0263	-0.2217	4.8768	337.6314	0.0000	GARCH(1,1)
N-Fin	0.0014	0.0304	-0.1367	4.6084	241.6727	0.0000	GARCH(3,3)
InvTrst	0.0010	0.02681	-0.2827	5.7055	693.6062	0.0000	GARCH(7,7)
PANEL B: 2nd March 1998 –31st October 2000							
N-All	0.0019	0.0337	-0.2122	4.0796	36.4985	0.0000	GARCH(2,2)
N-100	0.0020	0.0347	-0.1519	3.9569	27.3397	0.0000	GARCH(2,2)
N-30	0.0020	0.0366	-0.0499	3.8963	22.0631	0.0000	GARCH(1,1)
N-Ind	0.0018	0.0303	-0.4117	4.1201	52.4218	0.0000	GARCH(1,1)
N-Serv	0.0014	0.0331	0.1021	4.2310	42.2367	0.0000	GARCH(1,1)
N-Fin	0.0022	0.0377	-0.0475	3.8092	18.0074	0.0001	GARCH(3,3)
InvTrst	0.0199	0.3812	-0.3558	5.1997	144.9334	0.0000	GARCH(5,5)
PANEL C: 1st March 2001 – 29th December 2006							
N-All	0.0012	0.0225	-0.2164	4.7788	202.1985	0.0000	GARCH(4,4)
N-100	0.0012	0.0272	-0.2126	7.0920	1021.143	0.0000	GARCH(1,1)
N-30	0.0015	0.0272	-0.0635	5.0375	251.4396	0.0000	GARCH(2,2)
N-Ind	0.0011	0.0219	-0.0977	4.4181	123.6354	0.0000	GARCH(2,2)
N-Serv	0.0011	0.0255	-0.1442	4.3472	114.5117	0.0000	GARCH(2,2)
N-Fin	0.0013	0.0241	-0.0928	5.0117	246.2325	0.0000	GARCH(3,3)
InvTrst	0.0018	0.0255	-0.0193	3.8912	48.0100	0.0000	GARCH(5,5)

* The GARCH model which is estimated in order to calculate the correction factor for adjusting the returns for conditional heteroscedasticity.

Table 9. Unit Root Test Results of Logaritmic Price Levels of Indices Derived from the GARCH Adjusted Returns

Index	Leybourne type Augmented Dickey-Fuller Unit Root Test*				KPSS Stationarity Test**		
	t-value	Sign.***	Max. Augm.	Forward/ Backward	Max. t-value	Sign.***	Length of Autocorrelation
PANEL A: 2nd March 1998 – 29th December 2006							
N-All	-0.1133	¤	45	Forward	162.806	+++	0
N-100	-0.3231	¤	45	Forward	160.104	+++	0
N-30	-0.1748	¤	45	Forward	162.347	+++	0
N-Ind	0.0328	¤	45	Forward	175.559	+++	0
N-Serv	-0.2324	¤	45	Forward	102.922	+++	0
N-Fin	-0.2969	¤	45	Forward	155.144	+++	0
InvTrst	-0.7248	¤	45	Forward	168.452	+++	0
PANEL B: 2nd March 1998 –31st October 2000							
N-All	-1.0255	¤	45	Forward	51.5183	+++	0
N-100	-0.9807	¤	45	Forward	52.5159	+++	0
N-30	-0.9882	¤	45	Forward	53.5033	+++	0
N-Ind	-0.8743	¤	45	Forward	50.6005	+++	0
N-Serv	-0.9990	¤	45	Backward	47.7679	+++	0
N-Fin	-1.0422	¤	45	Forward	54.9112	+++	0
InvTrst	-0.6661	¤	45	Forward	48.5948	+++	0
PANEL C: 1st March 2001 – 29th December 2006							
N-All	-0.3308	¤	45	Backward	139.9020	+++	0
N-100	-0.8745	¤	45	Backward	136.7002	+++	0
N-30	-0.0081	¤	45	Forward	129.2950	+++	0
N-Ind	0.2845	¤	45	Forward	127.2264	+++	0
N-Serv	-0.3977	¤	45	Forward	132.5169	+++	0
N-Fin	-0.6577	¤	45	Backward	137.6130	+++	0
InvTrst	-0.0076	¤	45	Forward	139.7303	+++	0

* Null hypothesis of augmented Dickey-Fuller unit root test: Ho = variable is unit root.

** Null hypothesis of KPSS stationarity test: Ho= variable is stationary.

*** ¤ the null hypothesis cannot be rejected, +++: the null hypothesis is rejected at 1% significance level.

The null hypothesis of the Leybourne type augmented Dickey-Fuller test is the variable is unit root. However the null hypothesis of the KPSS test is the variable is stationary. Charemza and Syczewska (1998) state that the critical values of each test for testing their null hypotheses are not sufficient to perform a joint test for investigating the stationarity and calculated the required critical values for a joint test. We also implemented these critical values in the first stage of the bilinear tests. The test results are presented in Table 9.

The summarized results of Leybourne type augmented Dickey-Fuller test in Table 9 show that the null hypothesis of unit root cannot be rejected for all indices in all periods. The unit root feature of indices is also supported by the results of KPSS test. According to the test results, the null hypothesis of stationarity is rejected at 1% significance level for all indices in the full period and both subperiods.

The strong evidence about the nonstationarity of all index returns provided from two linear unit root tests satisfy the initial condition for testing the bilinear structure of the unit root. In the second stage of the test, the significance of the b coefficient, the bilinear term, in equation (26) is tested. The results of the bilinear unit root test are summarized in Table 10.

The bilinear test results presented in Panel A of Table 10 show that the null hypothesis of insignificant bilinear coefficient or, no rational bubble is rejected for all indices. These results can be interpreted as important evidence in favor of the existence of the rational bubbles in ISE. The test results also show that the bilinear coefficients of ISE National-All, ISE National-100, ISE National-30, ISE National-Industrials, ISE National-Financials and ISE Investment Trusts Indices are statistically significant at 1% level in the full period. However the test results of ISE National-Services reject the insignificant bilinear coefficient at 5% level.

The results of the subperiods are different than the full period. The test results of the first subperiod 2nd March 1998 –31st October 2000 are presented in the Panel B of Table 10. The evidence of the presence of rational bubbles can be seen in this pre financial crisis period when we analyse ISE National-All Shares, ISE National-100 and ISE National-30 indices. The null hypothesis of no bilinear term is rejected at 5% significant level for these indices. This can be interpreted as the evidence of the existence of rational bubbles in ISE in this subperiod. The test results of ISE National-Industrials, ISE National-Financials and ISE Investment Trusts also support this evidence. However the result of ISE National-Services index is controversial. According to the test results we cannot reject the insignificance of the bilinear term for the indices, except ISE National-Services index.

The analysis of the 1st March 2001–29th December 2006 period also presents different results than the results of the full period. In this subperiod, the indices which represent the general market, namely ISE National-All Shares, ISE National-100 and ISE National-30 indices, have statistically significant bilinear terms. Thus we can say that the unit root bilinearity is a general characteristic for the whole market and the rational bubbles exist in all three periods. However in the second subperiod, we cannot see the evidence of the presence of rational bubbles in ISE National-Industrials, ISE National-Services and ISE Investment Trusts indices.

Table 10. Bilinear Test Results of GARCH Adjusted Returns

Index	B-max	Significance[a]	Max. Aug.
PANEL A: 2nd March 1998 – 29th December 2006			
N-All	2.9986	+++	5
N-100	2.9149	+++	5
N-30	2.5543	+++	5
N-Ind	3.0439	+++	5
N-Serv	1.8430	++	1
N-Fin	2.4523	+++	5
InvTrst	2.5658	+++	3
PANEL B: 2nd March 1998 –31st October 2000			
N-All	2.2092	++	1
N-100	1.9246	++	4
N-30	1.9729	++	4
N-Ind	2.6742	+++	1
N-Serv	0.5723	¤	6
N-Fin	1.5310	+	4
InvTrst	1.6042	+	3
PANEL C: 1st March 2001 – 29th December 2006			
N-All	2.1000	++	4
N-100	1.9698	++	1
N-30	1.9165	++	1
N-Ind	-1.0429	¤	10
N-Serv	1.0772	¤	1
N-Fin	1.4874	+	4
InvTrst	0.9207	¤	6

[a] +++: Significant at 1% level,
++: Significant at 5% level,
+: Significant at 10% level,
¤: Statistically insignificant.

As an overall result, we found the evidence of the existence of rational bubbles in the indices which have great representative features in ISE, such as ISE National-All Shares, ISE National-100 and ISE National-30 indices in all sample periods. These results are parallel to the previous findings for different stock markets. For example Capelle-Blanchard and Raymond (2004) analysed the presence of bubbles in French, German, Japanese, UK and US stock markets from 1973 to 2002. They also could not reject the existence of bubbles in these markets. Similar results also come from the analysis of Lardic and Priso (2004) in France, Italy, UK, Belgium, Spain, Canada, Australia and Germany stock markets. The results are also in favor of accepting the existence of rational bubbles for most of the countries.

7. CONCLUSION

The detection of the divergence between fundamental value and market prices has important aspects on the investors who are trading in the stock market and as well as the whole economy. The importance of the possible presence of the bubbles in stock prices attracted the academic interest in this area and result in a great number of research with different bubble test methods which are still continuously developing.

We investigated the presence of rational bubbles in ISE between 1998-2006 by implementing linear and nonlinear unit root tests to the monthly and daily data of ISE National-All, ISE National-100, ISE National-30, ISE National-Industrials, ISE National-Services, ISE National-Financials and ISE Investment Trusts indices.

Considering the possible effects of the financial crises in the Turkish economy in November 2000 and February 2001, we decided to exclude these periods from our analysis. Thus we implemented our analysis to the full period of March 1998-November 2006 as well as two subperiods of March 1998-October 2000 and March 2001-December 2006.

In the first stage, we applied linear unit root test procedures to ISE monthly data. The first test is based on implementing augmented Dickey-Fuller unit root and KPSS stationarity tests to the price-dividend ratio of the indices which are stated above. The results are in favor of the presence of rational bubbles in all indices for at least one model in the full period and both subperiods. Considering the weakness of this classical test, a further test which enables time-varying discount rates is implemented to the data. The augmented Dickey-Fuller and KPSS test results of the loglinear model also support the previous results. We reach the track of the existence of rational bubbles in all indices when we apply augmented Dickey-Fuller test, however the results of KPSS tests are in favor of the nonexistence of rational bubbles in N-Serv index in the full period and the second subperiod. The potential weaknesses of linear test methods as well as the advantages of nonlinear models motivated to use the bilinear test method in detecting rational bubbles in ISE as a second stage.

When the test results of nonlinear models are considered, the evidence is in favor of the existence of rational bubbles in all indices in the full period. But the results of the subperiods are contradictory for some indices. In the first and second subperiods we cannot accept unit root bilinearity for ISE-National Services index. The results also reject the significance of the bilinear term for ISE-National Industrials and ISE Investment Trusts indices in the second subperiod.

Comparing this evidence with the evidence of linear tests, we are inclined to favor nonlinear unit root test results in this research. Because there is an important number of previous evidence of nonlinear structure of financial time series and the bilinear test procedure is considered to be robust in capturing the sudden and unexpected changes in the time series. Thus we can conclude that as a general structure, the market prices diverge from the fundamental values and so rational bubbles present in ISE but this structure can change according to the sample periods and sector indices that are under the investigation.

REFERENCES

Abreu, B.D. & Brunnermeier, M.K. (2003). Bubbles and Crashes, *Econometrica,* 71, 173-204.

Blanchard, O.J. & Watson M. (1982). Bubbles, Rational Expectations and Financial Markets. In P. Watchtel (Ed.), *Crises in the Economic and the Financial Structure,* (295-315) Lexington: Lexington Books.

Bohl, M. T. (2003). Periodically Collapsing Bubbles in the US Stock Market?, *International Review of Economics and Finance,* 2, 385-397.

Boucher, C. (2003). Testing for Rational Bubbles with Time Varying Risk Premium and Non-Linear Cointegration: Evidence from the US and French Stock Markets, www.univ-orleans.fr/deg/GDRecomofi/ Activ/boucher_nice.pdf, 20.08.2006.

Brooks, C. & Katsaris, A. (2003). Rational Speculative Bubbles: An Empirical Investigation of the London Stock Exchange, *Bulletin of Economic Research,* 55, 319-346.

Brunnermeier, M. K. (2001). *Asset Pricing Under Asymmetric Information: Bubbles, Crashes, Technical Analysis, and Herding,* Oxford: Oxford University Press.

Cajueiro, D.O. & Benjamin, M.T. (2005). Testing for Rational Bubbles in Banking Indices, Phsyca, 366, 365-376.

Campbell, J. & Shiller, R. J. (1987). Cointegration and Tests of Present Value Models, *Journal of Political Economy,* 95, 1062-1088.

Campbell, J. & Shiller, R. J. (1988). The Dividend Price Ratio and Expectations of Future Dividends and Discount Factors, *Review of Financial Studies,* 1, 195-227.

Campbell, J. Y., Lo A. W. & MacKinlay A. C. (1997). *The Econometrics of Financial Markets,* Princeton, NJ: Princeton University Press.

Capelle-Blanchard, G. & Raymond, H. (2004). Empirical Evidence on Periodically Collapsing Stock Price Bubbles, *Applied Economic Letters,* 11, 61-69.

Chang, T., Chang, H., Chu H. & Su, C. (2005). Does Rational Bubbles Exist in the Taiwan Stock Market? Evidence from a Nonparametric Cointegration Test, *Economics Bulletin,* 3, 1-9.

Charemza, W. W. & Syczewska, E. M. (1998). Joint Application of the Dickey-Fuller and KPSS Tests, *Economic Letters,* 61, 17-21.

Charemza, W.W. & Makarova, S. (2002). *Bilini Version 1.03: Collection of GAUSS Procedures for Linear and Bilinear Unit root Process,* University of Leicester, Mimeo.

Charemza, W. W., Lifshits, M. & Makarova, S. (2005). Conditional Testing for Unit root Bilinearity in Financial Time Series: Some Theoretical and Empirical Results, *Journal of Economic Dynamics and Control,* 29, 63-93.

Craine, R. (1993). Rational Bubbles: A Test, *Journal of Economic Dynamics and Control,* 17, 829-846.

Cunado, J., Gil-Alana, L. A. & de Gracia F. P. (2005). A Test for Rational Bubbles in the NASDAQ Stock Index: A Fractionally Integrated Approach, *Journal of Banking and Finance,* 29, 2633-2654.

De Bondt, W.F.M. & Thaler, R. H. (1985). Does the Stock Market Overreact?, *Journal of Finance,* 40, 793-803.

De Long J., Schleifer, A., Summers, L. & Waldmann J. (1990a). Positive Feedback Investment Strategies and Destabilizing Rational Speculation, *Journal of Finance, 45,* 379-396.

De Long J., Schleifer, A., Summers, L. & Waldmann, J. (1990b). Noise Trader Risk in Financial Markets, *Journal of Political Economy,* 98, 703-738.

De Long J., Schleifer, A., Summers, L. & Waldmann, J. (1991). The Survival of Noise Traders in Financial Markets, *Journal of Business,* 64, 1-19.

Dezhbakhsh and Demirguc-Kunt (1990). On the presence of Speculative Bubbles in Stock Prices, *Journal of Financial and Quantitative Analysis,* 25, 101-112.

Diba, B.T. (1990). Bubbles and Stock-Price Volatility. In Dwyer, G.P.Jr & Hafer, R.W. (Eds.) *Stock Market: Bubbles, Volatility and Chaos,* Boston: Kluwer.

Diba, B. T. & Grossman, H. I. (1988a). Explosive Rational Bubbles in Stock Prices?, *American Economic Review,* 78, 520-530.

Diba, B. T. & Grossman, H. I. (1988b). The Theory of Rational Bubbles in Stock Prices, *The Economic Journal,* 98, 746-754.

Evans, G. W. (1991). Pitfalls in Testing for Explosive Bubbles in Asset Prices, *American Economic Review,* 81, 922-930.

Flood, R. P. & Garber, P. (1980). Market Fundamentals versus Price Level Bubbles: The First Tests, *Journal of Political Economy,* 88, 745-770.

Froot, K. & Obstfeld, M. (1991). Intrinsic Bubbles: The Case of Stock Prices, *American Economic Review,* 81, 1189-1214.

Fukuta, Y. (2002). A Test for Rational Bubbles in Stock Bubbles, *Empirical Economics,* 27, 587-600.

Grossman, S. & Shiller, R. (1981). The Determinants of the Variability of Stock Market Prices, *American Economic Review,* 71, 222-227.

Gurkaynak, R. S. (2005). *Econometric Tests of Asset Price Bubbles: Taking Stock,* FEDS Working Paper No. 2005-04.

Hardouvelis, G. A. (1988). Evidence on Stock Market Speculative Bubbles: Japan, The United States and Great Britain, *Federal Reserve Bank of New York Quarterly Review,* Summer, 4- 16.

Hart, O. D. & Kreps, D. M. (1986). Price Destabilizing Speculation, *Journal of Political Economy,* 94, 927-952.

Horvath, M. T. & Watson, M. W. (1995). Testing for Cointegration When Some of the Cointegrating Vectors are Known, *Econometric Theory,* 11, 952-984.

Ikeda, S. & Shibata, A. (1992). Fundamentals-Dependent Bubbles in Stock Prices, *Journal of Monetary Economics,* 16, 353-373.

Kleidon, A. W. (1986). Variance Bounds Tests and Stock Price Valuation Models, *Journal of Political Economy,* 94, 953-1001.

Koustas, Z. & Serletis, A. (2005). Rational Bubbles or Persistent Deviations from Market Fundamentals, *Journal of Banking and Finance,* 29, 2523-2539.

Lamont, O. (1998). Earnings and Expected Returns, *Journal of Finance,* 53, 1563-1587.

Lardic, S. & Priso, A. M. (2004). Rational Stock Price Bubbles: Is There any International Evidence?, *Finance India,* 18, 559-576.

Larsen, E.S. (1997). Theories and Tests for Bubbles, Norges Universitetet, Tromso, www.nfh.uit.no/dok/bubbles%20small.pdf, 20/08/2006.

Lucas, R.E. Jr. (1978). Asset Prices in an Exchange Economy, *Econometrica,* 46, 1429-1445.

Peel, D. & Davidson, J. (1998). A Nonlinear Error Correction Mechanism Based on the Bilinear Model, *Economic Letters*, 58, 165-170.

Rappoport, P. & White, E. N. (1993). Was There a Bubble in the 1929 Stock Market?, *The Journal of Economic History,* 53, 549-574.

Rosser, J.B.Jr. (2000). *From Catastrope to Chaos: A General Theory of Economic Discontinuities* (2nd edition). Kluwer Academic.

Siegel, J. J. (2003). What is an Asset Price Bubble? An Operational Definition, *European Financial Management,* 9, 11-24.

Shiller, R. J. (1981). Do Stock Prices Move too much to be Justified by Subsequent Changes in Dividents?, *American Economic Review,* 71, 421-436.

Shleifer, A. & Summers, L. H. (1990). The Noise Trader Approach to Finance, *The Journal of Economic Perspectives,* 4, 19-34.

Taipalus, K. (2006). *Bubbles in the Finnish and US Equities Markets,* Helsinki: Bank of Finland Studies.

Timmermann, A. (1995). Cointegration Tests of Present Value Models with a Time-Varying Discount Factor, *Journal of Applied Econometrics,* 10, 17-31.

Tirole, J. (1982). On the Possibility of Speculation Under Rational Expectations, Econometrica, 50, 1163-1181.

Tirole, J. (1985). *Asset Bubbles and Overlapping Generations, Econometrica,* 53, 1499-1527.

Van Norden, S. & Schaller, R. (1993). The Predictability of Stock Market Regime: Evidence from the Toronto Stock Exchange, *Review of Economics and Statistics,* 75, 505-510.

West, K. D. (1987). A Specification Test for Speculative Bubbles, *Quarterly Journal of Economics,* 102, 553-580.

In: Economics of Emerging Markets
Editor: Lado Beridze, pp. 203-224

ISBN: 978-1-60021-850-7
© 2008 Nova Science Publishers, Inc.

Chapter 8

ANALYST ORIGIN AND THEIR FORECASTING QUALITY ON THE LATIN AMERICAN STOCK MARKETS[*]

Jean-François Bacmann[†]

RMF Investment Management, Quantitative Analysis, Huobstrasse 16,
CH-8808 Pfäffikon SZ.

Guido Bolliger[‡]

Olympia Capital Management, 21-25 Rue Balzac, F-75008 Paris, France

ABSTRACT

This paper investigates the relative performance of local, foreign, and expatriate financial analysts on Latin American emerging markets. We measure analysts' relative performance with three dimensions: (1) forecast timeliness, (2) forecast accuracy and (3) impact of forecast revisions on security prices. Our main findings can be summarized as follows. Firstly, there is a strong evidence that foreign analysts supply timelier forecasts than their peers. Secondly, analyst working for foreign brokerage houses (i.e. expatriate and foreign ones) produce less biased forecasts than local analysts. Finally, after controlling for analysts' timeliness, we find that foreign financial analysts' upward revisions have a greater impact on stock returns than both followers and local lead analysts forecast revisions. Overall, our results suggest that investors should better rely on the research produced by analysts working for foreign brokerage houses when they invest in Latin American emerging markets.

---

[*] The first version of this article was entitled "Who are the best? Local versus foreign analysts on Latin American stock markets". It was written at a time when Bacmann was affiliated to the University of Neuchâtel and Bolliger to the University of Neuchâtel as well as the International Center FAME. The views expressed in this article are individual views of the authors and do not necessarily reflect their employers' opinions.

[†] Phone: ++4155 417 77 10 . Fax: ++4155 417 77 11. Email: Jean-Francois.Bacmann@rmf.ch
[‡] Phone: ++331 4953 7426. Fax: ++331 4256 7009. Email: guidobolliger@olympiagroup.com

Keywords: analysts' forecasts, home bias, international diversification, emerging markets, herding behaviour.
JEL Classification: G14, G15, G24

1. INTRODUCTION

Past research suggests that geographic proximity is related to information flow. However, the empirical evidence on the impact of geographic proximity on the quality of investors' information is mixed. Brennan and Cao (1997) report that US investors are less informed about foreign markets conditions than are local investors. Kang and Stulz (1997) find no evidence that foreign investors outperform in Japan. Using US mutual fund holdings, Coval and Moskowitz (2001) show that investors located near potential investments have significant informational advantages relative to the rest of the market. According to Choe et al. (2000), foreign investors on the Korean market are disadvantaged relative to domestic individual investors. Inversely, Seasholes (2000) reports that foreigners act like informed traders in emerging markets. He finds that foreign investors profits come from trading stocks of large firms with low leverage and liquid shares. Similarly, Grinblatt and Keloharju (2000) exihibit evidence that foreign investors on the Finnish stock market generate superior performance than local investors. It is likely that the previous mixed findings are driven by the information available to the investors. This is why our research does not focus on the relative performance of investors but on the relative performance of analysts located at the upstream side of them.

Research devoted to financial analyst forecast accuracy documents that some groups of analysts display a better forecasting ability than others. Stickel (1992) finds that Institutional Investor All-American analysts provide more accurate earnings forecasts and tend to revise their forecasts more frequently than other analysts. Clement (1999) investigates the origin of financial analysts differential accuracy. He documents a negative relationship between financial analysts relative accuracy and the complexity of their stock portfolio. On the other hand, he shows that analysts' performance improves with their age and that analysts working for big research houses with more resources available, outperform their peers. Agency problems such as corporate financing business conflicts, have also an impact on financial analysts' performance. Lin and McNichols (1999) and Michaely and Womack (1999) show that analysts whose employer is affiliated with a company through an underwriting relationship issue more optimistic forecasts than unaffiliated analysts.

The present paper is directly related to these two streams of research. The objective is to investigate the relative performance of local, expatriate, and foreign analysts on Latin American emerging markets. Local analysts are those who work for local research firms. Expatriate analysts work for foreign brokerage houses but are located in the country. Finally, foreign analysts work for foreign research firms with no local presence. Ex-ante, three main reasons may be at the origin of differential performance across the three groups of analysts: geographical distance, agency problems, and available resources.

Residence may give local and expatriate analysts several advantages compared to foreign ones. First, they may have a better knowledge of the local economy. Local economy has been shown to have a significant impact on emerging stock markets ;see Harvey (1995). Second, they may be more familiar with the institutional context in which the companies evolve.

Institutional factors have a significant influence on the properties of financial analyst forecasts ; see Hope (2003). Third, they may have a better knowledge of the local culture. Finally, they may have a better human network in the country. This network may give them access to relevant private information. On the other hand, being closer from the analyzed firms, they may be more subject to agency problems such as conflict of interests. Foreign and expatriate analysts usually work for important international research firms. These big research firms have more resources available, they have the financial capacity to attract the best analysts, and their international expertise may help them to better anticipate international macro-economic fluctuations. Overall, if geographic proximity improves the quality of the information available to analysts, local and expatriate analysts should outperform their foreign counterparts. On the other hand, if the quantity of resources available to the analysts, their reputations as well as their expertise are the key determinant of their performance, foreign and expatriate analysts should outperform local ones. Finally, if conflict of interests, caused by tighter investment banking relationships between firms and banks having a local representation, have an important influence on the quality of financial analysts' output in these markets, foreign analysts should outperform both local and expatriate ones.

We conduct our investigation on Latin American markets for two reasons. First, due to geographical considerations, Latin American markets have always presented a great interest for US institutional investors. As a consequence, they create an important demand for financial analysts services on these markets. Second, as underlined by Choe et al. (2002), private information is likely to be more important on emerging stock markets than on developed ones.

We measure analysts' relative performance with three dimensions: (1) forecast timeliness, (2) forecast accuracy and (3) impact of forecast revisions on security prices. Our main findings can be summarized as follows. Firstly, there is a strong evidence that foreign analysts supply timelier forecasts than their peers. In particular, we detect a greater number of leaders among foreign analysts than among analysts with local residence. This finding suggests that both local and expatriate analysts have a tendency to revise their earnings forecasts in order to accommodate the opinions of foreign analysts. Secondly, analyst working for foreign brokerage houses (i.e. expatriate and foreign ones) produce less biased forecasts than local analysts. Lead foreign and expatriate analysts produce much more accurate forecasts than other analysts suggesting that leaders have an important informational advantage over other analysts. Finally, after controlling for analysts' timeliness, we find that foreign financial analysts' upward revisions have a greater impact on stock returns than both followers and local lead analysts forecast revisions. This suggests that the market considers forecast revisions provided by foreign leader analysts as being more informative than the revisions provided by their local counterparts.

Our research has important practical implication: investors should better rely on the research produced by analysts working for foreign brokerage houses when they invest in Latin American emerging markets. Moreover, our paper complements previous research in three ways. Firstly, we contribute to the literature on the importance of geography in economics by showing that location has an impact on the quality of the information provided by analysts. If foreign (local) investors rely mostly on foreign and expatriate (local) analysts' research in order to take their investment decisions, our results may explain the superior performance of foreign investors on some markets; see Seasholes (2000) and Grinblatt and Keloharju (2000). Secondly, by showing that analysts' location/affiliation has a significant impact on their forecast accuracy, we contribute to the large amount of literature which investigates the origins of financial analysts forecasts' bias. Thirdly, we complement, and somehow contradict, the recent research which also investigate the impact of analysts' location on forecast accuracy. Malloy (2003), Chang (2003), and Orport (2002) document that analysts located closer to the companies they follow make more accurate forecasts than their more distant counterparts. As underlined by Kini et al. (2003), the almost opposite conclusion drawn from our investigation may be due to differences in the industrial structure of the countries examined in these different papers. If, in Latin America, a good understanding of the sectors is a major determinant of forecast accuracy, a foreign (and to some extent an expatriate) analyst who focuses on a sector in multiple countries may have an advantage over a local analyst who focuses on multiple local firms across multiple sectors. Of course, the reverse may be true for other markets. This shows that the conclusions drawn from these studies may not be generalized to all countries.

The paper proceeds as follows. Section 2 presents the data used in this study. Section 3 investigates the relative timeliness of financial analysts. Section 4 tests for differences in forecast accuracy. Section 5 examines the impact of forecast revisions on security prices; and Section 6 concludes.

2. DATA AND OVERVIEW STATISTICS

The analysts' forecasts[1] are provided by Institutional Broker Estimate System (I/B/E/S) for 7 Latin American emerging markets: Argentina, Brazil, Chile, Colombia, Mexico, Peru and Venezuela. One year earning per share (EPS) forecasts are used from 1993 to 1999. We use the Nelson Directory of Investment Research to classify financial analysts. The Nelson Directory of Investment Research provides the name and the coordinates of each analyst that follows a particular company. Financial analysts who work for local brokerage houses are classified as local, those who work for foreign brokerage houses with residence in the country as classified as expatriate, and those who work for foreign brokerage houses without residence in the country are classified as foreign. Stock prices are extracted from Datastream. To be included in the sample, a forecast should meet the following conditions:

1. Realized EPS has to figure in the I/B/E/S Actual File.
2. The forecast must be issued between the end of previous fiscal year and current year earning reporting date.
3. The forecast must be issued by an analyst listed in the Nelson Directory of Investment Research.
4. The company for which the forecast is issued must be followed by at least 3 analysts of each group during a given year.

The last condition restricts the sample to big and medium-sized companies. The final sample includes 61'209 EPS forecasts. Table 1 shows that local analysts have produced 59% more forecasts than their foreign counterparts and more than twice much forecasts than expatriate analysts. The number of analysts and brokerage houses active on Latin American markets has sensibly increased between 1993 and 1999. This is due to the increasing coverage of the I/B/E/S database but also to the increasing attractiveness of these markets for foreign investors.

Table 1. Summary statistics by year

Year	No. Forecasts			No. Analysts			No. Brokers			No. Stocks
	Local	Foreign	Expatriate	Local	Foreign	Expatriate	Local	Foreign	Expatriate	
1993	1670	783	432	74	56	41	35	18	10	84
1994	4937	2345	2263	114	84	87	49	36	16	208
1995	4999	2526	1989	236	123	122	51	32	20	200
1996	4764	2864	1899	257	163	147	57	37	17	180
1997	5229	3888	2056	245	238	170	56	33	16	212
1998	4508	3694	2141	244	232	175	50	24	15	205
1999	3674	2624	1924	182	176	148	41	19	11	170
Total	29781	18724	12704	719	584	365	93	61	27	351

This table reports yearly statistics for the data. No. Forecasts represents the number of annual earnings forecasts made each year. No. Analyst represents the number of analysts who produced a forecast during the fiscal year t. The total number of analysts who produced an earning forecast during the entire period is indicated in the last row. No. Brokers represents the number of banks (or brokerage companies) for which analysts work each year. The total number of brokers identified during the entire period is indicated in the last row. No. Stocks is the number of firms in the sample. The total number of firms for which forecasts were produced during the period is indicated in the last row.

Table 2. Summary statistics by country

Country	No. Forecasts			No. Analysts			No. Brokers			No. Stocks
	Local	Foreign	Expatriate	Local	Foreign	Expatriate	Local	Foreign	Expatriate	
Argentina	5114	2685	1835	135	215	86	22	36	9	45
Brazil	11897	7238	6349	293	244	191	30	31	19	160
Chile	2224	1530	697	67	150	39	11	25	4	29
Colombia	160	364	174	6	43	15	2	17	2	11
Mexico	12905	7700	3753	242	286	128	21	35	12	82
Peru	651	927	226	27	111	27	7	32	3	17
Venezuela	110	279	97	1	66	15	1	18	2	7

This table reports statistics by country and by industry. *No. Forecasts* represents the number of annual earnings forecasts made each year. *No. Analyst* represents the number of analysts who produced a forecast during the fiscal year *t*. *No. Brokers* represents the number of banks (or brokerage companies) for which analysts work in each country. *No. Stocks* is the number of firms in the sample.

---

[1] Note that we make no distinction between individual analysts and team of analysts.

Table 2 shows that most of the forecasts (81%) are concentrated on Brazil and Mexico. In addition, in each country excepting Brazil, foreign analysts tend to be more numerous than local and expatriate ones. However, from Table 1, we see that this finding is reversed at the aggregated level: local analysts are more numerous than foreign ones and the difference between foreign and expatriate is smaller. Thus, foreign analysts tend to follow several different markets while local and expatriate analysts are more focused on specific markets.

Non-tabulated results indicate that the average number of analysts employed by foreign brokerage houses amounts to 7.9 while it amounts to 5.5 for local ones suggesting that, on average, foreign brokerage houses are bigger than local ones. Our sample contains 91 companies out of 351 that have quoted American Depositary Receipts (ADR). Lang et al. (2002) show that non-U.S. companies listed on U.S. exchanges have richer informational environment than other non-U.S. firms. Therefore, we will control for ADR listing in the subsequent analysis.

Table 3 shows that expatriate analysts are the less active ones. On average, they produce a forecast every 77 day while their foreign and local peers do it every 73, respectively 71 day. Similarly, expatriate analysts revise less frequently than their counterparts: on average 1.33 times per firm each year against 1.92 times for foreigners and 2.45 for locals. Although the frequency of forecast revisions gives an insight on the activity of financial analysts, this does not indicate that more active analysts have advantages in collecting and processing information. They may simply change their mind several times to accommodate the opinions of others. Therefore, in the subsequent section, we propose to measure analysts' relative activity with their timeliness.

Table 3. Frequency of forecast issuance and revision

Panel A: number of calendar days elapsed between forecasts			
	Mean	Min	Median	Max
Local analysts	70.63	1.00	59.00	344.00
Foreign analysts	73.00	1.00	59.75	372.00
Expatriate analysts	77.29	1.00	65.75	362.00
Panel B: number of revisions per analyst			
	Mean	Min	Median	Max
Local analysts	2.45	0.00	1.00	50.00
Foreign analysts	1.92	0.00	1.00	19.00
Expatriate analysts	1.33	0.00	1.00	11.00

This table reports summary statistics on financial analysts' activity. Panel A presents statistics about the number of calendar days that separate two consecutive forecasts by analyst for a particular company in a given year. Panel B reports statistics on the number of revisions by analyst for a particular company in a given year.

3. ANALYSTS' TIMELINESS

3.1. Empirical Design

Cooper, Day and Lewis (2001, thereafter CDL) show that timely analysts' (leaders) forecast revisions provide greater value to investors than other analysts' (followers) forecasts. They argue that timeliness is an important and necessary indicator of financial analysts' relative performance. Using forecast accuracy alone to assess the relative performance of financial analysts can lead to misclassification errors because less informed analysts can improve the accuracy of their forecasts by simply mimicking timely skilled analysts.

The leader to follower ratio (*LFR*) developed by CDL is used to distinguish leaders from followers.[2] This ratio is computed for each analyst/firm/year unit. It is distributed as $F_{(2KH, 2KH)}$,[3] where H is the number of other analysts following a particular firm in a given year and K is the total number of forecasts provided by the analyst during the year for that firm. Similar to CDL, analysts having *LFR* significantly greater than 1 at the 10% level are considered as leaders. Moreover, each analyst is required to produce at least 3 forecasts per year for the firm under consideration. As mentioned CDL, this restriction minimizes the possibility for an analyst to be classified as leader thanks to a single lucky forecast.

In order to test whether a group (local or foreign) tends to lead the other one, we compare the number of local leaders to the foreign ones. However, since the total number of analysts is different between the 2 groups, such a comparison is not directly possible. Thus, the proportion of leaders in a given group g, L_g, is compared to the proportion of analysts in group g in the sample, P_g. In order to determine whether a group of analysts has significantly more (less) leaders than its proportion in the population suggests, we test the following hypothesis:

$$H_0 : L_g = P_g \text{ vs } H_1 : L_g \neq P_g.$$

Consequently, the following normally distributed statistic is computed:

$$Time_g = \frac{\left(L_g - P_g\right)}{\sqrt{P_g \cdot \left(1 - P_g\right)}} \cdot \sqrt{N},$$

where:

$$L_g = \frac{Number\ of\ leaders\ in\ group\ g}{Total\ number\ of\ leaders},$$

---

[2] A precise description of the *LFR* computation methodology is given in the Appendix.
[3] CDL derive the distribution of the *LFR* by assuming that the time elapsed between the arrival of two subsequent revisions follows an exponential distribution.

$$P_g = \frac{Number\ of\ analysts\ from\ group\ g}{N},$$

$N = Total\ number\ of\ analysts$.

Table 4. Financial analysts' timeliness

Panel A: LFR for Latin America						
	Analysts' origin	No. observations	No. leaders	% leaders	% observations	Difference
		N		L_g	P_g	
Latin America	Local	5599	621	47.7	49.6	-1.9***
	Foreign	3457	444	34.1	30.6	3.5***
	Expatriate	2226	236	18.1	19.7	-1.6***
Panel B: LFR by country						
Country	Analysts' origin	No. observations	No. leaders	% leaders	% observations	Difference
		N		L_g	P_g	
Argentina	Local	938	90	45.9	53.6	-7.7***
	Foreign	476	62	31.6	27.2	4.4***
	Expatriate	337	44	22.4	19.2	3.2***
Brazil	Local	1948	231	44.6	46.5	-1.9***
	Foreign	1247	176	34.0	29.7	4.2***
	Expatriate	998	111	21.4	23.8	-2.4***
Chile	Local	315	26	43.3	48.1	-4.8***
	Foreign	246	29	48.3	37.6	10.8***
	Expatriate	94	5	8.3	14.4	-6.0***
Colombia	Local	4	0	0.0	20.0	-20.0***
	Foreign	12	3	100.0	60.0	40.0***
	Expatriate	4	0	0.0	20.0	-20.0***
Mexico	Local	2323	264	52.6	52.0	0.6
	Foreign	1388	163	32.5	31.0	1.4***
	Expatriate	760	75	14.9	17.0	-2.1***
Peru	Local	65	10	58.8	44.8	14.0***
	Foreign	58	6	35.3	40.0	-4.7
	Expatriate	22	1	5.9	15.2	-9.3***
Venezuela	Local	6	0	0.0	12.8	-12.8***
	Foreign	30	5	100.0	63.8	36.2***
	Expatriate	11	0	0.0	23.4	-23.4***

This table reports the number of analysts identified as leaders as well as the test of the null hypothesis, which is stating that the proportion of leaders in a given group equals the proportion of analysts from the given group in the total sample. The last column represents the difference between the percentage of leaders in a given group, L_g, and the percentage of analysts from the given group, P_g. The significance of this difference is determined by the following normally distributed

statistic: $Time_g = \dfrac{\left(L_g - P_g\right)}{\sqrt{P_g \cdot \left(1 - P_g\right)}} \cdot \sqrt{N}$. Panel A reports results for all Latin American markets. Panel

B reports results by country

***, **, * denote significance at the 1%, 5%, and 10% levels, respectively.

3.2. Results for Analysts' Timeliness

According to the LFR statistic, 1301 leaders out of 11282 observations are detected. Table 4 shows the breakdown of the leaders according to their origin. The proportions of local and expatriate analysts within the leaders are significantly smaller than their proportions within the full sample.[4] On the other hand, there are more leaders among foreign analysts than their proportion in the sample would suggest. These results indicate that, on average, foreign analysts lead while local and expatriate analysts herd. Analysts with local residence have a tendency to issue their forecasts shortly after foreign analysts and their revisions do not induce other analysts to revise their own forecasts.

Panel B of Table 4 shows the breakdown of the leaders across the different countries. The individual country results are consistent with those obtained for Latin America. The exceptions are Brazil and Peru. In Brazil, the proportion of expatriate analysts identified as leaders is significantly more important than their proportion in the population. The same is true for local analysts in Peru.

In summary, the above results indicate that foreign analysts have a greater tendency to lead than analysts with local residence. This holds at the aggregated level as well as for most of the individual stock markets. The implications of these findings in terms of forecast accuracy and earnings forecasts' informativeness are investigated in the following two sections.

4. FORECAST ACCURACY

4.1. Empirical Design

Forecast accuracy is the most widely used measure of the quality of an analyst's research. Indeed, the more accurate earnings forecast is, the more accurate the price extracted from any valuation model will be. Forecast accuracy is measured using the average percentage forecast error adjusted for the horizon bias.[5] Analyst i's percentage forecast error at date t is,

$$FE_{ijt} = \frac{FEPS_{it} - EPS}{|EPS|},$$

where:

$FEPS_{it} = $ analyst i's EPS forecast for company j at date t,

$EPS = $ reported earning per share at the end of the forecast horizon.

In order to correct for the horizon bias, CDL forecast accuracy regression is used. Compared to the matching forecasts methodology used by Stickel (1992), this operation is

---

[4] The inverse is automatically true for foreign leaders.
[5] Prior studies such as Kang, O'Brien and Sivaramkarishnan (1994) show that forecast bias increases with forecast horizon.

much less data-consuming and better suited for our study. Each FE_{ijt} is regressed on the length of time from forecast release to earning announcement date. The residuals from this regression are used to measure forecast accuracy. Formally,

$$FE_{ijt} = \alpha + \beta \cdot T + \varepsilon_{ijt},$$ (1)

where:

$T =$ number of days until the earnings announcement date,

$\varepsilon_{ijt} =$ residual forecast error for analyst i on firm j at date t.

The relative accuracy of each group of analysts is computed in three successive steps. First, for a given firm, the average residual forecast error is computed for each analyst,

$$MFE_{ij} = \sum_{t=1}^{K} |\varepsilon_{ijt}| / K,$$

where:

$MFE_{ij} =$ mean forecast error by analyst i for firm j,

$K =$ number of forecasts issued by analyst i for firm j during a given year.

Second, for each firm/year, individual analysts' mean forecast errors are averaged over all analysts of a given group g,

$$MGFE_{gj} = \sum_{i \in g} MFE_{ij} / N_j^g,$$

where:

$MGFE_{gj} =$ mean group forecast error for firm j,

$N =$ number of analysts from group g following firm j during a given year.

Finally, the mean difference forecast error between 2 groups is computed as

$$MDFE = \sum_{j=1}^{J} \left[MGFE_{Aj} - MGFE_{Bj} \right] / J$$

where J is the number of company/year units. In order to assess whether one group of analysts produces more (less) accurate forecasts than the other, the following hypothesis is tested:

$$H_0 : MDFE = 0 \ vs \ H_1 : MDFE \neq 0 \, .$$

A parametric mean test, a Wilcoxon sign rank test of equality of medians as well as a non-parametric binomial sign test are performed to test the hypothesis.

4.2. Results for Forecast Accuracy

The slope coefficient of equation (1) equals 0.01 and is significantly different from zero.[6] Emerging market analysts' bias decreases significantly with the distance between forecast release date and earnings announcement date. The intercept is not statistically different from zero.

Hypothesis tests and descriptive statistics for the mean difference forecast errors ($MDFE$) are reported in Table 5. Panels A through C report the difference across each category of analysts for all Latin American countries, for individual countries as well as for different security categories. The distribution of the MDFEs appears to be highly skewed by the presence of some extreme observations. As this may bias the results of the parametric tests, we will only consider the non-parametric results of column 7 and 8 for our analysis and conclusions.

Panel A shows that the median MDFE is positive for the whole sample and each individual countries indicating that local analysts' average forecast error is greater than foreign analysts' one. The Wilcoxon sign rank test and the binomial test reject the null hypothesis of equal forecasting skills at the aggregate level as well as for five of the individual countries. The superior ability of foreign analysts to predict firms earnings does not depend on size. Surprisingly, this superior ability disappears for American Depositary Receipts, which have a richer information environment and are the least distant firms for foreign analysts. Conflicts of interest due to increased investment and commercial banking relationship with foreign banks following U.S. exchange listing may explain this finding.

The results in panel B indicate that, excepting for Venezuela, the average error is greater for local analysts forecasts than for expatriate ones. The difference between both groups of analysts is statistically significant at the Latin American level but only weakly or not significant at the country and security category levels.

As indicated by the results in panel C, no difference between the forecasting skills of expatriate and foreign analysts can be found. As reported, in panel D, there is a strong evidence that leaders produce more accurate forecasts than follower analysts. Their mean forecast error appears to be much smaller than that of follower analysts. This is particularly true for local and foreign leaders for which the null hypothesis is rejected at the 1% level. The leader-follower criterion appears more important than the geographical one. However, no comparison is performed across leaders from each analyst group as the number of firm/year units for which leaders of both types are simultaneously identified is very low. Two important conclusions can be drawn about the behavior of financial analysts on Latin American markets. First, contrary to what has been documented by CDL, leader analysts do not "trade accuracy for timeliness". Indeed, foreign analysts are able to release timelier and more

---

[6] Results are not shown. They are available on request by the authors.

accurate forecasts. Second, follower analysts do not exactly reproduce the earnings per share forecasts issued by leader analysts. Even if their forecast releases closely follow leader analysts' ones, they avoid to reproduce exactly the information released by leader analysts.

Table 5. Financial analysts relative forecast accuracy

Distribution of the Mean Difference Forecast Errors (*MDFE*)								Sign of *MDFE*	
Panel A: Difference in forecast accuracy between local and foreign analysts									
Sample	N	Mean		Stdev	Min	Median		Max	% Local > Foreign	
Latin America	1263	-0.16		7.98	-238.88	0.02	***	62.10	54.95	***
Argentina	191	-0.01		0.88	-9.22	0.02	**	4.59	58.64	***
Brazil	557	-0.55		11.68	-238.88	0.02		47.11	53.68	**
Mexico	332	0.22		3.52	-4.97	0.02		62.10	53.31	
Chili	112	0.11	**	0.50	-1.96	0.03	**	3.31	55.36	
Peru	38	0.23		0.98	-0.42	0.05		5.46	60.53	*
Colombia	21	0.32	*	0.83	-0.38	0.10	**	3.54	71.43	**
Venezuela	12	-0.06		0.43	-1.13	0.02		0.36	50.00	
High Market Value	493	-0.01		6.54	-121.27	0.02	**	62.10	54.56	**
Small Market Value	323	0.16		2.25	-9.22	0.02	*	35.44	53.25	
ADR	277	0.04		0.88	-5.35	0.02		10.51	53.07	
Panel B: Difference in forecast accuracy between local and expatriate analysts									
Sample	N	Mean		Stdev	Min	Median		Max	% Local > Expatriate	
Latin America	1263	0.61	*	12.89	-20.69	0.01	**	402.14	52.26	*
Argentina	191	0.05		0.89	-4.24	0.02		10.27	53.40	
Brazil	557	1.04		18.48	-20.69	0.01		402.14	51.35	
Mexico	332	0.45		7.65	-13.31	0.01		136.34	52.41	
Chili	112	0.08	*	0.46	-0.76	0.00		3.03	50.89	
Peru	38	0.29	*	1.03	-0.65	0.08	*	5.59	60.53	*
Colombia	21	0.24		0.80	-0.36	0.02		3.20	61.90	*
Venezuela	12	-0.09		0.33	-0.75	-0.07		0.55	41.67	
High Market Value	493	0.63		9.60	-3.35	0.00		163.62	49.49	
Small Market Value	323	0.00		2.65	-20.69	0.02		35.23	52.94	
ADR	277	0.05		0.67	-3.61	0.01		6.81	52.71	
Panel C: Difference in forecast accuracy between expatriate and foreign analysts									
Sample	N	Mean		Stdev	Min	Median		Max	% Expatriate > Foreign	
Latin America	1263	-0.77		18.81	-641.02	0.00		19.46	50.75	
Argentina	191	-0.06		1.35	-12.48	0.01		4.41	52.88	
Brazil	557	-1.59		28.10	-641.02	-0.01		19.46	48.29	
Mexico	332	-0.23		4.45	-74.23	0.01		18.11	52.41	
Chili	112	0.03		0.38	-2.58	0.05	**	0.91	58.04	**
Peru	38	-0.06		0.22	-0.45	-0.08	**	0.53	34.21	**
Colombia	21	0.08		0.22	-0.25	0.04		0.50	52.38	
Venezuela	12	0.03		0.47	-1.28	0.10		0.52	66.67	*
High Market Value	493	-0.65	*	8.29	-120.94	0.01		3.71	52.54	

Table 5. Continued

Sample	N	Mean	Stdev	Min	Median		Max	% Expatriate > Foreign	
Small Market Value	323	0.16	1.97	-11.16	0.01		19.46	51.39	
ADR	277	-0.02	0.67	-4.70	0.01		3.71	52.71	
Panel D: Difference in forecast accuracy between leaders and followers									
Sample	N	Mean	Stdev	Min	Median		Max	% Leaders > Followers	
Local Leaders	426	-0.04	1.31	-11.04	-0.05	***	17.08	39.20	***
Foreign Leaders	350	-3.74	70.33	-1315.50	-0.58	***	12.09	40.57	***
Expatriate Leaders	198	0.07	6.13	-40.74	-0.02		73.38	44.95	*

This table presents descriptive statistics as well as hypothesis tests for the Mean Difference in Forecast Errors (*MDFE*). In Panel A, the third column reports the average difference between local analysts' forecast errors and foreign analysts' forecast errors. Column 6 reports the median difference between local analysts' forecast errors and foreign analysts' forecast errors. Column 8 reports the percentage of firm/year units for which the average forecast error of local analysts was greater than the average forecast error of foreign ones. In Panel B, the third column reports the average difference between local analysts' forecast errors and expatriate analysts' forecast errors. Column 6 reports the median difference between local analysts' forecast errors and expatriate analysts' forecast errors. Column 8 reports the percentage of firm/year units for which the average forecast error of local analysts was greater than the average forecast error of expatriate ones. In Panel C, the third column reports the average difference between expatriate analysts' forecast errors and foreign analysts' forecast errors. Column 6 reports the median difference between expatriate analysts' forecast errors and foreign analysts' forecast errors. Column 8 reports the percentage of firm/year units for which the average forecast error of expatriate analysts was greater than the average forecast error of foreign ones. In Panel D, the third column reports the average difference between lead analysts' forecast errors and follower analysts' forecast errors. Column 6 reports the median difference between lead analysts' forecast errors and follower analysts' forecast errors. Column 8 reports the percentage of firm/year units for which the average forecast error of lead analysts was greater than the average forecast error of follower ones. A parametric mean test is performed on column 3 numbers, a Wilcoxon signed rank test of equality of medians is performed on column 6 numbers, and a non-parametric sign test is performed on column 8 numbers. Note that in Panel D, the total number of firm/year units for each group of leader is lower than the number of leaders that has been identified. This is explained by the fact that there can be several leaders for a particular company in a given year.
***, **, * denote significance at the 1%, 5%, and 10% levels, respectively.

Overall, this section shows that foreign analysts foreign analysts have a better ability to analyze Latin American firms' earnings potential than their local peers. There is no significant difference between the performance of foreign and expatriate analysts and only a weak difference between expatriate and local analysts in the favor of expatriate ones. These finding indicate that analysts who work for foreign institutions may have greater resources, expertise and/or talent than their local peers. Finally, timely analysts are the most accurate ones. Consequently, lead analysts do not give up forecast accuracy when releasing more timely forecasts.

5. Impact of Forecast Revisions on Security Prices

5.1. Empirical Design

This section investigates whether one group of analysts' revisions provides more information to investors. The objective is to determine whether the stock price reaction following forecast revisions differs between the different groups of analysts. The reaction around forecast revisions for a given firm is proxied by the cumulative excess return during the forecast release period (days 0 and +1). This cumulative excess return is computed as the difference between the buy-and-hold returns for the firm's common stock and the value-weighted Datastream country index.

The incremental information content of each revision is measured by the scaled distance relative to the consensus forecast.[7] More precisely:

$$FSUR_{ijt} = \frac{FEPS_{ijt} - CF_{jt-1}}{\sigma(CF_{jt-1})}$$

where:

$FSUR_{ijt} =$ forecast surprise following analyst i's revision for firm j at date t,

$CF_{jt-1} =$ consensus EPS forecast for firm j at date $t-1$,

$\sigma(CF_{jt-1}) =$ standard deviation of the consensus forecast[8] at date $t-1$.

The consensus forecast is based on the average of the forecasts issued by analysts (excluding analyst i) during the 2 months preceding date t. Each analyst is required to provide at least 3 forecasts per year for the firm and each consensus forecast is required to contain at least 2 individual forecasts.

The impact of forecast revisions on security prices is measured by the following cross-sectional regression equations:

$$CAR_{jt} = \beta_0 + \beta_1 FSUR_{ijt} + \beta_2 LOC_i + \beta_3 FOR_i + \beta_4 LNSIZE_{jt} + \varepsilon_{jt} \tag{2}$$

$$CAR_{jt} = \beta_0 + \beta_1 LOC_i \times FSUR_{ijt} + \beta_2 FOR_i \times FSUR_{ijt} + \beta_3 EXPAT_i \times FSUR_{ijt} + \beta_4 LNSIZE_{jt} + \varepsilon_{jt} \tag{3}$$

$$CAR_{jt} = \beta_0 + \beta_1 FSUR_{ijt} + \beta_2 LOCLEAD_{ij} + \beta_3 FORLEAD_{ij} + \beta_4 EXPATLEAD_{ij} + \beta_5 LNSIZE_{jt} + \varepsilon_{jt} \tag{4}$$

---

[7] Our results are not sensitive to the choice of the scaling factor.

[8] Similar to Stickel (1992), a standard deviation less than 0.25 is arbitrarily set to 0.25 to mitigate small denominators. Our results are not affected by this operation.

$$CAR_{jt} = \beta_0 + \beta_1 LOCLEAD_{ij} \times FSUR_{ijt} + \beta_2 FORLEAD_{ij} \times FSUR_{ijt}$$
$$+ \beta_3 EXPATLEAD_{ij} \times FSUR_{ijt} + \beta_4 FOL_i \times FSUR_{ijt} + \beta_5 LNSIZE_{jt} + \varepsilon_{jt} \tag{5}$$

where:

$CAR_{jt} =$	cumulative excess return for firm j during the forecast release period (days 0 and +1),
$LOC_i =$	dummy variable set to 1 if analyst i is a local one and 0 otherwise,
$FOR_i =$	dummy variable set to 1 if analyst i is foreign and 0 otherwise,
$LNSIZE_j =$	logarithm of the market value (in USD) of common stock at fiscal year end,
$EXPAT_i =$	dummy variable set to 1 if analyst i is an expatriate and 0 otherwise,
$LOCLEAD_{ij} =$	dummy variable set to 1 if analyst i is a local analyst that has been identified as leader for company j and 0 otherwise,
$FORLEAD_{ij} =$	dummy variable set to 1 if analyst i is a foreign analyst that has been identified as leader for company j and 0 otherwise,
$EXPATLEAD_{ij} =$	dummy variable set to 1 if analyst i is an expatriate analyst that has been identified as leader for company j and 0 otherwise,
$FOL_{ij} =$	dummy variable set to 1 if analyst i has been identified as follower for company j and 0 otherwise,

Equations (2) and (4) measure the abnormal return associated with the different groups of analysts' forecast revisions. Equation (3) and (5) measures the proportion of abnormal return explained by each group of analysts' forecast revisions. The size variable is a proxy for the differences in firms' information environment[9] but also for foreign investors' ownership since they tend to concentrate their investments on high-capitalization liquid firms.

5.2. Results for the Impact of Forecast Revisions on Security Prices

Table 6 reports the mean cumulative abnormal return during the forecast release period. The price reaction depends on the size of the revision. The cumulative abnormal returns display important standard deviations and consequently only the stock returns associated with the bottom 50% sub-sample display statistically significant price reactions. Conversely, other revisions do not impact on prices. This is consistent with Stickel (1992, 1995) who documents a non-linear relation between forecast revisions and price reactions. Therefore, the regressions are restricted to revisions of a given magnitude.

Results for the cross-sectional regressions (2) and (3) are reported in table 7. First, panel A results indicate that, following downward revisions, there is no difference in the average

---

[9] Stickel (1995), among others, reports that buy and sell recommendations induces a greater price reaction for smaller companies than for larger ones.

size of the stock price reaction across groups. On the other hand, following large upward revisions (top 10%), the average cumulative abnormal return is significantly smaller for local analysts than for expatriate ones. The same is true for foreign analysts but the regression coefficient is only marginally significant. Second, results reported in panel B indicate that the stock price reaction following analysts forecast revisions is only significant for expatriate analysts large upward revisions. Unfortunately, the null hypothesis of equality across coefficients cannot be rejected by the F-tests presented in columns 7 through 9.

Table 6. Stock price reactions following forecast surprises

	All FSUR		Bottom 10%	Bottom 50%		Top 50%	Top 10%
Mean (%)	-0.07	**	-0.16	-0.12	**	-0.02	-0.17
Standard deviation (%)	4.39		4.73	4.52		4.27	4.42
N	16699		1670	8352		8347	1670

This table reports some descriptive statistics about the cumulative abnormal returns (CARs) following forecasts' revisions. Cumulative abnormal returns are computed as the difference between the buy-and-hold return for the firm's common stock and the value-weighted Datastream country index during the forecast release period (days 0 and 1). The column All FSUR reports statistics on CARs for all forecast surprise level. Bottom 10% reports CARs for forecast surprises located in the top 10% of the distribution. Bottom 50% reports statistics for CAR's located in the bottom 50% of the distribution. In the column Top 50%, statistics are reported for CAR's located in the top 50% of the distribution. Top 10% reports statistics for CAR's located in the top 10% of the distribution.
***, **, * denote significance at the 1%, 5%, and 10% levels, respectively.

Table 7. Stock price reactions following analyst forecast revisions

Panel A: $CAR_{jt} = \beta_0 + \beta_1 FSUR_{ijt} + \beta_2 LOC_i + \beta_3 FOR_i + \beta_4 LNSIZE_{jt} + \varepsilon_{jt}$

FSUR Cutoff	β_0	β_1	β_2	β_3		β_4		N
Bottom 10%	-0.46	0.09	-0.24	0.02		0.08		1670
	(-0.60)	(0.63)	(-0.77)	(0.05)		(0.88)		
Bottom 50%	-0.59 *	0.07	0.07	0.17		0.06		8352
	(-1.91)	(1.03)	(0.51)	(1.17)		(1.55)		
Top 50%	0.03	-0.04	-0.20	-0.27	**	0.02		8347
	(0.09)	(-0.56)	(-1.57)	(-1.97)		0.58		
Top 10%	1.07	0.20	-0.60 **	-0.52	*	-0.16	*	1670
	(1.35)	(1.42)	(-2.13)	(-1.68)		(-1.73)		

Table 7. Continued

Panel B: $CAR_{jt} = \beta_0 + \beta_1 LOC_i \times FSUR_{ijt} + \beta_2 FOR_i \times FSUR_{ijt} + \beta_3 EXPAT_i \times FSUR_{ijt} + \beta_4 LNSIZE_{jt} + \varepsilon_{jt}$									
FSUR Cutoff	β_0	β_1	β_2	β_3	β_4	$\beta_1 = \beta_2$	$\beta_1 = \beta_3$	$\beta_2 = \beta_3$	N
Bottom 10%	-0.56	0.13	0.05	0.06	0.08	0.40	0.25	0.01	1670
	(-0.76)	(0.86)	(0.30)	(0.35)	(0.87)				
Bottom 50%	-0.50 *	0.13	0.13	0.03	0.06	0.99	0.56	0.02	8352
	(-1.73)	(1.52)	(1.52)	(0.25)	(1.55)				
Top 50%	-0.14	-0.11	-0.03	0.12	0.02	0.42	2.89	* 1.04	8347
	(-0.51)	(-1.25)	(-0.29)	(0.98)	(0.53)				
Top 10%	0.64	0.13	0.22	0.35 **	-0.16	0.46	2.24	0.65	1670
	(0.84)	(0.81)	(1.36)	(1.99)	(-1.74)				

This table presents the coefficients obtained by regressing the cumulative abnormal returns following forecast revisions on the magnitude of the revision, firm size, and dummy variables indicating analysts' status. Revisions are dated within the firm's current fiscal year over the 1993-1999 period. CAR_{jt} is the cumulative abnormal return to security i during the release period (days 0 and +1). $FSUR_{ijt}$ is the forecast surprise following analyst i's revision at date t. $LNSIZE_{jt}$ is the natural logarithm of the market value (in USD) of common stock at fiscal year end. LOC_i is a dummy variable that takes a value of 1 if analyst i is employed by a local brokerage house and 0 otherwise. FOR_i is a dummy variable that takes a value of 1 if analyst i is employed by a foreign brokerage house without local residence and 0 otherwise. $EXPAT_i$ is a dummy variable that takes a value of 1 if analyst i is employed by a foreign brokerage house with local residence and 0 otherwise. All coefficients are multiplied by 100. T-statistics are based on White (1980). For each regression the adjusted R^2 are less than 0.01.
***, **, * denote significance at the 1%, 5%, and 10% levels, respectively.

Table 8 reports the results for the cross-sectional regressions (4) and (5). First, as reported in panel A, the average cumulative return does not differ between leader and follower analysts. Second, as indicated by panel B results, there is a significant market reaction following foreign and expatriate leaders large upward revisions (top 10%). The F-tests indicate that the regression coefficients associated to foreign leaders' revisions are significantly higher than those associated to local leaders and followers' revisions.

Overall, this section shows that there are almost no significant differences in the incremental information contained in financial analysts forecasts revisions. However, the market seems to consider the forecasts issued by local and, to some extent, by expatriate leaders as being more informative than those issued by other analysts. This is consistent with the view that foreign leaders' revisions have a greater information content than other analysts' revisions.

6. CONCLUSIONS

Foreign financial analysts' EPS forecasts are more timely than expatriate and local analysts' forecasts. Building on CDL methodology, 1301 leader analysts are identified. Out of these leaders, 444 are foreign. This is significantly greater than the proportion of foreign analysts' forecasts in the sample. Conversely, analysts with local residence display a significant tendency to follow the "crowd".

In terms of forecast accuracy, analysts working for foreign brokerage houses are better at predicting firms' EPS than local analysts. Surprisingly, we detect no significant differences in forecast accuracy for companies with quoted ADRs. This may indicate that foreign and expatriate analysts' superior performance vanishes for companies with richer information environment.

Finally, stock prices react positively to upward forecast revisions released by foreign and expatriate leader analysts. The coefficient associated to foreign leaders forecast surprises is significantly greater than that associated to follower forecast surprises. It is also marginally greater than the coefficient associated to local leaders forecast surprises.

We see that foreign analysts outperform their local peers across all our performance measures. This suggests that residence does not give local financial analysts an advantage relative to their foreign counterparts. The difference between foreign and expatriate analysts' performance is less evident. Foreign analysts outperform their expatriate peers for one out of three performance measures. This suggests that agency problems, due to tighter investment banking relationships between resident analysts' firms and local companies, are not influencing financial analysts' objectivity on Latin American markets. Overall, our results are consistent with better information and greater sophistication on the part of analysts employed by foreign brokerage houses. This superiority may be linked to the superior resources available to analysts who work for important international brokerage houses, to the better international expertise of these analysts, or to their greater talent.

The present results are consistent with a better information on the part of foreign investors. Foreigners' portfolio profits on emerging markets, such as those documented by Seasholes (2000), may be driven by the better ability of foreign analysts at analyzing firms' situation for their clients. However, further research is needed to understand which category of investors (foreign or domestic) trade around foreign and local analysts' revisions. Finally, the practical implication of this investigation is that investors should rely more heavily on foreign financial analysts' forecasts than on local ones when they invest in Latin American markets.

Table 8. Stock price reactions following leaders and followers forecast revisions

Panel A: $CAR_{jt} = \beta_0 + \beta_1 FSUR_{ijt} + \beta_2 LOCLEAD_{ij} + \beta_3 FORLEAD_{ij} + \beta_4 EXPATLEAD_{ij} + \beta_5 LNSIZE_{jt} + \varepsilon_{jt}$

FSUR Cutoff	β_0	β_1	β_2	β_3	β_4	β_5	N
Bottom 10%	-0.56	0.09	-0.63	0.52	-0.61	0.09	1670
	(-0.76)	(0.64)	(-1.19)	(0.86)	(-0.59)	(0.92)	
Bottom 50%	-0.48	0.07	-0.24	-0.03	-0.30	0.06	8352
	(-1.66)	(1.05)	(-1.15)	(-0.10)	(-0.72)	(1.57)	
Top 50%	-0.17	-0.03	0.17	-0.33	0.22	0.02	8347
	(-0.62)	(-0.52)	(0.78)	(-1.17)	(0.64)	(0.64)	
Top 10%	0.60	0.20	-0.18	0.78	0.97	-0.16 *	1670
	(0.79)	(1.38)	(-0.40)	(1.24)	(1.23)	(-1.72)	

Panel B: $CAR_{jt} = \beta_0 + \beta_1 LOCLEAD_{ij} \times FSUR_{ijt} + \beta_2 FORLEAD_{ij} \times FSUR_{ijt} + \beta_3 EXPATLEAD_{ij} \times FSUR_{ijt} + \beta_4 FOL_{ij} \times FSUR_{ijt} + \beta_5 LNSIZE_{jt} + \varepsilon_{jt}$

FSUR Cutoff	β_0	β_1	β_2	β_3	β_4	β_5	$\beta_1=\beta_2$	$\beta_1=\beta_3$	$\beta_2=\beta_3$	$\beta_2=\beta_4$	$\beta_3=\beta_4$	N
Bottom 10%	-0.55	0.24	0.04	0.46	0.07	0.08	0.26	0.23	0.77	0.01	1.04	1670
	(-0.75)	(0.76)	(0.14)	(1.05)	(0.51)	(0.86)						
Bottom 50%	-0.50 *	0.26	0.12	0.42	0.05	0.06	0.19	0.14	0.50	0.07	1.19	8352
	(-1.73)	(1.03)	(0.46)	(1.04)	(0.68)	(1.56)						
Top 50%	-0.14	-0.11	0.33	0.34	-0.05	0.02	1.41	1.32	0.00	1.64	1.48	8347
	(-0.53)	(-0.45)	(1.11)	(1.26)	(-0.78)	(0.55)						
Top 10%	0.64	0.10	0.88	0.60 ***	0.17 **	-0.16 *	3.60 *	1.35	0.35	4.41 **	1.44	1670
	(0.85)	(0.37)	(2.80)	(1.96)	(1.18)	(-1.73)						

This table presents the coefficients obtained by regressing the cumulative abnormal returns following forecast revisions on the magnitude of the revision, firm size, and dummy variables indicating analysts' status. Revisions are dated within the firm's current fiscal year over the 1993-1999 period. CAR_{jt} is the cumulative abnormal return to security i during the release period (days 0 and +1). $FSUR_{ijt}$ is the forecast surprise following analyst i's revision at date t. $LNSIZE_{jt}$ is the natural logarithm of the market value (in USD) of common stock at fiscal year end. $LOCLEAD_{ij}$ is a dummy variable that takes a value of 1 if analyst i is a local leader and 0 otherwise. $FORLEAD_{ij}$ is a dummy variable that takes a value of 1 if analyst i is a foreign leader and 0 otherwise. $EXPATLEAD_{ij}$ is a dummy variable that takes a value of 1 if analyst i is an expatriate leader and 0 otherwise. FOL_{ij} is a dummy variable that takes a value of 1 if analyst i is a follower and 0 otherwise. All coefficients are multiplied by 100. T-statistics are based on White (1980). For each regression the adjusted R^2 are less than 0.01.

***, **, * denote significance at the 1%, 5%, and 10% levels, respectively.

APPENDIX

Leader-to-Follower Ratio

The Leader-to-Follower Ratio (LFR) for a particular analyst a who provides forecasts for firm j is expressed a follows:

$$LFR_a^j = \frac{T_{0,a}^j}{T_{1,a}^j}, \tag{6}$$

where T_0 and T_1 are respectively the cumulative lead- and follow time for the K forecasts made by analyst a on firm j during a particular fiscal year. They are defined as follows:

$$T_{0,a}^j = \sum_{k=1}^{K}\sum_{h=1}^{H} t_{jhk}^0 \tag{7}$$

$$T_{1,a}^j = \sum_{k=1}^{K}\sum_{h=1}^{H} t_{jhk}^1 \tag{8}$$

t_{jmk}^0 (t_{jmk}^1) denotes the number of days by which forecast h precedes (follows) the k-th forecast may by analyst a for firm j. H is the number of forecasts made by other analysts that precede and follow the release of the k-th forecast of analyst a. The above figure provides an illustration of the idea underlying the LFR ratio. The forecast issued by analyst a for firm j at date t is denoted as $F_{a,t}^j$.

From this example, we see that analyst 2 issues a forecast on day 25. The preceding forecast was issued 20 days before on day 5. The following forecast is released soon afterward, on day 27. Taking into account only these one preceding and one following forecasts, analyst 2's LFR ratio is $\frac{20}{2}=10$. Analyst 2 would therefore classified as a leader.

To the same extent, analyst 3 is a follower analyst. He issues a forecast right after analysts 2 and no one free-rides on its forecast since the next to issue a forecast is analyst 4, only 23 days later. Its LFR would then be $\frac{1}{23}\cong 0.04$.

ACKNOWLEDGEMENTS

The authors thanks Michel Dubois, Christophe Pérignon, René Stulz, Ernst-Ludvig Von Thadden, and participants at FAME doctoral workshop, 5th Conference of the Swiss Society for Financial Market Research, 2002 FMA European meeting, 2002 EFMA meeting, and 2002 FMA US meeting for their helpful comments.

The authors acknowledge the contribution of Thomson Financial for providing earnings per share forecast data, available through the Institutional Brokers Estimate System. This data has been provided as part of a broad academic program to encourage earnings expectations research.

The authors aknowledge the financial support of the Swiss National Science Fondation (grant nr. 1214-065220).

REFERENCES

Brennan, M.J. and H.H. Cao, 1997, International portfolio investment flows, *Journal of Finance* 52, 1851-1880.

Brown, L.D., 1997, Analyst forecasting errors: Additional evidence, *Financial Analysts Journal,* November/December, 81-88.

Chang, C., 2002, *Information footholds: Expatriate analysts in an emerging market,* Working Paper, Haas School of Business, U.C. Berkeley.

Choe, H., Kho, B.C. and R.M. Stulz, 2000, *Do domestic investors have more valuable information about individual stocks than foreign investors?,* Working paper, Seoul National University and Ohio State University.

Cooper, R.A., Day, T.E. and C.M. Lewis, 2001, Following the leader: A study of individual analysts' earnings forecasts, *Journal of Financial Economics* 61, 383-416.

Coval, J.D. and T.J. Moskowitz, 2001, The geography of investment: Informed trading and asset prices, *Journal of Political Economy* 109, 811-841.

Grinblatt, M. and M. Keloharju, 2000, The investment behaviour and performance of various investor types: A study of Finland's unique data set, *Journal of Financial Economics* 55, 43-67.

Harvey, C.R., 1995, Predictable risk and returns in emerging markets, *Review of Financial Studies* 8, 773-816.

Hope, O., 2003, *Accounting policy disclosures and analysts' forecasts,* Contemporary Accounting Research, Forthcoming.

Kang, S., O'Brien, J. and K. Sivaramakrishnan, 1994, Analysts' interim earnings forecasts: Evidence on the forecasting process, *Journal of Accounting Research* 32, 103-112.

Kang, J. and R.M. Stulz, 1997, Why is there a home bias? An analysis of foreign portfolio equity ownership in Japan, *Journal of Financial Economics* 46, 2-28.

Kini, O., Shehzad, M., Rebello, M. and A. Venkateswaran, 2003, *On the determinants of international analyst research coverage,* Working Paper, Robinson College of Business, Georgia State University.

Lang, M.H., Lins, K.V. and D. Miller, 2003, ADRs, analysts, and accuracy: Does cross listing in the U.S. improve a firm's information environment and increase market value, *Journal of Accounting Research,* Forthcoming.

Lin, H. and M.F. McNichols, 1998, Underwriting relationships, analysts' earnings forecasts and investment recommendations, *Journal of Accounting and Economics* 25, 101-127.

Malloy, C.J., 2003, The geography of equity analysis, Journal of Finance, Forthcoming.

Michealy, R. and K.L. Womack, 1999, Conflict of interest and the credibility of underwriter analyst recommendations, *Review of Financial Studies* 12, 653-686.

Orpurt, S.F., 2003, *Local asymmetric information advantages: International evidence from analysts' European firm earnings forecasts,* Working Paper, Graduate School of Business, University of Chicago.

Seasholes, M., 2000, *Smart foreign traders in emerging markets,* Working paper, Harvard Business School, Cambridge, M.A.

Stickel, S., 1992, Reputation and performance among security analysts, Journal of Finance 47, 1811-1836.

Stickel, S., 1995, The anatomy of the performance of buy and sell recommendations, *Financial Analysts Journal,* September/October, 25-39.

White, H., 1980, A heteroscedasticity-consistent covariance matrix estimator and a direct test for heteroscedasticity, *Econometrica* 48, 817-838.

In: Economics of Emerging Markets
Editor: Lado Beridze, pp. 225-237

ISBN: 978-1-60021-850-7
© 2008 Nova Science Publishers, Inc.

Chapter 9

SECURITIES MARKETS IN EMERGING ECONOMIES: AN OVERVIEW OF THE MAIN ISSUES

Silvio John Camilleri[*]

Banking and Finance Department,
Faculty of Economics, Management and Accountancy,
University of Malta, Tal-Qroqq, Msida MSD 2080, Malta

ABSTRACT

This chapter surveys the salient concepts relating to the role and development of emerging securities markets. It considers both general securities markets activity as well as the operations of exchanges which facilitate securities trading. The section relating to general securities activity discusses the liberalisation of securities markets in recent years, the risks related to portfolio investment in emerging markets and the impacts of the gradual integration of these markets with global ones.

Part of the business activity of securities exchanges is migrating overseas through the tendency for larger companies to cross-list on major exchanges. This chapter thus explores how emerging economy exchanges may assert their role in international financial markets through supplementing traditional business streams with new ones, enhancing liquidity and using appropriate technology. Finally, the chapter illustrates how securities activity in emerging economies should be supplemented by the appropriate legal and regulatory framework.

Keywords: Emerging Markets; Financial Integration; Liberalisation; Securities Markets.
JEL Classification: G15, G18, G20, G28, O16

1. INTRODUCTION

The primary function of securities markets is to channel funds from savers to productive users. In this way, securities markets offer profitable opportunities to investors and provide

---

[*] E-mail address: silvio.j.camilleri@um.edu.mt

capital to the real sector. Most emerging securities markets grew steadily during the last decades witnessing increased portfolio flows, share of market capitalisation in world markets and number of listings. Such trends are clearly visible in Asian markets [Ding and Charoenwong, 2006], and similar progress is evident in other emerging markets in Latin America, Eastern Europe and North Africa. Portfolio investment in these markets was facilitated by the pronounced increase in emerging country funds marketed by global asset managers. Asia nowadays accounts for a large portion of total portfolio investment in emerging markets. Despite the above, equity finance still comprises a modest portion of corporate funding in emerging economies which were traditionally bank-dominated. For instance, according to Purfield *et. al.* [2006] the portion of equity financing of total corporate funding amounts to around 10% in emerging Asian countries, and this figure is in the region of 3.7% in non-Asian ones.

Portfolio investment towards emerging economies is at times repatriated at short notice, largely around intermitting times of financial crises. This suggests that it is important for emerging economies to nourish resiliency in their financial systems, and this pre-supposes implementation of international standards relating to investor protection, corporate governance and an adequate setup of subsidiary legislation.

This chapter surveys the main issues relating to the development of securities markets in emerging economies, encompassing both general securities markets activity as well as the role of exchanges in facilitating securities trading. In this way, the scope of the chapter is broad given that it aims to tackle the main concepts and to highlight their possible interactions; indeed most of these topics may be comprehensively studied on their own merits.

Section 2 of the chapter explores the impacts of liberalisation of securities markets, and the risks associated with portfolio investment in emerging economies. The section discusses how emerging securities markets are becoming integrated with developed ones and the related effects on diversification and contagion possibilities. Section 3 is concerned with the development prospects for securities exchanges in emerging economies. It reviews the issues impinging on the progress of these exchanges which include increased internationalisation and the drive to augment securities business and consolidate liquidity. Section 4 explores how securities markets in emerging economies should be complemented with an adequate legal and regulatory framework in order to maintain a competitive edge. Section 5 concludes.

This chapter emphasises relatively recent literature. Given the range of issues involved, it is not possible to describe any particular study in detail or to delve into the respective methodologies. Whilst most of the research papers cited in the chapter focus on emerging stock markets, other studies focusing on general financial markets, or stock markets in industrialised countries are occasionally referred to, especially in the context of those issues which are relevant to both emerging and industrialised markets.

2. THE LIBERALISATION
OF EMERGING SECURITIES MARKETS AND RELATED ISSUES

The liberalisation of financial services industries in emerging economies was encouraged by increased cross-border trade and this materialised in increased investment flows towards these countries [Phylaktis and Ravazzolo; 2002]. Financial liberalisation in the context of securities markets may be defined as the removal of restrictions on cross-border equity and debt investment flows. Bekeart and Harvey [2000] suggested alternative definitions of capital market liberalisation, such as the earliest date of an American Depository Receipt (ADR) issue or a country fund launch. Given that liberalisation is a process, the latter events are likely to occur on different dates usually clustered around a particular period.

2.1. Impacts of Securities Markets Liberalisation

Research has converged on the point that allowing overseas investors to access the home market may lead to a higher degree of pricing efficiency, partly because overseas investors include professional fund managers (Niarchos and Alexakis [1998], Tian and Wan [2004] and Kim *et. al.* [2005]). This should translate into a more efficient channelling of funds from savers to productive users.

Theoretical and empirical studies which considered the longer-term connection between securities markets and economic growth yielded mixed results since such relationship may differ depending on whether it is analysed in the context of an emerging economy as opposed to a developed one. For instance Minier [2003] empirically studied various developed and emerging countries and found that a positive relationship between stock market development and economic growth may not emerge in countries with low market capitalisation. In addition, the setting up of a (small) stock exchange might not lead to automatic growth effects. Beck and Levine [2004] analysed panel data from 40 emerging and developed countries and concluded that stock markets and banks contribute towards economic growth, however it is unclear whether stock markets provide a valuable service distinct from banks, as opposed to the possibility that financial development spurs growth irrespective of whether this emanates from the banking sector or the securities market. Whilst such mixed results were partly explained through an array of factors including the legal setup and investor protection, further research is needed to account for these diverse country experiences.

One factor which complicates the analysis of financial liberalisations is that the latter are typically accompanied by wider reforms and this makes it difficult to single out the real effects which are exclusively attributable to liberalisation. Bekaert *et. al.* [2001] addressed this problem by accounting for variables representing developments in the macroeconomic environment, banking sector and stock markets, and concluded that equity market liberalisations in emerging countries may be associated with real GDP growth.

Other studies point at adverse effects of financial liberalisation. For instance, according to Devereux and Smith [1994] the liberalisation of securities activity enhances the potential for international risk sharing and this may reduce savings rates and economic growth. Stiglitz [2000] noted that capital market liberalisation exposes countries to factors outside their economy, such as changes in investors' perceptions regarding the risk of the home market. The author argued that short-term capital flows are not usually appropriate to fund longer-term corporate requirements, and at times it might be prudent to implement restrictions on short-term capital flows. Similarly, Lin [2006] argued that the increased potential for mass selling activities around financial crises may reduce the benefits of liberalisation. Whilst policies to curtail destabilising capital flows might be sensible, the issue of capital controls remains controversial given that these may hinder cross-border portfolio investment.

The effects of stock market liberalisation were also analysed at a micro level, on the grounds that as a firm's stock becomes available to overseas investors it should facilitate access to funds, lowering the cost of capital. In addition, increased market surveillance adds on to the onus of the firm to offer an efficient risk-return combination. These effects may eventually spill over to other firms in the same economy. Mitton [2006] analysed a sample of firms from 28 developing countries that were opened up to foreign investment and found evidence of improvements in operating performance including higher growth, investment, profitability and efficiency.

The role of financial liberalisation on economic development has been extensively analysed and readers are referred to Auerbach and Siddiki [2004] for a detailed survey. Further research is required to explore the inherent country characteristics which impinge on the success of liberalisation programmes and how liberalisation affects listed and unlisted firms and the setting up of new ones. In addition the relationship between stock market liberalisation and financial stability has not yet been settled; whilst the availability of an alternative funding source may make the economy more resilient to shocks in one particular financing channel, it may potentially increase the exposure to external shocks.

2.2. Risks of Financial Investment in Emerging Economies

The risks relating to financial investment may differ in the context of emerging economies as compared to developed ones, given that some kinds of risks may become pronounced in emerging markets. Goriaev and Zabotkin [2006] in an empirical study of the Russian stock market, noted that investors take account of both country and firm-specific risks, and securities pricing is sensitive both to actual risks and to participants' perceptions of such risks.

One salient risk relating to cross-border investment emanates from political factors. Research shows that political risk is priced in emerging market securities [Bekaert et. al.; 1997] and emerging economies may reduce the cost of funds through reducing political risk. Whilst most emerging economies implemented reforms to reduce political risk, other countries may still be in need of more significant efforts to achieve this objective. For instance, Girard and Omran [2007] considered the current state of various Arab capital markets and argued that institutional reforms are needed to reduce political risk, such as curtailing corruption and improving legal frameworks to ensure rule and contract enforceability.

The risks of emerging market investment may exacerbate during financial crises. Experience shows that financial crises are usually caused by a variety of factors such as overvalued exchange rates, bank balance sheets unprepared for financial or real asset volatility, and deficiencies in financial system supervision. Emerging economies should therefore strive to make their financial systems more resilient to external shocks through emphasising prudential regulation and supervision and upgrading their settlement systems to make them less prone to liquidity shocks. The former problems tend to be amplified by the tendency of portfolio investors to withdraw funds at the first signs of financial distress, reducing liquidity in the emerging economy and amplifying asset price volatility. In fact, Reynolds [2001] argued that liberalisation has made emerging markets more vulnerable to global financial crises.

The overall risk of particular markets is often gauged by measuring volatility, and research has also focused on whether liberalisation may lead to volatility changes. One may argue that as speculative capital moves in and out of emerging markets, it may impact on stock prices and induce higher volatility. Yet, one may also expect that as emerging markets become integrated with their overseas counterparts, they should become more informationally efficient, and therefore less prone to excess volatility. Research presents mixed evidence on volatility changes following liberalisation; for instance Jayasuriya [2005] considered changes in stock return volatility following liberalisation in eighteen emerging markets and found that whether countries experience lower or increased volatility might depend on market characteristics. In particular, when markets allocate significant priorities to higher transparency, investor protection and ancillary factors, they are likely to experience reduced volatility. Cuñado et. al. [2006] analysed long-term time series for six emerging markets and argued that past research might have overstated volatility changes. They concluded that financial liberalisation might have reduced average volatility in these markets, whereas the higher post-liberalisation volatility inferred by other researchers might have been due to occasional large shocks.

Further risks associated with emerging market investment emanate from deficiencies of the broader legal and regulatory setup such as transparency and corporate governance requirements. This is discussed in Section 4 of this chapter.

2.3. The Integration of Emerging Markets with Global Ones

Integration should be considered as a distinct issue from liberalisation. Whereas the latter term is associated with removal of restrictions on capital market activity, integration requires actual cross-border capital flows, information availability and possibly ADR activity. Integration implies that assets of comparable risk in different countries should promise similar expected returns.

As markets become more integrated, the diversification prospects traditionally offered by emerging economies may be reduced as returns become more correlated across markets. According to Purfield et. al. [2006], the correlation between global equity markets and Asian ones has increased since the 1990s, and this trend seems representative of emerging markets in general. Contrasting evidence was presented by Hunter [2006] who found no significant evidence of integration between Latin American stock markets and international ones. The degree of integration seems to change around crisis periods, a finding confirmed in other literature such as Yang et. al. [2003] in the context of Asian stock markets.

Empirical studies on the effects of financial integration suggest mixed results; whilst integration may result in increased portfolio flows towards emerging markets and upgrades of country credit ratings [Bekaert and Harvey; 2003] it is not clear whether this may translate into significant real effects. For instance Edison et. al. [2002] considered a sample of 57 countries in various stages of development, and they did not reject the null hypothesis that integration does *not* accelerate economic growth. Various researchers maintained that financial integration makes emerging markets more prone to currency devaluations, capital flight and contagion. Grabel [2003] thus argued that measures which are not usually provided for in neo-liberal policies may be needed to curb financial crises. These include transaction taxes and trip wires that warn investors when signs of distress emerge. If such measures curb the former risks, they may translate in lower risk premiums.

The integration of emerging capital markets may also have implications for contagion possibilities given that financial or economic instability may spread across markets. The empirical evidence on contagion may be sensitive to the definition of the term; in particular whether contagion is considered as contemporaneous comovement across markets, or whether it entails a significant increase in such comovement following a particular shock. Inferences tend to be hampered by the facts that correlations are unstable over time [Longin and Solnik; 1995], and that correlation estimates tend to be biased upwards given that volatility typically increases during crises [Forbes and Rigobon; 2002]. Whereas these factors lead to debates on scientific conclusions, the notion that markets are prone to instability imported from overseas seems to be generally accepted. In particular, developed markets may be prone to crises originating in emerging markets in terms of higher risk premium demands [Dungey et. al.; 2006]. In addition, contagion effects might have been more pronounced in case of "smaller" crises which have so far been sidelined by researchers, such as the Brazilian one of 1999 [Collins and Gavron; 2005].

Theoretical and empirical literature relating to the integration of stock markets has flourished, and readers are referred to Kearney and Lucey [2004] for a detailed survey.

3. SECURITIES EXCHANGES IN EMERGING MARKETS

Exchanges assist in the efficient running of securities activities. Through providing liquidity and price discovery, exchanges facilitate secondary market trading and foster the primary issues of securities. Most exchanges in emerging economies were established in conjunction with government privatisation programmes and some of them are characterized by small size and meek liquidity. This section considers the main issues impinging on the progress of emerging exchanges which include increased internationalisation, the drive towards augmenting securities business and consolidating liquidity, and the competitive edge which may potentially be gained through technology.

3.1. The Internationalization Challenge

Technological improvements and deregulation have enhanced investors' ability to access information about securities issued overseas and to trade such instruments. This internationalisation process facilitated the issuers' task of marketing securities to overseas investors, commonly by issuing Global Depository Receipts (GDRs). The latter securities are backed by underlying shares and pay dividends similarly to the underlying shares. US and major European exchanges often attract significant GDR activity migrating from emerging markets. Factors which may account for such cross-listings include issuers aiming to exploit new sources of capital and reducing funding costs, and investors seeking overseas profitable opportunities.

The impacts of cross-listing activity are not confined to the particular issuer, but extend to the trading activity on the home (and possibly the host) exchange. Karolyi [2004] showed how the ADR activity emanating from twelve Latin American and Asian emerging markets resulted in more cross-border capital flows and increased integration. The author also found empirical evidence of adverse effects emanating from decreased trading activity in the home markets, fragmentation of trading activity, and the possibility of hindering development of the home market. Auguste *et. al.* [2006] noted that cross-listed shares may have served as a means of facilitating capital flight during the Argentine crisis.

The effectiveness of internationalization was also investigated in previous literature. For instance Karolyi [2004] noted that trading activity in some depository receipts may be minimal due to negligible interest in the originating markets on part of international investors. Similarly, Pirrong [1999] and Baruch *et. al.* [2003] constructed theoretical models predicting that the order flow for a given product tends to converge to a single exchange. There are reasons to expect the home market to be a more liquid venue for securities, given that home traders may be following the particular security more closely and are more likely to trade immediately on new information. Notwithstanding this, O'Hara [2001] cited practical examples illustrating how the venue where the order flow migrates to may be unpredictable; in particular trading does not always migrate to the largest venue.

One salient issue is that the larger and more liquid securities are more likely to be successful in cross-listing overseas and if the order flow relating to such securities migrates from the home markets, this would imply considerable lost business [Levine and Schmukler; 2003]. Moel [2001] found that such decline in liquidity may result in reduced ability of the local stock market to promote economic growth.

When drafting a course of action on how emerging exchanges may deal with internationalisation, one should identify the factors that encourage firms to cross-list in order to address them. Possible motivations for cross-listing, include the ability to tap funds at a lower cost, broadening the investor base, and the prestige related to listing on a larger market. Reese and Weisbach [2002] studied a cross section of US bank depositary receipts and argued that one motivation for listing abroad is to protect the interests of minority shareholders. Similar evidence was found by Pagano *et. al.* [2002]. La Porta *et. al.* [1997] and Pagano and Volpin [2005] presented evidence of a positive correlation between shareholder protection and stock market development and this implies that increased shareholder protection in the home market should encourage local trading activity.

One policy adopted by exchanges to tackle internationalization was to create alliances with peers in order to reduce operating costs and to augment the importance of their trading venues. Exchanges may collaborate in activities which offer potential for economies of scale if conducted jointly. These include order execution, data warehousing, clearing and settlement, information dissemination and marketing functions. Exchanges may also outsource particular functions, as discussed by Claessens *et. al.* [2003].

There is still significant potential for further research relating to internationalisation and ADR activity, primarily given that trends may change over time. This is also related to the notion that ADR activity should be considered as a continuing process, rather than a series of events clustered around a particular period, as outlined by Karolyi [2004]. A detailed review of the literature relating to cross-listing activities goes beyond the scope of this chapter and readers are referred to a survey by Karolyi [2006].

3.2. Increasing Business

Two pre-conditions for stock exchange survival are competitiveness and profitability, entailing that institutions monitor their expenditures and revenues. As for the expenditure side, cost cutting strategies might not be optimal since they can make markets less attractive [Claessens et. al.; 2003]. On the other hand, if exchanges attempt to increase revenues through higher fees, it might be difficult to attract new listings and to avoid migration of stocks [Pagano et. al.; 2002]. One alternative strategy which exchanges may adopt is to increase the volume of business to benefit from scale and scope economies.

Enhancing listing and trading activity on exchanges is a two sided effort, in the sense that both the demand and supply of securities have to be nurtured. Encouraging investors to approach the market entails an adequate legal setup in line with international standards which safeguards shareholders' rights and guarantees efficient dispute resolution. In addition securities market regulation has to be enforced. In enhancing the supply of securities, exchanges can target first-time listing companies through programmes set up with this specific aim. Yet, according to Claessens et. al. [2003] such initiatives had limited success in the context of newly set up European exchanges. Attracting first time-listing companies implies that exchanges have to cater for differing listing processes and requirements, and therefore most exchanges organise different tier markets.

O'Hara [2001] advocated that exchanges should lay particular emphasis on medium-sized companies in order to attract both domestic listings and possibly regional cross-listings. This rests on the notion that larger companies are likely to cross-list on global exchanges rather than smaller emerging markets, whilst smaller companies tend to remain at home and therefore these are not likely to generate significant cross-listing activity.

Finally, exchanges may consider generating higher revenues by diversifying in related services such as settlement systems. Derivatives constitute another alternative offering potential for increasing business, although these require well-developed underlying markets, increased safeguards to foster financial stability, effective transparency and disclosure requirements, and possible regulatory amendments in respect of short-selling restrictions and contract enforceability [Purfield et. al.; 2006].

3.3. Enhancing Liquidity

Liquidity may be defined as the degree to which a trader may promptly transact assets at reasonable cost. Larger exchanges have a competitive edge in terms of their ability to offer liquidity at low cost. This implies that increasing liquidity should be a top priority across emerging market exchanges; indeed liquidity may be deemed as one pre-condition for attracting portfolio investment.

Liquidity generation is a major objective of the trading protocols adopted by exchanges. Increasingly, modern markets are relying on automated systems such as electronic order-matching facilities, where queued orders are executed through price and time priorities. Such systems are usually cost-effective and transparent however they might be insufficient to ensure liquidity for less traded stocks. Therefore exchanges may consider including human input such as the services of market makers. Clayton et. al. [2006] noted that less developed markets tend to encourage market making activities on the grounds that completely automated systems rely on the continuous participation of traders, which may not always be forthcoming.

Trading protocols feature different elements designed to enhance liquidity and price discovery such as call auctions and dealership systems. Transparency may be a complex issue since whilst it enhances fairness, it may also facilitate market manipulation and information may be used to free-ride on other traders' strategies. The impacts of trading protocol features on liquidity may differ across markets and the interactions of such features have not been explored in detail. As discussed by O'Hara [2001] the optimal trading design is likely to depend on the characteristics of the particular market, and therefore trading venues should not replicate the procedures adopted by other venues. Comerton-Forde and Rydge [2006] considered the market setup of various Asia-Pacific exchanges in industrialised and emerging economies. The authors noted that these exchanges collectively differ when compared to other international ones and they may improve through fostering pre-trade transparency and by offering different trading mechanisms intended to suit the needs of different investor types.

Inferring whether a particular protocol is optimal for generating liquidity is not a straightforward task. Indeed, according to Purfield et. al. [2006] liquidity problems may arise from the "wider framework" such as inadequate investor protection. In this way, enhancing liquidity may also entail upgrading market regulations relating to transparency and corporate governance, apart from changes in the trading procedures.

3.4. Technology

Exchanges should aim to process transactions at a low cost in the interest of profitability and competitiveness; technology is a decisive factor which impinges on how this objective may be achieved. Hasan et. al. [2003] analysed time series data for a cross section of industrialised and emerging market exchanges and considered the impact of technology on operating efficiency. The authors found evidence of revenue and cost inefficiencies across various exchanges, and these are particularly pronounced for exchanges in Latin America and the Asia-Pacific region. The authors concluded that technological improvements, organisational structure and market competition may be associated with higher operating efficiency. Improvements in technology may also reduce fragmentation, if these enable exchanges to manage the trading flow across different venues.

Cost savings may be realised by using the software and/or hardware of other exchanges. According to Schmiedel [2001], agreements which permit exchanges to join forces and invest in tailor-made systems may enhance operating efficiency. In addition, shared costs make it easier for exchanges to reap the benefits of economies of scale related to investing in a new trading system.

4. THE BROADER FRAMEWORK OF SECURITIES MARKETS ACTIVITY

In order to ensure that emerging capital markets foster the interest of overseas investors, these should be complemented with a regulatory infrastructure of international standard and an adequate base of international operators which bring the markets more in line with developed country practices. La Porta *et. al.* [2006] focused on the legal framework governing securities issues in 49 stock markets, and presented evidence that appropriate securities laws such as disclosure requirements, contribute to stock market development since they facilitate the formalisation of private contracts between issuers and investors. In the theoretical model of Shleifer and Wolfenzon [2002], firms located in countries with better investor protection can raise more funds, due to a reduction in agency costs which increases production efficiency. Chung [2006] analysed ADR data for stocks originating from various countries, and found that firms originating in countries with better investor protection are more liquid. This may be attributed to the possibility that reduced investor protection exacerbates information asymmetries, resulting in liquidity providers posting wider bid-ask spreads.

Different emerging markets face different obstacles in upgrading their regulatory frameworks. Mensah [2000] described the factors hindering the implementation and enforcement of international corporate governance practices in African countries. These include:

- Dominant state enterprises and family-owned businesses which may have incentives *not* to follow international standards;
- Laws and administrative procedures which do not provide for a "level playing-field";
- Limitations in legal systems which result in inconsistent enforcement of subsidiary legislation; and
- Insufficient institutional investors and human resource capabilities to insist on reforms.

5. CONCLUSION

This chapter discussed the salient trends shaping the operations of securities markets in emerging economies. It explored how liberalisation may further impact on the risks and the degree of integration of emerging markets, and the related challenges which should be addressed if the latter markets are to develop further. As the diversification prospects offered by emerging economies become less obvious, these countries should strive to curtail political risk in order to retain the interest of overseas investors.

Other challenges are specifically related to emerging market exchanges. These include the drive to augment listings and liquidity as portions of the current business get cross-listed overseas. The way in which such challenges are addressed may impinge on the survival of these exchanges and according to Claessens *et. al.* [2000] some economies such as Eastern European ones in transition may end up without exchanges. Yet this may not necessarily be the case; as outlined by Kavajecz [2002] it might not be optimal for a country to depend on an overseas exchange since the ability to raise capital might be compromised should political disagreements arise. Claessens *et. al.* [2003] also outlined the necessity for countries to have their own exchanges whose practices such as listing fees and market tiers are in line with the profiles of home companies.

Smaller emerging exchanges should serve as a means through which smaller companies may tap funds. Such companies may be well known within their region however they may find the marketing campaigns and fees involved in listing on a major exchange to be prohibitive. The above factors emphasize the importance that exchanges and other institutions involved in securities activity should be equipped with the appropriate human resources and technological systems to effectively address future challenges.

REFERENCES

Auerbach, P., & Siddiki, J.U. (2004). Financial liberalisation and economic development: An assessment. *Journal of Economic Surveys*, 18(3), 231-265.

Auguste, S., Dominguez, K.M.E., Kamil, H., & Tesar, L.L. (2006). Cross-border trading as a mechanism for implicit capital flight: ADRs and the Argentine crisis, *Journal of Monetary Economics.* 53, 1259-1295.

Baruch, S., Karolyi, A., & Lemmon, M.L. (2003). Multi-market trading and liquidity: Theory and evidence. *Unpublished Working Paper*.

Beck, T., & Levine, R. (2004). Stock markets, banks, and growth: Panel evidence. *Journal of Banking & Finance*, 28, 423-442.

Bekaert, G., Erb, C.B., Harvey, C.R., & Viskanta, T.E. (1997). What matters for emerging market investments?. *Emerging Markets Quarterly*, 1(2), 17-46.

Bekaert, G., & Harvey, C.R. (2000). Foreign speculators and emerging equity markets. *Journal of Finance*, 55, 565-614.

Bekaert, G., & Harvey, C.R. (2003). Emerging markets finance. *Journal of Empirical Finance*, 10, 3-55.

Bekaert, G., Harvey, C.R., & Lundblad, C. (2001). Emerging equity markets and economic development. *Journal of Development Economics*, 66, 465-504.

Chung, H. (2006). Investor protection and the liquidity of cross-listed securities: Evidence from the ADR market. *Journal of Banking & Finance*, 30, 1485-1505.

Claessens, S., Lee, R., & Zechner, J. (2003). The future of stock exchanges in European Union Accession Countries. Report published by the Corporation of London.

Claessens, S., Djankov, S., & Klingebiel, D. (2000). Stock markets in transition economies. The World Bank, Financial Sector Discussion Paper No. 5.

Clayton, M.J., Jorgensen, B.N., & Kavajecz, K.A. (2006). On the presence and market-structure of exchanges around the world. *Journal Of Financial Markets*, 9, 27-48.

Collins, D., & Gavron, S. (2005). Measuring equity market contagion in multiple financial events. *Applied Financial Economics*, 15, 531-538.

Comerton-Forde, C., & Rydge, J. (2006). The current state of Asia-Pacific stock exchanges: A critical review of market design. *Pacific-Basin Finance Journal*, 14, 1-32.

Cuñado, J., Biscarri, J.G., & de Gracia, F.P. (2006). Changes in the dynamic behavior of emerging market volatility: Revisiting the effects of financial liberalization. *Emerging Markets Review*, 7, 261-278.

Devereux, M.B., & Smith, G.W. (1994). International risk sharing and economic growth. *International Economic Review*, 35, 535-551.

Ding, D.K., & Charoenwong, C. (2006). Editorial: Asian market microstructure. *International Review of Financial Analysis*, 15, 288-290.

Dungey, M., Fry, R., González-Hermosillo, B., & Martin, V. (2006). Contagion in international bond markets during the Russian and the LTCM crises. *Journal of Financial Stability*, 2, 1-27.

Edison, H.J., Levine, R., Ricci, L., & Sløk, T. (2002). International financial integration and economic growth. *Journal of International Money and Finance*, 21, 749-776.

Forbes, K.J., & Rigobon, R. (2002). No contagion, only interdependence: Measuring stock market comovements. *Journal of Finance*, 57, 2223-2261.

Girard, E., & Omran, M. (2007). What are the risks when investing in thin emerging equity markets: Evidence from the Arab world. *International Financial Markets, Institutions and Money*, 17, 102-123.

Goriaev, A., & Zabotkin, A. (2006). Risks of investing in the Russian stock market: Lessons of the first decade. *Emerging Markets Review*, 7, 380-397.

Grabel, I. (2003). Averting crisis? Assessing measures to manage financial integration in emerging economies. *Cambridge Journal of Economics*, 27, 317-336.

Hasan, I., Malkamäki, M. & Schmiedel, H. (2003). Technology, automation, and productivity of stock exchanges: International evidence. *Journal of Banking & Finance*, 27, 1743-1773.

Hunter, D. (2006). The evolution of stock market integration in the post-liberalization period: A look at Latin America. *Journal of International Money and Finance*, 25, 795-826.

Jayasuriya, S. (2005). Stock market liberalization and volatility in the presence of favorable market characteristics and institutions. *Emerging Markets Review*, 6, 170-191.

Karolyi, G.A. (2006). The world of cross-listings and cross-listings of the world: Challenging conventional wisdom. *Review of Finance*, 10, 99-152.

Karolyi, G.A., (2004). The role of American depositary receipts in the development of emerging equity markets. *Review of Economics and Statistics,* 86(3), 670-690.

Kavajecz, K., (2002). Comment on "The future of stock exchanges in emerging economies: Evolution and prospects by S. Claessens, D. Klingebiel, & S.L. Schmukler,", In R.E. Litan and R. Herring (Eds.). *Brookings-Wharton Papers on Financial Services,* (pp. 203-208). Washington, D.C.: The Brookings Institution.

Kearney, C., & Lucey, B.M. (2004). International equity market integration: Theory, evidence and implications. *International Review of Financial Analysis*, 13, 571-583.

Kim, J., Kartsaklas, A., & Karanasos, M. (2005). The volume-volatility relationship and the opening of the Korean stock market to foreign investors after the financial turmoil in 1997. *Asia-Pacific Financial Markets*, 12, 245-271.

La Porta, R., Lopez-de-Silanes, F., Shleifer, A., & Vishny, R. (1997). Legal determinants of external finance. *Journal of Finance*, 52, 1131-1150.

La Porta, R., Lopez-de-Silanes, F., & Shleifer, A. (2006). What works in securities laws?. *Journal of Finance*, 61, 1-32.

Levine, R., & Schmukler, S.L. (2003). Migration, spillovers, and trade diversion: The impact of internationalization on stock market liquidity. Unpublished Working Paper.

Lin, A.Y. (2006). Has the Asian crisis changed the role of foreign investors in emerging equity markets: Taiwan's experience. *International Review of Economics and Finance*, 15, 364-382.

Longin, F., & Solnik, B. (1995). Is the correlation in international equity returns constant: 1960-1990?. *Journal of International Money and Finance* , 14, 3-26.

Mensah, S. (2000). *Corporate governance in Africa.* Address Presented at the Consultative Meeting on Corporate Governance in Africa; Nairobi, Kenya, 30 October 2000.

Minier, J.A. (2003). Are small stock markets different?. *Journal of Monetary Economics*, 50, 1593-1602.

Mitton, T. (2006). Stock market liberalization and operating performance at the firm level. *Journal of Financial Economics*, 81, 625-647.

Moel, A. (2001). The role of American depositary receipts in the development of emerging markets. *Economia*, 2(1), 209-257, Fall.

Niarchos, N.A. & Alexakis, C.A. (1998). Stock market prices, 'causality' and efficiency: Evidence from the Athens stock exchange. *Applied Financial Economics*, 8, 167-174.

O'Hara, M. (2001). Designing markets for developing countries. *International Review of Finance*, 2, 205-215.

Pagano, M., Röell, A.A., & Zechner, J. (2002). The geography of equity listing: Why do companies list abroad?. *Journal of Finance*, 56(6), 2651-2694.

Pagano, M., & Volpin, P. (2005). Shareholder protection, stock market development, and politics. *Working Paper No. 105, European Corporate Governance Institute.*

Phylaktis, K. & Ravazzolo, F. (2002). Measuring financial and economic integration with equity prices in emerging markets. *Journal of International Money and Finance*, 21, 879-903.

Pirrong, C., (1999). The organization of financial exchange markets: Theory and evidence. *Journal of Financial Markets*, 2, 329-357.

Purfield, C., Hiroko, O., Kramer, C., & Jobst, A. (2006). Asian equity markets: Growth, opportunities, and challenges. *IMF Working Paper.*

Reese, W.A. Jr., & Weisbach, M.S. (2002). Protection of minority shareholder interests, cross-listings in the United States, and subsequent equity offerings. *Journal of Financial Economics*, 66, 65-104.

Reynolds, C. (2001). A conceptual model of global business growth in Southeast Asia. *Journal of the Asia Pacific Economy*, 6, 76-98.

Schmiedel, H. (2001). Technological development and concentration of stock exchanges in Europe. Bank of Finland Discussion Paper No. 21-2001.

Shleifer, A., & Wolfenzon, D. (2002). Investor protection and equity markets. *Journal of Financial Economics*, 66, 3-27.

Stiglitz, J.E. (2000). Capital market liberalization, economic growth, and instability. *World Development*, 28, 1075-1086.

Tian, G.G., & Wan, G.H. (2004). Interaction among China-related stocks: Evidence from a causality test with a new procedure. *Applied Financial Economics*, 14, 67-72.

Yang, J., Kolari, J.W., & Min, I. (2003). Stock market integration and financial crises: The case of Asia. *Applied Financial Economics*, 13, 477-486.

In: Economics of Emerging Markets
Editor: Lado Beridze, pp. 239-253

Chapter 10

FREQUENCY-DOMAIN VERSUS TIME-DOMAIN ESTIMATES OF RISK AVERSION FROM THE C-CAPM: THE CASE OF LATIN AMERICAN EMERGING MARKETS

Ekaterini Panopoulou[*]

University of Piraeus, Greece and Trinity College Dublin

ABSTRACT

Campbell (2003) confirms the equity premium puzzle in an international context based on the Consumption-CAPM and cross-country evidence on implausibly large coefficients of relative risk aversion. In this paper we adopt a spectral approach to re-estimate the values of risk aversion over the frequency domain for six Latin American emerging markets. We complement our analysis with the traditional time series approach and confirm the results of existing literature of large coefficients of relative risk aversion. Our frequency domain findings, however, indicate that at lower frequencies risk aversion falls substantially across countries, thus yielding in many cases reasonable values of the implied coefficient of risk aversion.

Keywords: Equity premium puzzle; Consumption-CAPM; risk aversion; frequency domain; emerging markets.
JEL Classification: G10; C13

---

[*] Correspondence to: Ekaterini Panopoulou, Department of Statistics and Insurance Science, University of Piraeus, 80 Karaoli & Dimitriou str., 18534, Piraeus, Greece. Email: apano@unipi.gr. Tel: 0030 210 4142728. Fax: 0030 210 4142340.

1. INTRODUCTION

Economists accept as a stylized fact that average stock returns are substantially higher than average returns on short-term debt instruments. The failure of financial theory to explain the magnitude of these excess returns has led to this phenomenon being labeled as the "equity premium puzzle" by Mehra and Prescott (1985). Standard asset pricing models can only match the data if investors are extremely risk averse. In particular, the coefficient of relative risk aversion must be implausibly large for traditional models to reconcile the large differential between real equity returns and real returns available on short-term debt instruments.[1] Of course, we expect different financial assets to deliver large variations in returns, but typically financial economists have explained such differentials by attributing them to differences among the covariances of asset returns and investors consumption, e.g. the Consumption Capital Asset Pricing Model (C-CAPM) of Lucas (1978) and Breeden (1979). The more traditional version of CAPM assumes a perfect correlation between the stock market return and the consumption path of the typical investor. This allows us to measure asset risk as its covariance with the market return. However, in their path breaking work, Mehra and Prescott (1985), using annual US data from 1889 to 1978, showed that the covariance of equity returns with consumption growth was insufficient to explain the observed equity premium of over 6%. In fact, they could only account for a premium of approximately 0.35%.

Much of the resulting empirical literature has focused on the US markets where longer data series exist, but Campbell (1996, 2003) focuses on some smaller stock markets and finds evidence that an equity premium is also a feature of these markets. Specifically, Cambbell (2003) reports evidence from 11 countries that imply extremely high values of risk aversion, which usually exceed many times the value of 10 considered plausible by Mehra and Prescott (1985), and claims "...that the equity premium puzzle is a robust phenomenon in international data". Using the same theoretical setup as in Campbell (2003) and a dataset from six Latin America emerging markets, we adopt both a time series and a spectral approach to re-estimate the values of risk aversion over the frequency domain.[2]

Our approach allows for long-term consumption dynamics by performing a dynamic analysis of the link between consumption and returns at several frequencies rather than over the time domain. As pointed out by Granger and Hatanaka back in 1964, according to the spectral representation theorem a time series can be seen as the sum of waves of different periodicity and, hence, there is no reason to believe that economic variables should present the same lead/lag cross-correlation at all frequencies. We incorporate this rationale into the context of the single-factor C-CAPM by using well-developed techniques to estimate the coherency (the analog of the correlation coefficient in the time domain) between returns and consumption over the frequency domain along with the related spectra of the series (the analog of variance).[3] In this way, we can separate different layers of dynamic behavior of consumption and returns by distinguishing between the short run (fluctuations of 2 to 6 quarters), the medium run or business cycle (lasting from 8 to 32 quarters), and the long run

---

[1] Kocherlakota (1996) provides an excellent survey of the topic.
[2] Some studies have investigated the implications of spectral analysis within economic applications, mostly by interpreting (high) low-frequency estimates as the (short) long-run component of the relationship under scrutiny; see, for instance, Engle (1974, 1978).
[3] See Hamilton (1994) for a general overview of spectral analysis.

(oscillations of duration above 32 quarters). Our findings indicate that at lower frequencies risk aversion falls substantially across countries, thus yielding in many cases reasonable values of the implied coefficient of risk aversion.

The paper is structured as follows. Section 2 presents the theoretical model, while our frequency domain technique is developed in Section 3. Section 4 discusses our data and its properties, while Section 5 presents the empirical results. Concluding remarks are contained in Section 6.

2. MEASURING RISK AVERSION AND THE EQUITY PREMIUM

The equity premium puzzle can be presented in different ways. We adopt the approach of Campbell (1996, 2003) which follows the seminal papers of Lucas (1978), Mehra and Prescott (1985) on the equity premium puzzle. Specifically, we assume that there is a representative agent who maximizes a time-separable utility function:

$$MaxE_t \sum_{j=0}^{\infty} \delta^j U(C_{t+j}) \tag{1}$$

where δ is the discount factor, C_{t+j} is the investor's future consumption stream and $u(C_{t+j})$ is the period utility derived from such consumption. This problem yields the following Euler equation to describe the optimal consumption and investment path of the investor;

$$U'(C_t) = \delta E_t[(1 + R_{i,t+1})U'(C_{t+1})] \tag{2}$$

with $1 + R_{i,t+1}$ representing the gross rate of return available on asset i. The investor equates the loss in current consumption with the expected gain in discounted consumption next period.

Consistent with other studies, we employ a time-separable power utility function:

$$Max \sum_{j=0}^{\infty} \delta^j \frac{C_{t+j}^{1-\gamma}}{1-\gamma} \tag{3}$$

where γ is the coefficient of relative risk aversion. The features of this utility function are well known and have had their validity questioned in the literature.

Specifically, this utility allows risk premia to remain stable over time even if both aggregate wealth and the economy increase. In this respect, aggregation of different investors with different wealth levels but the same power utility function into a single representative investor can be performed. On the downside, however, the tight link between the elasticity of intertemporal substitution which is equal to the reciprocal of the coefficient of relative risk aversion is preserved. Epstein and Zin (1991) and Weil (1989) introduced a more general utility function that breaks the aforementioned link.

Despite some shortcomings of the power utility specification, we retain this specification in this study for two reasons. Firstly, it facilitates comparison with other studies. Secondly, Kocherlakota (1996) reports that modifications to preferences such as those proposed by Epstein and Zin (1991), habit formation due to Constantinides (1990) or "keeping up with the Joneses" as proposed by Abel (1990) fail to resolve the puzzle.

Combining equations (2) and (3), we get the familiar expression,

$$1 = E_t\left[(1+R_{i,t+1})\delta\left(\frac{C_{t+1}}{C_t}\right)^{-\gamma}\right]. \tag{4}$$

Following Hansen and Singleton (1983) and Campbell (1996), we assume that the joint conditional distribution of asset returns and consumption is lognormal, with time-varying volatility. Taking logs of equation (4), we get

$$0 = E_t r_{i,t+1} + \log\delta - \gamma E_t[\Delta c_{t+1}] + 0.5(\sigma_{it}^2 + \gamma^2\sigma_{ct}^2 - 2\gamma\sigma_{i,ct}) \tag{5}$$

where $r_{i,t} = \log(1+R_{i,t})$, $c_t = \log(C_t)$, σ_{it}^2 and σ_{ct}^2 denote the conditional variance of log returns and log consumption growth respectively, and $\sigma_{i,ct}$ represents their conditional covariance. The log risk premium is

$$E_t\left[r_{i,t+1} - r_{f,t+1}\right] + \frac{\sigma_{it}^2}{2} = \gamma\sigma_{ict} \tag{6}$$

where the variance term on the left-hand side of equation (6) is Jensen's Inequality adjustment term due to using expectations of log returns. Therefore the log risk premium is a function of the coefficient of relative risk aversion multiplied by the covariance of stock returns with consumption growth. In this respect, riskier assets get a larger risk premium as these assets are the ones that have a high covariance with consumption and produce low returns when consumption is low.

Letting then $e_{i,t+1} \equiv E_t[r_{i,t+1} - r_{f,t+1}]$ denote the excess return over the risk free rate, we get that the excess return on any asset over the riskless rate is constant and therefore the risk premium on all assets is linear in expected consumption growth with the slope coefficient, γ, given by:

$$\gamma = \frac{e_{i,t+1} + 0.5\sigma_i^2}{\sigma_{i,c}} \tag{7}$$

Equation (7) provides a working formula for the estimation of the coefficient of relative risk aversion by simply calculating the sample moments of excess returns and consumption growth. This type of calculation is refereed to as the 'time-domain' estimate of relative risk aversion.

3. ECONOMETRIC METHODOLOGY

In this section, we present an alternative econometric methodology employed to study the behavior of the equity premium and the coefficient of relative risk aversion over the frequency domain.

Departing from the time domain to the frequency domain we can rewrite (7) for each frequency.[4] After dropping the time subscript for simplicity, we get that the coefficient of risk aversion over the whole band of frequencies ω, where ω is a real variable in the range $0 \le \omega \le \pi$, is given by:

$$\gamma_\omega = \frac{e + 0.5 f_{ee}(\omega)}{f_{ec}(\omega)} \tag{8}$$

where e denotes the excess log return of the stock market over the risk-free rate. As is well known, the cross-spectrum, $f_{ec}(\omega)$, between e and c is complex-valued and can be decomposed into its real and imaginary components, given here by:

$$f_{ec}(\omega) = C_{ec}(\omega) - i Q_{ec}(\omega),$$

where $C_{ec}(\omega)$ denotes the *co-spectrum* and $Q_{ec}(\omega)$ the *quadrature spectrum*. The measure of comovement between returns and consumption over the frequency domain is then given by:

---

[4] In general, the spectrum of a process, say x_t, can be written as $f_{xx}(\omega) = \rho_0 + 2 \sum_{k=1}^{\infty} \rho_k \cos(k\omega)$, where ρ_k is the k-order autocovariance function of the series. In turn, we can consider the multivariate spectrum, $F_{yx}(\omega)$, for a bivariate zero mean covariance stationary process $Z_t = [y_t, x_t]^T$ with covariance matrix $\Gamma(\cdot)$, which is the frequency domain analog of the autocovariance matrix. The diagonal elements of $F_{yx}(\omega)$ are the spectra of the individual processes, $f_{yy}(\omega)$ and $f_{xx}(\omega)$, while the off-diagonal ones refer to the cross-spectrum or cross spectral density matrix of y_t and x_t. In detail,

$$F_{yx}(\omega) = \frac{1}{2\pi} \sum_{k=-\infty}^{\infty} \Gamma(k) e^{-ik\omega} = \begin{bmatrix} f_{xx}(\omega) & f_{yx}(\omega) \\ f_{xy}(\omega) & f_{yy}(\omega) \end{bmatrix}$$, where $F_{yx}(\omega)$ is an Hermitian, non-negative definite matrix, i.e. $F_{yx}(\omega) = F_{yx}^*(\omega)$, with * denoting the complex conjugate transpose since $f_{yx}(\omega) = \overline{f_{xy}(\omega)}$. See Hamilton (1994) for a more detailed presentation of spectral analysis.

$$c_{ec}^2(\omega) \equiv \frac{\left|f_{ec}(\omega)\right|^2}{f_{ex}(\omega)f_{cc}(\omega)} = \frac{C_{ee}^2 + Q_{cc}^2}{f_{ee}(\omega)f_{cc}(\omega)} \tag{9}$$

where $0 \leq c_{ec}^2(\omega) \leq 1$ is the squared *coherency*, which provides a measure of the correlation between the two series at each frequency and can be interpreted intuitively as the frequency-domain analog of the correlation coefficient.[5]

The spectra and co-spectra of a vector of time-series for a sample of T observations can be estimated for a set of frequencies $\omega_n = 2\pi n / T$, $n = 1, 2, ..., T/2$. The relevant quantities are estimated through the periodogram, which is based on a representation of the observed time-series as a superposition of sinusoidal waves of various frequencies; a frequency of π corresponds to a time period of two quarters, while a zero frequency corresponds to infinity.[6]

4. TIME-DOMAIN AND FREQUENCY DOMAIN PROPERTIES
OF THE DATA

4.1. Data

Our dataset comprises quarterly equity and macroeconomic data for the Latin American emerging markets, namely Argentina, Brasil, Chile, Colombia, Mexico and Peru. The source for equity data is the Morgan Stanley Capital International (MSCI) indices adjusted for dividends for emerging markets. The indices are denominated in local currency and the domestic money market rate is employed. In this respect, we calculate the equity premium that a domestic investor faces in contrast to calculating returns in a foreign currency, for example in US dollars and adjusting them for the US risk free rate.[7] Data on population, household consumption, GDP deflator, and a short-term interest rate, mainly a 3-month T-bill rate are available at the IFS Statistics Database (International Monetary Fund). Real personal consumption per capita was calculated by dividing personal consumption with the population and adjusting it for price changes utilizing the GDP deflator.[8] Additionally, seasonal adjustment of the consumption series was also undertaken for the cases that consumption data were unadjusted. Our dataset is the longest available for each country at hand. Specifically, the samples employed are as follows: Argentina (1988:Q1- 2005:Q4), Brasil (1988:Q1-

---

[5] Engle (1976) gives an early treatment on the frequency-domain analysis and its time-domain counterpart.

[6] Consistent estimates of the spectral matrix can be obtained by either smoothing the periodogram, or by employing a lag window approach that both weighs and limits the autocovariances and cross-covariances used. We use here the Bartlett window, which assigns linearly decreasing weights to the autocovariances and cross-covariances in the neighborhood of the frequencies considered and zero weight thereafter, with the lag, k, set using the rule $k = 2\sqrt{T}$, as suggested by Chatfield (1989).

[7] The approach of calculating US denominated excess returns would signal the equity premium faced by an international investor investing in the emerging markets. Such an approach is taken by Salomons and Grootveld (2003).

[8] Population data are reported annually. The series were converted to quarterly by means of linear interpolation.

2005:Q4), Chile (1988:Q1- 2005:Q4), Colombia (1993:Q1-2005:Q4), Mexico (1988:Q1-2005:Q4) and Peru (1993:Q1-2005:Q4).

4.2. Descriptive Statistics

Table 1 reports summary statistics for stock market excess returns and consumption growth. Excess returns are calculated by subtracting the return on the relevant short-term risk-free asset from the return in the stock market index and consumption growth is the difference in the logarithm of seasonally adjusted personal consumption per capita GDP deflated. For each country we report the mean and standard deviation in annualized percentage points of the series and countries under scrutiny.[9] The table shows that Latin American countries share the same stylized facts with developed countries (Campbell, 2003).

First, Latin American stock markets have delivered average returns of 7% or more in excess of the risk free rate. Specifically, Chile, Colombia and Peru just exceed 7%, whereas the excess return in Mexico is 17%. These figures are roughly equivalent to the figures for the developed markets examined by Campbell (2003). In his dataset, excess returns range between 3% and 14%. Quite interestingly, the respective figures for Argentina and Brasil reach the impressive 170% and 146% for the period under examination.

Second, the annualized volatility of stock returns ranges from 25% to 35% for Chile, Colombia, Mexico and Peru. As expected, the higher Argentinean and Brasilian excess returns are followed by higher risk as depicted in their volatility that reaches 461%. Comparing the volatility of these emerging markets with the developed ones, we have to note that the volatility of the former is on the upper part of the latter which experience a volatility of 15% to 27%.

Table 1. Descriptive Statistics

Country	Excess return (mean)	Excess return (standard deviation)	Consumption Growth (mean)	Consumption Growth (standard deviation)
Argentina	170.44	461.01	7.50	13.31
Brasil	146.45	131.78	18.04	21.40
Chile	7.75	24.99	14.46	4.48
Colombia	7.22	35.25	14.85	3.51
Mexico	16.60	29.58	22.09	9.42
Peru	7.06	29.30	12.63	5.97

Notes: Means and standard deviations are given in annualized percentage points. Means are multiplied by 400 and standard deviations by 200.

---

[9] To annualize the raw quarterly data, means are multiplied by 400 and standard deviations by 200 given that in serially uncorrelated data standard deviations increase with the square root of the interval.

Third, consumption growth is rather elevated and depicts higher volatility compared to developed countries. This is expected since developing countries normally experience faster growth that undergoes larger swings. The fastest growth in consumption is for Mexico (22%), followed by Brasil (18%), while the lowest one is the Argentinean one with annualized growth of almost 8%. In any case these figures are 4 to ten times greater than the growth in developed countries. The least volatile economy in our dataset is Colombia, while the ones with the greater volatility are Argentina and Brasil.

5. EMPIRICAL RESULTS

5.1. Time-domain Techniques

We follow Campbell (2003) and present two measures of risk aversion. The first one termed RRA1 is calculated directly from (7), while the second one, denoted by RRA2 assumes a unitary correlation of excess returns and consumption growth. Although this is a counterfactual exercise, we follow closely Campbell (2003) and postulate a unitary elasticity between returns and consumption growth to account for the sensitivity of the implied risk aversion on the smoothness of consumption rather than its low correlation with excess returns. Table 2 reports the average equity premium, the unconditional correlation between excess returns and consumption along with the two estimates of relative risk aversion for the countries at hand.

In detail, the second column reports the mean equity premium given by the left part of equation (6)[10] (i.e. adjusted with the respective variance term).[11] Quite interestingly, there is a great dispersion among the values of the equity premia for the Latin American countries. The higher one is the one of the Argentinean market that exceeds 1200% per, followed by Brasil which is over 200% with the lowest one being the one that corresponds to Peru of just over 10%. The huge numbers for Argentina and Brasil combine two effects, both the increased mean of average excess returns and the respective increased volatility. The correlation between the returns and consumption also exhibits great variation among countries. The lowest is reported in Argentina and Mexico (4%) and the highest one in Brasil (51%). The lower correlations should normally correspond to higher estimates of risk aversion while the higher ones to the lower estimates. This is true as column 3 (Table 2) suggests that reports these estimates.

Specifically, this traditional approach yields the usual finding (see also Campbell 1996, 2003). The estimated coefficients of relative risk aversion of 502 for Argentina, 175 for Mexico and 81 for Peru are much larger than suggested by economic theory.[12] This is often interpreted as an equity premium puzzle. While still outside the economically accepted range,

---

[10] This approach has been advocated by Jobson and Korkie (1981), amongst others, in relation to the application of Modern Portfolio Theory.

[11] The equity premium is given in annualized percentage points. The calculations, however, are done in natural units.

[12] Mehra and Prescott (1985) impose an upper limit of 10 on 'reasonable' values of the coefficient of RRA. However, others such as Kandel and Stambaugh (1991) argue that this parameter could be much higher (up to 30) in financial markets and still imply reasonable economic behaviour.

the estimates of 36 and 16 for Chile and Brasil, respectively certainly move the relative risk parameter in the right direction.[13]

We repeat the analysis for the hypothetical situation where the correlation between stock returns and consumption growth is unity. This case gives the model the best chance of explaining the premium. Indeed, the estimated coefficients are reduced. With the exception of Argentina (RRA= 20) and Colombia (RRA=11), the remaining estimates of risk aversion are all within the economically acceptable values. What it shows is that the extreme risk aversion displayed in the actual data is driven mainly by an almost complete dis-connect between stock returns and consumption.

5.2. Frequency-domain Techniques

Before moving on with the estimates of relative risk aversion, we report some evidence on the comovement between returns and consumption growth in the frequency domain along with the estimated spectra of the series at hand. Tables 3A-3F report the coherency and the variance decomposition of excess returns and consumption growth over the frequency domain (columns 3-5). Column 1 states the respective frequency as a fraction of π, while column 2 reports the time-domain analogue of the frequency in quarters. Zero frequency corresponds to an infinite horizon, while a frequency of π corresponds to a 2-quarter horizon.

Overall our estimates suggest that the correlation (measured by coherency) between returns and consumption growth exhibits an upward trend as we move from high to low frequencies with the exception of Colombia. More in detail, coherency in the long-run is around 99% for Argentina, Brasil and Chile, 67% for Mexico, 32% for Peru and just 9% for Colombia. The Colombian co-spectrum is rather inverse exhibiting higher correlation in the short-run rather than the long-run. On the whole, the short-run correlation (2 to 6 quarters) between returns and consumption growth ranges from 13% in Peru to 90% in Argentina, while the business-cycle correlation (8 to 32 quarters) fluctuates between 8% in Colombia to 78% in Argentina and Brasil.[14]

Table 2. Time Domain Estimates of Relative Risk Aversion

Country	Equity premium (mean)	Correlation	RRA1	RRA2
Argentina	1233.11	0.04	502.01	20.10
Brasil	233.29	0.51	16.12	8.27
Chile	10.87	0.27	35.51	9.71
Colombia	13.43	<0	---	10.87
Mexico	20.97	0.04	175.48	7.53
Peru	11.36	0.08	81.43	6.49

Notes: Equity premium is given in annualized percentage points. RRA1 is calculated from (7) and RRA2 by imposing a unitary correlation between excess returns and consumption growth.

---

[13] The negative correlation between excess returns and consumption for Colombia does not allow us to calculate the RRA coefficient.

[14] The respective figures are calculated by averaging their frequency domain counterparts over the relevant frequencies.

Table 3A. Frequency Domain Estimates of Relative Risk Aversion (Argentina)

Frequency	(Quarters)	Coherency $f_{ec}(\omega)$	Returns Variance $f_{ee}(\omega)$	Consumption Variance $f_{cc}(\omega)$	RRA1	RRA2
0	(inf)	0.995	1.663	0.610	1.25	1.25
1/16	(32.000)	0.987	1.437	0.476	1.39	1.38
1/8	(16.000)	0.940	1.067	0.233	1.99	1.92
3/16	(10.667)	0.776	0.895	0.070	3.95	3.48
1/4	(8.000)	0.448	0.834	0.025	8.74	5.85
3/8	(5.333)	0.792	0.733	0.056	4.39	3.90
1/2	(4.000)	0.936	0.706	0.144	2.52	2.44
5/8	(3.200)	0.981	0.794	0.245	1.88	1.87
3/4	(2.667)	0.986	0.925	0.290	1.73	1.71
13/16	(2.462)	0.976	1.007	0.243	1.90	1.88
7/8	(2.286)	0.953	0.938	0.139	2.53	2.47
15/16	(2.133)	0.876	0.755	0.053	4.28	4.01
1	(2.000)	0.651	0.640	0.023	7.67	6.19

Notes: Frequency is expressed as a fraction of π. RRA1 is calculated from (8) and RRA2 by imposing a unitary correlation between excess returns and consumption growth.

Table 3B. Frequency Domain Estimates of Relative Risk Aversion (Brasil)

Frequency	(Quarters)	Coherency	Returns Variance	Consumption Variance	RRA1	RRA2
0	(inf)	0.989	0.634	1.294	0.76	0.75
1/16	(32.000)	0.969	0.413	0.852	0.98	0.97
1/8	(16.000)	0.826	0.150	0.318	2.22	2.02
3/16	(10.667)	0.606	0.085	0.170	4.37	3.40
1/4	(8.000)	0.740	0.067	0.149	4.65	4.00
3/8	(5.333)	0.799	0.043	0.164	5.14	4.59
1/2	(4.000)	0.646	0.030	0.200	6.14	4.93
5/8	(3.200)	0.637	0.035	0.404	4.05	3.23
3/4	(2.667)	0.602	0.032	0.591	3.60	2.79
13/16	(2.462)	0.209	0.027	0.434	7.72	3.53
7/8	(2.286)	0.587	0.044	0.220	5.17	3.96
15/16	(2.133)	0.548	0.051	0.146	6.16	4.56
1	(2.000)	0.270	0.025	0.121	13.34	6.93

Notes: See Table 3A.

Table 3C. Frequency Domain Estimates of Relative Risk Aversion (Chile)

Frequency	(Quarters)	Coherency	Returns Variance	Consumption Variance	RRA1	RRA2
0	(inf)	0.976	0.003	0.012	3.51	3.47
1/16	(32.000)	0.943	0.001	0.000	45.37	44.07
1/8	(16.000)	0.993	0.003	0.000	48.73	48.54
3/16	(10.667)	0.593	0.006	0.000	85.63	65.96
1/4	(8.000)	0.354	0.008	0.000	185.63	110.38
3/8	(5.333)	0.864	0.001	0.000	218.04	202.72
1/2	(4.000)	0.964	0.003	0.000	119.81	117.66
5/8	(3.200)	0.846	0.002	0.000	215.19	197.92
3/4	(2.667)	0.943	0.004	0.000	77.07	74.86
13/16	(2.462)	0.668	0.006	0.000	179.88	146.98
7/8	(2.286)	0.987	0.003	0.000	177.33	176.20
15/16	(2.133)	0.868	0.001	0.000	411.44	383.23
1	(2.000)	0.331	0.000	0.000	1696.00	975.16

Notes: See Table 3A.

Table 3D. Frequency Domain Estimates of Relative Risk Aversion (Colombia)

Frequency	(Quarters)	Coherency	Returns Variance	Consumption Variance	RRA1	RRA2
0	(inf)	0.093	0.010	0.001	22.34	6.81
1/16	(32.000)	0.061	0.009	0.001	30.71	7.61
1/8	(16.000)	0.035	0.008	0.001	51.13	9.53
3/16	(10.667)	0.059	0.007	0.000	55.82	13.60
1/4	(8.000)	0.170	0.006	0.000	62.59	25.79
3/8	(5.333)	0.304	0.005	0.000	83.65	46.10
1/2	(4.000)	0.371	0.004	0.000	103.01	62.70
5/8	(3.200)	0.268	0.003	0.000	155.69	80.63
3/4	(2.667)	0.178	0.003	0.000	244.71	103.19
13/16	(2.462)	0.119	0.002	0.000	356.00	123.03
7/8	(2.286)	0.089	0.002	0.000	441.08	131.25
15/16	(2.133)	0.039	0.003	0.000	643.67	127.02
1	(2.000)	0.053	0.004	0.000	531.75	122.52

Notes: See Table 3A.

Table 3E. Frequency Domain Estimates of Relative Risk Aversion (Mexico)

Frequency	(Quarters)	Coherency	Returns Variance	Consumption Variance	RRA1	RRA2
0	(inf)	0.674	0.006	0.006	8.60	7.06
1/16	(32.000)	0.618	0.005	0.004	12.90	10.15
1/8	(16.000)	0.389	0.003	0.001	36.69	22.88
3/16	(10.667)	0.188	0.004	0.001	60.99	26.43
1/4	(8.000)	0.345	0.005	0.001	45.56	26.76

Table 3E. Continued

Frequency	(Quarters)	Coherency	Returns Variance	Consumption Variance	RRA1	RRA2
3/8	(5.333)	0.504	0.003	0.000	56.87	40.36
1/2	(4.000)	0.588	0.002	0.000	93.57	71.75
5/8	(3.200)	0.477	0.002	0.000	107.61	74.33
3/4	(2.667)	0.242	0.006	0.000	114.33	56.23
13/16	(2.462)	0.233	0.008	0.000	108.09	52.20
7/8	(2.286)	0.030	0.006	0.000	334.33	58.33
15/16	(2.133)	0.310	0.004	0.000	116.19	64.68
1	(2.000)	0.285	0.003	0.000	136.24	72.68

Notes: See Table 3A.

Table 3F. Frequency Domain Estimates of Relative Risk Aversion (Peru)

Frequency	(Quarters)	Coherency	Returns Variance	Consumption Variance	RRA1	RRA2
0	(inf)	0.324	0.003	0.001	15.51	8.83
1/16	(32.000)	0.320	0.004	0.001	16.51	9.34
1/8	(16.000)	0.258	0.003	0.001	22.68	11.53
3/16	(10.667)	0.174	0.003	0.000	38.08	15.89
1/4	(8.000)	0.116	0.003	0.000	72.84	24.80
3/8	(5.333)	0.150	0.002	0.000	102.77	39.79
1/2	(4.000)	0.156	0.003	0.000	120.48	47.57
5/8	(3.200)	0.141	0.003	0.000	137.56	51.66
3/4	(2.667)	0.126	0.004	0.000	152.96	54.22
13/16	(2.462)	0.126	0.004	0.000	159.15	56.48
7/8	(2.286)	0.090	0.004	0.000	207.61	62.26
15/16	(2.133)	0.081	0.004	0.000	237.79	67.71
1	(2.000)	0.112	0.004	0.000	216.75	72.47

Notes: See Table 3A.

As aforementioned the spectra of the series under scrutiny (reported in columns 4-5 of Tables 3A-3F) can be interpreted as the variance decompositions over various frequency bands (stated as a fraction of π). As can be readily observed, the variability of returns and consumption growth exhibit substantial changes over the frequency domain. Specifically, the variability of consumption is generally muted for 2 to 16 quarters; however, for horizons exceeding 16 quarters a steep increase is prevalent. As the time horizon approaches infinity, the variance of consumption is thirty times greater than its short-run value in Brasil for example.[15] Similar patterns are observed in all the countries under scrutiny. Turning to the spectra of returns, we have to note that in general the variance of returns increase as we move to the end of spectrum (long-run) but these increases are milder compared with the ones prevailing the consumption growth.

---

[15] The concentration of variance in low frequencies is an indication of short-term correlation in consumption growth, such as an AR(1) with a positive coefficient, rather than an indication of non-stationarity of the process, which can be ruled out for the series at hand.

These findings have direct implications for the subsequent analysis, i.e. the estimation of the coefficient of risk aversion, since the variance of consumption growth and returns are inversely related to the coefficient of risk aversion and coherence is positively related to relative risk aversion. Consequently, we expect that as the lower frequencies are taken into account, risk aversion will decrease.

Column 6 (Tables 3A-3F) reports the coefficient of relative risk aversion calculated from (8) (RRA1) while column 7 reports the respective coefficient after imposing a unitary correlation coefficient between returns and consumption (RRA2). Starting with Argentina, we have to note that both RRA1 and RRA2 are sufficiently reduced even at high frequencies. Specifically RRA1 reduces to 1.25 in the long run from 7.67 in the short run. Marginal reductions prevail when RRA2 is considered. This stems from the high coherency between returns and consumption growth over roughly the entire spectrum.

Turning to Brasil, a similar pattern is observed with RRA1 decreasing from 13.34 to 0.76 over the spectrum, while the respective figures are 6.93 and 0.75 for RRA2. Our results for Chile are more impressive as the short-term RRA1 is estimated at the enormous value of 1696 in the short-run and falls to 3.51 in the infinite horizon with similar reductions prevailing RRA2 as well. With respect to Colombia, the low correlation between consumption and returns in the short-run leads to high relative risk aversion of 531.75, whereas in the low frequency a somewhat increased coherency and increased variability in returns and consumption leads to a reduced estimate of 22.34. These gains are further amplified when the unitary coefficient is imposed and as such RRA2 reduces to 6.81. Our results for Mexico and Peru paint a similar picture suggesting that risk aversion at high frequencies is found to be extremely large while it considerably reduces at the low frequencies with estimates at 8.60 and 15.51 respectively. This picture continues to hold under the assumption of a unitary elasticity between excess returns and consumption growth that leads to further reductions to 7.06 and 8.83, respectively.

On the whole, the estimates of relative risk aversion improve substantially at low frequencies and range from 0.76 (Argentina) to 22.34 (Colombia). When a unitary correlation coefficient is imposed, these estimates are slightly reduced for all the countries at hand and range from 0.75 to 8.83. This improvement in the estimates of relative risk aversion for the lowest frequency is driven by the spectral properties of the data at hand. As we move to lower frequencies, the variability of consumption growth increases significantly matching the variability of excess returns and as such the covariance of returns and consumption increases. This property is coupled for most of the countries at hand with a rise in the estimated coherency (i.e. the correlation in the frequency domain) between consumption and returns.

6. CONCLUSION

We re-investigate the presence of an equity premium puzzle in six Latin America emerging stock markets. We attempt to re-address the empirical issue of implausibly high risk aversion within the context of the C-CAPM by looking at the pattern of risk aversion over the frequency domain. Our results show that as lower frequencies are taken into account, risk aversion falls substantially across countries and, in many cases, is consistent with more reasonable values of the coefficient of risk aversion.

Specifically, the traditional time series approach yields the usual finding of high risk aversion with estimates of relative risk aversion of 502 for Argentina, 175 for Mexico and 81 for Peru. However, the estimates of 36 and 16 for Chile and Brasil, respectively certainly move the relative risk parameter in the right direction. When repeating the analysis by imposing a unit coefficient between stock returns and consumption growth, the estimated coefficients are reduced. With the exception of Argentina (RRA= 20) and Colombia (RRA=11), the remaining estimates of risk aversion are all within the economically acceptable values.

Turning to our frequency domain estimates, we get substantially improved estimates of relative risk aversion at low frequencies that range from 0.76 (Argentina) to 22.34 (Colombia). Our findings mainly stem from the fact that the variability of consumption growth increases significantly matching the variability of excess returns and as such the covariance of returns and consumption increases, as we move to lower frequencies. This property is coupled for most of the countries at hand with a rise in the estimated coherency (i.e. the correlation in the frequency domain) between consumption and returns. Furthermore, when a unitary correlation coefficient is imposed, these estimates are slightly reduced for all the countries at hand and range from 0.75 to 8.83.

This evidence shows some improvement towards understanding the dynamics of the C-CAPM in the Latin America countries by reconciling its standard single-factor version with lower values of risk aversion and thus the equity premium over the frequency domain appears to be less of a puzzle.

REFERENCES

Abel, A.B. (1990). Asset Prices under Habit Formation and Catching up with the Joneses. *American Economic Review*, 80, 38-42.

Breeden, D.T. (1979). An Intertemporal Asset Pricing Model with Stochastic Consumption and Investment Opportunities. *Journal of Financial Economics*, 7, 265-296.

Campbell, J.Y. (1996). Consumption and the Stock Market: Interpreting International Experience. *Swedish Economic Policy Review*, 3, 251-299.

Campbell, J.Y. (2003). Consumption-Based Asset Pricing, *Handbook of the Economics of Finance*, George Constantinides, Milton Harris, and Rene Stulz eds., North-Holland, Amsterdam, Vol 1B, 803-887.

Cochrane J. (2005) `Financial markets and the real economy', *Foundations and Trends in Finance*, 1, 1, 1-101.

Constantinides, G. (1990). Habit Formation: A Resolution to the Equity Premium Puzzle. *Journal of Political Economy*, 98, 519-543.

Chatfield C. (1989). *The Analysis of Time Series*, London: Chapman and Hall.

Engle R.F. (1974). Band spectrum regression, *International Economic Review*, 15, 1, 1-11.

Engle R.F. (1976). Interpreting spectral analysis in terms of time-domain models, *Annals of Economic and Social Measurement*, 5, 89-109.

Engle R.F. (1978). Testing price equations for stability across spectral frequency bands, *Econometrica*, 46, 4, 869-881.

Epstein, L. and S.E. Zin (1991). Substitution, Risk Aversion and the Temporal Behaviour of Consumption Growth and Asset Returns: An Empirical Investigation. *Journal of Political Economy*, 99, 263-286.

Granger C.W.J. and M. Hatanaka (1964). *Spectral Analysis of Economic Time Series*, Princeton: Princeton University Press.

Hamilton, J.D. (1989). A new approach to the economic analysis of nonstationary time series and the business cycle, *Econometrica*, 57, 357-384.

Hamilton J.D. (1994) *Time Series Analysis*, Princeton: Princeton University Press.

Hansen, L.P. and K.J. Singleton (1983). Stochastic Consumption, Risk Aversion and the Temporal Behavior of Asset Returns. *Journal of Political Economy*, 91, 249-268.

Jobson, J.D. and B. Korkie (1981). Putting Markowitz Theory to Work. *Journal of Portfolio Management*, 70-74.

Kandel, S., and R.F.Stambaugh (1991). Asset returns and intertemporal preferences. *Journal of Monetary Economics*, 27, 39-71.

Kocherlakota, N.R. (1996). The Equity Premium: It's still a Puzzle. *Journal of Economic Literature*, 34, 42-71.

Lucas, R. (1978). Asset Prices in an Exchange Economy. *Econometrica*, 46, 1429-1445.

Mehra, R. and E. Prescott (1985). The Equity Premium: A Puzzle. *Journal of Monetary Economics*, 15, 145-161.

Salomons, R. and H. Grootveld (2003). The equity risk premium: emerging vs developed markets. *Emerging Markets Review*, 4, 121-144.

Weil, P. (1989). The equity premium puzzle and the risk-free rate puzzle. *Journal of Monetary Economics*, 24, 401-421.

In: Economics of Emerging Markets
Editor: Lado Beridze, pp. 255-276

ISBN: 978-1-60021-850-7
© 2008 Nova Science Publishers, Inc.

Chapter 11

MOMENTUM AND MARKET STATES IN LATIN AMERICAN EMERGING MARKETS

Luis Muga and Rafael Santamaría
Public University of Navarre

ABSTRACT

In this chapter we examine how investor overconfidence and self-attribution bias affects the profitability of momentum strategies in emerging markets, in light of the assumptions made by Cooper et al. [2004] for the US stock market and later applied to the Spanish stock market by Muga and Santamaría [2006]. Consistent with our initial hypotheses, behavioural biases of this kind are found to have little influence in the emerging markets considered, (Argentina, Brazil, Mexico, and Chile) due to the impact of the periodical economic crises experienced by these countries during the study period (1994-2004). Nevertheless, a more detailed analysis of the winner and loser portfolios for the different strategies revealed some evidence of momentum consistent with the presence of disposition investors in these markets.

1. INTRODUCTION

Since Jegadeesh and Titman [1993] first drew attention to the momentum effect in the US market, it has remained one of the most hotly debated anomalies in the financial economics literature, manifesting itself in medium-term return continuation, such that stocks with the best (worst) returns in the past continue to yield the best (worst) returns in the future.

In order to exploit this effect, Jegadeesh and Titman [1993] designed a series of self-financing strategies based on buying winners, that is, stocks with the highest returns over a formation period of three to twelve months, and selling losers, that is, stock with the lowest returns over the same formation period. These strategies were held for a period ranging from 3 to 12 months (the holding period). Portfolios were renewed at the beginning of each month.

The positive returns reported by Jegadeesh and Titman [1993] for this type of strategy potentially challenge the weak form of the market efficiency hypothesis, which states that it is not possible to systematically obtain risk-adjusted profits exclusively on the basis of time series price data. An investor should therefore not be able to obtain abnormal returns by trading on past returns, as with the momentum strategy.

The profitability of these apparently simple strategies laid open a series of questions, some of which have been resolved by researchers over the last ten years, and others that remain unanswered to the present day. Can this effect be generalized beyond the original study sample to other markets and time periods? Once the momentum effect appears, will it be exploited by investors and as a result then fade? Are returns to these strategies due to risk factors omitted by the CAPM, or do we need to seek some other explanation for the pattern? In this chapter, we analyse these questions by trying to characterize the momentum effect for an emerging market setting with evidence for a group of Latin American countries. Thus, section two presents an overview of the profitability of these strategies in a variety of different markets. Section three summarises some of the theories that have been put forward to explain the possible causes of the momentum effect. Section four describes the database used for the analysis. Section five details some of the features of the momentum effect in emerging markets and provides an indirect comparison of some of the behavioural theories regarding the source of momentum in Latin American markets. Finally, section six concludes with a summary of the main findings and conclusions, together with some suggestions for further research.

2. MOMENTUM STRATEGY RETURNS: INTERNATIONAL EMPIRICAL EVIDENCE

The general outlines for detecting the momentum effect were established in the pioneer study by Jegadeesh and Titman [1993], using different combinations of 3, 6, 9 and 12-month formation and holding periods. The same authors also introduced the possibility of skipping a week between the formation and holding period in order to allow for possible short-term reversal, [Jegadeesh 1990]. Thus, they analysed a total of 32 different strategies by combining formation and holding periods of different lengths, some with a skipped period, some without.

Their database was compiled from NYSE and AMEX stocks for 1965 to 1989. The returns to these strategies ranged between a monthly 0.32% (t=1.1) for the three month formation, three month holding period combination without skipping a month (3x3), and 1.49% per month (t=4.28) for a combination of 12 month formation period, three month holding period skipping a month in between (12x1x3). All the strategies tested in their study proved significant[1], except the one already mentioned (3x3). Since their work was published, it has become common to use (6x6) or (6x1x6) strategies, which in their case yielded monthly returns of 0.95% and 1.10%, respectively.

---

[1] Jegadeesh and Titman [1993] themselves point out that, when applying the overlapping portfolio method presented in their study, there is no need to adjust the t statistic to overcome possible autocorrelation in returns to the strategies analysed.

According to the market efficiency hypothesis, once a return pattern has been detected, it ought to fade gradually, unless there is no way of exploiting it or the profits are not worth the risks or costs involved. However, a later article by the same authors, Jegadeesh and Titman [2001], reported positive returns to this type of strategy in the US market during the 1990s. Specifically, for the representative strategy (6x6), they observed significant monthly returns of 1.39%, which is even higher than in their original sample. The literature provides further evidence of the momentum effect in the US market in the works of authors such as Chan, Jegadeesh and Lakonishok [1996], Lee and Swaminathan [2000], and Grinblatt and Moskowitz [2004].

The fact that evidence consistent with a momentum effect has emerged for the US stock market might suggest that the pattern is specific to that market. There are however several articles that report a similar pattern in other developed markets. Thus, Rouwenhorst [1998], for example, found evidence of the momentum effect in twelve European countries[2] for the period 1980-1995. This author observed significant returns to the representative strategies of 1.16% (6x6) and 1.28% (6x1x6) across his sample, which is highly consistent with those reported for the US market. The literature has also provided evidence of the momentum effect in individual analyses of some of these markets, some examples being Glaser and Weber [2003] for the German market, Hon and Tonks [2003] for the UK, Mengoli [2004] for Italy, and Forner and Marhuenda [2003] and Muga and Santamaría [2007a] for Spain.

The published findings for return patterns in emerging markets are less conclusive, however. Hameed and Kusnadi [2002], for example, in their study of 6 Pacific basin countries[3] report significant returns only for their country-neutral strategy (0.37% monthly) while Rouwenhorst [1999] reports significant monthly returns of 0.39% for a (6x6) strategy using a sample of stocks from 20 emerging economies. Evidence of a weakened momentum effect in emerging markets can also be found in works such as Van der Hart et al. [2003] and Griffin et al. [2003].

More recently, Muga and Santamaría [2007b] presented evidence of the momentum effect in a sample of stocks from 4 Latin American markets over a period between 1994 and 2004 with a monthly return of 1.34% for the (6x1x6) strategy. After an individual country analysis, however, the representative strategy was found to be significant only in Chile and Argentina, while the observed returns for the Mexican and Brazilian markets were positive but non-significant.

Thus it can be said that, despite plentiful evidence of the presence of the momentum effect in developed markets, the evidence for emerging markets is less clear.

There are various possible reasons for this. First of all, the possible causes of abnormal returns to these strategies may not be the same in both types of market. Nevertheless, it might also be that the causes are the same and it is only the impact that differs. Finally, results might be significantly influenced by institutional and micro-structural factors. Progress in solving this issue is hampered by the fact that there is still no consensus in the literature over the

---

[2] Specifically, Rouwenhorst [1998] reports positive returns for the representative momentum strategy (6x6) in Austria, Belgium, Denmark, France, Germany, Italy, the Netherlands, Norway, Spain, Switzerland and the UK. Non-significant returns to this strategy were found for Sweden.

[3] Hammed and Kusnadi [2002] checking for a momentum effect in Hong Kong, Malaysia, Singapore, South Korea, Taiwan, and Thailand, found no significant evidence of this effect when analysing each of these markets individually.

sources of the profitability of this type of strategy. In the next section we offer an overview of some of the theories that have been put forward to explain return patterns.

3. POSSIBLE SOURCES OF MOMENTUM RETURNS

Since the publication of the seminal works [see Jegadeesh and Titman, 1993 or Rouwenhorst, 1998] risk exposure spread, or beta spread, between the winner and loser portfolios momentum returns has been rejected as the cause of momentum. For market risk to explain returns to momentum strategies, the winner portfolio, for which the investor takes a buying position, would need to be more exposed to this type of risk than the loser portfolio, where the selling position is taken. However, Jegadeesh and Titman [1993] show the CAPM beta coefficient to be even higher for loser stock portfolios, making it even riskier than the winner portfolio. They also show that when momentum returns are CAPM risk-adjusted, there is an increase in abnormal returns[4].

The real debate surrounding the nature of momentum returns, nevertheless, probably arose when Fama and French [1996] admitted that their widely accepted three-factor pricing model was unable to explain momentum returns. This gave way to several alternative theories, such as the possible presence of omitted risk factors in the traditional asset pricing models, the possibility that these factors might vary in time, that momentum profits may not be enough to offset the associated transaction costs, or that the strategy may not be directly implementable, due to the short-selling restrictions affecting some markets.

Some of the papers in this line of research are Harvey and Siddique [2000], Fuertes, Miffre and Tan [2005] or Muga and Santamaría [2007c] who find a partial explanation for momentum returns using asymmetric risk factors linked to stock skewness and kurtosis. Other important contributions have been made by Chordia and Shivakumar [2002] and Avramov and Chordia [2006] whose findings are consistent with an explanation linked to the variables that capture the economic cycle[5], or Wu [2002] whose explanation was obtained by incorporating conditional data into asset pricing models. The results, nevertheless, remain inconclusive and subject to various interpretations. To cite a few final references that fall within this rationalist approach, Lesmond, Schill and Zhou [2004] and Korajczyk and Sadka [2004] examine the transaction costs involved in the implementation of momentum strategies, reaching contradictory conclusions with respect to their impact, and Ali and Trombley [2006] show the importance of short-selling restrictions when putting these strategies into practice.

The publication of the above cited work by Fama-French [1996] triggered a number of theories departing from the traditional asset pricing models and agent rationality framework to find possible explanations for momentum returns within the framework of the *behavioural finance* theory. All of this was driven by the fact that the "rational" approaches, while having found partial explanations for the phenomenon, had failed to provide conclusive evidence.

Some of the main works in this vein include Barberis, Shleifer, and Vishny (1998) who posit a model in which investors' conservatism and representativeness bias trigger the

---

[4] This result appears widely throughout the literature [see Rouwenhorst 1998, Muga and Santamaría 2007c, or Fuertes, Miffre and Tan 2005]

[5] Griffin, Ji and Martin [2003] performed a world-wide search for evidence of the momentum effect, analysing its relationship with the variables that capture the general state of the economy.

appearance of the momentum effect, and also Daniel, Hirshleifer and Subrahmanyam [1998] who suggest that momentum is due to the presence of investors with behavioural biases, in their case self-attribution and overconfidence. Finally, Hong and Stein [1999] developed a model in which momentum was attributed to slow diffusion of information and the presence of momentum traders basing their trading decisions on past returns.

The works cited above all share the belief that the presence of different types of agents in the market leads to a stock price overreaction destined to end in long term reversal. Thus, as well as medium-term momentum, these behavioural models predict long term reversal in stock prices. Following these considerations, Jegadeesh and Titman [2001] are inclined to give more credit to some kind of behavioural theory to explain the momentum effect in the US market, where such reversal is observed. Their main argument is that, assuming risk-based causes, momentum strategies should yield continuing returns[6].

Another behavioural model, but with a clearly different starting point, since it does not assume behavioural bias, is the proposal made by Grinblatt and Han [2005], who show that the presence of disposition investors, who characteristically hold on to loser stocks longer than winner stocks, will, in the presence of an imperfectly elastic demand function, generate a price underreaction to public information. This will lead to a spread between market prices and fundamentals, and this, together with investor heterogeneity, will trigger momentum in asset returns. These authors base their model on the Prospect Theory and the notion of mental accounting, which suggest that investors use the purchase price of their stock as a reference point for subsequent decisions. In an analogous manner, George and Hwang [2004] claim that investors take the 52 week-high as a valid reference, observing similar effects to those described by Grinblatt and Han [2005].

Some of these behavioural theories have been empirically tested, by authors such as Hong, Lim and Stein [2000], who observe a stronger momentum effect in small firms with less analyst coverage, which they interpret as empirical support for Hong and Stein's [1999] slow information diffusion model. Meanwhile, Daniel and Titman [1999] find higher momentum in low BTM ratio stocks, that is, growth stocks relatively harder to value and on which self-attribution and overconfidence bias[7], to which momentum is attributed in the model developed by Daniel et al. [1998], may have more impact. One possible means to validate these behavioural models is that used by Cooper, Gutierrez and Hameed [2004], who use the market state as a proxy for the impact of behavioural biases among investors. These authors claim that self-attribution and overconfidence might be more manifest after up-market periods and that higher momentum should therefore be observed at such times. If this *were* the cause, moreover, the momentum effect should revert in the long term, as supported by their empirical evidence from the US market. Such results are not observed in other markets, however, suggesting that this explanation can not be generalized [Muga and Santamaría, 2006].

Summing up, it can be said that neither line of thought has managed to find a full explanation for momentum returns, either because of the indirect tests needed to validate the behavioural theories, or because the rationalist theories have proven unable to provide a global explanation for the phenomenon. Some studies have therefore tried to distinguish

---

[6] Such long-term continuation of returns to momentum strategies should be observable assuming a constant level of exposure to this type of risk in both the winner and loser portfolios used to implement the strategy.

[7] Similar reasoning is used in Muga and Santamaría [2007d] where higher momentum is found in new economy assets, in the Spanish stock market.

generically between the two possible causes by decomposing returns into components or aggregate technical statistics.

As already mentioned, one of the characteristics of momentum returns that has been used in the attempt to ascertain the causes, is the long-term profitability of these strategies. Thus, on observing long-term reversal, Jegadeesh and Titman [2001] are more inclined to adopt explanations based on investor behaviour, although they themselves advise caution in interpreting their findings. In an attempt to investigate the issue further, Jegadeesh and Titman [2002] perform a decomposition of returns to momentum strategies based on one made by Lo and Mackinlay [1990], concluding that momentum profits are most likely to be explained by behavioural models, having rejected cross-sectional spread in expected returns and autocorrelation in the return generator factor as possible causes, while being unable to rule out autocorrelation in individual stock returns.

One of the procedures most widely-used in the literature to discern between possible causes of the momentum effect is the bootstrap technique. Conrad and Kaul [1998], using bootstrap analysis with replacement, attribute returns to momentum strategies to cross-sectional dispersion in stock returns, which is consistent with general asset pricing models. The said bootstrap procedure is harshly criticized by Jegadeesh and Titman [2002], however, who claim that if the procedure were to be repeated without replacement, the results would change dramatically, and that the cause of momentum returns might lie in the autocorrelation of individual stock returns, which is consistent with the behavioural theories. More recently, Karolyi and Kho [2004] carried out a comparison between these two procedures using several alternative return generation models, after which they concluded that both are susceptible to potential biases, and the results of previous studies should therefore be interpreted with caution. Muga and Santamaría [2007e], in a study using data drawn from the Spanish stock market, introduced a methodological innovation into the procedure by resampling blocks of returns in the same period to avoid destroying any cross sectional patterns in the stock returns, and, after comparing the results of the procedures with and without replacement, gave more credit to those obtained without replacement, which suggest that the most likely explanation for profits to momentum strategies lies in behavioural finance theories.

Another type of general statistical technique that might help to distinguish between the potential causes of the momentum effect is stochastic dominance test. Fong, Wong and Lean [2005] working with international indexes, show that better past performers stochastically dominate poorer performers, which allows them to conclude that a preference for the winner portfolio over the loser portfolio is not consistent with explanations based on general asset-pricing models. Muga and Santamaría [2007e] and [2007b] report similar findings for the Spanish stock market and Latin American markets, respectively, that is, the winner portfolio stochastically dominates the loser, which allows them to conclude that not even when using individual stocks do general asset pricing models appear to be able to explain momentum returns.

In short, when attempting to differentiate between the potential causes of the momentum effect, the use of general statistical techniques has in most cases provided evidence to suggest that, apart from partial explanations linked to "rational" factors, it appears impossible to find a full explanation for the momentum effect without taking investor behaviour into account. This, together with the difficulty of measuring risk in emerging markets, due to weaknesses in conventional asset pricing models, Estrada and Serra [2005], is why we focus in this paper on the role played by behavioural theories in explaining the momentum effect in these markets.

We are fully aware that ours is a partial analysis, thus, the two approaches will probably be complementary.

4. THE DATA BASE

The data used for this analysis are monthly returns on assets listed in the following Latin American stock indexes: "Indice General" (Argentina), "Bovespa" (Brazil), "IPSA" (Chile) and "IPC" (Mexico) for the estimation period January 1994 to January 2005, supplied by Bloomberg[8], as well as the stock market indexes. In some cases, where the low liquidity of the shares means that there is no monthly return data for some of the stocks, an equal-weighted index of all the securities in the sample during that period is used instead.

With the exception of the General Index, which lists all the stocks traded in the Buenos Aires stock exchange, all the rest are selective indexes listing only the blue chip securities in each market. Although this selection enables us to avoid the serious problems that can arise from infrequent trading in these markets, past international evidence shows that the results may be affected, since several studies report stronger momentum in small securities. [See Hong, Lim and Stein 2000, Jegadeesh and Titman 2001, Hameed and Kusnadi 2002 or Muga and Santamaría 2007a][9].

5. EMPIRICAL EVIDENCE

5.1. Particular Features of the Momentum Effect in Emerging Markets

The empirical evidence to explain the momentum effect in emerging markets is scant indeed. Recently, Muga and Santamaría [2007b], using general statistical techniques, such as bootstrap and stochastic dominance tests, found evidence to reject asset pricing models with insatiable and risk averse investors as a means to explain the momentum effect, thus establishing one finding that leaves scope for the use of behavioural theories to explain momentum returns in Latin American markets. There is, however, still no evidence to show which of the above theories best fits the data for emerging markets.

As shown in previous sections of this chapter, the evidence of the momentum effect in emerging markets is weaker than for developed markets. Nevertheless, using investor behaviour theories, it is hard to predict whether such markets will present higher or lower momentum strategies. On the one hand, the average size of listed companies is smaller, and there is less analyst coverage; two features that would lead one to expect higher returns, according to the model proposed by Hong and Stein [1999]. On the other hand, there are arguments to suggest a weaker momentum effect in markets that are periodically shaken by

---

[8] The stocks that are included are those listed in the above-mentioned indexes at the end of the estimation period. Among the listed stocks there were a few isolated cases that had to be removed from the database for lack of time-series return data. This left a total of 173 stocks: Argentina (60), Brazil (40), Chile (40) and Mexico (33).

[9] The Buenos Aires stock exchange has the Merval index, but for most of the estimation period it listed so few stocks that it was hardly worth including in the analysis presented in this paper. The fact is that, at the end of the estimation period, only 11 stocks were listed on this index. Furthermore, the Merval25 index does not go back far enough to have been of use in this analysis.

economic crises with potentially serious consequences for return continuation, which is a key factor in momentum strategy returns.

Taking the behavioural theory perspective, Cooper, Gutierrez and Hammeed [2004] claim that the momentum effect increases following an up-market period, while Chordia and Shivakumar [2002] use a rationalist approach to show higher returns in economic growth periods. If these periods are very short or frequently interrupted by sudden severe crises, it appears reasonable to suppose that returns to momentum strategies, at least as usually perceived, will decline, unless there are other compensatory factors.

Among other possible explanations, there is the potential impact of disposition-prone investors on asset pricing, but it is impossible to hypothesise to what extent the response of developed and emerging markets might differ in this respect. Only a link with the phenomenon of "house money" [see Thaler and Johnson 1990] would support this as a cause of increased momentum.

5.2. Momentum and Market State in Latin American Markets

To test for a link between the momentum effect and market state, as posited for the US market by Cooper, Gutierrez and Hameed [2004] and later particularized to the Spanish market by Muga and Santamaría [2006], we will present evidence of the momentum effect in the 4 Latin American countries considered (Chile, Brazil, Argentina, and Mexico) following upward and downward market states.

According to the hypotheses presented in Cooper, Gutierrez, and Hameed [2004], the momentum effect should manifest itself more strongly after a period of market gains. One of the theoretical arguments used to support this hypothesis is that the impact of self-attribution and overconfidence prone investors ought to be greater after an up-market period. Therefore, if the momentum were due to this cause, it should revert in the long term [Daniel et al. 1998]. While not refuting the probable increase in the impact of self-attribution and overconfidence prone investors following upward market trends, Muga and Santamaría [2006], present their own evidence for the Spanish stock market, to show that even stronger momentum can be observed following downward market trends. These authors show that the disposition effect [Grinblatt and Han 2005] influences investors in both up- and down-market periods, and is a potential cause of the momentum effect observed in financial markets. Portfolio-specific characteristics may, nevertheless, strengthen the effects during either up- or down-market periods. More specifically, therefore, the peculiar behaviour of winner and loser portfolios in the Spanish stock market produces a stronger disposition effect following downward trends in this particular market, hence the inference that the relationship between the momentum effect and the market state is less obvious than that suggested in Cooper, Gutierrez and Hameed [2004]. Rather, in the context of a behavioural model, it is necessary to take into account different investor types when attempting to explain the momentum effect. The omission of any of them may limit the explanatory capacity of the method used to explain momentum in a given market.

Thus, as explained earlier, these issues have yet to be particularized to emerging markets. The specific expectation is that there will be less impact from self-attribution and overconfidence prone investors, due to the periodic economic crises that beset these countries.

The extent of the disposition effect is hard to predict because it depends on the performance of the winner and loser portfolios around the reference price, in each market state.

The methodology employed throughout this study basically follows that of Cooper, Gutierrez and Hameed [2004], where momentum profits in each formation period are calculated in event time, irrespective of what strategies might be implemented in successive periods. This departs from the "calendar-time" method proposed by Jegadeesh and Titman [1993] and presents a problem of high correlation in momentum portfolio returns, making adjustments to the t statistic necessary in order to assess the level of significance[10]. This drawback is offset, however, by the advantage that it enables us to observe long-run return performance, which is not possible when using Jegadeesh and Titman's [1993] overlapping portfolio method. Specifically, in each of the markets considered in the study, stocks were sorted in a given month according to their past formation period[11] returns, whereupon a buying position was taken on the highest-performing quintile in the formation period, which were used to form the winner portfolio, and a selling position was taken on the lowest-performing quintile during the same period, from which the loser portfolio was formed. The momentum profits were then calculated by constructing time series return data for each consecutive month, from 1 to 48 months after the formation period. The raw returns[12] are cumulated to form the event-time returns to the momentum strategy.

$$CAR_{T+K_2} = \sum_{K=K_1}^{K_2} R_{K,T+K}^{mom}$$

where ($R_{k,t+k}^{mom}$) is the raw profit for each momentum strategy, and the (K_1, K_2) pairs correspond to the periods to be analyzed, which, in our case, are (1,6); (1,12) or (13,48). The first two holding periods will allow us to evaluate the impact of the momentum effect in these markets and the third will enable us to determine the long term performance.

Finally, the following regression:

$$CAR_{t+K_2} = \beta_{UP} . D_{UP} + \beta_{DOWN} . D_{DOWN} + \varepsilon_{t+K_2}$$

allows us to test various hypotheses. Specifically, we check to see if momentum strategies yield zero mean returns in any market state and whether mean returns to momentum strategies are invariant between up-markets and down-markets.

When presenting their results, Cooper, Gutierrez and Hameed [2004] consider a market to be in an upward trend when the cumulative returns of the previous 36 months are positive, in which case that month takes a value of 1 for the variable D_{UP} and 0 for the variable D_{DOWN}. A down-market is one in which the cumulative returns of the previous 36 months are zero or negative, in which case the corresponding values are assigned to the dummy variables. To

---

[10] The t statistic was adjusted using the Newey-West [1987] procedure.
[11] The formation periods are the 6 and 12 month periods typically used in the literature.
[12] Cooper, Gutierrez and Hameed [2004] also use CAPM and Fama-French adjusted returns, but, since there is sufficient evidence to show that these evaluation models are unable to explain the momentum effect and are also difficult to apply to emerging markets, Estrada and Serra [2005], they are not used in the present study.

increase the robustness of the results, periods of less than 36 months can also be used to define the market state. In this chapter, given that emerging market up-trends and down-trends may be relatively shorter-lived than in developed markets, we considered markets to be in an upward trend if the cumulative returns over the previous 12 months were positive and in a downward trend otherwise[13].

The results for the momentum effect, and their performance in up- and down-market states, approximated with the past 12 months cumulative returns for the Argentine market, are shown in Table 1. A significant momentum effect can be observed for the 6-month formation period. Momentum profits for the 12 month formation period, however, while positive, are not significant. Significant long term return reversal can be observed in both cases.

Table 1. Momentum effect in Argentina across market states: Event time raw returns

Strategies	Momentum		Up-Market		Down-Market		Wald Test	
MOM66	1.43	*	1.89	*	0.94		0.7	
MOM612	0.82	#	2.25	*	-0.56		12.3	*
T+13, T+48	-0.91	*	-0.37		-1.68	*	4.9	*
MOM126	0.81		1.21		0.41		0.3	
MOM1212	0.16		1.10	*	-0.67		2.7	#
T+13, T+48	-0.87	#	-0.37		-1.55	*	8.9	*

This table reports the mean monthly returns to the different momentum strategies based on different combinations of formation and holding periods, and the long run mean monthly returns, measured in event time, sorted by market state (up-market, down-market). Assuming an up-market state for positive returns over the last 12 months of the "Indice General" and a down-market otherwise. It also includes the Wald test for difference in the coefficients associated with up-market and down-market states. * and # denote returns and coefficients significant at the 5% and 10 % levels according to the t statistic adjusted by the Newey West (NW) procedure.

Table 2. Momentum effect in Brazil across market states: Event time raw returns

Strategies	Momentum		Up-Market		Down-Market		Wald Test	
MOM66	0.69	#	0.96		0.38		0.2	
MOM612	0.53		0.62		0.42		0.1	
T+13, T+48	0.38		0.18		0.78		0.9	
MOM126	1.13	#	1.08	#	1.17		0.1	
MOM1212	0.81		0.41		1.20		0.7	
T+13, T+48	0.65	*	0.29		1.79	*	7.6	*

This table reports the mean monthly returns to the different momentum strategies based on different combinations of formation and holding periods, and the long run mean monthly returns, measured in event time, sorted by market state (up-market, down-market). Assuming an up-market state for positive returns over the last 12 months of the "BOVESPA Index" and a down-market otherwise. It also includes the Wald test for difference in the coefficients associated with up-market and down-market states. * and # denote returns and coefficients significant at the 5% and 10 % levels according to the t statistic adjusted by the Newey West (NW) procedure.

---

[13] When using the 36 month cumulative index return as the market state proxy, as suggested by Cooper et al. [2004], results are usually similar to those presented in this chapter, although the frequency of market crises in emerging markets may make this a less consistently reliable market state indicator, as will be shown later. The results are available from the authors upon request.

Momentum profits on the Brazilian market (see Table 2) are even more modest, with a 10% significant momentum effect for holding periods of 6 months, and non-significant momentum for 12 month holding periods. Long run returns are positive, albeit significant only for 12 month formation periods.

It is the Chilean market that shows the strongest evidence of the anomaly (see Table 3) with significant positive returns for all the combinations of formation and holding periods analyzed. In this market, moreover, strategies with a 12 month formation period present 10% significant return continuation.

Finally, the results for the Mexican market (see Table 4) reveal a momentum effect with significant positive returns for a 6-month formation period, and for the 12-month formation / 6-month holding period combination. These profits nevertheless fade in the long term.

Table 3. Momentum effect in Chile across market states: Event time raw returns

Strategies	Momentum		Up-Market		Down-Market		Wald Test	
MOM66	1.59	*	1.50	*	1.67	*	0.1	
MOM612	1.09	*	0.82	#	1.26	*	0.6	
T+13, T+48	0.04		-0.35	#	0.37	#	7.3	*
MOM126	1.20	*	1.28	#	1.15	*	0.0	
MOM1212	0.71	*	0.56		0.79	#	0.1	
T+13, T+48	0.51	#	0.10		0.78	*	9.8	*

This table reports the mean monthly returns to the different momentum strategies based on different combinations of formation and holding periods, and the long run mean monthly returns, measured in event time, sorted by market state (up-market, down-market). Assuming an up-market state for positive returns over the last 12 months of the "IPSA" and a down-market otherwise. It also includes the Wald test for difference in the coefficients associated with up-market and down-market states. * and # denote returns and coefficients significant at the 5% and 10 % levels according to the t statistic adjusted by the Newey West (NW) procedure.

Table 4. Momentum effect in Mexico across market states: Event time raw returns

Strategies	Momentum		Up-Market		Down-Market	Wald Test	
MOM66	0.93	*	1.30	*	0.28	2.7	#
MOM612	0.69	*	1.03	*	0.14	2.7	#
T+13, T+48	-0.18		-0.07		-0.39	0.4	
MOM126	0.93	*	1.34	*	0.26	2.4	#
MOM1212	0.24		0.71	*	-0.46	6.7	*
T+13, T+48	0.11		0.05		0.23	0.2	

This table reports the mean monthly returns to the different momentum strategies based on different combinations of formation and holding periods, and the long run mean monthly returns, measured in event time, sorted by market state (up-market, down-market). Assuming an up-market state for positive returns over the last 12 months of the "IPC" and a down-market otherwise. It also includes the Wald test for difference in the coefficients associated with up-market and down-market states. * and # denote returns and coefficients significant at the 5% and 10 % levels according to the t statistic adjusted by the Newey West (NW) procedure.

To sum up, except in the Brazilian market, the evidence indicates the presence of momentum, consistent with the findings of Muga and Santamaría [2007b], while the long-term performance of the strategies differs across the different countries, with strongly negative returns in the Argentine market contrasting with strongly positive returns in the Brazilian market, thus preventing general conclusions at this stage of the analysis.

Having described the overall return performance of momentum strategies in these markets, we next compared performances after upward and downward market trends. Table 1, shows significant positive returns to the different strategies, revealing the presence of a momentum effect following upward trends in the Argentine market. The results fail to confirm the presence of the anomaly in this market following downward trends, however, because none of the returns are significant. Furthermore, there is significant return spread between up and down markets for strategies using longer holding periods (12 months). Finally, the long-term return performance in this market also differs, such that the negative return following up-market periods during the months following the holding period, that is, from month 13 to month 48, is much weaker than after down-market periods. Thus, there is no evidence of the reversal of momentum. This long-term performance runs contrary to what one would expect if up-market momentum were driven by overconfidence and self-attribution bias.

The momentum profits for Brazil, for up- and down-market periods, shown in Table 2, fail to provide any significant conclusions, since there are no appreciable differences between the two market states considered. The presence of a momentum effect in the Brazilian stock market during the sample period therefore remains unconfirmed.

Turning to Chile, in Table 3, there is again no significant momentum return spread between markets states, despite the fact that, unlike the case of Brazil, where there was no discernible sign of the anomaly, significant positive momentum returns can be observed for the different formation and holding periods considered. The long-term performance following down-markets, however, shows significant return continuation. The up-market performance is less clear. For a formation period of 12 months it is possible to appreciate long-term fading of the effect. Where the 6 month formation period is applied, however, one can observe 10% significant weak reversal. This last result would indeed be compatible with a momentum effect caused by self-attribution and overconfidence bias, despite the very slight degree of reversal.

Finally, Table 4 shows significantly higher momentum returns following upward trends in the Mexican market. These returns fade in the long term, moreover, without reaching the point of reversal, which again appears to be inconsistent with momentum driven by self-attribution and overconfidence bias.

Summing up, the market state variable appears affect momentum profits in two of the four markets analyzed, in the sense predicted by Cooper, Gutierrez and Hameed [2004], specifically, the Argentine and Mexican markets both present significantly higher momentum returns after up-markets. There appears to be no significant long-term reversal in these returns in either of these markets, however. In the cases of Chile and Brazil, no significant differences can be observed between up-market and down-market periods. In other words, the former always shows an observable momentum effect, while in the latter, momentum returns are not significantly distinct from zero.

Leaving long term momentum strategies momentarily aside, the results for the Mexican and Argentine markets, where there is an increase in momentum profits following up-market periods, might prove to be consistent with momentum driven by overconfidence and self-attribution bias. However, as already discussed, given the peculiar characteristics of emerging markets that are frequently altered by economic shocks and crises, investors would appear unlikely to display such typically optimistic biases when interpreting their own information. In order to obtain a more detailed analysis of the source of momentum profits, we decided to discriminate the results between the two portfolios used to implement the strategy, that is, winners and losers.

5.3. Winner and Loser Portfolios and Market State

Another potential source of momentum profits in any stock market is the presence of disposition investors, Grinblatt and Han [2005]. Although there is in theory no reason why the presence and impact of such investors should differ between market states, certain features of momentum portfolio performance may prove more or less advantageous according to the state of the market, as demonstrated in Muga and Santamaría [2006]. The impact of these investors is due to their tendency to sell winners and hold on to losers in order to fulfil their particular utility function.

Thus, if, in a market with a high proportion of disposition investors, there is a positive news announcement for some asset, the said agents will tend to overreact by selling winner stocks, thus triggering a supply excess that will slow down information adjustment and lead to a continuation of positive returns. Bad news, on the other hand, causes prices to fall below the reference point of these investors, whose utility function prevents them from selling at a loss. Since this reduces stock supply, information will again be slow to adjust and the result in his case will be negative continuation.

Following the behaviour pattern of these investors, therefore, the observed momentum effect should be stronger when the winner portfolio presents positive returns, asset prices therefore rise above the reference point, and lead to positive continuation, while negative returns to the loser portfolio are followed by negative continuation. This situation can arise irrespective of the state of the market. However, if both the winner and loser portfolios present positive returns, disposition-prone investors will be inclined to sell stock from both in order to realize capital gains and the effect on the momentum portfolio will be less pronounced. A similar process occurs when both portfolios yield negative returns and disposition-prone investors are inclined to hold on to both portfolios.

According to Grinblatt and Han [2005], moreover, there is no reason why the momentum effect arising from the presence of disposition traders should revert in the long term.

In light of the evidence presented above, this section will give the results for winner and loser momentum portfolios in those countries showing evidence of the anomaly[14] for a representative strategy based on a 6-month formation period[15]. The results for Argentina are shown in Figure 1, which gives the cumulative returns per market state to the portfolios used in the momentum strategies.

---

[14] Results for the Brazilian market are not shown, since no significant returns to the various strategies were found either for the aggregate period or for an UP/DOWN market breakdown taking the past 12 month cumulative Brazilian stock market index return as the market state variable.

[15] The results for the 12 month formation period strategies yield similar conclusions for the winner and loser portfolio performance and their impact on possible momentum effect explanatory sources.

ARGENTINA UP MARKET WINNERS AND LOSERS

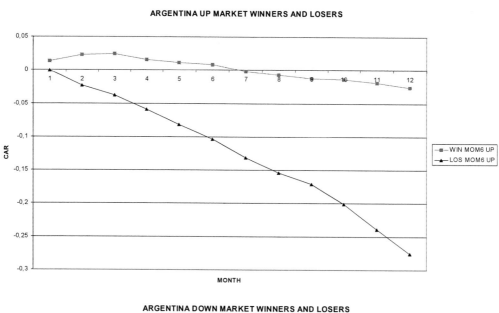

ARGENTINA DOWN MARKET WINNERS AND LOSERS

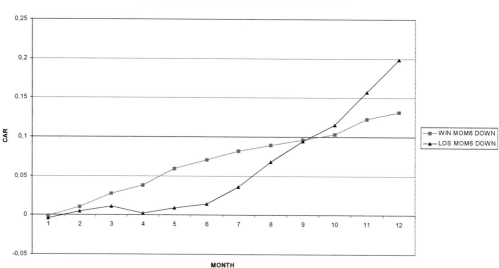

Figure 1. The cumulative return of the winner and loser portfolios used to implement the momentum strategy with a formation period of 6 months, in event time, during up-market and down-market periods, respectively in the Argentine stock market.

Following a period of market gains, the winner portfolio can be seen to yield positive returns for the first 6 months of the holding period, while returns to the loser portfolio are negative. Disposition investors may therefore have an impact on momentum strategies. Table 1 shows that long term returns are negative although not significant, which is consistent with the reasoning set out above. After periods of market losses, both the winner and the loser portfolios show positive returns with no evidence of momentum.

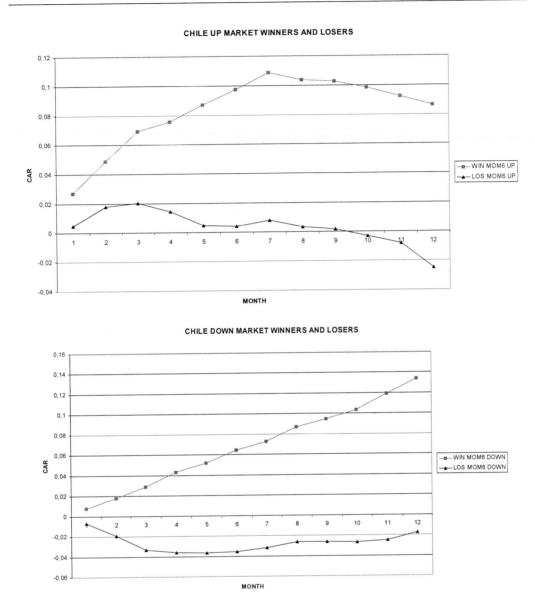

Figure 2. The cumulative return of the winner and loser portfolios used to implement the momentum strategy with a formation period of 6 months, in event time, during up-market and down-marketperiods, respectively in the Chilean stock market.

Figure 2 displays the results for the Chilean market, which hold particular interest because they include a momentum effect in both up-market and down-market states. Furthermore, of the four countries included in the analysis, Chile was the least affected by economic crises during the sample period, which is why the Chilean market is more likely to feature investors acting upon self-attribution and overconfidence bias, cited by Daniel et al. [1998] as a source of momentum. Thus, in up-market states, for a 6-month formation period, positive returns can be observed in both the winner and loser portfolios, so the impact of disposition trading will be low. Given the relative lack of economic crises in this market, it is reasonable to expect momentum driven by some other type of behavioural bias with possible long-run reversal. This is in fact what can be observed in Table 1, which shows negative monthly returns of -0.35% in years 2 to 4. Meanwhile, in down-market states, positive returns to the winner portfolio are observed alongside negative returns to the loser portfolio, thus creating the necessary conditions for disposition trading to have a positive impact on momentum returns. The improbability of a significant proportion of investors being affected by overconfidence and self-attribution bias in such periods decreases the likelihood of long-term reversal, as Table 3 shows.

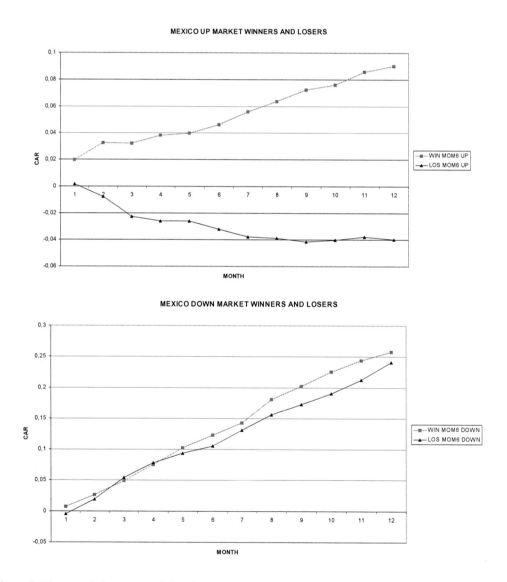

Figure 3. The cumulative return of the winner and loser portfolios used to implement the momentum strategy with a formation period of 6 months, in event time, during up-market and down-market periods, respectively in the Mexican stock market.

Finally, Figure 3 gives the cumulative return trends of the winner and loser portfolios for strategies based on a 6-month formation period in up- and down-market states in the Mexican stock market. Following periods of market gains, the winner portfolio shows positive returns and the loser portfolio negative returns. This again encourages disposition traders, increases their impact on momentum strategies, and reduces probability of long-term reversal. The Mexican market shows no evidence of momentum after down-market states. Both the winner and loser portfolios present positive returns.

Though based on indirect evidence only, these results confirm the ideas set out in this chapter: that is, the momentum effect in emerging markets does not appear to be consistent with an increase in overconfidence and self-attribution bias following periods of market gains, probably because of the relative vulnerability of these markets to frequent economic and financial crises. Thus, the positive returns observed in the Argentine and Mexican markets appear to be due to the presence of disposition traders rather than investor self-attribution or overconfidence. Chile stands out from the rest of our sample by showing positive momentum returns after both up-markets and down-markets. The absence of any major crises in this country, unlike Mexico, which was hit by the *"tequila crisis"* at the beginning of our sample period or Argentina, which suffered the *"corralito"* at the turn of the millenium, allow for an analysis of the momentum effect differentiated by market state.

5.4. Emerging Markets, Winners, Losers, and Crises. A Discussion of our Findings

Although the evidence described in the preceding sections appears largely to confirm our initial hypothesis, we believe it is necessary to explore the results further in light of the existing evidence for other more developed markets, specifically the US market, the behaviour of which is described in Cooper et al. [2004] and the Spanish stock market described in Muga and Santamaría [2006].

The evidence presented in these two studies is consistent with the momentum effect appearing after periods of market gains as a result of the presence of traders acting under overconfidence and self-attribution bias. In the Latin American markets, however, the impact of this type of investor can be appreciated only in the Chilean market, although in a somewhat weakened form, given that the reversal of up-market momentum is 10% statistically significant only for 6-month formation period strategies. We hypothesise that this is due to the fact that periods of market gains tend to be shorter in these emerging markets, due to the effects of periodic crises. Thus, from Table 1 of Cooper et al [2004], it can be seen that there were a total of 674 up-market months (84%) versus 124 down-market months (16%) for the dummy for examining market state, i.e. the past 36 month cumulative index returns. Muga and Santamaría [2006], observing the Spanish market over a shorter sample period, report 245 up-market months (65%) versus 130 down-market months (35%). The market states calculated for the countries included in the present study were as follows: Argentina 65 up (49%) to 67 down (51%), Brazil 73 up (55%) to 59 down (45%), Chile 68 up (51%) to 64 down (49%), and Mexico 85 up (64%) to 47 down (36%). In addition to a general tendency for up-market periods to outnumber down-market periods, the former clearly last longer than in emerging markets. Figure 4 in Cooper et al. [2004] shows periods of over 10 years without a down-market month in the US market. Muga and Santamaría [2006] work with up-market periods of up to 90 consecutive months in the Spanish market. The longest up-markets in the Latin American setting, however, last 18 months in Argentina, 48 months in Brazil, where there is no sign of a momentum effect, 24 months in Mexico, and 39 months in Chile (these 39 would have been 82 if the analysis had been performed on the index returns prior to the start of our sample period).

These data, together with the results observed in the reviewed literature, show that both the number of up-market periods as well as their length and intensity may be determinant in the momentum-driving effect of overconfident and self-attribution biased traders following periods of market gains in developed countries, where expectations are less overshadowed by the threat of economic crises. Thus, in a market such as that of the US, there is clear evidence of positive momentum following up-market periods, due to the activity of this type of investors [Cooper et al 2004]. The Spanish market also shows evidence of this phenomenon, although it is somewhat weaker [Muga and Santamaría 2006]. In emerging markets, however, there appears to be no evidence to support this, except, as shown in the present study, in the case of Chile, where there was a relatively prolonged period of market gains at the beginning of the sample period.

In short, it appears that the presence of periodic economic crises in emerging markets, and specifically in the sample of Latin American countries analysed in this study, has such an effect on the state of the market. For this cause, the presence of investors with self-attribution and overconfidence bias is not sufficient to maintain returns in up-market states as in developed countries. This may be one of the reasons why the anomaly has traditionally had a weaker observed impact in emerging markets.

The frequent changes in market state observed in emerging countries, moreover, may render the traditional market-state proxies useless in that context. The cases of Argentina and Mexico, shown in Figures 1 and 3 are illustrative in this respect. In both cases it can be seen that in situations defined in this chapter as down-markets, both the winner and loser portfolios show positive returns, while, in what have been defined as up-market periods, returns are positive to the winners and negative to the losers[16]. Despite this restriction when interpreting the data, due to the incomparability of the proxies across developed and emerging markets, we believe that the conclusions of this study still remain completely valid. That is, from the behavioural finance perspective, the characteristics of emerging markets prevent overconfident and self-attribution biased investors from affecting momentum returns with the same force as in developed markets. This may be one of the reasons for the lower momentum returns traditionally observed in emerging markets. There are, however, various potential market conditions that may be favourable to the appearance of momentum driven by another type of investor behaviour, such as disposition trading [Grinblatt and Han 2005], which generates a type of return persistence that will not necessarily revert in the long term.

Finally, it is worth noting that, with the exception of the General Index, which lists all the stocks traded in the Buenos Aires stock exchange, the sample stocks are selective indexes listing only the blue chip securities in each market. This stock sample was chosen for the liquidity of the assets, which may substantially affect the results by excluding assets that, due their small size, lower analyst coverage, or other characteristics likely to attract momentum

---

[16] The behavioural anomaly in the market state proxy is aggravated if the past 36 month cumulative return index is used to discriminate the variable, which is why we present the results with the variable based on the past 12 months return index for each market.

traders, produce a higher level of return continuation. In this respect, Muga and Santamaría [2007d] show that the characteristics of some assets are such that they become a focal point for momentum traders. The characteristics in question usually tend to linked them to a particular sector of industry, as in the recent case of New Economy firms.

6. CONCLUSION

This chapter has examined returns to momentum strategies in Latin American emerging markets, concentrating on behavioural finance explanations, since the use of general statistical techniques has permitted us to conclude that, although there may be partial explanations tied to "rational" factors, the momentum effect does not appear to be entirely explicable unless to investor behaviour is taken into account. Since we are aware that the latter approach also results in a partial analysis, we believe that a more flexible view including the two perspectives, should lead to some common ground that can help us to gain a fuller insight into the economic issues involved.

Within the behavioural finance setting, analysis of the role of investor behaviour in different market states has proven to be one of the most successful indirect methods. Specifically, Cooper et al [2004] reveal the explanatory power of overconfidence and self-attribution bias for the momentum effect observed in the US market. Their findings are qualified by Muga and Santamaría [2006] who note that these are not the only biases able to explain the momentum effect, since, if that were the case, momentum would be significant only in periods of market gains, or would at least be substantially stronger than in down-market periods. Results for the Spanish stock market do not fulfil this prediction, however, since these authors find that they can be explained when disposition trading is brought into the analysis.

This chapter has tested momentum performance against the state of the market in four major Latin American stock markets, in order to seek further empirical evidence particularized to emerging markets with significantly different characteristics from those of the US market, which is the typical reference.

In line with the literature, the momentum effect detected in the markets considered in the present analysis is less pronounced than that observed in other more developed market settings. Furthermore, when momentum is tested against the state of the market, overconfidence and self-attribution are found to have little explanatory power for the intensity of the effect. This, despite departing from the findings reported by Cooper et al. [2004], does not contradict their results, since such behavioural biases are unlikely in the presence of frequent financial crises. All these issues taken in conjunction, together with the fact that the impact of disposition traders varies with the performance of the winner and loser portfolios against the reference price, allow us to explain the variation in patterns across markets.

In short, although the results appear to depart from those obtained by Cooper et al. [2004] and Muga and Santamaría [2006] for developed markets, there is no essential difference, given that, first, emerging markets do not appear to create the necessary conditions for overreaction and overconfidence traders to affect stock return continuation and, second, the impact of disposition traders largely depends on the performance of the winner and loser portfolios under different states of the market, and, as already suggested by Muga and

Santamaría [2006], it is impossible to make an a priori hypothesis concerning the pricing impact of this type of investor.

ACKNOWLEDGEMENTS

The authors would like to thank the helpful comments made by anonymous referees. This paper has received financial support from the ERDF and the Spanish Ministry of Education and Science (SEJ2006-14809-C03)

REFERENCES

Ali, A. Trombley M.A. (2006) "Short sales constraints and momentum in stock returns" *Journal of Business Finance and Accounting*, 33, 587-615.

Avramov, D. Chordia, T. (2006) "Asset pricing models and financial market anomalies" *Review of Financial Studies* , 19, 1001-1040.

Barberis, N Shleifer, A. Vishny, R (1998) "A model of investor sentiment" *Journal of Financial Economics*, 49, 307 – 343.

Chan, L. K. C. Jegadeesh, N. Lakonishok, J. (1996) "Momentum strategies" *Journal of Finance,* 51, 1681 – 1713.

Chordia, T. Shivakumar, L. (2002) "Momentum, business cycle and time varying expected returns" *Journal of Finance*, 57, 985 – 1019.

Conrad, J. Kaul, G. (1998) "An anatomy of trading strategies" *Review of Financial Studies*, 11, 489 – 519.

Cooper, M.J. Gutierrez, R.C. Hameed, A. (2004) "Market states and momentum" *Journal of Finance*, 59, 1345-1365.

Daniel, K. Hirshleifer, D. Subrahmanyam, A. (1998) "Investor psychology and security market under and overreactions" *Journal of Finance*, 53, 1839 – 1885.

Daniel, K. Titman, S. (1999) "Market efficiency in an irrational world" *Financial analysts Journal*, 55, 28-40.

Estrada J., Serra P. (2005) "Risk and return in emerging markets: Family matters" *Journal of Multinational Financial Management*, 15, 257-272.

Fama, E. F. French K. R. (1996) "Multifactor explanation of asset pricing anomalies" *Journal of Finance*, 51, 55 – 84.

Fong W.M, W.K.Wong, H.H. Lean (2005) "International momentum strategies: a stochastic dominance approach", *Journal of Financial Markets*, 8, 89-109.

Forner, C. Marhuenda, J. (2003) "Contrarian and momentum strategies in the Spanish stock market" *European Financial Management*, 9, 67 – 88.

Fuertes, A.M. Miffre, J. Tan, H.W. (2005) "Momentum profits and non normality risks" Available at SSRN: http://ssrn.com/abstract=755645

George T.J., Hwang Ch-Y (2004) "The 52-week high and momentum investing" *Journal of Finance*, 59, 2145-2176.

Glaser, M. Weber, M. (2003) "Momentum and turnover: Evidence from the German Stock market" *Schmalenbach Business Review*, 55, 108-135.

Griffin J.M, Ji X., Martin J.S. (2003) "Momentum investing and business cycle risk: evidence from pole to pole" *Journal of Finance*, 58, 2515-2548.

Grinblatt; M. Han, B. (2005) "Prospect Theory, Mental Accounting, and Momentum" *Journal of Financial Economics*, 78 , 311 -339.

Grinblatt, M., Moskowitz, T. J. (2004) "Predicting stock price movements from past returns: the role of consistency and tax loss selling" *Journal of Financial Economics*, 71, 541-579

Hameed, A., Kusnadi, Y. (2002) "Momentum strategies: Evidence from pacific basin markets" *Journal of Financial Research*, 25, 383 – 397.

Harvey, C. R. Siddique, A. (2000) "Conditional Skewness in asset pricing tests" *Journal of Finance*, 55, 1263 – 1295.

Hon, M. T., Tonks, I. (2003) "Momentum in the United Kingdom stock market" *Journal of Multinational Financial Management*, 13, 43 –70.

Hong, H. Lim, T. Stein, J.C. (2000) "Bad news Travels slowly: Size, analyst coverage and the profitability of momentum strategies" *Journal of Finance* , 55, 265 – 295.

Hong, H. Stein, J. C. (1999) "An unified Theory of underreaction, momentum trading and overreaction in asset markets" *Journal of Finance*, 54, 2143 – 2184.

Jegadeesh, N. (1990) "Evidence of predictable behavior of security returns" *Journal of Finance*, 45, 881 – 898.

Jegadeesh, N., Titman, S. (1993) "Returns to buying winners and selling losers: Implications for stock market efficiency" *Journal of Finance*, 48, 65 – 91.

Jegadeesh, N., Titman, S. (2001) "Profitability of momentum strategies: an evaluation of alternative explanations." *Journal of Finance*, 56, 699 – 720.

Jegadeesh, N., Titman, S. (2002) "Cross sectional and time series determinants of momentum returns" *Review of Financial Studies*, 15, 143 – 158.

Karolyi, G. A., Kho, B-C. (2004) "Momentum strategies: Some Bootstrap tests" *Journal of Empirical Finance*, 11, 509 – 536.

Korajczyc R. and Sadka R. (2004) "Are momentum profits robust to trading costs?" *Journal of Finance*, 59, 1039-1082.

Lee, C. M. C. Swaminathan, B. (2000) "Price, momentum and trading volume" *Journal of Finance*, 55, 2017 – 2069.

Lehmann, B (1990) "Fads martingales and market efficiency" *Quarterly Journal of Economics*, 105, 1 –28.

Lesmond, D. A., Schill, M. J., Zhou, C. (2004) "The illusory nature of momentum profits" *Journal of Financial Economics*, 71, 349 - 380.

Lo, A. W., Mackinlay, A. C. (1990) "Data snooping biases in tests of financial asset pricing models" *Review of Financial Studies*, 3, 431 – 468.

Mengoli S. (2004) "On the source of contrarian and momentum strategies in the Italian equity market" *International Review of Financial Analysis*, 13, 301-331.

Muga, L and Santamaria, R., (2006) "Momentum, Market States and Investor Behavior" Available at SSRN: http://ssrn.com/abstract=892756.

Muga, L., Santamaría, R. (2007a) "The stock market crisis and momentum. Some evidence for the Spanish stock market during the 1990s" *Applied Financial Economics*, 17, 469 - 486.

Muga, L., Santamaría, R. (2007b) "Momentum effect in Latin American Emerging Markets" *Emerging Markets Finance and Trade*, Forthcoming.

Muga, L, Santamaría R. (2007c) "Riesgo asimétrico y efecto momentum. Evidencia empírica en el mercado de valores español" *Investigaciones Económicas*, Forthcoming.

Muga L. y Santamaría R. (2007d) "New Economy Firms and Momentum" *Journal of Behavioral Finance*, Forthcoming.

Muga, L. y Santamaría, R. (2007e) "The momentum effect: Omitted risk factors or investor behaviour? Some evidence from the Spanish stock market" *Quantitative Finance*, Forthcoming.

Newey, W.K., West, K.D. (1987) "A simple positive definite, heteroskedasticity and autocorrelation consistent matrix" *Econometrica*, 55, 703-705.

Rouwenhorst, K. G. (1998) "International momentum strategies" *Journal of Finance*, 53, 267 – 284.

Rouwenhorst, K. G. (1999) "Local return factors and turnover in emerging stocks markets" *Journal of Finance*, 54, 1439-1464.

Thaler, R.V. Johnson, E (1990) "Gambling with the house money and trying to break even: The effects of prior outcomes in risky choice" *Management Science*, 36, 643-660.

Van der Hart J., Slagter E., Van Dijk, D.(2003) "Stock selection strategies in emerging markets" *Journal of Empirical Finance*, 10, 105-132.

Wu, X. (2002) "A conditional multifactor model of return momentum" *Journal of Banking and Finance*, 26, 382 – 395.

In: Economics of Emerging Markets
Editor: Lado Beridze, pp. 277-316

ISBN: 978-1-60021-850-7
© 2008 Nova Science Publishers, Inc.

Chapter 12

EMERGING BONDS MARKETS CRISES AND CONTAGION: EXTREME DEPENDENCE

Diego Nicolás López[*]

ABSTRACT

Recent financial crises suggest the importance of the diffusion mechanism, at an international level, of emerging bonds markets shocks. Using extreme value analysis for the sovereign debt spreads of emerging markets, the present paper explores the extreme dependence of the Colombian risk premium to international financial markets. The architecture of capital markets can lead a collapse of emerging markets, where fundamentals do not determine the position liquidation totally. The relation between the Colombian country risk and the United States asset markets shows that an increase in global uncertainty defines a "*Flight to quality*" and therefore an additional increase in the contagion probability for the emerging markets bonds.

JEL Classification: C52; G15
Keywords: Contagion, Copula, Financial Crisis, Emerging Markets, Extreme Value Theory.

INTRODUCTION

Recent financial crises have diffused faster between emerging markets in general, and even have affected countries with sound fundamentals.

Moreover, the link with the country originally affected was not significant. The more recent crises have been characterized by contagion such as, Mexico in 1994, South East Asia in 1997, Russia in 1998, Brazil in 1999, as Turkey and Argentina in 2001 (Exhibit 1). In each one of these cases, a shock over one country trigger a series of extreme events in other

---

[*] Email: diegonicolaslopez@hotmail.com. The ideas expressed in this document are personal and do not represent those of the institution I belong. I want to thank Juan Camilo Cabrera, Mauricio Cárdenas, Andrés Escobar,

countries, having among its many symptoms the increase in the sovereign debt spread. The main target of this work is to accomplish an analysis of the extreme dependence of an emerging sovereign bonds spreads sample having for reference the Colombian country risk. The objective is to analyse the different interactions between emerging markets, conditionally to high volatility spreads periods. Thus, we analyse the direct effect over the Colombian country risk under an extreme dependence structure. Using a copula function overcomes the econometric difficulty in measuring and defining contagion.

We want to explore if there exist a contagion phenomena towards the risk premium of the colombian external debt during high volatility periods and the principal characteristics that has this transmission.

At the same time, we go far beyond the current literature carrying on an analysis based on multivariate extreme values for the bonds of emerging countries, work that has not been accomplished having for principal target the relation with the colombian debt spread. In the first part of the paper, a literature review about international shocks propagation is made. In the second part, we study the empirical literature, which has been the principal tool of analysis. This is the theoretical support of the empirical model build next. In a third part, we analyse the stylised facts for daily frequency financial series. In a fourth part, we develop an univariate analysis that estimates the marginal probability distributions. In a fifth part, we estimate the joint distribution of the stochastic process. In the sixth part, we present the corresponding results.

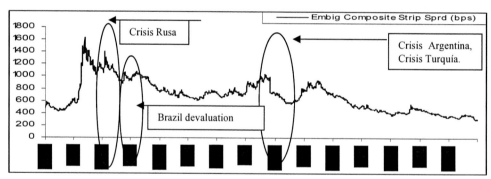

Source: J.P Morgan. Financial stress episodes are characterized by an increase in the country risk of similar countries from the point of view of investors as the case of Brazil, Russia, and Turkey, Argentina.

Exhibit 1. Recent financial crises in emerging markets.

Luis Fernando Melo, Enrique Pinzón, Miguel Urrutia, and Andrés Villaquirán for useful discussions and helpful comments. Finally, the remaining errors are my own totally responsibility.

LITERATURE REVIEW

1. Theoretical Literature

The contagion literature can be divided in two groups. The first one analyses the contagion phenomena under the *"balance of payments crisis"* point of view. The second one focuses on the dependence between financial markets, arguing for the international diversification of portfolios, and the capital market architecture. Because of incomplete markets or information asymmetries, emerging markets shows multiple equilibriums.

1.1. Non Crisis Contingent

Forbes and Rigobon (2000a) introduce a difference between the non-crisis contingent and the crisis contingent literature. The first one refers to the shocks that trigger an international propagation, with no change in the transmission channel after the initial shock.

The propagation is justified by economic links between related countries. In this literature the principal channels of contagion are international commerce, as aggregates random shocks.

Spillovers of international commerce refer to significant devaluations, those that can affect the exportations of others countries. This is formally derived in Gerlach and Smets (1995) and empirically by Eichengreen, Rose, and Wyplosz (1997). Aggregate random shocks, equivalent to an external shock, affect in a simultaneously way the fundamentals of a group of countries. Masson (2000) defines those as big changes in industrialized countries who trigger a crisis in emerging markets. In this case, a hike in international interest rates is considered as an exogenous liquidity shock.

1.2. Crisis Contingent

The focus of this document refers to the propagation of international shocks, under the point of view in which the transmission mechanism has changed after the initial shock. The transmission is not justified by economical fundamentals or real links between markets, making that countries with sound fundamentals could be affected. The principal explanation has been given by multiple equilibriums, endogenous liquidity shocks, and herd behaviour. Multiple equilibriums are realized when a crisis in one market becomes a sunspot in other market as in Masson (2000). The change towards a bad equilibrium is accomplished by investors expectations without a necessarily significant change in fundamentals.

An endogenous liquidity model is presented by Valdes (1996), as in Calvo (1999a). In this case, information asymmetries play an important role. Informed agents confront a liquidity shock, while the uninformed cannot distinguish between a shock and a bad signal. The rational agent, but uninformed, over react to the signal emitted by the informed investor.

The herd behaviour is presented in Calvo (1996). If there is an inadequate research of fundamentals, it is optimal to sell simultaneously in two markets when a problem appears in one of them.

In this paper, we will focus on the crisis contingent models. Contagion between two countries is defined as the surpass of a threshold for the sovereign debt of country X_1 fact that increase the probability of exceeding the threshold for the debt spread of another country X_2 independently of fundamentals.

$$P(X_2 > x_2 | X_1 > x_1) > P(X_2 > x_2 | X_1 \leq x_1) \tag{1}$$

When a *crash*, defined as the excess of a threshold, occurs somewhere in the world, the probability of a simultaneous crash in another country increases.

In this case, the contagion measure depends of the conditionally marginal probability under periods of speculative pressure as in Straetmans (2001).

2. Empirical Literature

Most of the empirical literature lies on the long-term relationship between markets and assets. In general, this literature is concerned with long periods of analysis for the dependence between markets without emphasis on the crisis period in particular. Recently, some studies have concentrated in the relationship between financial markets in the short run. Longin y Solnik (1995) shows that the interaction between financial markets is higher in periods of high volatility.

Likewise, Koedijk, Schafgans and de Vries (1990), remarks that while average risks have decreased, *"extreme risks"* have surged, defining those extreme risks, as large changes in the underlying asset returns.

2.1. Correlation as a Measure of Dependence

The background of the empirical treatment of this theme is based on a frequency data that is at least monthly. The approaches in this way have been dominated by linear regressions as by comparisons between correlations. An example of this literature is Kofman y Martens (1997). Another focus has been based on vector autoregressive as in Von Furstenberg and Jeon (1989).

More specifically, dichotomous models support recent approximations. In this case it is established the relationship between the evolution of fundamentals and the probability of a crisis occurrence as in Kaminsky and Reinhart (1998).

This type of analysis in general has emphasised on the relationship between variables in the long run. However, contagion is eminently a short run phenomena between financial markets, characteristic that implies daily frequency data.

On the other hand, linear correlation is a measure of dependence for multivariate normal distributions. The properties of dependence in the world of elliptical distributions are unsustainable in the non-elliptical world. The Pearson correlation is not a measure of dependence of a random variable vector as in Embrechts, McNeil, Strautman (1999). Correlation is a measure of dependence only in the particular case of normal multivariate distribution.

Then, it is a stylised fact that financial series are non-normal, non stationary, non lineal and heteroscedastics.

Following Embrecht et al (1999) the correlation is defined when variances are finite; in this case, daily data of financial series exhibit fat tails, so correlation is not an adequate tool for studying the dependence over the tails of the distribution. Correlation quantifies a dependence measure over the central moments of the distribution, not only for the tails of the distribution where extreme events are concentrated. An appropriate measure must extract the entire dependence structure.

Furthermore, Pearson correlation is not robust to heteroscedasticity as shown in Forbes and Rigobon (1999),and in Boyer, Gibson, Loretan (1999).

Daily financial series follow an autoregressive conditional volatility process, where volatility clusters in periods of crises following the phenomena known as "*Volatility Clustering*"[1], reason why correlation is not an adequate tool for carrying a dependence analysis between financial markets. The properties that a dependence measure must accomplish have been analysed by Nelsen (1998). A dependence measure δ must:

- δ Must be defined for every pair (X_1, X_2)

- $\delta(X_1, X_2) = \delta(X_2, X_1)$; The measure of dependence must be symmetric.

- $0 \leq \delta(X_1, X_2) \leq 1$;

- $\delta(X_1, X_2) = 0$; If and only if X_1 y X_2 are independents.

- $\delta(X_1, X_2) = 1$; If and only if X_1 y X_2 are comonotonic or counter monotonic.

- $\delta(X_1, X_2) = \delta(T_1(X_1), T_2(X_2))$; The measure of dependence must be invariant to monotonic transformations in the marginals.

Pearson correlation does not describe appropriately the dependence measure criteria given the fact that correlation depends on the joint density function, and at the same time on the marginal distributions. In contrast, a copula accomplishes this criteria and represent the true statistical dependence because it links the marginal distributions of a group of individual risks to the joint distribution. Hence, Longin y Solnik (2000) have proposed the extreme value approximation in a multivariate scenario, having for objective the analysis of the dependence between financial assets.

3. Stylised Facts

3.1. Non Normality, Non-stationarity, Non-linearity, Heteroscedasticity

The database is a daily spread[2] sample, in basic points, of the Emerging Market Bond Index Global[3].

Observations start the 02/01/98 until 10/06/05. The sample represents a speculative period. The end of the sample is established as the day in which the new issues of Argentina's sovereign debt have been added to the EMBIG index, since this date, new bonds are added to the index replacing the defaulted bonds of this country. The capital market open again his

---

[1] See Pagan (1996).

[2] Returns and risk premiums controls the common movements generated by the American treasuries yield curve in the analysis.

[3] The Emerging Markets Bond Index Global (EMBIG) published by J.P. Morgan reply totals returns for a debt instrument denominated in dollars and issued by sovereign entities from the emerging markets.

doors to this type of issues, representing a decrease in the uncertainty and hence defining the end of a period characterized by high levels of risk aversion.

The sovereign debt spreads used are: Argentina, Brazil, Bulgaria, Colombia, China, Ecuador, Philippines, Malaysia, Morocco, Mexico, Nigeria, Panama, Peru, Poland, Russia, South Africa, Thailand, Turkey, and Venezuela. In addition, we incorporate the EMBIG Asia index, representative of the Asian emerging markets in general. Also for a complete analysis we carry on a comparison with the principal United States assets; we incorporated in this sample the Moody's Seasoned Aaa Corporate Bond Yield index, the Moody's Seasoned Baa Corporate Bond Yield, the Spx Vix index from the Cboe, the S&P 500 index, the Nasdaq index, the Morgan Stanley Equity Latin America MSCI index, as the High Yields index of Merril Lynch[4].

The first building block of the econometric model is the identification of the principal statistical characteristics of the series.

By this way, daily financial series are leptokurtic, so they present fat tails. Then they are not normal. Also, they present a unitary root, consequently they are not stationary[5].

Series are not independent and identically distributed over time, there exist evidence of non linearity dependence, which is a signal of chaos in the series and finally they present periods of volatility cluster, so they are heretoscedastics[6].

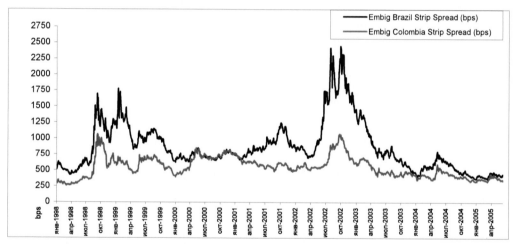

Fuente: J.P Morgan. Bloomberg.

Figure 1. Colombia and Brazil debt spreads.

---

[4] The Us High Yield bonds, is composed by ratings below the threshold Baa/BBB. The volatility index Vix is a weighted average of the implied volatility for put and call options for the S&P500. This index is *"forward looking"*, and represents expectations about the future volatility. The value increases as a result of an increase in the uncertainty. The value diminishes for periods of low volatility, those who are linked to periods of less financial stress.

[5] An increase in the yield, means investor losses in his profits and losses book, the return is,

$$- \left(\frac{P_t - P_{t-1}}{P_{t-1}} \right) \approx - \left(\ln(P_t) - \ln(P_{t-1}) \right)$$. (See exhibit N°2).

[6] A complete explanation of the stylised facts in financial series, as the techniques that have been built to model these characteristics can be found in Pagan A, *"The econometrics of financial markets"*. (1996). Journal of Empirical Finance.

Univariate normality could be verified by the Jarque Bera test. For every one of the series of the sample the null hypothesis of normality is rejected at the 1% level of confidence. Most of the level series have a skewness different to zero and a kurtosis major than three (Table 1).

Series are neither lineal. The BDS test rejects the null hypothesis of linearity for every one of the series in levels (Table 1).

This result is evidence of serial autocorrelation, non-stationary, heteroscedasticity or chaos.

The Dickey Fuller test tells us that the series presents a unitary root, besides the autocorrelogram shows a high persistence path. The Q statistics of Ljung Box are highly significant; hence series are non stationary[7] (Table 1).

At the same time, we analyse the autocorrelogram of second order as the Arch test, which identify an autoregressive conditional heteroscedastic process for most of the series[8] (Table 2).

3.2. Modelling the Marginal Dynamics

It is necessary to model the particular dynamics of the mean and the conditional volatility, in order to obtain a white noise tail distribution, given the stylised facts presented in the first part of the text. Thus, we use the filter developed in Mc Neil and Frey (2000).

3.2.1. Debt Spreads Filter: ARMA-GARCH

Filtering the series is a two-stage process, resulting on the conditional tail distribution for the heteroscedastics returns series of the sovereign debt.

1- we estimate an AR(1)-GARCH(1;1) model. The mean follows an AR(1) process with a GARCH(1;1) error (Table 2).

$$X_t = \varphi_t + \sigma_t \varepsilon_t$$
$$\varphi_t = \lambda X_{t-1} \tag{2}$$
$$\sigma_t^2 = \alpha_0 + \alpha_1 (X_{t-1} - \varphi_{t-1})^2 + \beta_1 \sigma_{t-1}^2$$

$$\alpha_0 > 0; \alpha_1, \beta_1 \geq 0; \alpha_1 + \beta_1 \leq 1; |\lambda| < 1 \ ; E(\varepsilon_t) = 0 \ ; E(\varepsilon_t^2) = 1 ; \varepsilon_t \sim iid \ ;$$

This process could be written as:

$$X_t = \sum_{k=0}^{\infty} \lambda^k y_{t-k}$$
$$y_t = \sigma_t \varepsilon_t \tag{3}$$
$$\sigma_t^2 = \alpha_0 + \alpha_1 y_{t-1}^2 + \beta_1 \sigma_{t-1}^2$$

---

[7] The Vix is the only stationary series without a difference.
[8] There is not enough evidence to reject the null hypothesis that data does not follow an Arch process in his principal lags order for the Ecuador Embig and the Asia Embig.

Where $(y_t)_{t \in Z}$ is a GARCH(1;1).

From this model, we obtain the standardized residuals:

$$(\hat{z}_{t-n+1},...,\hat{z}_t) = \left(\frac{X_{t-n+1} - \hat{\varphi}_{t-n+1}}{\hat{\sigma}_{t-n+1}} ,...., \frac{X_t - \hat{\varphi}_t}{\hat{\sigma}_t} \right) \tag{4}$$

Running the BDS test for the residuals, it does not exist enough statistical evidence to reject the null hypothesis that, residuals are distributed independent and identically for most of the series [9](Table 2).

Also, it does not exist enough statistical evidence, for each one of the series, to reject the null hypothesis that residuals do not follow an ARCH process in their principal lags. The filter output or residuals are homoscedastic series and independent and identically distributed (Table 2).

2- from the standardized residuals that are a white noise process for most of the series (Table 2) we use the extreme value theory (EVT) searching for an accurate estimation of the univariates probabilities.

The second moments are not enough to explain the diffusion phenomena. Following the contagion definition established in this document, we are interested in large catastrophic movements in the spreads. The extreme value theory and in particular the *"Peaks over threshold"[10]* methodology is focused on those events that exceed a high threshold, so we model this events in a different manner in contrast to the rest of the distribution.

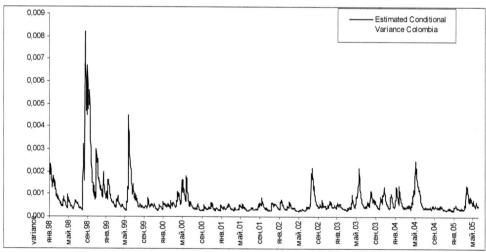

Fuente: Author's Calculation. Heteroscedasticity is an important part of the tails of the distribution.

Figure 2. Conditional variance estimation for the Colombian debt spread.

---

[9] After the filter, the Embig China and the Embig Thailand are the unique series that are not independent and identically distributed (iid). The use of the extreme value theory under non-lineal series creates unstable results, for that reason be careful with the interpretation of this two series.

[10] This approach offers a parametric shape of the distribution tail and extrapolate the probabilities in the tail where by definition those probabilities are hard to estimate. See appendix (a) for a better explanation.

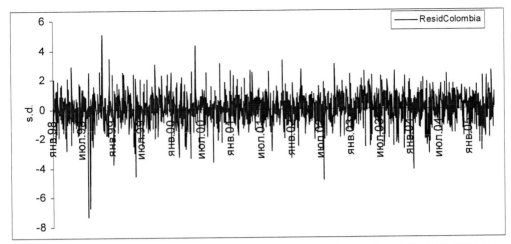

Fuente: Author's calculations. The standardized residuals for each AR(1)-GARCH(1;1) are denominated in standard deviations of the original returns.

Figure 3. ARMA GARCH filtered residuals for the Colombian debt spread.

METHODOLOGY

4. Univariate Analysis. Marginal distributions

For the estimation of a conditional probability of simultaneous *crash*, we must estimate three probabilities in two stages. In the first stage, we calculate the two univariate probabilities of the excess returns, in particular $P(X_1 > x_1)$ and $P(X_2 > x_2)$.

In the second stage, we estimate the bivariate probability of excesses, that means, $P(X_1 > x_1 \cap X_2 > x_2)$. By this approach we have non endogeneity, omitted variables or heteroscedasticity problems in the estimation.

4.1. Extreme Value Theory

The methodological solution is based on the *"outliers"* of the series. We could appreciate that the extreme events occur at the same time for most of the countries (Table 3).

The determination of the threshold by three different ways, assure the robustness of the model in the univariate stage. The proximity of the different thresholds confirms a lack of sensibility to the number of observations used by each method. The different methods used are the mean excess graph, the hill estimator plot, and the minimization of the mean square error of the hill estimator through a bootstrapping approach[11].

4.2. Mean Excess Discontinuity

Under this methodology, we take the observations of the residual series losses that exceed a defined threshold, u, then we model in a separate form the observations chosen in comparison to the total distribution. The estimation is by maximum likelihood over the

---

[11] Bootstrapping is a historical simulation technique based on random subsampling.

Generalized Pareto Distribution (GPD). This is a two parameters distribution with functional form:

$$G_{\xi,\beta} = \begin{cases} 1 - (1 + \xi x / \beta)^{-1/\xi} & \xi \neq 0 \\ 1 - \exp(-x/\beta) & \xi = 0 \end{cases} \tag{5}$$

Where $\beta > 0$, y $x \geq 0$ when $\xi \geq 0$ y $0 \leq x \leq -\beta/\xi$ when $\xi < 0$.

The distribution is called generalized in the sense that it comports others distributions implicitly, as the ordinary Pareto distribution when $\xi > 0$, the exponential distribution when $\xi = 0$ and the Pareto II distribution when $\xi < 0$. ξ Is the shape parameter and β is the scale parameter. If $\xi > 0$, the shape parameter reflects fat tails. The excess distribution over a threshold, u, is defined as:

$$Fu(y) = P\{X - u \leq y | X > u\} \tag{6}$$

For $0 \leq y \leq x_0 - u$, where $x_0 \leq \infty$ is the final point in the right side of Fu.

The excess distribution represents the probability that a loss exceeds the threshold u by a quantity y, given the information that we have exceeded the threshold.

Using the following limit theorem, developed in Balkema and de Haan (1974) as in Pickands (1975), the convergence of the maximums distribution towards a Generalized Pareto Distribution can be demonstrated, assuming that the random variable sequences are iid, as ours residuals estimated, we have then:

$$\lim_{u \to x_0} \quad \sup_{0 \leq y \leq x_0 - u} \quad \left| F_u(y) - G_{\xi,\beta(u)}(y) \right| = 0 \tag{7}$$

$$F_u(y) = G_{\xi,\beta(u)}(y) \tag{8}$$

Assuming that N_u from n data exceeds the threshold, the GPD is fitted to N_u excesses using the maximum likelihood estimation.

One way of defining the threshold is graphically. If the excess over the threshold $(X-u)$ follows a Generalized Pareto Distribution with parameters $\xi < 1$ and β, the excess over the threshold u is:

$$e(u) = E\left[X - u | X > u\right] = \frac{\beta + \xi u}{1 - \xi}; \tag{9}$$

These are the expected losses, conditionally to the excesses over a defined threshold. These mean excess function is linear in the threshold u, special feature that make it prone to choose an appropriate value of the threshold.

The excess distribution function could be written as:

$$1 - F(x) = (1 - F(u))(1 - F_u(x - u)) \tag{10}$$

And, the tail estimator could be expressed as:

$$F(\hat{x}) = 1 - \frac{N_u}{n}\left(1 + \hat{\xi}\frac{x - u}{\hat{\beta}}\right)^{-1/\hat{\xi}} \tag{11}$$

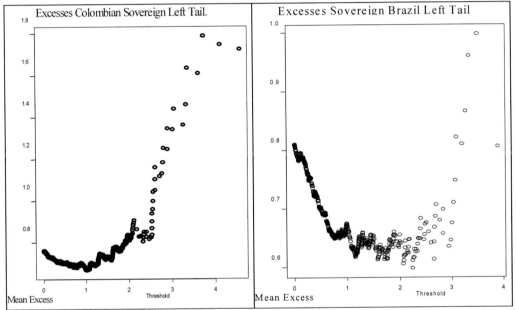

Fuente: Author's Calculation. The threshold is defined when the mean excess is non continuous and data follows a positive lineal trend.

Figure 4. Mean excess. Colombia spread, Brazil spread.

The number of observations in the tail of the distribution such as: $N = k$. This gives a threshold for the statistic (k+1).

The residuals ordered are $u_1 \geq u_2 \geq ... \geq u_n$; The Generalized Pareto distribution whose parameters are ξ and β fit the residuals excess over a determined threshold, it is $\left(u_{(1)} - u_{(k+1)}, ..., u_{(k)} - u_{(k+1)}\right)$. From the functional form of the tail estimator we can take quantils over the unconditionals tails, with an associated probability p.

Table 1. Debt spreads descriptive statistics

	Mean	Maximum	Minimum	Std.Dev	Skewness	Kurtosis	Jarque-Bera	Prob	Observations	Bds stat dim 6	Prob	ADF Test Statistic	10% Critical Value	5% Critical Value
ARGENTINA	2974,962	7222	381	2348,892	0,186322	1,247335	248,6953	0	1859	0,541174	0	-0,601506	-2,5679	-2,8636
ASIA	302,7682	926	182	100,4254	3,086389	15,32121	14710,54	0	1859	0,535926	0	-2,579926	-2,5679	-2,8636
BRAZIL	858,4368	2451	372	377,4958	1,454563	5,347241	1082,291	0	1859	0,537767	0	-2,202651	-2,5679	-2,8636
BULGARIA	508,8838	1679	62	302,3005	0,358858	2,732952	45,42389	0	1859	0,552491	0	-1,486512	-2,5679	-2,8636
CHINA	113,1501	364	39	51,81876	1,043775	5,035421	658,4583	0	1859	0,526245	0	-1,870880	-2,5679	-2,8636
COLOMBIA	552,2813	1076	261	160,2875	0,572125	3,084432	101,969	0	1859	0,524895	0	-2,564833	-2,5679	-2,8636
ECUADOR	1575,764	4764	592	951,2388	1,516258	4,505747	887,9382	0	1859	0,551208	0	-1,866180	-2,5679	-2,8636
HIGHYIELD	387,9461	511,685	321,235	50,91225	1,147404	2,86817	409,2526	0	1859	0,574724	0	0,444832	-2,5679	-2,8636
MALAYSIA	236,787	1141	76	165,639	2,940323	13,30097	10897,76	0	1859	0,554768	0	-1,734588	-2,5679	-2,8636
MEXICO	365,8591	1149	152	171,1225	1,390139	5,094496	938,552	0	1859	0,539252	0	-1,753107	-2,5679	-2,8636
MOODYAAA	6,50184	8,12	4,76	0,783619	-0,105433	1,971509	85,37911	0	1859	0,542617	0	-0,623630	-2,5679	-2,8636
MOODYBAA	7,390226	9,08	5,64	0,768894	-0,350378	2,023603	111,8815	0	1859	0,546155	0	-0,600335	-2,5679	-2,8636
MOROCCO	432,5412	1606	128	207,5942	0,933402	5,342869	695,1105	0	1859	0,527977	0	-1,991863	-2,5679	-2,8636
MSCILATAM	955,2717	1668,95	522,22	224,6484	0,717822	3,482104	177,6505	0	1859	0,54004	0	-0,563467	-2,5679	-2,8636
NASDAQ	2205,193	5048,62	1114,21	779,99	1,468228	4,612307	869,2614	0	1859	0,556469	0	-1,538317	-2,5679	-2,8636
NIGERIA	1169,588	2937	389	561,4718	0,715064	2,836261	160,4997	0	1859	0,531881	0	-1,987809	-2,5679	-2,8636
PANAMA	404,6477	769	236	76,32097	0,403543	3,218156	54,14173	0	1859	0,508747	0	-2,852201	-2,5679	-2,8636
PERU	526,1269	1061	229	158,2386	0,243576	2,527937	35,64334	0	1859	0,519913	0	-1,859783	-2,5679	-2,8636
PHILLIPINES	477,0145	993	300	109,3717	1,496476	6,583987	1688,803	0	1859	0,523073	0	-2,771066	-2,5679	-2,8636
POLAND	180,581	410	17	82,90698	-0,279597	2,007253	100,5598	0	1859	0,541327	0	-1,318165	-2,5679	-2,8636
RUSSIA	1306,859	7063	160	1491,381	1,698567	4,754724	1132,407	0	1859	0,570045	0	-1,269754	-2,5679	-2,8636
SOUTHAFRICA	281,3249	757	85	127,7742	0,866875	3,770108	278,769	0	1859	0,545008	0	-1,437009	-2,5679	-2,8636
SP500	1161,911	1527,46	776,77	168,5978	0,106624	2,388735	32,46431	0	1859	0,530535	0	-1,881505	-2,5679	-2,8636
THAILAND	164,5788	951	31	123,8258	2,609367	12,36412	8901,666	0	1859	0,542256	0	-2,762990	-2,5679	-2,8636
TURKEY	593,7509	1188	236	214,8282	0,38009	2,233774	90,237	0	1859	0,530266	0	-1,853242	-2,5679	-2,8636
VENEZUELA	896,192	2658	388	320,6782	1,137671	6,630161	1421,767	0	1859	0,527901	0	-2,503375	-2,5679	-2,8636
VIX	22,78196	45,74	11,1	6,366798	0,679238	3,526631	164,4283	0	1859	0,454844	0	-3,607435	-2,5679	-2,8636

Source: Author's Calculation. Series without differencing.

Table 2. Estimated parameters. ARMA-GARCH filter

	F stat ARCH test	Prob	AR(1)	Prob	C	Prob	ARCH(1)	Prob	GARCH(1)	Proba	Bds stat dim 6	Prob	F stat ARCH test	Prob
ARGENTINA	60,368260	0	0,039572	0,1354	4,94E-05	0	0,281974	0	0,701649	0	0,000189	0,9629	0,02117	0,884331
ASIA	1,011537	0,314666	0,059417	0,0201	2,15E-05	0	0,128017	0	0,830013	0	0,002483	0,5088	0,20783	0,648529
BRAZIL	10,448260	0	0,148458	0	2,42E-05	0	0,12507	0	0,844551	0	0,004178	0,1761	0,01141	0,914964
BULGARIA	12,038390	0	-0,020964	0,4107	4,59E-05	0	0,131037	0	0,813317	0	0,002707	0,4798	1,93459	0,164424
CHINA	39,393040	0	-0,274778	0	0,000167	0	0,15237	0	0,745589	0	0,025475	0	0,01817	0,892778
COLOMBIA	22,332130	0,000002	0,129449	0	2,32E-05	0	0,095996	0	0,869049	0	0,002672	0,4523	0,57647	0,447796
ECUADOR	1,339270	0,247312	0,125972	0	8,41E-06	0	0,096023	0	0,908962	0	0,008101	0,0207	0,02868	0,865535
HIGHYIELD	23,038610	0,000002	0,479422	0	2,75E-07	0	0,450052	0	0,671107	0	-3,44E-05	0,9249	0,04870	0,825359
MALAYSIA	11,016930	0,00092	0,017063	0,4993	9,44E-05	0	0,108685	0	0,724405	0	0,019821	0,0001	0,05521	0,814263
MEXICO	15,861490	0	0,074002	0,0039	4,67E-05	0	0,126444	0	0,811646	0	0,000536	0,8754	0,68060	0,409488
MOODYAAA	12,607570	0,000394	0,04736	0,0449	9,27E-07	0,002	0,053628	0	0,931329	0	0,002141	0,4964	0,31622	0,573959
MOODYBAA	23,206350	0,000002	0,037357	0,1117	1,14E-06	2E-04	0,052834	0	0,920551	0	0,00109	0,7236	0,98291	0,321611
MOROCCO	80,572260	0	-0,123905	0	0,000163	0	0,134809	0	0,767539	0	0,004342	0,3538	1,56892	0,210522
MSCILATAM	69,183030	0	0,171527	0	1,70E-05	0	0,112878	0	0,81557	0	-0,000852	0,7979	0,59345	0,441186
NASDAQ	61,865460	0	-0,027174	0	1,15E-06	0	0,065354	0	0,933613	0	0,002276	0,4196	1,71287	0,190775
NIGERIA	10,811320	0,001028	-0,103966	0	0,000103	0	0,077936	0	0,856503	0	0,002421	0,5773	0,00064	0,979812
PANAMA	27,457550	0	0,071664	0	5,65E-05	0	0,143801	0	0,735623	0	-0,000832	0,8181	0,65930	0,416911
PERU	15,429590	0,000089	0,083273	0	8,71E-05	0	0,127562	0	0,759031	0	0,003205	0,3775	0,09592	0,756822
PHILLIPINES	12,741900	0,000367	0,078154	0	2,94E-05	0	0,137625	0	0,805775	0	0,001064	0,7656	0,12891	0,719611
POLAND	12,029680	0	-0,214759	0	8,04E-05	0	0,11448	0	0,867093	0	0,00906	0,0063	0,00050	0,982154
RUSSIA	14,741680	0,000127	0,100437	0	7,93E-05	0	0,20187	0	0,751528	0	-0,005019	0,1635	0,02016	0,887114
SOUTHAFRICA	34,798410	0,062279	-0,147985	0	4,93E-05	0	0,102389	0	0,86023	0	0,013225	0,001	0,11846	0,730752
SP500	53,892350	0	-0,024789	0	1,47E-06	0	0,076117	0	0,915957	0	-0,00132	0,6706	0,96310	0,326535
THAILAND	20,244850	0	-0,20587	0	0,000225	0	0,133817	0	0,828652	0	0,051388	0	0,28264	0,595041
TURKEY	93,143540	0	0,113317	0	3,98E-05	0	0,120121	0	0,831149	0	0,004386	0,2422	1,91204	0,166903
VENEZUELA	10,384900	0	0,112612	0	3,11E-05	0	0,21975	0	0,750837	0	-0,005551	0,0883	0,41258	0,520742
VIX	4,266035	0,03902	-0,048009	0	0,000115	4E-04	0,071762	0	0,890155	0	0,003889	0,2024	0,92748	0,335644

Source: Author's Calculation. Estimated parameters for the first difference (Logarithmic returns) of the series.

Table 3. Historical minimums for the spreads residual series

	Min 5	Min 4	Min 3	Min 2	Min 1
Argentina	07-08-98 / -4,37772296	13-01-99 / -6,80766969	29-10-01 / -3,88329127	04-12-01 / -3,87776988	29-01-04 / -3,66884662
Brazil	18-05-98 / -5,2952334	07-08-98 / -4,33017884	04-01-00 / -4,4530578	29-07-02 / -3,49357097	02-07-02 / -3,28128429
Bulgaria	07-08-98 / -3,6366897	13-01-99 / -5,60607763	21-05-99 / -4,30636782	11-07-01 / -3,85212561	09-02-04 / -4,527527
China	29-07-98 / -5,597622	29-01-99 / -8,7704829	14-09-01 / -6,57450293	31-12-02 / -7,08797288	06-05-04 / -4,23597807
Colombia	10-08-98 / -7,30309087	21-08-98 / -6,73096825	27-05-99 / -4,56981698	20-04-04 / -4,85154864	29-01-00 / -5,3272826
Ecuador	20-08-98 / -7,12923304	13-01-99 / -3,98003003	09-05-02 / -5,21406959	20-04-04 / -4,12855524	10-03-05 / -3,90161932
Asia	21-08-98 / -6,85394789	28-04-00 / -4,71507926	01-08-03 / -5,01123876	30-04-04 / -11,0507863	25-06-04 / -2,93485909
Philippines	21-08-98 / -5,37109777	30-03-00 / -4,11030264	12-10-00 / -3,97416676	01-08-03 / -3,55021901	17-09-01 / -4,34647836
HighYield	27-04-98 / -4,24676681	11-08-98 / -4,70817887	08-10-98 / -5,97923186	14-09-01 / -18,2838836	07-05-99 / -4,24236842
Malaysia	09-01-98 / -3,97719356	10-02-98 / -5,34050633	02-09-98 / -6,17160458	10-10-02 / -8,10203635	26-06-03 / -5,32787646
Morocco	07-08-98 / -5,43066451	12-01-04 / -6,26277515	30-03-04 / -5,40151212	05-08-04 / -5,65660803	17-03-03 / -6,0809794
Mexico	07-08-98 / -5,14039093	13-01-99 / -4,98965338	30-03-00 / -3,65836804	06-06-02 / -3,37059094	03-01-03 / -3,63567076
AAA	08-10-98 / -5,38508991	30-04-99 / -3,60484033	06-08-99 / -3,17673786	02-01-03 / -3,12932206	22-02-05 / -3,63946171
BAA	08-10-98 / -5,66705166	04-09-99 / -3,11858086	09-01-01 / -3,14865057	08-05-02 / -3,93482324	02-04-04 / -3,63646663

	Min 5	Min 4	Min 3	Min 2	Min 1
MSCILatam	27-08-98 / -3,64971091	13-01-99 / -4,0915637	04-01-00 / -4,98420175	13-09-01 / -7,17956652	19-04-05 / -4,90756419
Nasdaq	31-08-98 / -4,56883579	19-04-99 / -3,49265616	04-01-00 / -3,78169533	17-09-01 / -3,87018019	15-04-04 / -3,8866085
Nigeria	07-08-98 / -4,18080964	19-04-00 / -3,86243844	28-08-02 / -10,1517191	24-03-03 / -5,74312507	20-06-02 / -4,74117188
Panama	20-08-98 / -4,17818255	21-08-98 / -3,84544111	21-06-02 / -4,11249886	27-02-04 / -4,5548235	01-08-03 / -5,05368794
Peru	13-01-99 / -4,59548924	30-03-00 / -5,13771256	18-09-00 / -4,74005205	23-10-00 / -6,12052561	29-01-04 / -4,11603039
Poland	21-08-98 / -4,15977185	13-01-99 / -2,72943384	16-03-04 / -4,02730786	08-12-04 / -2,65567759	20-04-05 / -3,81272225
Russia	18-05-98 / -3,92224642	13-01-99 / -3,16547482	12-05-99 / -3,23575859	29-01-04 / -3,70397398	28-02-05 / -5,80239662
sp500	31-08-98 / -4,55323224	04-01-00 / -4,80720032	14-04-00 / -4,36522156	12-03-01 / -3,65595122	22-10-03 / -3,67977114
SouthAfrica	10-06-98 / -4,20379954	21-08-98 / -6,19574373	27-08-98 / -7,74112334	31-12-98 / -6,430158	26-06-02 / -14,6308536
Thailand	04-04-00 / -5,49668884	26-04-01 / -6,96867273	30-05-01 / -7,06970591	29-08-02 / -7,01815221	01-08-03 / -5,49720213
Turkey	21-08-98 / -5,41083304	31-01-00 / -7,61813571	20-02-01 / -5,31846796	06-07-01 / -6,06354483	04-05-05 / -5,58313208
Venezuela	18-05-98 / -3,5968418	07-08-98 / -7,39987868	20-08-98 / -3,8234535	07-01-99 / -3,546464	01-08-03 / -3,79687502
Vix	27-04-98 / -3,48738896	12-03-01 / -3,41543193	17-09-01 / -5,28961512	03-09-02 / -3,58401553	02-04-04 / -3,62016405

Source: Author's Calculation. The extreme negative events dates are very close between countries. In yellow are those days between the fifteen days before and after the Russian devaluation of the 17/08/98.

Table 4. Generalized Pareto Distribution (GPD) estimated parameters

	Negative Residuals					Positives Residuals					Tail (-)	Tail (+)	Data (-)	Data (+)
	Threshold	Xi	ses	Beta	ses	Threshold	Xi	ses	Beta	ses				
Poland	1,25481	0,00422	0,08014	0,49943	0,05933	1,25169	0,27752	0,09470	0,46428	0,05694	130	153	924	926
Russia	0,91058	-0,02076	0,07958	0,57273	0,06008	1,80081	0,35824	0,15793	0,61606	0,12735	214	50	891	961
Nasdaq	1,60065	0,15625	0,10602	0,35931	0,05095	1,50078	0,08132	0,08946	0,39907	0,05148	111	115	876	981
AAA	1,49761	-0,00259	0,08363	0,56990	0,06964	1,70084	0,12941	0,13821	0,40332	0,07219	127	76	865	973
BAA	1,25016	-0,00289	0,06758	0,59820	0,06019	1,50220	-0,03659	0,08953	0,50181	0,06627	181	107	873	961
Vix	1,37805	0,00063	0,05660	0,58424	0,05681	1,60669	-0,19454	0,10458	0,48865	0,07357	161	83	872	985
S&P 500	1,52176	0,08566	0,09688	0,51482	0,06828	1,61463	-0,14741	0,10310	0,47578	0,06901	123	95	901	956
Phillipines	1,25115	0,01383	0,08994	0,65945	0,07998	1,75820	0,24835	0,13936	0,45127	0,08043	152	77	922	929
Brazil	1,25103	0,00087	0,12600	0,63741	0,09309	1,50183	0,11470	0,11464	0,36412	0,05489	184	104	879	978
Panama	1,25564	-0,00371	0,09395	0,68923	0,08555	1,60413	0,05505	0,11203	0,58927	0,08989	153	93	929	921
Mexico	1,40476	-0,07678	0,07600	0,77031	0,08925	1,50111	-0,02738	0,10970	0,59952	0,09119	131	90	873	971
Venezuela	1,25991	0,13963	0,08430	0,47758	0,05364	1,59637	0,26354	0,13116	0,41505	0,06860	178	92	901	953
Argentina	1,30534	0,03275	0,08632	0,76304	0,09406	1,75888	0,35643	0,18836	0,60797	0,13739	131	57	1000	856
Bulgaria	1,25263	0,17693	0,11807	0,55886	0,08207	1,75234	0,07612	0,13339	0,65200	0,11049	127	92	903	939
MsciLatam	1,41254	0,14567	0,10169	0,57425	0,07652	1,49185	-0,01581	0,11730	0,50337	0,07695	134	104	902	955
Peru	1,51372	0,11935	0,10705	0,64719	0,09325	1,75476	0,13014	0,14844	0,47557	0,08961	106	73	905	947
Colombia	1,40513	0,14442	0,09309	0,62322	0,07975	1,35045	0,01098	0,08646	0,56853	0,07044	129	127	889	966
Ecuador	1,25215	0,30627	0,11919	0,43793	0,06277	1,76553	0,39436	0,17393	0,59028	0,12863	144	50	928	928
Nigeria	1,25326	0,13427	0,08923	0,73031	0,09222	1,50168	0,01526	0,10422	0,84786	0,12399	124	95	950	906
SouthAfrica	1,25774	0,16224	0,10139	0,69508	0,09498	1,74885	0,02272	0,12236	0,91549	0,16012	117	65	891	950
Malaysia	1,31062	0,09252	0,09681	0,83850	0,11156	1,53335	0,09568	0,09098	0,74788	0,10113	120	99	857	881
Morocco	1,30251	0,18195	0,12348	0,77274	0,12001	1,50508	0,15805	0,12269	0,71756	0,11279	131	101	866	937
Turkey	1,51051	0,21866	0,11234	0,68276	0,10035	1,50183	-0,11921	0,10401	0,60321	0,08876	106	91	867	987
Thailand	1,00023	0,21855	0,11491	0,75518	0,11033	1,75091	0,44050	0,19905	0,83941	0,19012	117	69	855	864
Asia	1,49655	0,35367	0,13509	0,55028	0,09072	1,75573	0,15399	0,15747	0,50799	0,10108	99	66	898	938
China	1,10255	0,35267	0,11897	0,57674	0,08139	1,26271	0,06762	0,10062	0,86905	0,11730	152	124	802	843
High Yield	1,50968	0,51508	0,16676	0,52963	0,10386	1,37670	0,18850	0,13850	0,42648	0,07655	69	75	820	1037

Source: Author's Calculation. ($\xi = Xi$).

$$VaR_q = u_q = u_{(k+1)} + \frac{\hat{\beta}_k}{\hat{\xi}_k}\left(\left(\frac{1-q}{k/n}\right)^{-\hat{\xi}_k} - 1\right)^{12} \tag{12}$$

The parameters β, ξ, are estimated by maximum likelihood.

Finally, the "*Expected Shortfall*"[2] is obtained by the combination of the excess mean of the distribution and the VaR equation:

$$ES_q = \frac{VaR_q}{1-\hat{\xi}} + \frac{\hat{\beta}-\hat{\xi}\hat{u}}{(1-\hat{\xi})} \tag{13}$$

The selection of a threshold is restricted to a "*trade off*" between choosing a high threshold, making the asymptotic theorem be irrelevant and choosing a lower threshold, in order to have enough observations for the estimation of the tail. The graphical technique for the determination of the threshold is based on the fact that the distribution of beyond threshold losses is linear in the threshold.

Then, we proceed to estimate the GPD. For most of the series we obtain a positive value for the parameter ξ, results that suggest fat tails (Table 4).

4.3. Graphic Method for the Hill Estimator

Another method is based on the determination of the threshold by the hill estimator plot[3]. Fat tail distributions have the characteristic that tails distributions decays slowly, while others functions decrease exponentially.

$$\lim_{q \to \infty} \frac{1-F(qx)}{1-F(x)} = x^{-\alpha}, x > 0, \alpha > 0. \tag{14}$$

In this particular case, F is in the maximum domain of attraction of the Frechet distribution, defining the tail behavior.

The tail index α tells us how fat is the distribution tail. Under independent and identically distributed observations we obtain the following maximum likelihood estimator:

$$\gamma = \frac{1}{\alpha} = \frac{1}{m}\sum_{j=0}^{m-1}\ln\left(\frac{X_{[n-j]}}{X_{[n-m]}}\right) \tag{15}$$

---

[1] VaR is the abbreviation of Value at Risk, it suggest the worst that could happen, given a level of confidence, with a position in determined asset.

[2] The "*Expected Shortfall*" is a subadditive risk measure. It means the worst that could happen given the fact that we have exceeded a threshold. It is defined as: $ES_t = E(Loss_t | Loss_t > VaR_t)$. See appendix (a) for a better explanation.

[3] See Hill (1975).

This is the Hill estimator, smaller the Alpha, higher is the Hill estimator, and the tail distribution will be fatter.

$X_{[n-m]}$ Defines the break point and so the beginning of the tail distribution. We have the same "*trade off*" between bias and variance. If $X_{[n-m]}$ is too high, we will be too close to the mean of the total distribution and Alpha will be biased. On the opposite side, if $X_{[n-m]}$ is too low, we will be far in the tails, then the estimator will be very volatile, when we sum one observation or we take one away. The *k-associated* values for the optimal threshold are defined graphically where the Hill estimator is the most stable possible (Figure N°5). Table 5, shows the corresponding threshold parameters by the Hill method for the determination of the tail distribution.

Table 5. Hill estimator parameters

	MSE Left Tail			MSE Right Tail		
	k	miu	alpha	k	miu	alpha
Poland	25	2,05864	0,2749	17	2,6731	0,1924
Russia	56	1,72896	0,2391	32	2,2481	0,3319
Nasdaq	30	2,06872	0,2437	21	2,2483	0,1781
AAA	20	2,58447	0,1512	27	2,2282	0,1656
BAA	34	2,23979	0,2214	25	2,2807	0,1385
Vix	33	2,31544	0,218	25	2,171	0,1364
S&P 500	60	1,94479	0,2203	51	1,9167	0,1859
Phillipines	20	2,72497	0,1748	60	1,8939	0,2401
Brazil	60	1,97357	0,2493	15	2,3901	0,1578
Panama	38	2,28642	0,2543	16	2,7515	0,1931
Mexico	28	2,55158	0,1803	15	2,57	0,1817
Venezuela	17	2,63132	0,0015	33	2,0783	0,2611
Argentina	19	2,78879	0,2597	60	1,7179	0,348
Bulgaria	60	1,6858	0,3379	15	3,0989	0,1879
MsciLatam	60	1,86105	0,3129	48	1,9216	0,2015
Peru	60	1,88654	0,2968	17	2,7049	0,1924
Colombia	18	2,70431	0,2825	36	2,1675	0,1832
Ecuador	29	2,29826	0,261	33	2,1054	0,3079
Nigeria	25	2,61678	0,2604	52	2,0852	0,2898
SouthAfrica	60	1,78841	0,3295	30	2,5469	0,2416
Malaysia	22	2,82783	0,2836	60	2,0318	0,2652
Morocco	20	2,8436	0,3582	19	3,0577	0,2222
Turkey	17	2,91471	0,371	34	2,056	0,2121
Thailand	19	2,66597	0,0003	15	4,4196	0,2858
Asia	60	1,79522	0,3576	60	1,798	0,2616
China	18	3,03982	0,3565	35	2,4902	0,2875
High Yield	29	2,09242	0,4198	15	2,2517	0,2202

Source: Author's Calculation. MSE = Mean Square Error. Miu = u.

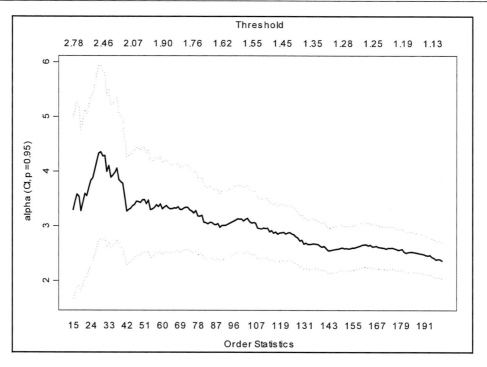

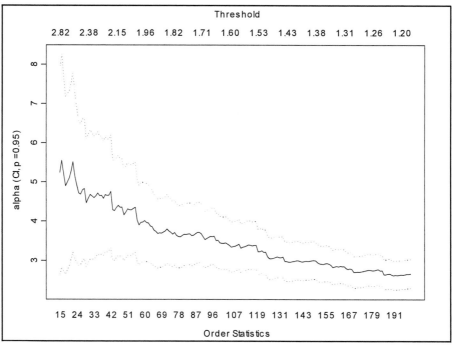

Fuente: Author's Calculation. The threshold is determined from the interval where the Hill estimator
becomes stable.

Figure 5. Hill estimator. Colombia spread, Brazil spread.

4.4. Mean Square Error Bootstrapping

Another method to determine the optimal threshold, is the minimization of the mean square error of the Hill estimator, that gives a numerical solution to the *"trade off"* between bias and variance. Using the asymptotical properties of the Hill estimator, we minimize the mean square error by a bootstrap simulation as in Hall (1990):

$$ECM(n_1,k_1) = E(\alpha_{n1}^{*}(k_1) - \alpha_n(k)|\chi)^2 \qquad (16)$$

Accordingly, we have three different methods to define the tail threshold and so the univariate probabilities (Appendix Figure N°3).

Comparing the determination of each one of the thresholds by each method (Table 6), we could see that the worst thing that could happen to an investor with a long position over every one of this debt issues is very close, and the results of the different methods do not differ in an ample measure[4].

The results of this univariate approach reveal the skewness between the tails of the distribution. The left tail is higher than the right tail for most of the cases. The average percentage of observations used in the left tail is 7,386% of the entire sample, while in the right tail we worked with 4,909% of the total observations. The probability that an investor has extreme losses is higher than the probability of presenting the same profit level (Table 6).

5. Multivariate Analysis: Joint Distribution

This is the second stage of the empirical model; in this part we estimate the joint probability of extreme events. Specifically, it is necessary to use a function that links the tails of the two distributions for the analysis of the residuals dependence. A first approach consists on the analysis of the concordance between variables.

The concordance is defined as large changes in one variable that are followed by large values in another variable. Likewise, low values in one variable are followed by low values in another variable. The concordance catches the extreme dependence that can surge of the non-linearity. For measuring the concordance we use de Kendall's Tao:

$$\tau = \tau_{x,y} = \left[P(X_1 - X_2)(Y_1 - Y_2) > 0 \right] - \left[P(X_1 - X_2)(Y - Y_{21}) < 0 \right] \qquad (17)$$

This is the probability of concordance less the probability of disconcordance. Another measure is the Spearman Rho:

---

[4] By the Hill graphical method the Value at risk is defined as: $VaR_{(hill)} = u\left(\left(\frac{n}{k}(1-q) \right)^{-\alpha(n)} \right)$, the result of the estimation of k, u, α are detailed in Table 5.

$$\rho_s = \frac{\sum_{i=1}^{n} \left(R_I - \bar{R} \right)\left(S_i - \bar{S} \right)}{\sqrt{\sum_{i=1}^{n} \left(R_i - \bar{R} \right)^2} \sqrt{\sum_{i=1}^{n} \left(S_i - \bar{S} \right)^2}} \tag{18}$$

These two measures quantify the monotonic degree of dependence between two variables. For the sample, the correlation between the spreads residuals is significant (Table 7). Nevertheless, the high degree of concordance seen through the Tao and Rho, suggests that a part of the dependence is concentrated on the tails of the distribution. The results for the Kendall Tao and the Spearman Rho are very close to the "*Frechet upper bound*"[5] evidence that the spreads of the sample are an increasing transformation of the Colombian spread. Hence, the country risk increase in a simultaneously way. Although, for the representative safe assets series, Aaa and Baa assets in the United States, the Tao and the Rho are very close to the "*Frechet lower bound*" evidence of a negative dependence for extreme events. When one of these two series over reacts, the Colombian spread moves in the opposite direction (Table 7).

5.1. Joint Distribution Identification

A copula can be defined as a dependence function between random variables. It is a function that links the marginal with the multivariate distribution. The copula represents the entire dependence structure.

$$F(z_1, z_2; \theta) = C(F_1(z_1), F_2(z_2); \theta) \tag{19}$$

C is the copula function; it is unique as it was demonstrated by the Sklar theorem[6]. A huge number of copula families exist, but for the extreme value modeling few are adequate. The families that matter in this case are copulas associated with a generalized extreme value distribution.

Let a bivariate vector of random variables (X_1, X_2) with distribution functions F_1 and F_2 as a copula function C, the probability of a contagion phenomena is:

$$P(X_2 > x_2 | X_1 > x_1) > P(X_2 > x_2 | X_1 \leq x_1) \tag{20}$$

$$P(X_2 > F_2^{-1}(\alpha_2) | X_1 > F_1^{-1}(\alpha_1)) \geq P(X_2 > F_2^{-1}(\alpha_2) | X_1 \leq F_1^{-1}(\alpha_1)) \tag{21}$$

$$\lambda = \lim_{u \to 1^-} P\{X_2 \geq F_2^{-1}(u) | X_1 > F_1^{-1}(u)\}^{[7]} \tag{22}$$

---

[5] See appendix (a) for a better explanation.
[6] See Sklar (1959).
[7] Lambda is the coefficient of "*upper tail dependence*". It is the asymptotic result of the contagion definition used in the paper.

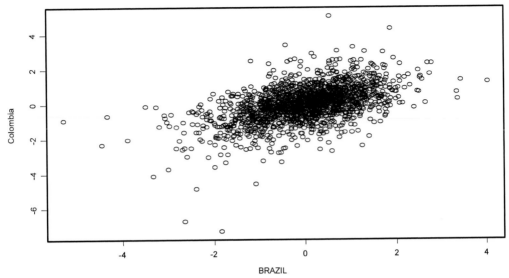

Fuente: Author's Calculation. Extreme events outside the ellipse are larger for falls in the return, equivalent to an increase in the spread.

Figure 6. Modeling the tails bivariate distribution. Colombia residual, Brazil residual.

Lambda[8] is the dependence index, defining the conditional probability that a *crash* occurs in a market, given the fact that a *crash* has occurred in another similar market.

Our approach uses for tool the estimation of the joint distribution for the determination of the probability of a conditional *crash*, using a copula we extract all the dependence information. Specifically, it is necessary to adopt the better functional form for the copula function. The copula family will be defined by the goodness of fit between the empirical and the diverse theoretical copulas, as by the main characteristics of each family.

5.2. Calculating the Empirical Copula

This estimator calculates the frequency of exceeding two different thresholds for a couple of variables.

$$C_n\left(\frac{i}{n},\frac{j}{n}\right)=\frac{1}{n}\sum_{k=1}^{n}I\{X_{1k}\leq x_{1(i)};X_{2k}\leq x_{2(j)}\} \tag{23}$$

The empirical copula is the starting point for exploring a finite sample of copulas, $\overline{C}\subset C$, and to find the function that better fit the data. The empirical copula (Exhibit 7) shows us the divergence with the assumption of normality; consequently the contour graphs for the empirical copula are very distant from the contour graphs of the bivariate normal distribution. This suggests that the copula fitness must deal with positive and the negative dependence in the tail distribution.

---

[8] See appendix (b) for a better explanation.

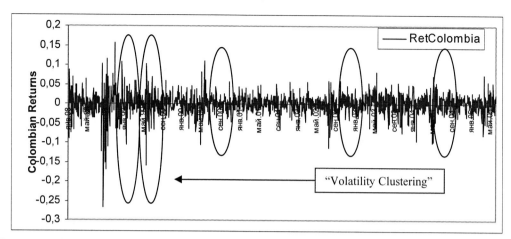

Source: Author's Calculation. Spreads first difference. An increase in the spread, a fall in returns, means losses for the investor P/L.

Exhibit 2. Colombia spread returns.

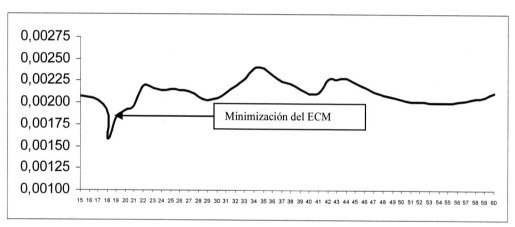

Source: Author's Calculation. From the resulting of the minimization of the MSE, we calculate the VaR.

Exhibit 3. Mean square error. Hill estimator bootstrapping.

5.3. Goodness of Fit between the Empirical and Different Theoretical Copulas Families

We make a goodness of fit quantifying the area between the empirical and the theoretical copulas searching for the best modeling of the stochastic process.

The better fits are attained by copulas derived from the "*Archimedean*" family, in the case of the BB1, the BB4 and the Gumbel functional forms.

Table 6. Univariate probabilities. GPD method, and Hill

	VaR (gpd)	VaR (hill)	sfall 0,95 (-)	sfall 0,99 (-)	VaR (gpd) (+)	VaR (hill) (+)	sfall 0,95 (+)	sfall 0,99 (+)	Left Tail	Rigth Tail
Poland	1,772630689	1,738858519	2,27637	3,08986	1,909768074	2,204410058	2,79931	4,61274	7,027%	8,270%
Russia	1,79491691	1,826149006	2,33802	3,19766	1,825496731	1,964359899	2,77962	4,88420	11,555%	2,700%
Nasdaq	1,960264468	1,886463003	2,44826	3,34813	1,852886524	1,933064901	2,31845	3,11900	5,977%	6,193%
AAA	2,110651003	2,299986518	2,67302	3,58344	1,886052477	2,021221512	2,37686	3,25507	6,910%	4,135%
BAA	2,099223239	2,119257063	2,68996	3,64382	1,898111173	2,083333502	2,36382	3,09886	9,869%	5,834%
Vix	2,141579316	2,179023384	2,72302	3,66514	1,849209203	1,979266309	2,21430	2,72619	8,670%	4,470%
S&P 500	2,061740581	2,071525322	2,66532	3,72275	1,925421622	1,939913627	2,29618	2,83392	6,624%	5,116%
Phillipines	2,044445045	2,354871239	2,71978	3,82607	2,001213646	2,013922915	2,67299	4,01538	8,212%	4,160%
Brazil	2,164304958	2,13282366	2,79959	3,82837	1,788849601	1,983484819	2,23300	3,02485	9,908%	5,600%
Panama	2,075431932	2,17260178	2,75461	3,85167	2,026430659	2,243432039	2,67464	3,76549	8,270%	5,027%
Mexico	2,216592602	2,35528227	2,86905	3,86508	1,868035344	2,076118832	2,44180	3,34519	7,104%	4,881%
Venezuela	1,983277309	2,627517392	2,65575	3,86930	1,894536805	1,881779664	2,56480	3,90840	9,601%	4,962%
Argentina	2,051994459	2,169132492	2,85362	4,19842	1,942275631	1,932222519	2,97007	5,22991	7,058%	3,071%
Bulgaria	1,886860407	1,855818639	2,70219	4,22032	2,202368938	2,500921767	2,93705	4,20779	6,895%	4,995%
MsciLatam	2,090206002	2,03493556	2,86610	4,29171	1,881282515	1,923628019	2,37076	3,14861	7,216%	5,600%
Peru	2,093585302	2,051321413	2,90706	4,35048	1,966536373	2,221027046	2,54494	3,58052	5,724%	3,942%
Colombia	2,12294549	2,094824598	2,95927	4,49512	1,903009412	2,053893005	2,48399	3,42736	6,954%	6,846%
Ecuador	1,84499592	2,032933985	2,73178	4,58541	1,810288926	1,895669071	2,79387	5,03230	7,759%	2,694%
Nigeria	2,001182014	2,214007615	2,95320	4,67529	2,133139945	2,170249597	3,00393	4,42276	6,681%	5,119%
SouthAfrica	1,984305799	1,972755829	2,94638	4,72857	2,037021376	2,279239309	2,96587	4,51189	6,355%	3,531%
Malaysia	2,216564177	2,340681635	3,22441	4,98685	2,163068336	2,205368176	3,05671	4,61164	6,904%	5,696%
Morocco	2,250212833	2,156290814	3,19670	5,28606	2,091141789	2,5021082	3,05341	4,81693	7,266%	5,602%
Turkey	2,184751446	2,059535309	3,24728	5,29691	1,857807197	1,899826464	2,35885	3,09262	5,717%	4,908%
Thailand	1,850683512	2,665253205	3,05491	5,37763	2,187457341	3,266560858	4,03146	8,35106	6,806%	4,014%
Asia	1,998569768	1,991325436	3,11326	5,54627	1,933927551	1,917635496	2,56682	3,72276	5,392%	3,595%
China	2,083577661	2,284711693	3,50899	6,59701	2,235171518	2,36060754	3,23003	4,93384	9,240%	7,538%
High Yield	1,825866218	1,809324499	3,25390	6,83315	1,539734919	1,713562233	2,09559	3,15227	3,716%	4,039%

Source: Author's Calculation. Sfall = Expected Shortfall.

Table 7. Concordance measures

	Pearson Correlation	t stat	p value	Kendalls Tau Empirical Copula	Spearmans Rho Empirical Copula	Kendalls Tau	Spearman Rho
AAA	-0,307565	-13,9216	0	0,8589447	0,968504	-0,2359757	-0,341431
Argentina	0,3169358	14,3923	0	0,4726965	0,6506408	0,2196448	0,3223714
Asia	0,4474138	21,5469	0	0,7300058	0,8962963	0,324278	0,4669401
BAA	-0,3143621	-14,2626	0	0,9303556	0,9885967	-0,2396501	-0,3473207
Brazil	0,5061904	25,2794	0	0,8923644	0,9768512	0,3442862	0,4925896
Bulgaria	0,3099721	14,042	0	0,7578884	0,9107542	0,1931485	0,2828483
China	0,1850843	8,1117	0	0,9023592	0,980623	0,1277836	0,1896523
Ecuador	0,3321496	15,1666	0	0,376424	0,5303499	0,2467405	0,3605758
High Yield	0,1273108	5,5282	0	0,265027	0,3618243	0,05405398	0,0797648
Malaysia	0,24564	10,9138	0	0,6688973	0,8428979	0,1783141	0,2628404
Mexico	0,5450044	27,9965	0	0,8417637	0,9578104	0,3867258	0,5479392
Morocco	0,1389808	6,0445	0	0,5518704	0,745091	0,09003677	0,1335303
MsciLatam	0,3468471	15,9273	0	0,785005	0,9319485	0,2152439	0,3156112
Nasdaq	0,25467	11,3426	0	0,5970733	0,7859569	0,1656518	0,2440621
Nigeria	0,2235483	9,8781	0	0,798868	0,9356664	0,1968803	0,2903545
Panama	0,4791406	23,5109	0	0,6836817	0,8526992	0,3306803	0,4728485
Peru	0,4930545	24,4089	0	0,7816034	0,9328941	0,3427682	0,4932103
Phillipines	0,4581359	22,1984	0	0,6663498	0,8460907	0,315644	0,4521779
Poland	0,394439	18,4873	0	-0,3560236	-0,4873968	0,3017125	0,4343636
Russia	0,3495805	16,0703	0	-0,3851039	-0,5133605	0,2860861	0,4124317
S&P 500	0,2592966	11,5633	0	0,9461973	0,9902304	0,1636347	0,2427403
SouthAfrica	0,35545	16,3787	0	0,8517817	0,9652051	0,2513782	0,3627926
Thailand	0,1721845	7,5284	0	0,6418561	0,8196451	0,1147986	0,1693481
Turkey	0,4236986	20,1463	0	0,7177409	0,8950285	0,305814	0,4409844
Venezuela	0,3912646	18,3115	0	0,8455645	0,9629466	0,2846441	0,4115216
Vix	0,2546675	11,3424	0	0,8690683	0,9734541	0,1594404	0,2360781

Source: Author's Calculation.

Table 8. Estimation parameters of different copulas

Copula	Parameter	Argentina	Asia	Brazil	Bulgaria	China	Ecuador	High Yield	Malaysia	Mexico	Morocco	MsciLatam	Nasdaq	Nigeria	Panama	Peru	Phillipines	S&P 500	SouthAfrica	Thailand	Turkey	Venezuela	Vix
Normal	Normal Copula Delta	0.33312	0.46844	0.50985	0.30503	0.19552	0.36892	0.09430	0.26650	0.53236	0.13914	0.33894	0.25956	0.27211	0.48295	0.49771	0.46008	0.26392	0.36644	0.17768	0.44350	0.41181	0.25422
Frank	Frank Copula Delta	2.07711	3.22553	3.46519	1.82032	1.18825	2.35592	0.48917	1.65349	4.06996	0.82614	2.03576	1.53509	1.84061	3.30878	3.43381	3.15790	1.51256	2.42725	1.06689	3.01670	2.77820	1.47759
Kimeldorf Sampson	Theta Archimedean Copula	0.41551	0.66751	0.77135	0.40850	0.22270	0.48971	0.14055	0.31094	0.91225	0.16994	0.46345	0.26644	0.31901	0.72884	0.75354	0.70090	0.29084	0.49969	0.19281	0.60615	0.58278	0.30022
Gumbel	Gumbel Copula Delta	1.23128	1.39810	1.43930	1.20101	1.16639	1.27014	1.03438	1.16914	1.50969	1.07055	1.22528	1.16737	1.18566	1.41709	1.42672	1.38450	1.16037	1.28013	1.10949	1.36997	1.32796	1.15322
Galambos	Galambos Copula Delta	0.47752	0.65497	0.69978	0.44034	0.34128	0.51996	0.00000	0.40770	0.77251	0.27657	0.47041	0.41017	0.42065	0.67481	0.68555	0.63660	0.40243	0.52554	0.32801	0.62358	0.58020	0.39048
Husler Reiss	Husler and Reiss Delta	0.81673	1.00851	1.06914	0.77106	0.64633	0.85669	0.00000	0.73242	1.13153	0.56969	0.81218	0.74741	0.73606	1.02383	1.04223	0.98741	0.73903	0.65597	0.63487	0.98058	0.92106	0.76633
BB1 Theta	Lower Tail Dependence and Concordance	0.25922	0.35520	0.44255	0.31173	0.15459	0.31151	0.14055	0.19935	0.54292	0.14832	0.35439	0.11781	0.18503	0.42072	0.44787	0.44636	0.17624	0.30412	0.11407	0.28964	0.34116	0.20604
BB1 Delta	Upper Tail Dependence and Concordance	1.11349	1.21631	1.21615	1.06658	1.05342	1.12598	1.00000	1.08275	1.23161	1.01702	1.07498	1.11653	1.10028	1.20619	1.20109	1.16810	1.08726	1.13765	1.06446	1.22337	1.16487	1.06898
BB2 Theta	Lower Tail Dependence and Concordance	0.00021	0.00019	0.00019	0.00045	0.22083	0.00020	0.07324	0.00016	0.00020	0.16940	0.00027	0.00019	0.00013	0.00027	0.00023	0.00017	0.00017	0.00023	0.19167	0.00015	0.00018	0.00023
BB2 Delta	Upper Tail Dependence and Concordance	1968.93879	3495.04951	4071.37770	909.87033	4137.40077	2389.49918	832.82	1901.76347	4489.32242	3.28658	1688.02604	1424.34564	2403.52840	2742.36329	3341.27946	2812.47568	1664.92598	2156.99151	0.00000	3990.39945	3163.03281	1313.55628
BB3 Theta	Upper Tail Dependence and Concordance	1.16578	1.21920	1.23061	1.15740	1.11785	1.17829	1.07371	1.13951	1.24542	1.09406	1.16420	1.14125	1.14214	1.23970	1.22815	1.21806	1.13678	1.18508	1.11530	1.21309	1.19760	1.13341
BB3 Delta	Lower Tail Dependence and Concordance	0.28262	0.39495	0.44893	0.29299	0.17805	0.33224	0.13469	0.22770	0.51752	0.15034	0.32545	0.19379	0.22710	0.42851	0.44292	0.42827	0.21583	0.32514	0.15771	0.36152	0.36681	0.22694
BB4 Theta	Upper Tail Dependence and Concordance	0.26537	0.37090	0.45096	0.32064	0.16020	0.32333	0.14055	0.20243	0.55299	0.14674	0.35966	0.11413	0.20355	0.43534	0.46019	0.46604	0.17090	0.32484	0.12312	0.30503	0.35452	0.20821
BB4 Delta	Lower Tail Dependence and Concordance	0.33629	0.45136	0.45950	0.26932	0.24735	0.34691	0.03714	0.29662	0.47510	0.18438	0.28518	0.35086	0.30284	0.44135	0.43893	0.39066	0.31463	0.35062	0.25987	0.45708	0.39113	0.26078
BB5 Theta	Upper Tail Dependence and Concordance	1.23120	1.39110	1.43917	1.20018	1.11639	1.27014	1.03438	1.16914	1.50969	1.04580	1.20806	1.00000	1.18566	1.41709	1.42672	1.38450	1.00000	1.28013	1.10773	1.36997	1.32796	1.12105
BB5 Delta	Lower Tail Dependence and Concordance	0.07348	0.03174	0.07566	0.09808	0.02881	0.02935	0.00000	0.03170	0.03080	0.19677	0.17218	0.41017	0.02849	0.03357	0.03108	0.03136	0.40243	0.02875	0.11155	0.03387	0.03034	0.20963
BB6 Theta	Upper Tail Dependence and Concordance	1.10000	1.15000	1.15000	1.10000	1.05000	1.15000	1.05000	1.10000	1.20000	1.05000	1.10000	1.10000	1.10000	1.15000	1.15000	1.15000	1.10000	1.15000	1.05000	1.15000	1.15000	1.10000
BB6 Delta	Lower Tail Dependence and Concordance	1.18201	1.31548	1.31548	1.18201	1.05736	1.18201	1.07993	1.18201	1.49573	1.07993	1.18201	1.18201	1.18201	1.31548	1.31548	1.31548	1.18201	1.31548	1.07993	1.31548	1.31548	1.18201
BB7 Theta	Upper Tail Dependence and Concordance	1.12711	1.24262	1.25208	1.08153	1.19145	1.14308	1.00000	1.08629	1.25486	1.01694	1.20826	1.13418	1.09489	1.24128	1.22211	1.18990	1.10086	1.15611	1.07524	1.25516	1.26400	1.08026
BB7 Delta	Lower Tail Dependence and Concordance	0.34545	0.53760	0.63932	0.35488	0.51269	0.52212	0.00000	0.26189	0.78222	0.31397	0.41694	0.19081	0.26444	0.60241	0.57363	0.60190	0.23599	0.41318	0.15297	0.46367	0.48075	0.26690
Normal Mix	P	0.81268	0.76881	0.50000	0.57677	0.00000	0.55624	0.16676	0.07333	0.61616	0.45120	0.20172	0.03985	0.51345	0.66044	0.33522	0.46613	0.50001	0.74163	0.62509	0.76184	0.35867	0.50001
	Delta 1	0.25016	0.36363	0.50985	0.50731	0.40671	0.14366	0.51823	0.84608	0.72074	0.00000	0.69615	0.94432	0.08081	0.65598	0.71959	0.73742	0.26392	0.21513	0.21513	0.32602	0.74320	0.25422
	Delta 2	0.69683	0.82643	0.50985	0.01666	0.14366	0.51269	0.12031	0.22202	0.29093	0.00000	0.24623	0.23297	0.49298	0.15203	0.22111	0.21959	0.26392	0.81665	0.04621	0.83425	0.23341	0.25422
Joe	Joe Copula Theta	1.26419	1.47754	1.51407	1.21510	1.12463	1.30676	1.02031	1.18751	1.58662	1.06479	1.23073	1.20290	1.20946	1.49117	1.49849	1.43950	1.18080	1.32324	1.12482	1.45055	1.38148	1.16523

Source: Author's Calculation.

Table 9. Probabilities: bivariates peaks over thresholds

		AAA	Argentina	Asia	BAA	Brazil	Bulgaria	China	Ecuador	High Yield	Malaysia	Mexico	Morocco	MsciLatam	Nasdaq	Nigeria	Panama	Peru	Phillipines	Poland	Russia	S&P 500	SouthAfrica	Thailand	Turkey	Venezuela	Vix
3 s.d	P(Yx)																										
	P(Yx x Yy)																										
	P(Yx)P(Yy)																										
	P(Yx|Yy)																										
	P(Yx|Yy)																										
4 s.d	P(Yx)																										
	P(Yx x Yy)																										
	P(Yx)P(Yy)																										
	P(Yx|Yy)																										
5 s.d	P(Yx)																										
	P(Yx x Yy)																										
	P(Yx)P(Yy)																										
	P(Yx|Yy)																										
	P(Yx|Yy)																										
6 s.d	P(Yx)																										
	P(Yx x Yy)																										
	P(Yx)P(Yy)																										
	P(Yx|Yy)																										
	P(Yx|Yy)																										
10 s.d	P(Yx)																										
	P(Yx x Yy)																										
	P(Yx)P(Yy)																										
	P(Yx|Yy)																										
	P(Yx|Yy)																										

Source: Author's Calculation.

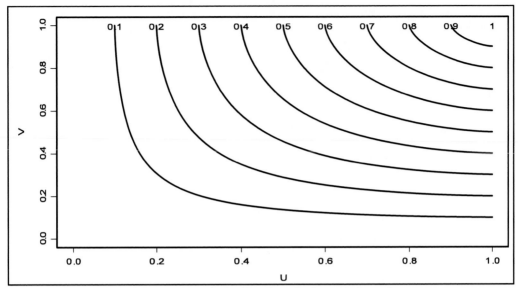

Source: Author's Calculation. Data historical calibration of a theoretical copula.

Exhibit 4. Gumbel theoretical copula. (Contour graphs).

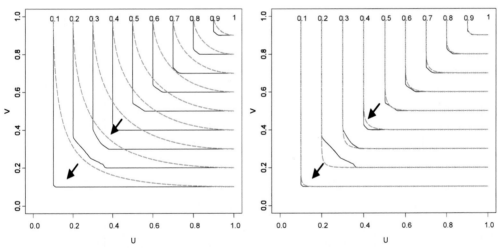

Source: Author's Calculation. Goodness of fit between the empirical copula (black lines), the normal copula (orange lines), and the Gumbel (orange lines in the second square).

Figure 7. Modeling the bivariate excesses distribution. Fit between the empirical and the theoretical copula (Contour graphs).

5.4. Maximum Likelihood Estimation of Different Copulas Families

Following Longin and Solnik (2001) we emphasize in the "*Archimedean*" copulas family. Then we calibrate the principal theoretical copulas families based on the historical data of our sample (Appendix Exhibit 4). For the bivariate normal, the Kimeldorf Sampson Copula, Joe, Gumbel, Galambos, and the Husler Reiss copula, the delta parameter increases when the dependency increase (Table 9). These copulas differ in their functional forms and in the shape of the probability density, which models the probabilistic behavior of random variables. In our case we calibrate the different families searching for a better robustness of the model to the selection of a specific copula. Therefore, the results interpretation is based on the copulas of the *"Archimedean"* family because it has the better fit to the empirical copula, and also it has key properties that are important in this kind of analysis. In fact, these copulas include the total dependence and independence case asymptotically. Also, it is a more parsimonious model because of the estimation of only one parameter.

The normal copula is the normal bivariate distribution. Which is denoted:

$$C(u_1, u_2) = \Phi_\beta(\Phi^{-1}(u_1), \Phi^{-1}(u_2)) \tag{24}$$

$$C(u_1, u_2) = \int_{-\infty}^{\phi^{-1}(u_1)} \int_{-\infty}^{\phi^{-1}(u_2)} \frac{1}{2\pi\sqrt{1-\beta^2}} \exp\left(-\frac{1}{2}\left(\frac{x^2 - 2\beta xy + y^2}{1-\beta^2}\right)\right) dxdy \tag{25}$$

Where Φ is the cumulative density function of a $N(0;1)$ and Φ_β the cumulative density function of a bivariate normal distribution with correlation coefficient β.

The functional form of the extreme value copulas is:

$$C(u_1^t, \ldots, u_n^t) = C^t(u_1, \ldots, u_n) \cdot t > 0. \tag{26}$$

The *"Archimedean"* copulas family has for functional form:

$$C(u, v) = \varphi^{-1}(\varphi(u) + \varphi(v)) \tag{27}$$

Where φ is a function in C^2, and $\varphi(1) = 0$, $\varphi'(x) < 0$, $\varphi''(x) > 0$. Con $0 \leq x \leq 1$.
The Gumbel copula is an *"Archimedean"* Copula. That is:

$$C(u_1^t, u_2^t) = \left[\exp(-[(\ln u_1)^\alpha + (-\ln u_1)^\alpha]^{1/\alpha})\right]^t = C^t(u_1, u_2) \tag{28}$$

At the same time, the copulas families that have two parameters δ, θ are useful for capturing more than one type of dependence. For example, the positive tail dependence, and the negative tail dependence. If there exist dependence in negative tails, then, an increase in the spread of one country, negative movements for an investor, will be followed by increases in the spread of another country.

For the BB1[1] copula, the Colombian debt spread exhibits the higher concordance, as showed by the higher theta of the estimation for Mexico (*0.54292*), Peru (*0.44787*), Philippines (*0.44636*), Brazil (*0.44255*) and Panama (*0.42072*) (Table 9).

---

[1] The BB1, BB2, BB4 Copula are built from the *"Archimedean"* Copula.

Those countries have for main characteristic that they are close in terms of they sovereign debt rate and exhibit for principal threat a high external leverage, as structural weaknesses in their public finance.

The smaller theta value, for the negative tail dependence of the Copula BB1, reflects the degree of disconcordance. Small values are obtained for the series of the Nasdaq (*0.11781*), High Yield (*0.14055*), Morocco (*0.14832*), S&P500 (*0.17624*), Nigeria (*0.18503*) and Malaysia (*0.19935*).

The fact that delta is close to zero suggests that the negative tail dependence between these variables is small (Table 8). Nigeria owns a small stock of external debt, in contrast with its big reserves of petroleum and gas followed by plans for its exploitation. Malaysia have for principal strength being an external lender in continuously growth, also it has a high international liquidity capacity. Therefore, there is no empirical evidence that the principal United States indexes, as Nigeria and Malaysia, are conditioning the increase in the Colombian spread, having those countries a higher international potential liquidity at the moment of paying there external debts.

6. ESTIMATION RESULTS

6.1. Bivariate Peaks over Threshold

Seeking the robustness of the multivariate model results, we calculate first a bivariate peaks over thresholds model. Then, we adjust a joint excesses model over a couple of thresholds.

We can see that the conditional probabilities are very small (Table 9). Also, the probability of a joint *crash* is higher than the one expected individually. The probability that Colombia exceeds 3 standard deviations given the fact that another spread has exceeded it, is conditioned in the lower cases by Baa (*0.0244*), Aaa (*0.0296*), Morocco (*0.1014*), High Yield (*0.1170*), and Malaysia (*0.1239*).

In comparison, the higher probabilities of contagion are given by the conditioning of Russia (*0.4836*), Poland (*0.4462*), Panama (*0.3678*), Brazil (*0.3580*), Mexico (*0.3569*), Venezuela (*0.3395*), and Peru (*0.3314*).

For six standard deviations the less contagious series are Baa (0.05313143), High Yield (0.05575592), Aaa (0.06538039), Morocco (0.07251475), Nigeria (0.1108772) and Malaysia (0.112077). In six standard deviations the most contagious series are Russia (0.810943), Mexico (0.7629098), Poland (0.7454879), Brazil (0.6350241), Panama (0.6178745), and Philippines (0.534747).

6.2. Emerging Sovereign Debt Spreads Dependence

For the analysis period we found a high dependence, in the negative tail, with countries near geographically even if this is not a constant rule. Also, the dependence is high for countries that belong to the same pair group or at least close in terms of the sovereign long term debt rating (Table 10).

Table 10. Tail dependence

	BB1		BB4		BB7	
	Lower Tail	Upper Tail	Lower Tail	Upper Tail	Lower Tail	Upper Tail
Thailand	0,003317529	0,0822117	0,004782294	0,06944055	0,01076708	0,09469109
Nasdaq	0,005145965	0,1395753	0,004323648	0,1386828	0,02644584	0,1574621
High Yield	0,007214396	0	0,007214396	7,84735E-09	0,007214396	0
Morocco	0,01010107	0,02306583	0,009621197	0,0232991	0,01336775	0,02295983
China	0,01417322	0,06907921	0,01601114	0,06067078	0,02676895	0,07380778
S&P 500	0,02685441	0,1082215	0,02415148	0,1104652	0,05301455	0,1230624
Nigeria	0,03321646	0,1224393	0,04286438	0,1013857	0,07271636	0,1166074
Malaysia	0,04030414	0,1031912	0,04160698	0,09663457	0,07088396	0,1071442
Vix	0,04429867	0,08748482	0,04410217	0,08469924	0,06733194	0,1003902
Argentina	0,09058797	0,1364194	0,094028	0,1273063	0,1344578	0,1503852
Bulgaria	0,1248246	0,08702056	0,1299602	0,07625337	0,1496198	0,101821
SouthAfrica	0,1348733	0,1608936	0,1476522	0,1384953	0,1868234	0,1786987
Ecuador	0,1386	0,1492433	0,1456368	0,135598	0,1865807	0,1662088
Turkey	0,1413973	0,2377554	0,1509974	0,2199225	0,2242677	0,2628634
MsciLatam	0,1621125	0,09439399	0,1641194	0,08798752	0,1896713	0,1093294
Venezuela	0,1747892	0,186892	0,1818346	0,1699645	0,2365008	0,2042399
Asia	0,2010134	0,2319503	0,2097727	0,215308	0,2755857	0,2531554
Panama	0,2551528	0,2234765	0,2618388	0,2079379	0,3164394	0,2521032
Phillipines	0,2646324	0,1898728	0,2733041	0,1696025	0,316131	0,2093574
Peru	0,2756729	0,2191363	0,2808771	0,2061451	0,3365133	0,2367257
Brazil	0,2758545	0,2318177	0,2788496	0,2212457	0,3381741	0,260502
Mexico	0,3546541	0,2444229	0,3570085	0,2324802	0,4122488	0,2626341

Source: Author's Calculation. Positive and negative tail for three types of extreme value copula. In yellow those countries that have for all the sample period a "Long term foreign currency rating" by Fitchratings below investment grade.

6.2.1. Extreme Dependence

Most of emerging markets series, present dependence in positives and negatives tails. This means that extreme events, even if they are positives or negatives, are linked. Analyzing the output of the lambdas estimation (interpreted as a probability) for the copula BB1 and BB4, in some countries, the tail positive dependence is higher than the dependence in the negative tail (Table 10). Thus, the sensibility to contagion is highly non lineal in the tails. In fact, the univariate results show that the different debt bonds are different types of assets. Also, factors whose dependence is lower have a higher probability of a rise, compared to the probability of a downfall (Table 10). For the Nasdaq (*0.005145965*), High Yield (0.007214396), Morocco (*0.01010107*), S&P500 (*0.02685441*), Nigeria (0.03321646), and Malaysia (0.04030414), these series have a joint probability *crash* with Colombia smaller than the one of a joint *boom*. On the other hand, the higher probabilities of contagion toward Colombia are defined by Mexico (*0.3546541*), Brazil (0.2758545), Peru (*0.2756729*), Philippines (*0.2646324*) and Panama (*0.2551528*) (Table 10). These series have a joint probability *crash* with Colombia higher than the joint probability of a *boom.*

The highest probability of contagion comes from Mexico, country desired by the appetite of international direct investment in the short term.

Also, Mexico as Colombia shares the same structural weaknesses in their public finances, as the same need to accomplish structural reforms with the objective of making sustainable the debt service.

Even if the most representatives tail negative dependences are countries near geographically, as in terms of real links, this is not the main rule, justifying the information extraction process. In fact, in the capital market, information matters before fundamentals. The crisis is transmitted from very distant countries in geographical terms, as the case of Philippines. Investor possibilities purchase spectrum, in emerging debt, are countries that do not differentiate even if they are very distinct and distant, this is the case for the associations between Argentina and Turkey, Brazil and Russia, as in this case, Philippines and Colombia. This last couple posses a high external leverage in common. Philippines has not sufficient fiscal flows, increasing its debt compared to its earnings. Increasing the futures flows uncertainty regards the debt service. Colombia has a high stock of external debt in comparison with his pair group in terms of sovereign ratings, as structural disequilibria in his public finances.

We made an average of the lambdas by groups of similar countries, as in Laurent (2001). Looking for the establishment of an interdependence measure to others countries, behind external shocks, whatever the origin of this last.

We calculate the lambda average for the tail negative dependence for the BB4 Copula. Making the average of the tail negative dependence for the series of United States assets (Nasdaq, High Yield, S&P500, Vix), the extreme dependence average is (*0.019947924*).

This is a small result, indicating the low degree of negative dependence from these assets towards the Colombian spread.

At the same time, analyzing the tail dependence with Asian countries (Malaysia, Philippines), we have a low level for Malaysia, but one elevated for Philippines.

In general, Asian countries except Philippines have a high liquidity capacity in terms of their international reserves, because of the current account excesses sustained for many years.

Now, the Embig Asia dependence to Colombia in the negative tail is (*0.2010134*). This means that even if the Asian crisis was transmitted to Colombia, this was not through Malaysia, but through Philippines and surely those Asian countries issuers of external sovereign debt that do not appear directly in the sample but that are represented in the Embig Asia.

Making the extreme dependence average for countries that are below the investment grade[2] for all the sample period (Mexico, Brazil, Peru, Philippines, Panama, Venezuela, Turkey, Ecuador, Argentina, Nigeria) we obtain an average of (*0.20672393*).

Finally, we made an average for the group of Colombian geographic neighbors, (Venezuela, Ecuador, Panama, Peru and Brazil); we obtain a lambda of (*0.22980738*).

This is higher than the aggregation of other Latin-American countries in the sample as Mexico and Argentina. Including this two countries the average is (*0.22858191*) a result that is higher than the aggregation for countries which posses a speculative rating.

Therefore, the geographical proximity has some influence in the conditioning mechanism. Any kind of shock independently of its origin, can influence the Colombian spread by the spreads of neighbors countries, and increase the country risk without being *totally* determined by fundamentals.

---

[2] Those bonds rated below investment grade are considered speculative, indicating that the default probability has exceeded an inflection point, increasing this from the threshold of the BBB- more than proportional to the next notches.

The dominant effect of a crisis is primarily defined in the geographical region in which the crisis is originated. Hence, in financial stress periods, investors seek to sell those assets that possess a high potential volatility, reducing the value at risk of the portfolio. Also, portfolios specialized in geographic zones, increase their appetite for high quality assets. This last strategy reinforces the fact that fundamentals do not totally determine a position sell, role played by the administration logic of a portfolio. Management that must match assets liquidity with liabilities in duration terms, and must define a minima expected profitability during a defined investment horizon, so the credit quality of an asset in a specific moment is crucial.

This result reinforce the fact that investors follow a sovereign rating as a market signal and behind a loss of confidence, or an increase in uncertainty, it is this market signal that will define investment decisions and so the portfolios management course.

Investors sell or liquidate a profitable position in one country behind a loss given in another one, whose sovereign risk rating is similar. Therefore, the earnings of the positive sell will compensate the losses of the marked negative position, hedging the portfolio profitability and the trading book, but punishing an asset that has not necessarily become riskier.

6.2.2. United States Assets Markets Dependence

The risk perception of the capital market is relative to a safe asset. A comparison with the principal assets of the United States is very important. In fact, the international investors compare the risk profitability relation in emerging markets with those associated to risk free assets and also new technology markets, as the junk bonds in matured markets. The risk-return comparison between assets for the risk averse investor deals with all the efficient frontier possibilities.

From an univariate point of view, the emerging markets bonds are riskier than the industrialized issues, but they show the same skewness (Table 6).

Analyzing the relation with the dependence of the Colombian risk country we found disconcordance in the principal United States indicators (Table 7).

It follows then that most of the United States assets index dependence concentrates rather in the positive tail than in the negative tail (Table 8). This is evidence of a "*Flight to quality*"[3] during stress episodes. Investors sells the riskier searching the safest asset, reason why emerging markets bonds can collapse together even if their fundamentals are sound. A higher international uncertainty leads an increase in the probability of contagion for the emerging bonds. Finally, the Colombian country risk is more linked to the negative tail dependence with the Vix than with the "*High Yield*" and with that last one more than with the Nasdaq (Table 10).

This result is explained by the fact that the Vix is representative of the risk aversion at an international level, when this one increases, there is a negative effect over the Colombian spread, phenomena that is not so direct with other indexes.

---

[3] "*Flight to quality*" refers to the investment flows from volatile assets to risk free assets, during periods of uncertainty or crisis.

CONCLUSION

This document deals with an empirical analysis of the international capital markets crisis based on extreme events. The proposed methodology solves the econometric modeling problem of the joint structure dependence between debt spreads applying the copula function.

Initial empirical results that are complemented by the analysis of the dependence with another class of asset as the United States capital markets index.

We found contagion evidence for the Colombian emerging bonds from the principal international risk factors for the analysis episode. Colombian debt spreads have a high probability of presenting extreme events during high volatile periods conditionally to countries near in geographical terms, as in international sovereign risk ratings, particularly the pair group, even if this last is composed by countries that are not necessarily close in spatial terms neither in economic real links. This last link argues for the information channel of contagion, which is leaded by the behavior under uncertainty of agents, rather than the movements in fundamentals, even if fundamentals matter. Following Calvo, the international capital market is composed essentially of two types of investors. Those informed and the uninformed. The first one is a leader and the second one is a follower. The uninformed accomplish a signal extraction process. The "*Russian virus*", which was an unexpected panic episode, was propagated through the market architecture, by the imperfections in the functioning of financial markets. The capital market can help spread and multiplies the initial shock and this paper is empirical evidence in that way. Poor research about a country and its fundamentals evolution, assuming that diversification will minimize risk, is not necessarily accomplished. Diversification fails in crisis episodes. Sudden stops of capitals generate an effect that is triggering an unstable equilibrium that could lead to the contagion effect between countries, affecting countries that do not deserve a punishment.

Behind this empirical evidence, given the fact that capital flows has a speculative character in the short run, an alternative for hedging against the contagion effect consist in the deepening or the lengthen of the duration as the increase in the diversification of the external debt in foreign currency. Thereby, deepen on the large part of the yield curve reduce the exposition to a scenario of low liquidity in which the "*roll over*" of the short term debt will find liquidity restrictions due to the behavior of investors and the market sentiment. The external debt curve must deepen ideally in the large part of the external curve, while liquidity needs must be supplied in the short section of the internal debt curve.

At the same time, for the market risk, the creation of repurchase mechanism over the issues of sovereign debt, as structured notes using put options since the issue of the bond on the primary market, could reduce the market risk of an investor. For the credit risk, special guarantees supplied by a higher credit quality agent, activating in periods of financial turmoil, could reduce the panic of the market, hedging the investor in stress moments.

Finally, attaining a sovereign risk rating at least equal or higher than investment grade constitute an attractive market signal behind the lack of information or confusion during crisis periods.

Thus, minimizing the information asymmetries in the capital markets and accessing to an insurance against sudden and extreme changes leaded by the allocation of international portfolios due to moments of lack of information. Speculative attacks that could potentially drag to the default of the sovereign debt and could go far beyond translating in a shock affecting the real business cycle of the economy.

Research the existence of changes in the conditional extreme dependence structure, for example through the use of information criteria, is the next step to this work. Given these facts, starting the statistical validation of changes in the dependence structure focused on the interpretation of specific macroeconomic events and the interpretation of the reasons of such extreme changes is a task that is left to a future inquiry.

APPENDIX

a. Extreme Value Theory: Peaks over Threshold Approach

Traditional approaches in statistics are normal based and focus on the entire probability distribution function. On the other hand, the extreme value theory is focused on the tails of the distribution.

Let m random variables be independent and identically distributed $X_1, ..., X_m$. And so, $M_n = \max[X_1, ..., X_n]$ where M_n represents the maximums of observed values over n data. The underlying distribution function is unknown. $: F(x) = P(X_i \leq x)$. The excess loss function distribution over a threshold u is defined as:

$$F_u(y) = P(X - u \leq y | X > u) \tag{29}$$

For $0 \leq y \leq x_0 - u$; with $x_0 = \sup\{x \in R : F(x) < 1\}$; this function represents the probability that a loss exceeds a threshold u, for a major quantity than y, knowing that we have exceeded a threshold u. This equation can be written as:

$$F_u(y) = P(X - u \leq y | X > u) = \frac{P(X \leq y + u \cap X \geq u)}{P(X \geq u)} = \frac{P(u \leq X \leq y + u)}{1 - P(X \leq u)} = \frac{P(X \leq y + u) - P(X \leq u)}{1 - F(u)}$$

$$F_u(y) = \frac{F(y + u) - F(u)}{1 - F(u)} \tag{30}$$

Balkema and de Haan (1974) as Pickands (1975) demonstrate that for $F_u(y)$ it is possible to find a function that, when the threshold u increases, the distribution function of excesses converges into a non-degenerative distribution.

$$\lim_{u \to x_0} \sup_{0 \leq y \leq x_0 - u} \left| F_u(y) - G_{\xi, \beta(u)}(y) \right| = 0 \tag{31}$$

As u gets large, we have then, $F_u(y) = G_{\xi, \beta}(y)$.

The distribution $F_u(y)$ converges into a generalized Pareto distribution, that is:

$$G_{\xi,\beta} = \begin{cases} 1 - (1 + \xi x / \beta)^{-1/\xi} & \xi \neq 0 \\ 1 - \exp(-x / \beta) & \xi = 0 \end{cases} \tag{32}$$

The distribution has two parameters: β that is a scale parameter, and ξ that is a shape parameter or tail index. When $\xi > 0$, the GPD has fat tails. Now, as $F_u(y) = \dfrac{F(y+u) - F(u)}{1 - F(u)}$ if u is large and $y > 0$, we arrive to: $F_u(y) = G_{\xi,\beta}(y)$. Defining $x = u + y$, a $F(x)$ estimator is:

$$(1 - F(u)) \times F_u(y) = F(y+u) - F(u) \tag{33}$$

$$F(x) = (1 - F(u)) \times G_{\xi,\beta}(x-u) + F(u); \tag{34}$$

The observations proportion that do not exceeds the threshold is F(u), then an estimator of this one is the observations proportion over the threshold: $\hat{F}(u) = \dfrac{(n - N_u)}{n}$; Where N_u is the excesses number over a threshold u. This is an empirical estimator of the tail distribution. Replacing in the last equation and using the functional form of the Generalized Pareto Distribution[4], we obtain:

$$\hat{F}(x) = \left(1 - \frac{N_u}{n}\right) + \frac{N_u}{n}\left(1 - \left(1 + \frac{\hat{\xi}(x-u)}{\hat{\beta}}\right)^{-1/\hat{\xi}}\right) \tag{35}$$

$$\hat{F}(x) = 1 - \frac{N_u}{n}\left(1 + \hat{\xi}\frac{(x-u)}{\hat{\beta}}\right)^{-1/\hat{\xi}} \tag{36}$$

The Generalized Pareto Distribution is based on the determination of a threshold u. This one must be large to obtain the convergence in distribution but must represent at the same time extreme values concentrated in the tail of the distribution and by definition scarce.

The value at risk of an asset is $q > F(u)$, this is equivalent to a quantile of the F distribution, so: $VaR_q = F^{-1}(q)$.

It could be obtained by inverting the tail estimator. By this way, we have, $\hat{F}^{-1}(q)$ and so:

---

[4] ξ, β Are estimated for the tail distribution by the maximum likelihood method.

$$VaR_q = u + \frac{\hat{\beta}}{\hat{\xi}}\left(\left(\frac{n}{N_u}(1-q)\right)^{-\hat{\xi}} - 1\right) \tag{37}$$

The "*Expected Shortfall*" is the expected size of a return exceeding the VaR.

$$ES(\alpha) = E[X|X > VaR(\alpha)] \tag{38}$$

Value at risk tells us the worst that we can loss if an extreme event is realized, while the expected shortfall tell us the expected loss given an extreme event.

The *expected shortfall* is the conditional value at risk. This one can be written as:

$$ES(\alpha) = VaR(\alpha) + E[X - VaR(\alpha)|X > VaR(\alpha)] \tag{39}$$

The second term is the distribution mean excesses over a threshold, the value at risk represent the threshold:

$$ES(\alpha) = VaR(\alpha) + \frac{\beta + \xi(VaR(\alpha) - u)}{1 - \xi} = \frac{VaR(\alpha)}{1 - \xi} + \frac{\beta - \xi u}{1 - \xi} \tag{40}$$

Thus, the "*peaks over threshold*" approach apply extreme value theory to an excess distribution over a defined threshold that could be defined as the value at risk.

b. Multivariate Extreme Value Theory: Copulas

A copula is the distribution function of a vector of random variables in R^n with marginal uniforms (0,1). It is a function such as C: $[0,1]^n \rightarrow [0,1]$.

In the bivariate case, it is a two-dimension distribution function in $[0,1]^2$, with marginal uniform (0,1). It is a C function that links the marginal distributions with the joint distribution, so: $F(x_1, x_2) = C(F_1(x_1), F_2(x_2))$[5];

A two-dimension copula is a function C with the following properties:

1. Dom $C = [0,1] \times [0,1]$
2. $C(0,u) = C(u,0) = 0$ and $C(u,1) = C(1,u) = u$ $\forall u \in [0,1]$;
3. C is increasing: $C(v_1, v_2) - C(v_1, u_2) - C(u_1, v_2) + C(u_1, u_2) \geq 0$. C is increasing in each component. Ever that:

---

[5] $F_n(X_n)$ Is a marginal distribution function.

$(u_1, u_2) \in [0,1]^2$

$(v_1, v_2) \in [0,1]^2$, such as, $0 \le u_1 \le v_1 \le 1$ y $0 \le u_2 \le v_2 \le 1$

The copula function of the random variables (X_1, X_2) is invariant under strictly increasing transformations: $\partial_x F_n(x) > 0$. It is then an exhaustive statistical of dependence. Also, if the marginal distributions are continuous based on Sklar's (1959) theorem the copula is unique. This theorem map a specific copula to each distribution.

In one hand, we have the marginal, and in the other we have the copula, the one that links the marginal and models the dependence between them.

We extract the unique copula C from a multivariate distribution F with continuous marginal $F_1, ..., F_n$ when:

$$C(F_1(x_1), F_2(x_2), ..., F_n(x_n)) = F(x_1, x_2, ..., x_n)$$
$$C(F_1(x_1), F_2(x_2), ..., F_n(x_n)) = P(X_1 \le x_1, X_2 \le x_2, ..., X_n \le x_N) \qquad (41)$$

$$C(F_1(x_1), F_2(x_2), ..., F_n(x_n)) = P(F_1^{-1}(U_1) \le x_1, F_2^{-1}(U_2) \le x_2, ..., F_n^{-1}(U_n) \le x_n)$$
$$C(F_1(x_1), F_2(x_2), ..., F_n(x_n)) = P(U_1 \le F_1(x_1), U_2 \le F_2(x_2), ..., U_n \le F_n(x_n))$$

The multivariate distribution represents the information that lies in the dependence structure between variables. Then, a copula must extract all this source of information. The "*Frechet upper bound*", as the "*Frechet lower bound*", represents the bounds within the dependence measure is defined. The first case will be denominated as C^+ and the second C^-. These are numerically defined as:

$$C^-(u_1, u_2) = \max(u_1 + u_2 - 1, 0)$$
$$C^+(u_1, u_2) = \min(u_1, u_2) \qquad (42)$$

For any kind of copula the following order must be respected:

$$C^- \prec C \prec C^+$$

Then, two random variables X_1 and X_2 are countermonotonics, $C = C^-$, if there exist a random variable X as $X_1 = f_1(x)$ and $X_2 = f_2(x)$ with f_1 non-increasing and f_2 non-decreasing. Two random variables X_1 and X_2 are comonotonic, $C = C^+$, if there exist a random variable X as $X_1 = f_1(x)$ and $X_2 = f_2(x)$ with f_1 non-increasing and f_2 non-decreasing.

The tail dependence is the dependence in the first quadrant of the positive or negative bivariate distribution. If a bivariate copula is defined as:

$$\lim_{u \to 1} \frac{\overline{C}(u,u)}{1-u} = \lambda_u \tag{43}$$

And if the limit exists, C has a positive tail dependence if $\lambda \in (0,1]$. It does not present a positive tail dependence if $\lambda = 0$. Where lambda is the parameter of tail dependence. Likewise, if:

$$\lim_{u \to 0} \frac{\overline{C}(u,u)}{u} = \lambda_L \tag{44}$$

And if the limit exists, C has a negative tail dependence if $\lambda \in (0,1]$. It does not present a tail dependence if $\lambda = 0$. Then,

$$\lambda_U = \lim_{u \to 1} P(U_1 > u | U_2 > u) = \lim_{u \to 0} P(U_2 > u | U_1 > u) \tag{45}$$

If there exist negative tail dependence, large negative movements in the price of an asset will be followed by large negatives movements in the price of another asset. λ Is the probability that a variable is extreme given that the other is extreme, in value at risk terms; we could write this measure as:

$$\lambda(VaR) = p(X_2 > F_2^{-1}(VaR) | X_1 > F_1^{-1}(VaR)) = p(U_2 > VaR | U_1 > VaR) = \frac{\overline{C}(u,u)}{1-u} \tag{46}$$

REFERENCES

[1]   Balkema, A., and L. De Haan (1974): "*Residual life time at great age.*" Annals of Probability, 2, 792-804.

[2]   Bouyé Eric, (2000) "*Copulas for Finance a Reading Guide and Some Applications.*" Financial Econometrics Research Center.

[3]   Boyer, B., M. Gibson, and M. Loretan (1999), "*Pitfalls in tests for changes in correlations.*" Board of Governors of the Federal Reserve System, International Finance Discussion Paper, 597.

[4]   Calvo, G. (1996), "*Capital Inflows and Macroeconomic Management: Tequila lessons, International Journal of Finance and Economics.*" International Journal of Finance and Economics,1, 207-223.

[5]   Calvo Guillermo. (1998) "*Understanding the Russian Virus with special reference to Latin America.*" (Working Paper).

[6]   Calvo, G (1999a), "*Contagion in Emerging Markets.*" University of Maryland, Working Paper.

[7]   Calvo, Guillermo (1999) *"Contagion in Emerging Markets: When Wall Street is a Carrier."* Working Paper, University of Maryland.

[8]   Danielsson J. and C. de Vries (1997), *"Tail index and quantile estimation with Very high frequency data."* Journal of Empirical Finance, 4, p. 241-257.

[9]   Eichengreen, B., A. Rose, and C. Wysplosz (1997). *"Contagious Currency Crises."* CEPR, Working Paper.

[10]   Embrechts, P., McNeil, A.J. and D. Straumann (1999), *"Correlation and dependency in risk management: properties and pitfalls."* Department of Mathematik, ETHZ, Zurich, Working Paper.

[11]   Forbes, K. and R. Rigobon (1999), *"Measuring Contagion: Conceptual and Empirical Issues."* Massachusetts Institute of Technology, Sloan School of Management, Working Paper.

[12]   Forbes, K. and R. Rigobon (2000a), *"Contagion in Latin-American: Definitions, Measurement, and Policy Implications. "*, NBER, Working Paper.

[13]   Forbes, K. and R. Rigobon (2000b), *"No Contagion, only interdependence."* Massachusetts Institute of Technology, Sloan School of Management, Working Paper.

[14]   Gerlacht, S. and F. Smets (1995). *"Contagious Speculative Attacks."* European Journal of Political Economy, 11, 45-63.

[15]   Hall P (1990). *"Using the bootstrap to estimate mean squared error and select smoothing parameter in nonparametric problems."* Journal of Multivariate Analysis, Vol. 32, Issue 2, P. 177-203.

[16]   Hill, B. (1975). *"A simple general approach to inference about the tail of a distribution."* The Annals of Statistics. Vol. 3, N°5, 1163-1174.

[17]   Kaminsky, G., and C. Reinhart (1998), *"On Crises, Contagion and Confusion."* University of Maryland, Working Paper.

[18]   Kaminsky, G., and S. Schmukler (1999), *"What triggers market jitters? A chronicle of the Asian Crisis."* Journal of International Money and Finance, 18, 537-560.

[19]   Koedijk K., Schafgans M. and C. de Vries (1990), *"The tail index of exchange rate returns."* Journal of International Economics, 29, p.93-108.

[20]   Kofman, P. and M. Martens (1997), *"Interaction between stock Markets: an analysis of the common trading hours at the London and New York stock exchange."* Journal of International Money and Finance, 16, 387-414.

[21]   Laurent Pierre and Jérôme Teiletche (2001). *"Emerging Sovereign Bond Markets: A view from the extremes."* Preliminary version.

[22]   Longin, F. and B. Solnik (1995), *"Is the correlation in international equity returns constant: 1960-1990?"* Journal of International Money and Finance, 14, 3-26.

[23]   Longin, F. and B. Solnik (2000), *"Correlation structure of international equity markets during extremely volatile periods."* CEPR, Discussion Paper, 2538.

[24]   Longin F. and B. Solnik (2001), *"Extreme correlation of international equity markets."* Journal of Finance, 56, p. 649-676.

[25]   Masson, P. (2000), *"Multiple Equilibria, contagion and emerging markets crises."* forthcoming in R. Glick, R. Moreno and M. Spiegel (eds), Financial Crises in Emerging Markets, Cambridge University Press.

[26]   McNeil, A.J. and R. Frey, (2000), *"Estimation of tail-related risk measures for heteroscedastic financial time series: an extreme value approach."* Journal of Empirical Finance 7, 271-300.

[27] Nelsen R. (1998), *"An Introduction to Copulas"*, Lecture *Notes in Statistics*, 139, Springer Verlag.

[28] Pagan A. *"The Econometrics of Financial Markets."* Journal of empirical finance. 3 (1996). 15-102.

[29] Pickands, J. (1975): *"Statistical inference using extreme order statistics."* The annals of Statistics, 3, 119-131.

[30] Roncalli, Costinot y Teiletche, (2000). *"Revisiting the dependence between financial markets with copulas."* (Work in Process). Groupe de Recherche Opérationnelle Crédit Lyonnais.

[31] Roncalli Thierry. *"La théorie des Extrêmes et la gestion des Risques de Marché."* GRO Crédit Lyonnais. (2004).

[32] Sklar, A (1959). *"Fonctions de répartition a n dimensions et leurs marges."* Publ. Inst. Statist. Univ. Paris, 8:229-231.

[33] Straetmans, S. (2001), *"Extreme financial returns and their comovements."* Tinbergen Institute Research Series, PhD Thesis N° 181, Erasmus University Rotterdam.

[34] Valdes, R. (1996), *"Emerging Market Contagion: Evidence and Theory."* MIT, Working Paper.

[35] Von Furstenberg, G.m. and B.n, Jeon (1989), *"International Stock Prices Movements: Links and Messages"*, *Brookings Papers on Economic Activity,* 1: 125-179.

In: Economics of Emerging Markets
Editor: Lado Beridze, pp. 317-327

Chapter 13

DO DIVIDENDS MATTER FOR STOCK RETURNS? EVIDENCE FROM THE BRAZILIAN MARKET

Andre Carvalhal da Silva[*]

Coppead Graduate School of Business, Federal University of Rio de Janeiro (UFRJ)
Rua Pascoal Lemme, 355 Ilha do Fundao, 21941-918, Rio de Janeiro, Brazil

ABSTRACT

There is evidence that value stocks have higher returns than growth stocks in markets around the world. Not much is known, however, about the performance of value strategies in the Brazilian market. The purpose of this paper is to analyze the performance of a very simple investment strategy based on the dividend yield. Using data from a 10-year period from 1995 to 2004, we provide evidence that the dividend yield has a moderate power to explain stock returns. The results using the Jensen alpha, and the Treynor and Sharpe ratios indicate that the most diversified portfolios do achieve risk-adjusted excess returns. All betas are significant and below unity suggesting that the dividend strategy has a lower risk than investing in the market. Building portfolios with the highest yielding stocks present more bull months (positive returns) than bear months (negative returns). Further, the magnitude of the returns in bull months is higher than in bear months.

1. INTRODUCTION

Investment strategies based on dividend yield are very popular in many countries due to their simplicity and alleged ability to outperform market indices. One of the most common strategies is the Dogs of the Dow Jones (DoD), which consists in investing in the highest yielding components of the Dow Jones [see Bary (1993, 1994) and O'Higgins and Downes (1990)].

[*] Tel.: (55-21) 2598-9878; Fax: (55-21) 2598-9872; E-mail: andrec@coppead.ufrj.br

The theoretical basis for the strategy can be traced to the theory of corporate dividend policy. The numerator of dividend yield is the dividend flow and the denominator is the stock's current price. Corporations strive to maintain stable dividend payouts to avoid sending undesirable signals to the markets about the company's future business prospects. If the market driven equity prices exceed (fall below) intrinsic market values, they will produce lower (higher) dividend yields, due to the more stable policy-driven dividend payout.

Recent empirical research is consistent with a high dividend yield strategy outperforming the market in many developed and emerging countries [Fama and French (1998)]. Capaul, Rowley and Sharpe (1993) also document the superior performance of the value investing strategies in six countries. Barry et al. (1997) find some evidence of the value effect in cross-sectional returns for 26 emerging markets during 1985-1995. Claessens et al. (1998) conclude that the dividend yield has a partial power to explain cross-sectional returns in a group of 18 emerging markets.

Fama and French (1992, 1993, 1996) argue that value strategies are fundamentally riskier and therefore the higher average returns reflect compensation for bearing this risk. Lakonishok, Shleifer and Vishny (1994) argue that value strategies yield higher returns because investors are able to identify mispriced stocks and not because they are fundamentally riskier. However, McQueen, Shields and Thorley (1997) report that the DoD strategy beats the market statistically but not economically. Moreover, McQueen and Thorley (1999) find that highest yielding stocks do not outperform the market after adjusting for risk. Finally, Hirschey (2000) argues that there is no robust evidence of an average return anomaly tied to the DoD strategy.

Although there is a vast literature on many developed and developing counties, not much is known about the performance of value strategies based on dividends in the Brazilian market. Fama and French (1998) document a huge value premium in Brazil. They find an average difference between dollar returns on the high and low book-to-market portfolios of 73.72% per year over the 1987 to 1995 period. However, this value premium is calculated using only the book-to-market ratio and not the dividend yield.

Leal et al. (2000) study a more recent period and conclude that the DoD does not yield significant risk-adjusted excess returns in Brazil from 1994 to 1998. Silva (2001) provides evidence that the DoD does not add value as an investment strategy in Brazil from 1994 to 1999.

The purpose of this paper is to analyze the performance of value strategies based on dividend yield in Brazil during a longer and more recent period. Using data from the Sao Paulo stock exchange for a 10-year period from 1995 to 2004, there is evidence that the dividend yield has a moderate power to explain stock returns. More important, a diversified portfolio of the highest yielding stocks does yield significant risk-adjusted excess returns.

This paper is structured as follows. In section 2, we present the data and the methodology used in the paper. Section 3 contains the main results of the time-series regressions and the implementation of the DoD strategy in Brazil. Section 4 discusses our findings and conclusions.

2. DATA AND METHODOLOGY

A. Brazilian Economic Environment

Table 1 reports various indicators of the economic environment in Brazil. Five characteristics of the Brazilian economy are particularly relevant: high interest rates, stable inflation in recent years, large GDP, low per capita GDP, and a declining country risk measured by the emerging markets bond index (EMBI).

In the beginning of the 1990's, the Brazilian inflation was very high and volatile, reaching extreme levels, such as 2,987% in 1990 and 2,148% in 1993. The high inflation rates were subdued in 1994 by the Real Plan and the introduction of a new currency. Annual inflation declined to 22.4% in 1995 and to 7.60% in 2004.

Nevertheless, interest rates are still high (41.2% in 1995 and 17.5% in 2004). Arida et al. (2005) argue that the high interest rate in Brazil is due to the existence of a large domestic currency short-term debt market under jurisdictional uncertainty. The interventionist nature of the Brazilian State increases jurisdictional uncertainty. For example, the currency convertibility does not exist and remittances abroad can be suspended at any time.

Brazil has one of the largest economies around the world, but has been growing at small rates when compared to other emerging markets, especially Asian countries. In 2004, Brazilian GDP reached approximately US$ 664 billion, but it is still smaller than 10 years before (US$ 770 billion). Further, the per capita GDP dropped from US$ 4,440 in 1995 to US$ 3,326 in 2004. While Brazilian per capita GDP was roughly 30% of the U.S. per capita GDP in 1980, it was only 8% of the U.S. per capita GDP in 2004.

Regarding the external sector, the export flow more than doubled from US$ 46 billion in 1995 to US$ 96 billion in 2004. The international reserves have been increasing recently, and the external debt has decreased. As a result, the country risk has declined substantially from 933 to 382 basis points.

Table 1. Brazilian Economic Environment

Indicator	1995	2000	2004
Macroeconomic			
Treasury bill rate (% per year)	41.22	16.19	17.50
Inflation (% per year)	22.41	5.97	7.60
GDP (US$ million)	770,350	644,984	663,783
Per capita GDP (US$)	4,440	3,515	3,326
International Transactions			
Exports (US$ million)	46,506	55,086	96,475
Reserves (US$ million)	51,475	33,011	52,934
Country risk (EMBI) (% per year)	933	749	382
External debt (US$ million)	92,347	190,316	135,702

Macroeconomic and international indicators of the economic environment in Brazil are reported at the end of 1995, 2000, and 2004.

Table 2. Stock Market Capitalization of Emerging Countries

Country	1995	2000	2004
Latin America			
Argentina	37,784	45,839	47,590
Brazil	147,636	226,152	474,647
Chile	71,262	60,401	136,493
Mexico	90,694	125,204	239,128
East Asia			
India	NA	NA	1,069,046
Indonesia	66,454	26,813	81,428
Korea	181,955	148,361	718,011
Malaysia	213,757	113,155	180,518
Philippines	58,786	25,261	39,818
Singapore	150,959	155,126	257,341
Taiwan	187,211	247,597	476,018
Thailand	135,907	29,217	123,885

Stock market capitalization (in US$ million) of emerging countries is reported at the end of 1995, 2000, and 2004.

Table 2 shows that the Brazilian market capitalization (US$ 474 billion) is the largest in Latin America and the fourth largest among emerging markets, behind India (US$ 1,069 billion), Korea (US$ 718 billion), and Taiwan (US$ 476 billion).

B. Sample and Portfolio Formation

Our sample consists of all firms listed on the Sao Paulo stock exchange from (some portion of) January 1995 to December 2004. Most of the data come from the Economatica, a financial database that contains a wide coverage of Brazilian stock market data. The sample does not include companies with incomplete or unavailable information, and firms whose shares were not traded on the stock market during the 1995–2004 period. The final sample consists of a total of 212 firms, which represent 59% of the number of firms at the end of 2004.

In each year t, all stocks are ranked on size (market value of equity in December of year t-1). The sample is divided and classified into three size groups based on the breakpoints for the bottom 30% (Small), middle 40% (Medium), and top 30% (Big). Independently, we also break the stocks into three dividend yield (DY) groups (Low, Medium, and High) according to the bottom 30%, middle 40%, and top 30%.

We construct 9 portfolios (S/L, S/M, S/H, M/L, M/M, M/H, B/L, B/M, B/H) from the intersections of the 3 size, and 3 DY groups, respectively. For example, the S/L portfolio contains the stocks that are in the small-size and low-DY groups. The portfolio SMB (small minus big) is the difference between the returns on the 3 small-stock portfolios, and the returns on the 3 big-stock portfolios. The portfolio HML (high minus low) is the difference between the returns on the 3 high-DY portfolios, and the returns on the 3 low-DY portfolios.

We use portfolios formed on size and DY because we seek to determine whether the mimicking portfolios SMB and HML capture common factors in stock returns related to size and dividend yield.

C. Time-Series Regressions

This paper uses the time-series regression approach of Black, Jensen, and Scholes (1972) in order to investigate whether the dividend yield helps explain stock returns. The following regression is estimated:

$$R_t - RF_t = a + b(RM_t - RF_t) + sSMB_t + hHML_t + e_t$$

where R_t is the return of each portfolio in month t, RF_t is the risk-free rate[1] in month t, RM_t is the market return[2] in month t, SMB_t (small minus big) is the return of the size factor in month t, HML_t (high minus low) is the return of the DY factor in month t. The regressions for each of the 9 portfolios are estimated using monthly returns in local currency from 1995 to 2004.

D. Implementation of the DoD Strategy

The DoD strategy was widely popularized by Bary (1993, 1994) and O'Higgins and Downes (1990). The DoD strategy consists in investing equal amounts in the highest yielding components of the Dow Jones. The idea is that the dividend yield is often an inverse indicator of popularity, and that buying Dow stocks when they are temporarily out of favor ("dog" stocks) is a shrewd way to beat the market.

At the end of the year, the portfolio is rebalanced and updated with the new DoD stocks. We test the most popular versions of the DoD strategy: the highest yielding stock by itself (Top 1), five highest yielding stocks (Top 5), ten highest yielding stocks (Top 10), fifteen highest yielding stocks (Top 15), and the twenty highest yielding stocks (Top 20).

We perform all our tests for one-year holding period on an absolute and on a risk-adjusted basis. To measure the risk-adjusted performance of the DoD, we employ three traditional measures of risk-adjusted performance: the Treynor (1965) and Sharpe (1966) ratios, and Jensen (1968) alpha.

Variables like price-to-earnings, book-to-market equity, and dividend yield are all scaled versions of a firm's stock price. Therefore, the DoD strategy would be capturing the information impounded in dividend yield which Fama and French (1992) found in the book-to-market equity ratio.

---

[1] Our proxy for the risk-free rate of return is the CDI (interbank certificate of deposit), the prime rate for one-day loans between financial institutions. This rate is the most commonly used investment benchmark in Brazil, yielding virtually the same as the equivalent one-day repo rates on government securities (the "Over/SELIC" rate). Thus we decide to use the benchmark widely followed by the market.

[2] We use the Sao Paulo stock exchange index (Ibovespa), since it is a representative indicator of the price performance of the main shares traded on the Sao Paulo stock exchange.

Table 3. Monthly Excess Returns for 9 Portfolios Formed on Size and Dividend Yield

Portfolio	Average Return	Standard Deviation
S/L	0.60%	10.05%
S/M	0.30%	9.22%
S/H	0.61%	9.50%
M/L	-0.08%	9.30%
M/M	-0.27%	7.46%
M/H	0.52%	7.19%
B/L	-0.22%	10.50%
B/M	-0.63	8.86%
B/H	-0.08%	8.17%

Monthly excess returns of each portfolio from 1995 to 2004. The excess return is measured by the difference between the portfolio returns and the risk-free rate of return (CDI). Each portfolio is named with two letters, related to size (small, medium, big) and dividend yield (low, medium, and high), respectively. For example, the S/L portfolio contains the stocks that are in the small-size and low-DY groups.

3. EMPIRICAL RESULTS

Table 3 shows the monthly excess returns[3] of each portfolio from 1995 to 2004. All portfolios formed by small companies present positive excess returns. In contrast, all portfolios formed by large firms present negative excess returns. This size effect seems to be consistent with the evidence provided by Fama and French (1998) for many countries.

Further, the returns on the portfolios formed by high-DY firms are larger than those on low-DY firms. This result seems to indicate that value stocks have higher returns than growth stocks (Fama and French (1998)). It is important to note that the excess returns are neither statistically nor economically significant, which means that no portfolio presents a return higher than the risk-free rate. This is not surprising since Brazilian interest rates have been one of the highest around the world during the sample period.

Table 4 reports the regressions for the three-factor model. The results indicate that the market, SMB and HML factors typically capture substantial time-series variation in stock returns.

The market factor has more explanatory power than SMB and HML, but the size and DY factors seem to be important to explain stock returns. The number of market, SMB and HML slopes statistically significant at the 1% level are 9 (out of 9), 4, and 4, respectively.

No intercept term is statistically different from zero, suggesting that the market beta, SMB, and HML do a good job in explaining stock returns. Moreover, the slopes on SMB and HML are related to size, and DY, respectively. Controlling for DY, the slopes on SMB decrease from smaller- to bigger-size portfolios. Similarly, controlling for size, the slopes on HML increase from lower- to higher-DY portfolios.

---

[3] The excess return is measured by the difference between the portfolio returns and the risk-free rate of return.

Table 4. Regressions of Excess Stock Returns on the Excess Market Return and the Mimicking Returns for Size (SMB) and Dividend Yield (HML)

Portfolio	a	b	s	h
S/L	0.00	0.68***	0.94***	-1.02***
	(0.47)	(0.00)	(0.00)	(0.00)
S/M	0.00	0.56***	0.93***	-0.21
	(0.76)	(0.00)	(0.00)	(0.15)
S/H	0.00	0.71***	0.82***	0.58***
	(0.92)	(0.00)	(0.00)	(0.00)
M/L	0.00	0.56***	0.23**	-0.73***
	(0.84)	(0.00)	(0.03)	(0.00)
M/M	0.00	0.43***	0.11	-0.21*
	(0.78)	(0.00)	(0.25)	(0.10)
M/H	0.00	0.53***	0.26***	0.00
	(0.30)	(0.00)	(0.00)	(0.97)
B/L	0.00	0.61***	-0.18*	-0.65***
	(0.59)	(0.00)	(0.08)	(0.00)
B/M	0.00	0.74***	-0.04	-0.03
	(0.31)	(0.00)	(0.49)	(0.71)
B/H	0.00	0.62***	-0.09	0.02
	(0.58)	(0.00)	(0.19)	(0.78)

The excess returns on the 9 size-DY portfolios are regressed on the excess market return, SMB, and HML. ***, **, * denote statistical significance at 1%, 5% and 10%, respectively; p-values in parentheses use heteroscedasticity and autocorrelation consistent covariance matrix.

$R_t - RF_t = a + b(RM_t - RF_t) + sSMB_t + hHML_t + e_t$

Table 5. Mean Monthly Returns for the DoD Strategies, Ibovespa and CDI

Portfolio	Average Return	Standard Deviation
Top 1	1.62%	32.17%
Top 5	2.47%*	14.80%
Top 10	2.97%***	11.04%
Top 15	2.99%***	9.34%
Top 20	2.81%***	8.67%
Ibovespa	1.49%	10.91%
CDI	1.86%***	0.74%

Mean monthly returns for each DoD strategy, for the market (Ibovespa) and for the risk-free rate of return (CDI) from 1995 to 2004. Five strategies are built depending on the number of high yielding stocks in the portfolio: Top 1, Top 5, Top 10, Top 15, and Top 20. ***, **, * denote statistical significance at 1%, 5% and 10%, respectively.

Table 5 shows the average monthly returns for each DoD strategy, for the market (Ibovespa) and for the risk-free rate of return (CDI). We can see that most DoD strategies (except for Top 1) present positive returns. The most diversified portfolios present the highest returns, ranging from 2.81% (Top 20) to 2.99% (Top 15) per month. As expected, the strategies with fewer stocks in the portfolio (Top 1 and Top 5) have greater variability measured by the standard deviation of returns. The return on the Ibovespa (1.49% per month) is not statistically different from zero, while the CDI present a significant average return of 1.86% per month. This result is consistent with the high interest rates in Brazil.

Table 6 shows the differential returns between each DoD strategy and the Ibovespa. Although all differential returns are positive, only one of them (Top 15) is statistically significant at 10%. Therefore, we conclude that there does not exist strong statistical evidence to support the argument that the DoD strategies outperform the market in Brazil.

In order to analyze risk-adjusted performance we employ Jensen's alpha, Treynor and Sharpe ratios. Table 7 shows these risk measures together with the betas of each DoD strategy. Most DoD strategies exhibit alphas close to zero. The most diversified portfolios (Top 15 and Top 20) present positive alphas statistically significant at 10%. The evidence using alphas does not indicate that the DoD strategies achieve statistically significant risk-adjusted excess returns. However, there is some evidence that the DoD strategies with greater number of firms in the portfolio outperform the market after adjusting for risk.

Table 6. Differential Returns of the DoD Relative to the Market

Portfolio	Average Return	Standard Deviation
Top 1	0.12%	31.12%
Top 5	0.98%	14.71%
Top 10	1.47%	11.12%
Top 15	1.49%*	9.65%
Top 20	1.32%	8.80%

Mean monthly differential returns of each DoD strategy relative to the market (Ibovespa). Five strategies are built depending on the number of high yielding stocks in the portfolio: Top 1, Top 5, Top 10, Top 15, and Top 20. * denotes statistical significance at the 10% level.

Table 7. Risk-Adjusted Performance of the DoD

Portfolio	Jensen's Alpha	Market Beta	Treynor Ratio	Sharpe Ratio
Top 1	0.00	0.77***	0.00	0.01
Top 5	0.00	0.50***	0.01	0.04
Top 10	0.01	0.49***	0.02	0.10
Top 15	0.01*	0.47***	0.02	0.12
Top 20	0.01*	0.49***	0.02	0.11
Ibovespa	-	-	-0.01	-0.03

Jensen's alpha, market beta, Treynor and Sharpe ratios of each DoD strategy. Ibovespa is our proxy for market return. Five strategies are built depending on the number of high yielding stocks in the portfolio: Top 1, Top 5, Top 10, Top 15, and Top 20. ***, **, * denote alpha and beta statistically different from zero at 1%, 5% and 10%, respectively.

Table 8. Bull and Bear Months of the DoD

Portfolio	Frequency of Bull Months	Frequency of Bear Months	Average Return in Bull Months	Average Return in Bear Months
Top 1	48%	52%	20.59%	-15.74%
Top 5	60%	40%	9.22%	-7.64%
Top 10	62%	38%	8.39%	-5.75%
Top 15	67%	33%	7.24%	-5.52%
Top 20	66%	34%	7.10%	-5.45%
Ibovespa	60%	40%	8.26%	-8.65%

Bull (positive returns) and bear (negative returns) months of each DoD strategy. Ibovespa is our proxy for market return. Five strategies are built depending on the number of high yielding stocks in the portfolio: Top 1, Top 5, Top 10, Top 15, and Top 20.

All betas are significant and below unity indicating that the DoD strategy has a lower risk than investing in the market and would appeal to investors who prefer conservative, lower risk portfolios. Further, all DoD strategies have positive Treynor and Sharpe ratios, which are higher than those of the market index. In fact, the Treynor and Sharpe ratios of the Ibovespa are negative. The most diversified portfolios (Top 10, Top 15 and Top 20) present the highest Treynor and Sharpe ratios. The evidence using the Treynor and Sharpe ratios does indicate that the DoD strategies achieve risk-adjusted excess returns.

Table 8 shows the performance of the DoD strategies during bull and bear markets. During the 10-year period, the Ibovespa rose in 60% of the months ("bull months"). More important, all DoD strategies (except for Top 1) rose in at least 60% of the months. The most diversified portfolios (Top 15 and Top 20) had 67% and 66% of bull months, respectively. Interestingly, the average return for the Top 15 and Top 20 in bull months (7.24% and 7.10%, respectively) is higher than in bear months (-5.52%, and -5.45%).

This superior performance also happens with the Top 1 and Top 5 strategies. It is important to note that, although the Top 1 has more bear than bull months, the average return is higher in bull months (20.59%) than bear months (-15.74%). In contrast, the Ibovespa has more bull than bear months, but the average return is lower in bull months (8.26%) than bear months (-8.65%). We can conclude that the DoD is less risky than the market, since it presents more positive than negative returns, and the positive returns during bull months are higher than the negative returns during bear months.

Overall, our results indicate that there is no strong statistical evidence to support the argument that the DoD strategies outperform the market in Brazil. However, there is some evidence that the most diversified portfolios (Top 15 and Top 20) tend to achieve statistically significant risk-adjusted excess returns. Further, the DoD is a lower risk strategy than investing in the market.

4. CONCLUSION

Recent empirical research is consistent with a high dividend yield strategy outperforming the market in many developed and emerging countries. Not much is known, however, about the performance of dividend strategies in the Brazilian market. The purpose of this paper is to analyze the performance of value strategies based on dividend yield in Brazil during a 10-year period from 1995 to 2004.

Our results tend to indicate that the dividend yield has a moderate power to explain stock returns in Brazil. Overall, there is no strong statistical evidence to support the argument that the DoD strategies outperform the market. However, the evidence using the Jensen alpha, and the Treynor and Sharpe ratios does indicate that the most diversified DoD portfolios (Top 15 and Top 20) achieve risk-adjusted excess returns. All betas are significant and below unity indicating that the DoD is a lower risk strategy than investing in the market. The DoD has more bull than bear months, and the magnitude of the return in bull months is higher than in bear months.

ACKNOWLEDGEMENTS

I would like to thank Carlos Roberto Ferreira Reis for his excellent research assistance and valuable discussions. All errors are my own. I also thank Coppead Graduate School of Business for its support.

REFERENCES

Arida, P., Bacha, E., Resende, A. (2005). Credit, interest, and jurisdictional uncertainty: conjectures on the case of Brazil. In: F. Giavazzi, I. Goldfajn, S. Herrera (eds.). *Inflation Targeting, Debt, and the Brazilian Experience from 1999 to 2003*. Cambridge, MIT Press.

Bary, A. (1993). Canny canines. *Barron's*, Dec 13.

Bary, A. (1994). Howling dogs. *Barron's*, Dec 26.

Barry, C., Goldreyer, E., Lockwood, L., and Rodriguez, M. (1997). Size and book-to-market effects: evidence from emerging equity markets. *Texas Christian University Working Paper*.

Black, F., Jensen, M., and Scholes, M. (1972). The capital asset pricing model: some empirical tests. In Michael C. Jensen, ed.: *Studies in the Theory of Capital Markets*, Praeger Publishers Inc.

Capaul, C., Rowley, I., and Sharpe, W. (1993). International value and growth stock returns. *Financial Analysts Journal*, Jan/Feb, 27-36.

Claessens, S., Dasgupta, S., and Glen, J. (1998). The cross-section of stock returns: evidence from the emerging markets. *Emerging Markets Quarterly* 4, 4-13.

Fama, E., and French, K. (1992). The cross-section of expected stock returns. *Journal of Finance* 47, 427-465.

Fama, E., and French, K. (1993). Common risk factors in the returns on stocks and bonds. *Journal of Financial Economics* 33, 3-56.

Fama, E., and French, K. (1996). Multifactor explanations of asset pricing anomalies. *Journal of Finance* 51, 55-84.

Fama, E., and French, K. (1998). Value versus growth: the international evidence. *Journal of Finance* 53, 1975-2000.

Jensen, M. (1968). Problems in selection of security portfolios: the performance of mutual funds in the period 1945-1964. *Journal of Finance* 23, 389-419.

Lakonishok, J., Shleifer, A., and Vishny, R. (1994). Contrarian investment, extrapolation and risk. *Journal of Finance* 49, 1541-1578.

Leal, R., Silva, A., Austin, M. (2000). Does this dog hunt? Testing the performance of the dogs of the dow in the U.S and in Brazil. *International Journal of Finance* 12, 1896-1912.

McQueen, G., Shields, K., and Thorley, S. (1997). Does the dow-10 investment strategy beat the dow statistically and economically? *Financial Analysts Journal*, Jul/Aug, 66-72.

O'Higgins, M., and Downes, J. (1990). *Beating the Dow*, New York: Harper Collins.

Sharpe, W. (1964). Capital asset prices: a theory of market equilibrium under conditions of risk. *Journal of Finance* 19, 425-442.

Silva, A. (2001). Empirical tests of the dogs of the dow strategy in Latin American stock markets. *International Review of Financial Analysis* 10, 187-199.

Treynor, J. (1965). How to rate management of investment funds. *Harvard Business Review* 43, 63-75.

In: Economics of Emerging Markets
Editor: Lado Beridze, pp. 329-347

ISBN: 978-1-60021-850-7
© 2008 Nova Science Publishers, Inc.

Chapter 14

CORPORATE FINANCIAL PERFORMANCE AND MARKET REACTION TO EMPLOYEE STOCK OWNERSHIP PLANS IN TAIWAN

Wei-Ning Chen[1],*, Dar-Hsin Chen[2],
and Po-Wei Lu[3]

[1]Department of International Business, Kainan University, Taiwan
[2]Department of Business Administration, National Taipei University, Taiwan
[3]Graduate Institute of Banking and Finance, Tamkang University, Taiwan

ABSTRACT

This study examines whether the financial performances of companies in Taiwan differ when the firms adopt employee stock ownership plans (ESOPs). The results of analyzing the market reactions, as reflected in the stock returns when an announcement is made in a board meeting regarding the adoption of an ESOP, indicate that the electronics and non-electronics industries differ significantly on terms of the ROE, profit margin and equity multiplier during the pre- and post-event periods. The total asset turnover rate in the non-electronics industry, however, does not differ significantly during the pre- and post-event periods. Reactions toward the adoption of an ESOP are observed in the market before the event occurs, and the electronics industry accounts for the most significant reaction. Moreover, we find that a negative relationship exists between the CAAR and firm size, and that there is a positive relationship between the CAAR and the market-to-book ratio and the debt ratio.

Keywords: Du Pont identity; Employee stock ownership plans; Event study
JEL Classifications: G30, G32, M43, M41

---

* Please address all correspondence to: Professor Dar-Hsin Chen, Department of Business Administration, National Taipei University, 151 University Rd., San Shia, Taipei County, 237 Taiwan. Tel: 886-2-2500-9820. Fax: 886-2-2502-9353. Email: dhchen@mail.ntpu.edu.tw.

1. INTRODUCTION

In recent years, the high technology industry in Taiwan has rapidly developed and its stock trading volume has accounted for the majority of the trading activities in the stock market. With the help of a unique employee stock option plan (ESOP), the stock price, once it goes up, will then give rise to numerous high-tech parvenus. During the high growth period of the electronics industry in the past, investors did not feel that shareholders' equity was significantly eroded by ESOPs. However, more recently, less economic prosperity and a series of accounting and financial scandals, the most well-known involving Enron and WorldCom, has caused foreign investors to question the rationality of ESOPs in Taiwan. The investors are concerned that the employees will benefit more than the shareholders, and this situation has led to a heated debate both within industry and academic circles.

As stated in earlier studies, when the stock market enters a bullish period there will be an increase in the stock price both before and after the date when a rights issue takes place as well as an abnormal return on the ex-right date. As a result, both shareholders and employees will benefit, and this will enhance the willingness of electronics companies to issue bonus stock, thus causing the company's capital value to be over inflated and diluting the stockholders' equity. However, when the stock market enters a bearish period and the downward cycle of the economy, the issue of ESOP, which results in a transfer of wealth from the shareholders' equity to the employees, is thereby highly questionable in the eyes of the concerned parties.

From the viewpoint of the investor, all of the shareholders must bear the capital cost of the ESOP as well as the risk of operating failure. On the contrary, the employees are able to enjoy the high dividend shares at no cost and with less risk. Furthermore, shares with high dividends reflect over inflated capital values and a dilution of earnings per share. If the growth of the company's earnings does not keep pace with the rate of inflation to maintain the capital's value, it will cause the stock price to fall in the long run.

Foreign companies regard employee dividends and their after-tax gains as part of the actual after-tax profit given to shareholders, after deducting employee dividends and the remuneration of the board of directors. However, in Taiwan, the preparation of an income statement requires that the financial statements first be audited, and then the board of directors will decide on the ratio of salaries and dividends. A general meeting of shareholders will then be held to decide whether this ratio will be upheld. Controversy will arise due to this difference.

In view of the above, the purpose of this study is to explore the reaction of the market in different sectors when information regarding the ESOP is announced by the board of directors. In addition, we look into whether the financial performance of companies with an ESOP is superior to that of those without. Furthermore, we will discuss the relationships between corporate size, growth potential, and the debt ratio in terms of the market's reaction to ESOP information.

2. LITERATURE REVIEW

Park and Song (1995) evaluated the efficiency of 232 companies in the U.S. based on their market net worth ratios and returns on assets for the period from 1979 to 1989. They stated that companies with ESOPs certainly have a positive affect on company operations in the long run. Meanwhile, these companies all have independent auditors that are responsible for monitoring the management's decision making to prevent the management team from making unfavorable decisions. These authors believed that the implementation of ESOPs can stimulate employee morale and increase efficiency; however, the possession of company stock by the management team might lead to an extension of voting power, which might endanger the interests of shareholders. Therefore, in addition to being an efficient motivating system, a well-supervised system is equally important.

DeFusco, Johnson, and Zone (1990) indicated that the implementation of ESOPs would lead to a wealth transfer effect for shareholders, and would induce the management team to engage in investments that entailed higher risk. In fact, the shareholders in such circumstances are equivalent to a buy option, and the value of the buy option increases along with the heightening of company asset variation risk. As a result, the management team that implements an ESOP will tend to engage in more risky activities so as to detract from the value attached to the company by the creditors.

Hung, Chen, and Jiang (2003) used financial information for the Taiwan IT industry from 1996 to 2001, along with the Du Pont Equation, as their research topic, and reviewed the financial performance of various companies. They used the profit margin as a substitute variable for operating efficiency, the asset turnover rate as a substitute variable for asset utilization, and the equity multiplier as a substitute variable for financial leverage to see if companies adopting ESOPs would have better financial performance. They found that, in terms of operating efficiency and asset utilization, companies with ESOPs outperformed those without ESOPs. Moreover, companies with ESOPs exhibited lower financial leverage than those without, which implied that implementing ESOPs tended to lower companies' financial risk.

Ding and Qian (2000) argued that the adoption of an ESOP had the characteristic of being associated with the employee's interests, in that it tended to reduce the problems associated with management and lowered the cost of financial reports. Furthermore, they also used the financial information of companies listed in Singapore from 1992 to 1995, along with Matsunaga's (1995) Pooled Multiple-Regression method, and concluded that ESOP was positively related to corporate size and future growth opportunities, and negatively related to the company's liquidity. Meanwhile, they also found that there was a significant cumulative abnormal return on the day of the ESOP announcement that continued until the fourth day. This indicated that investors in Singapore were optimistic with regard to the implementation of ESOPs, even though ESOPs are strictly regulated in Singapore.

3. DATA AND METHODOLOGY

Previous studies have suggested that ESOPs can effectively reduce the likelihood of problems arising between shareholders and the management team due to conflicts of interest. Thus, in this study we will first examine the differences in terms of financial performance between companies implementing ESOPs and those that do not by means of the Du Pont Identity. We will then probe into the reactions of Taiwan investors to companies with ESOPs when the ESOP information is announced, i.e., by seeking to determine whether or not there is an abnormal return in terms of the stock price, and whether or not the information is of value. Furthermore, a market model will be used to estimate the abnormal return and accrual to the cumulative abnormal return, in order to test whether the disclosure of information will give rise to an abnormal return on the stock price. Finally, a multiple regression model will be used to examine the relationships between ESOPs and corporate size, growth opportunities and the debt ratio.

The time period used extends from fiscal year 2002 to fiscal year 2004. The data employed are obtained from the Taiwan Economic Journal. The criteria used for selecting the stocks that make up the sample include the following: (1) Companies are listed on the TAIEX. (2) Non-financial sector companies are excluded to reduce bias since the financial industry is highly regulated by the government, thereby creating a distinctive rule for ESOP. (3) Full-value transaction stocks are excluded as these stocks are usually issued by companies with poor financial situations. (4) The data for the sampled companies must be based on the fiscal year system to ensure comparability and consistency in cross-sectional analysis. (5) To avoid interference, stocks that are ex-right and ex-bonus on the same day are excluded.

3.1. Hypotheses

3.1.1. ESOP and Company Performance

Wagner and Rosen (1985) stated that, compared with companies that have not implemented ESOPs, companies with ESOPs have a higher ROE, sales growth and operating profitability. In this study, we use the Du Pont Equation to measure company operating efficiency, the asset turnover rate, and the degree of financial leverage to examine the financial performance of companies both with and without ESOPs. If the ESOP conforms to the incentive program of both the management team and the shareholders' objective, we then use the following three hypotheses to test and verify whether companies with ESOPs outperform those without in financial terms:

Hypothesis 1: An ESOP can enhance the company's operating efficiency and hence increase its financial performance.

Hypothesis 2: An ESOP can strengthen the company's efficiency in asset utilization and hence increase its financial performance.

Hypothesis 3: An ESOP can reduce the company's financial risk by reducing financial leverage.

3.1.2. ESOP Information Disclosure and Market Efficiency

In practice, Taiwan credits the bonus share by the face value of the share, which is not reasonable from an accounting point of view. Based on the principles of accountancy, bonus shares should serve as an incentive for employees to work harder and create revenue and the relevant costs should be incurred as well. In this research we intend to find out how investors regard the information on the issuance of bonus shares to employees. If the Taiwan capital market is an efficient market, investors should realize that the ESOP in fact transfers the cost to them, and that the increase in the number of shares will inflate the company's capital value and dilute the EPS while the market should not be affected. Thus, we use the electronics and non-electronics sectors in our sample to investigate the reactions of market investors to the disclosure of information on the issuance of bonus shares.

> **Hypothesis 4:** *Ceteris paribus*, on the event day when the announcement is made, the average abnormal return (AAR) differs from zero;
>
> **Hypothesis 5:** *Ceteris paribus*, in the event window, the cumulative average abnormal return (CAAR) differs from zero;

That is, we examine whether or not the AAR and the CAAR calculated by the market model are different from zero in order to verify their influence on price when the information is announced, and hence determine whether the information is of value.

3.1.3. Regression Analysis of CAAR

We use multiple regression models to determine the effect on the CAAR of company size, growth opportunities, and the debt ratio.

> **Hypothesis 6:** *Ceteris paribus*, company size (Size) is negatively related to the market CAAR when the ESOP is announced;

According to Chang, Tsai, and Yeh's (1993) research on the TAIEX for 1986-1991, the TAIEX has the scale effect whereby the company stock price is negatively related to company size.

> **Hypothesis 7:** *Ceteris paribus*, growth opportunities are positively related to the market CAAR when the ESOP is announced;

Due to the asymmetry of information, the management team has more information on future growth plans than the shareholders, and when the objectives are inconsistent, future investment decisions will tend to be conservative and to result in a shortage of investments. In order for the management team to be more aggressive with regard to the investment plan, the use of the ESOP in order to align the objectives of employees with shareholders will be the preferred method.

> **Hypothesis 8:** *Ceteris paribus*, the debt ratio (Debt) is negatively related to the market CAAR when the ESOP is announced;

A high debt ratio implies that the majority of the capital comes from the creditors. In order to avoid excessively risky investments on the part of management and the transfer of wealth to shareholders, creditors will request a higher and more risky return than shareholders, and the market's response to ESOP information will be negative.

3.2. Methodology

3.2.1. Event Study

An event study is the method used to examine the relationship between the stock price and certain events in empirical studies. In this research, we use the date of the board meeting instead of the ex-right date as the event date, because the decisions regarding bonus shares are decided by the board, and whether they are upheld or not is decided by the general meeting. Both of these dates are earlier than the ex-right date. The estimation period used is 150 days. The longer the event period, the more easily the effect will be grasped. However, the model will be used to estimate the expected rate of return on the individual stock, as the market model assumes that the individual stock return is only related to the market return. We set the daily return rate of the TAIEX index as the independent variable and the individual company's daily return rate as the dependent variable, as follows:

$$R_{it} = \alpha_i + \beta_i R_{mt} + \varepsilon_{it} \tag{1}$$

where R_{it} is the daily return rate on the tth day for the ith stock; R_{mt} is the daily return rate on the tth day for the market index (volume weighted price index); α_i is the linear interception term; β_i is the systematic risk; and ε_{it} is the error term. If the individual stock is not affected by the research event, the expected return for a specific event date will be:

$$E(R_{it}) = \hat{\alpha}_i + \hat{\beta}_i R_{mt} \tag{2}$$

After estimating the expected return for the stock, the abnormal return (AR) can be obtained by subtracting the expected return from the actual return of the event period, that is:

$$AR_{it} = R_{it} - E(\hat{R}_{it}) \tag{3}$$

where AR_{it} is the abnormal return for company i on the tth event date; and $E(\hat{R}_{it})$ is the expected return for company I on the tth event date. The average abnormal return (AAR) is:

$$AAR = \frac{1}{N} \sum_{i=1}^{N} AR_{it} \tag{4}$$

where N is the sample size for each group; and AAR_t is the average abnormal return for each sample for all events on event date t. The $CAAR$ is the cumulative average abnormal return for selected samples in the event period accumulated from date t_1 to t_2.

$$CAAR_t(t_1,t_2) = \sum_{t_1}^{t_2} AAR_t = \frac{1}{N}\sum_{i=1}^{N}\sum_{i=t_1}^{t_2} AR_{it}$$ (5)

3.2.2. Regression Model

If the announcement of an ESOP has informational value, there exists a relationship between the CAAR and the company's characteristics. That is, CAAR is the dependent variable, and company size (*Size*), the company market-to-book ratio (*MBR*), and the debt ratio (*Debt*) are the independent variables. Then, the regression model will be:

$$CAAR_i = \alpha_0 + \beta_1 Size_i + \beta_2 MBR_i + \beta_3 Debt_i + \varepsilon_i$$ (6)

where, $Size_{i,t}$ is the replacement variable for company size based on the book value for company i in period t; and $MBR_{i\ t}$ is the market-to-book ratio in the tth period for company i. We follow Core and Guay's (2001) statement that the larger the intangible asset is, the greater the opportunity for growth. Therefore, we use the ratio of market value to book value as the replacement variable for the measurement of the company's growth opportunities (*Growth*). $Debt_{i,t}$ is the debt ratio in period t for company i; and ε_i is the error term.

The null hypotheses are $H_{O1}: \beta_1 < 0$, *ceteris paribus*, *Size* is negatively related to the market CAAR when the ESOP is announced; $H_{02}: \beta_2 > 0$, *ceteris paribus*, *Growth* is positively related to the market CAAR when the ESOP is announced; and $H_{03}: \beta_3 < 0$, *ceteris paribus*, *Debt* is negatively related to the market CAAR when the ESOP is announced.

4. EMPIRICAL RESULTS

From Table 1, it can be seen that on average about 75% of the sample for the electronics sector had decided to implement ESOPs during the sample period. This indicates that ESOPs are common in the electronics sector and have exhibited a growing trend, reaching a high of 86.09% in 2003. This may be due to the intense competition and eagerness for high-level talent in the industry. With the high employee turnover rate, it is hard to retain talent without a hefty ESOP. However, on average only about 25% of the non-electronics sector has implemented ESOPs and this share has decreased from 24.31% in 2001 to 13.90% in 2003. Due to the different characteristics of industries, the following empirical results are compared based on the electronics and non-electronics sectors.

Table 1. Percentage of ESOP Companies According to Industry and Year

	2001		2002		2003		01~03
	Number of Companies	%	Number of Companies	%	Number of Companies	%	Average %
Cement	0	0%	0	0%	1	0.45%	0.15%
Food	2	0.92%	0	0%	0	0%	0.31%
Plastic	2	0.92%	0	0%	1	0.45%	0.46%
Textile	2	0.92%	1	0.44%	2	0.90%	0.75%
Electric	12	5.51%	9	3.98%	11	4.72%	4.74%
Cable	2	0.92%	0	0%	0	0%	0.31%
Chemical	7	3.21%	6	2.65%	6	2.58%	2.81%
Glass	0	0%	0	0%	0	0%	0.00%
Paper	1	0.46%	0	0%	0	0%	0.15%
Steel	2	0.92%	2	0.89%	3	1.35%	1.05%
Rubber	0	0%	0	0%	1	0.45%	0.15%
Automobile	4	1.84%	4	1.77%	4	1.79%	1.80%
Electronic	165	75.69%	185	81.86%	192	86.10%	81.22%
Construction	2	0..92%	3	1.33%	2	0.90%	1.11%
Transport	1	0.46%	2	0.89%	1	0.45%	0.60%
Trading	0	0%	1	0.44%	1	0.45%	0.30%
Others	16	7.34%	13	5.75%	7	3.00%	5.37%
Total	218	100%	226	100%	233	100%	100%

4.1. Du Pont Identity Analyses

Table 2 presents the ratios of the Du Pont identity analysis for the electronics sector from 2001 to 2003 in order to test the significance of different ESOPs that have been implemented. The implementation of ESOP is defined as having to do with companies with earnings and stock dividends issued to employees. Companies with losses for the year that have issued bonuses from retained earnings are excluded from the sample. The financial ratio average for companies with ESOPs and for those without are tested using the Mann-Whitney-Wilcoxon method. The results show that, during 2001~2003, the sales profit margins for companies with ESOPs were larger than for those without, with significant differences in p-values of less than 0.05 for 2001 and 2002. This indicates that companies with ESOPs have better operating efficiency in the electronics sector.

As for asset turnover, the annual averages for the companies with ESOPs are larger than for those without. As for the equity multiplier, the annual averages for the companies with

ESOPs are smaller than for those without due to the dilution of shareholders' equity by employee bonus shares which has changed the capital structure of the companies with ESOPs. A P-value of 0.0059 for 2003 indicates that companies with ESOPs can reduce their financial risk through an increase in their shareholders' equity. As for the equity return rate, companies with ESOPs do have better operating effectiveness than those without.

Table 2. Du-Pont Equation Ratios for ESOP and non-ESOP Companies in 2001~2003 (Electronics)

Ratio	Year	Average for ESOP Companies (1)	Average for non-ESOP Companies (2)	P-value (3)= (2)-(1)
Profit Margin	2001	0.1335 (0.1231)	0.1144 (0.1051)	0.0671*
	2002	0.2294 (0.2779)	0.075 (0.0831)	0.0238**
	2003	0.1179 (0.1051)	0.0947 (0.0918)	0.6828
Asset Turnover	2001	1.0061 (0.8590)	0.9568 (0.6269)	0.0988*
	2002	1.005 (0.8067)	0.9829 (0.6232)	0.0761*
	2003	1.3347 (1.5694)	0.9022 (0.7410)	0.0155**
Equity Multiplier	2001	1.4369 (0.4681)	1.5528 (0.3549)	0.0482**
	2002	1.572 (0.4035)	1.7398 (0.6976)	0.0105**
	2003	1.5526 (0.4565)	1.5874 (0.4922)	0.0059**
ROE	2001	0.1356 (0.1192)	0.1223 (0.0880)	0.0285**
	2002	0.1187 (0.0760)	0.0836 (0.0874)	0.0068***
	2003	0.1322 (0.1186)	0.0918 (0.0597)	0.0220**

Note: Values inside parentheses represent the standard deviations.
*** 1% significance level.
** 5% significance level.
* 10% significance level.

In general, for the electronics sector, companies with ESOPs tend to have better operating efficiency as stated in Hypothesis 1. The adoption of an ESOP enhances cost control capabilities, which in turn increases profit margins. In regard to asset turnover, companies that implement ESOPs have higher asset turnover than those without, thus supporting Hypothesis 2. Through an ESOP, the management team can increase its asset utilization in order to further enhance operating efficiency. In terms of the equity multiplier, companies that implement ESOPs have significantly smaller equity multipliers than companies that do not. This is due to the dilution of shareholders' equity after the ESOP is implemented, and hence supports Hypothesis 3. Companies that implement ESOPs can lessen the financial risks involved in diluting company equity.

Table 3 shows the 2001~2003 average financial ratios for the non-electronics industries in the Du Pont Equation. We use the Mann-Whitney-Wilcoxon method to test the significance of differences between the ESOP and non-ESOP companies. In terms of profit margins, companies with ESOPs are significantly different from those without at the α=0.05 significance level. This indicates that companies that adopt ESOPs have better operating efficiency in the non-electronics industries. In terms of asset turnover, companies with ESOPs have higher turnover than companies without them. Therefore, for companies that adopt ESOPs, the view that there is better asset utilization is supported. In terms of the equity multiplier, since ESOPs lead to diluted company equity, those companies that implement the plan will have a smaller equity multiplier than those that do not. This demonstrates that companies with ESOPs undergo capital structure changes, and hence reduce their debt ratios and financial risk. However, in the case of the shareholders' ROE, in the non-electronics industries, companies with ESOPs are better off than those without in terms of effectiveness.

In general, for the non-electronics industries, companies with ESOPs tend to have better operating efficiency as stated in Hypothesis 1, which is similar to the electronics industry. The same conclusions have also been drawn in the electronics industry. In terms of asset turnover, Hypothesis 2 is inconclusive as only 1 out of 3 years exhibits significance. In terms of the equity multiplier, companies with ESOPs exhibit smaller equity multipliers than companies without ESOPs. This is due to the diluted equity caused by ESOPs, and thus Hypothesis 3 is supported. Companies with ESOPs can reduce their financial risks through equity dilution.

Table 3. Du-Pont Equation Ratios for ESOP and non-ESOP Companies in 2001~2003 (non-Electronics)

Ratio	Year	Average for ESOP Companies (1)	Average for non-ESOP Companies (2)	P-value (3) =(2)-(1)
Profit Margin	2001	0.1093 (0.1076)	0.0425 (0.7728)	0.0263**
	2002	0.0904 (0.0945)	0.0836 (0.0854)	0.0511*
	2003	0.1408 (0.2201)	0.1027 (0.1060)	0.0253**
Asset Turnover	2001	0.1957 (0.1703)	0.1557 (0.0666)	0.7730
	2002	0.1880 (0.1236)	0.1838 (0.0864)	0.7742
	2003	0.166 (0.0765)	0.1191 (0.0133)	0.0030***
Equity Multiplier	2001	1.6319 (0.3737)	2.2167 (2.5174)	0.0784*
	2002	1.6102 (0.4700)	2.0300 (1.3115)	0.0655*
	2003	1.6813 (0.4419)	2.1567 (1.9945)	0.0349**
ROE	2001	0.0305 (0.0169)	0.0254 (0.0266)	0.0849*
	2002	0.0354 (0.0315)	0.0247 (0.0215)	0.0030***
	2003	0.0753 (0.0496)	0.0316 (0.0354)	0.0220**

Note: Values inside parentheses represent the standard deviation.
*** 1% significance level.
** 5% significance level.
* 10% significance level.

Table 4. AAR and Test Statistics for the Electronics Industry

Day	AAR	t value		Rank test	CAAR	t value		Rank test	
-15	0.46%	2.423	**	0.460	2.47%	4.982	***	1.267	
-14	0.49%	2.651	***	0.650	2.96%	5.614	***	1.418	
-13	0.43%	1.616		0.360	3.39%	5.823	***	1.453	
-12	-0.03%	0.049		-0.530	3.36%	5.506	***	1.193	
-11	0.66%	3.260	***	1.070	4.02%	6.255	***	1.469	
-10	0.74%	3.793	***	1.570	4.76%	7.107	***	1.874	**
-9	0.40%	1.789	*	0.390	5.16%	7.321	***	1.907	*
-8	-0.36%	-1.773	*	-0.670*	4.80%	6.542	***	1.368	
-7	-0.12%	-0.550		-0.480	4.68%	6.157	***	1.189	
-6	0.97%	4.730	***	2.210	5.65%	7.170	***	1.178	*
-5	0.97%	4.850	***	1.970*	6.62%	8.155	***	2.155	*
-4	0.48%	2.266	**	0.490	7.10%	8.461	***	2.209	*
-3	0.61%	2.947	***	1.050	7.71%	8.917	***	2.394	**
-2	0.60%	3.678	***	1.470	8.31%	9.523	***	2.668	***
-1	-0.29%	-1.488		-0.880	8.02%	8.949	***	2.405	*
0	0.20%	0.896		0.030	8.22%	8.929	***	2.354	
1	0.68%	2.884	***	1.260	8.90%	9.339	***	2.570	**
2	0.70%	3.328	***	1.480	9.60%	9.827	***	2.821	***
3	0.52%	2.626	***	1.150	10.12%	10.156	***	2.996	***
4	0.52%	3.072	***	1.260	10.64%	10.565	***	3.187	***
5	0.32%	1.367		-0.040	10.96%	10.628	***	3.117	***
6	0.22%	1.410		0.050	11.18%	10.701	***	3.067	***
7	0.23%	1.035		0.030	11.41%	10.704	***	3.018	***
8	0.13%	0.799		0.140	11.54%	10.666	***	2.993	***
9	0.28%	1.406		0.410	11.82%	10.743	***	3.017	***
10	-0.24%	-1.132		-1.020	11.58%	10.365	***	2.785	***
11	-0.49%	-1.371		-0.930	11.09%	9.960	***	2.577	***
12	0.06%	0.180		0.000	11.15%	9.839	***	2.538	***
13	-0.38%	-1.986	**	-1.310	10.77%	9.352	***	2.375	***
14	0.07%	0.300		-0.010	10.84%	9.269	***	2.241	**
15	0.39%	2.163	**	0.800	11.23%	9.499	***	2.342	**

*** 1% significance level.
** 5% significance level.
* 10% significance level.

Announcement Effect of ESOPs

Table 4 lists the average abnormal returns and test statistics t in the electronics industry within a 41-day event period (-15, 15).[1] Table 4 shows that the AARs are positive for all pre-event dates except for -12, -8, -7, and -1. In addition, 14 out of the 20 pre-event dates are significant with a maximum AAR of 0.97% being obtained on the -6 day. On the event date, the AAR is 0.20%, which is relatively lower than for the other dates. We believe this may be due to most companies choosing to hold their board meetings in the afternoon to avoid affecting the market. After the event date, 7 out of the 20 dates have significant AARs. In contrast to the pre-event dates, the probability of a date having a significant AAR is lower for the post-event dates. Therefore, it is inferred that the ESOP information had been disclosed prior to the event date due to information leakage, and thus a higher AAR was recorded. After the event date, apart from day 4 on which there was a significant result, the remainder of the AARs were relatively lower, which shows that the ESOP information had been fully reflected in the stock market.

When the event period is divided into multiple sections and analyzed in terms of the CAAR, Table 5 shows that, among the 6 event windows, namely, (-20, 20), (-10, 10), (-20, 0), (-5, 5), (-1, 1), and (0, 20), only event window (-1, 1) was not significant. In addition, except for the event window (-5, 0) that had a CAAR that was less than half that of the event window (0, 5), the rest of the pre-event CAARs were greater than those following the event date. This shows that ESOP returns had been expected by investors, and had been reflected in the stock price. The CAARs for the entire event period (-20, 20) were found to be significantly greater than 0, indicating that the disclosure of ESOP information conveyed a positive message to the market.

Table 5. CAAR and Test Statistics for the Electronics Industry

Event Window	CAAR	t value		Rank test	
(-20,20)	12.17%	9.683	***	2.335	**
(-10,10)	7.57%	8.277	***	2.371	**
(-5,5)	5.32%	7.968	***	2.785	***
(-1,1)	0.58%	1.323		0.244	
(-20,0)	8.22%	8.929	***	2.354	**
(-10,0)	4.20%	6.374	***	1.852	*
(-5,0)	2.57%	5.368	***	1.688	*
(0,5)	2.94%	5.786	***	2.098	*
(0,10)	3.57%	5.333	***	1.434	
(0,20)	4.16%	4.795	***	0.916	

*** 1% significance level.
** 5% significance level.
* 10% significance level.

---

[1] Due to space limitations, the event period (-20, 20) results are not presented here but are available from the authors upon request.

Table 6. AAR and Test Statistics for the non-Electronics Industry

Day	AAR	t value		Rank test	CAAR	t value		Rank test
-15	0.06%	0.485		-0.330	2.13%	3.165	***	1.378
-14	0.33%	2.382	**	0.870	2.46%	3.745	***	1.612
-13	0.10%	-0.379		-0.690	2.56%	3.439	***	1.319
-12	0.21%	0.752		0.200	2.77%	3.217	***	1.169
-11	-0.08%	-0.861		-0.560	2.69%	2.725	***	0.903
-10	-0.41%	-1.741	*	-0.940	2.28%	1.650	*	0.300
-9	0.30%	1.376		1.030	2.58%	1.984	*	0.661
-8	-0.40%	-1.317		-1.350	2.18%	1.584		0.253
-7	0.26%	0.602		0.140	2.44%	1.411		0.112
-6	0.38%	0.800		0.790	2.82%	1.379		0.222
-5	0.77%	2.620	***	1.460	3.59%	1.853	*	0.542
-4	-0.07%	-0.035		-0.440	3.52%	1.835	*	0.565
-3	0.13%	0.804		0.560	3.65%	1.826	*	0.647
-2	0.18%	0.735		0.100	3.83%	1.973	**	0.656
-1	0.27%	0.476		0.690	4.10%	1.869	*	0.703
0	0.06%	-0.213		0.320	4.16%	1.804	*	0.777
1	-0.09%	-0.336		-0.102	4.07%	1.805	*	0.631
2	-0.17%	0.042		-0.110	3.90%	1.745	*	0.583
3	0.50%	2.022	**	0.930	4.40%	2.026	**	0.722
4	-0.10%	-0.716		-0.650	4.30%	1.779	*	0.570
5	-0.43%	-1.425		-1.050	3.87%	1.531		0.357
6	-0.15%	-1.189		-1.030	3.72%	1.440		0.196
7	-0.21%	-1.296		-1.140	3.51%	1.175		-0.004
8	0.04%	-0.104		-0.280	3.55%	1.102		-0.091
9	-0.65%	-2.081		-1.660*	2.90%	0.810		-0.283
10	-0.21%	0.315		-0.030	2.69%	0.719		-0.364
11	-0.06%	-1.292		-0.930	2.63%	0.475		-0.508
12	-0.08%	1.034		0.050	2.55%	0.605		-0.513
13	0.40%	0.429		0.610	2.95%	0.597		-0.433
14	0.06%	0.000		-0.330	3.01%	0.494		-0.531
15	0.11%	-0.063		-0.590	3.12%	0.430		-0.647

*** 1% significance level.
** 5% significance level.
* 10% significance level.

From the above, it can be concluded that, based on the inference of the accumulation rate of the CAAR, investors in the market had already anticipated that the ESOP information would be released by the board of directors prior to the meeting, and believed that even though this incentive system eroded the shareholders' equity, it was beneficial to the company's long-term development and operating performance. Hence, it was well reflected in the price. Since the stock market had already reacted, on the day the board meeting took place, the ESOP information did not give rise to a significant abnormal return. Furthermore, the abnormal return as compared to the period before the date on which the meeting was held was much smaller. On the day the event took place, the AAR was not significantly different from 0, and thus did not support Hypothesis 4. In the event window (-20, 20), the CAAR was significantly different from 0, and therefore Hypothesis 5 was supported.

From Table 6, it can be seen that the AAR was higher for the pre-event date period than the post-event period. However, only the -19, -18, -14, -10, and -6 dates of the pre-event period and the +3 and +9 events of the post-event period were significant. In terms of the CAAR, as shown in Table 7, the event windows (-20, 0), (-10, 0) and (-5, 0), prior to the board meeting, had higher CAARs than the event windows (0, 5), (0, 10) and (0, 20) did. This indicated that the market reacted to the ESOP information prior to the meeting, similar to the situation in the electronics sector.

Figure 1 shows that the AAR trends are similar for both the electronics and non-electronics industries. This indicates that investors reacted in the same manner in the market in both sectors. However, since the electronics industry is a technologically concentrated industry, ESOPs are inevitable if R&D talents are to be retained. On the other hand, market capital is generally concentrated in electronics stocks rather than in non-electronics stocks. Thus, even through the AAR trend for the non-electronics industry is similar to that for the electronics industry, the occurrence of significant abnormal returns is relatively low when compared to the electronics industry.

Table 7. CAAR and Test Statistics for the non-Electronics Industry

Event Window	CAAR	t value	Rank test
(-20,20)	2.94%	1.317	-0.297
(-10,10)	0.01%	-0.144	-0.805
(-5,5)	-0.43%	0.743	0.289
(-1,1)	0.24%	-0.042	-0.005
(-20,0)	4.16%	1.804**	0.777
(-10,0)	1.47%	-0.106	0.213
(-5,0)	1.34%	1.195	1.103
(0,5)	-0.23%	-0.227	-0.541
(0,10)	-1.41%	-1.315	-1.559
(0,20)	-1.17%	-2.518**	-2.174*

*** 1% significance level.
** 5% significance level.
* 10% significance level.

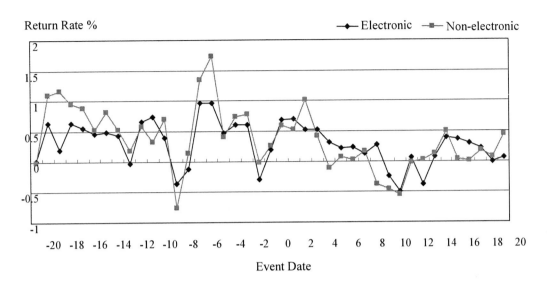

Figure 1. AAR for Electronic and non-Electronic Industries.

In terms of the entire event period, (-20, 20), the CAAR is not significantly greater than 0. This shows that the ESOP information, relatively speaking, does not have information value in the non-electronics industry. In terms of the AAR, both the electronics industry and the non-electronics industry displayed the same market reactions. The AAR before the event date was much higher than that after the event date. During the event period, the individual trading dates or the entire event period (-20, 20) were not as statistically significant as in the electronics industry. It is thus inferred that as capital is mostly concentrated in the electronics industry, greater concern is attached to electronic stocks by market investors as compared to non-electronics stocks. On the other hand, since ESOPs have been widely adopted by the electronics industry to recruit talents, investors still have great faith in their future even though they may dilute equity. Thus, once the non-electronics industries disclose ESOP information, investors in the market will tend to remain on guard and act conservatively. Their reactions are not as intense, however, as they would have been in the case of the electronics industry. On the day of the event, the AAR is not significantly different from 0 with the ESOP information, and thus Hypothesis 4 is not supported. The CAAR in the event window (-20, 20) is not significantly different from 0, and thus Hypothesis 5 is not supported either.

Besides, Figure 1 shows that both the electronics and non-electronics sectors displayed similar AAR trends, with high levels being reached on the pre-event dates -6 to -5. The rate of increase in the AAR prior to the event was greater than that after the event. This shows that, prior to the event, both sectors had fully reacted to the ESOP information. From Figure 2, we can see that the differential prior to the event date was less than that after the event date. It also indicates that if investors invest primarily in the electronics sector, the attainable cumulative return will be higher than they would have received if they had invested in non-electronics stocks. This is probably due to the fact that the market is still electronics-oriented and prices are therefore more sensitive to information.

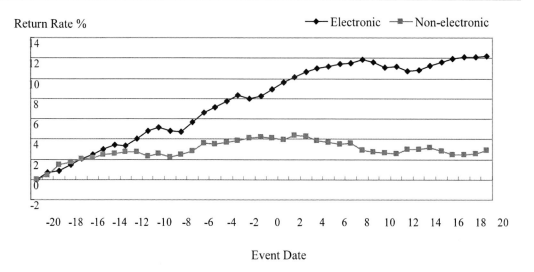

Figure 2. CAAR for Electronic and non-Electronic Industries.

Meanwhile, as compared to the Ding and Qian (2000) finding on the ESOP announcement effect in Singapore, investors in both Taiwan and Singapore affirmed the intrinsic value of the ESOP information, but the reactions were different. The abnormal return in the case of the Singapore ESOP information was significant only after the information was released. In this study we found that the TSE possesses a significant abnormal return prior to the occurrence of an event. This is likely to be due to the fact that the ESOP issue has been going around in the market for a long time. In addition, the difference in the time frame and regulations might have contributed to the variation in this result.

4.2. Regression Analysis

Since the ESOP information has given rise to a greater intrinsic value in the electronics sector, we therefore use the CAAR in the electronics industry for the event window (0, 5) as the dependent variable in the multiple regression model and use the growth opportunity, market-to-book ratio (MBR) and the debt ratio (Debt) as the independent variables to confer the relationships in between.

Table 8. Descriptive Statistics for Regression Variables

Variable	Mean	(%)	Medium	Max	Min
$CAAR_i$	0.588	0.331	0.322	0.670	0.001
$Size_i$	0.340	0.223	0.343	0.991	0.036
MBR_i	1.327	1.237	1.052	22.512	0.066
$Debt_i$	0.221	0.120	0.233	0.890	0.001

Note: $CAAR_i$ is the Cumulative Average Abnormal Return for the Electronics Industry in Event Window (0, 5).

Table 9. Correlation Analysis

Variable	iCAAR	iSize	iMBR	iDebt
iCAAR	1	-0.123	0.352	-0.015
iSize	-0.111	1	-0.073	0.212
iMBR	0.439	-0.021	1	0.332
iDebt	-0.032	0.129	0.219	1

Table 10. Regression Results for

$$CAAR_i = \alpha_0 + \beta_1 Size_i + \beta_2 MBR_i + \beta_3 Debt_i + \varepsilon_i$$

Variable	Coefficient	t-value	p-value
Intercept	1.741	3.242***	0.000***
$Size_i$	-0.016	-2.210***	0.000***
MBR_i	1.861	1.891***	0.046***
$Debt_i$	-0.004	-2.374***	0.000***
R-Squared 0.241		F-statistic 3.642***	
Adjusted R-Squared 0.296		Prob(F-statistic) 0.000	

*** 1% significance level.
** 5% significance level.
* 10% significance level.

Table 8 lists the descriptive statistics for the multiple regression variables including the mean, standard deviation, and minimum and maximum values. Among the variables, MBR has the largest level of dispersion. To avoid multicollinearity in the regression analysis, we investigated the relationship between the independent variables as stated in Table 9. We found that, apart from MBR that reached a medium level of correlation, the remaining variables exhibited only slight correlation. Thus the problem of collinearity was not found to exist among the variables.

The results of the analysis for the electronics industry sample in Table 10 show that the independent variable MBR is positively related to the CAAR and all other independent variables tend to exhibit a negative relationship. The coefficient for Size is negatively related to the market CAAR, and thus supports Hypothesis 6, namely, that, *ceteris paribus*, company size is negatively related to the market CAAR when the ESOP is announced. This indicates that a scale effect exists in the Taiwan capital market and that small-scale companies are more easily manipulated than large-scale companies and hence have better performance in terms of price. The coefficient for MBR is positively related to the CAAR, implying that ESOPs promote consistency in terms of their objectives for both management and shareholders, and thereby avoid the problem of inadequate investment on the part of management. Companies will then adopt more aggressive investment plans to increase company value and Hypothesis 7 is thus sustained. When the company leverage level or debt ratio is higher, an ESOP will have a negative effect on the stock price. This implies that when the company's capital mostly comes from creditors, the creditors will demand more of a risk premium than the shareholders and will thus prevent management from engaging in high-risk investments. On the other hand, creditors will try to avoid stock dividend distributions that may lead to increases in the number of shareholders and will transfer wealth to shareholders. Thus, the results support Hypothesis 8 and conform to Ding and Qian's (2000) results.

5. CONCLUSION

In this study, we use the Du-Pont Identity analysis to determine whether an ESOP has an effect on company performance, and analyze the announcement effect of the ESOP on the market investors. A regression analysis is conducted on the CAAR after the ESOP announcement. The results show that the adoption or non-adoption of the ESOP in the electronics industry significantly affects the company's performance. Among these results, the ROE has displayed the most significant disparities. The results for the non-electronics industries indicate that the adoption of ESOPs also contributes to an improvement in the company's operating capability, increased shareholder ROE, and reduced financial risks. By using the event study method, we find that both the electronics and non-electronics industries reacted prior to the event date. The reaction is most significant in the electronics industry and shows that investors prefer electronics stocks in the Taiwan stock market. Through a multiple regression model, it is inferred that the company's scale, market-to-book ratio and debt ratio affect the CAAR at the time that the information regarding the ESOP is released. After years of implementing ESOPs, the stock market regards ESOP information as having intrinsic value. Antedated reactions toward the information are also observed in the market before the event takes place.

REFERENCES

Chang, C. H., Y. C. Tsai, and S. Yeh, 1993, Determinants of Stock Prices in Taiwan: An Empirical Examination, *Globalization of Asian Economics and Capital Markets,* pp. 1-16.

Core, J. and W. Guay, 2001, Stock Option Plans for Non-executive Employees, *Journal of Financial Economics,* 61, pp. 253-287.

DeFusco, R. A., R. R. Johnson, and T. S. Zone, 1990, The Effect of Executive Stock Option Plans on Stockholders and Bondholders, *Journal of Finance, Vol. 45,* pp. 617-628.

Ding, David K. and S. Qian, 2000, Causes and Effects of Employee Stock Option Plans: Evidence from Singapore, *Pacific-Basin Finance Journal, Vol. 9,* pp. 563-599.

Hung, Y. S., H. L Chen and C. H. Jiang, 2003, ESOPs and Corporate Financial Performance: *An Empirical Analysis of the Information Technology Industry in Taiwan,* working paper, National Taiwan University of Science and Technology.

Matsunaga, S. R., 1995, The Effects of Financial Reporting Costs on the Use of Employee Stock Options, *Accounting Review, Vol. 70,* pp. 1-26.

Park, Sangsoon and Moon H. Song, 1995, Employee Stock Ownership Plans, Firm Performance, and Monitoring by Outside Blockholders, *Financial Management, Vol. 24,* pp. 52-65.

Wagner, Ira and Corey Rosen, 1985, Employee Ownership – Its Effects on Corporate Performance, *Employee Relations Today, Vol. 12,* pp. 73-79.

INDEX

D

E

T